Midwest Studies in Philosophy
Volume XXIV

D1452533

MIDWEST STUDIES IN PHILOSOPHY

EDITED BY PETER A. FRENCH
HOWARD K. WETTSTEIN

Many papers in MIDWEST STUDIES IN PHILOSOPHY are invited and all are previously unpublished. The editors will consider unsolicited manuscripts that are received by January of the year preceding the appearance of a volume. All manuscripts must be pertinent to the topic area of the volume for which they are submitted. Address manuscripts to MIDWEST STUDIES IN PHILOSOPHY, Department of Philosophy, University of California, Riverside, CA 92521.

The articles in MIDWEST STUDIES IN PHILOSOPHY are indexed in THE PHILOSOPHER'S INFORMATION CENTER.

Midwest Studies in Philosophy Volume XXIV
Life and Death: Metaphysics and Ethics

Editors

Peter A. French
University of South Florida

Howard K. Wettstein
University of California, Riverside

BLACKWELL PUBLISHERS • BOSTON, MA & OXFORD, UK

Copyright © 2000 Blackwell Publishers, Inc.

Blackwell Publishers,Inc.
350 Main Street
Malden, MA 02148 USA

Blackwell Publishers, Ltd.
108 Cowley Road
Oxford OX4 1JF
United Kingdom

ISBN 0-63121-593-X
ISBN 0-63121691-X (P)
ISSN 0363-6550

Midwest Studies in Philosophy
Volume XXIV
Life and Death: Metaphysics and Ethics

Midwest Studies in Philosophy
Volume XXIV

Midwest Studies in Philosophy, XXIV (2000)

Metaphysics as Prolegomenon to Ethics

JOEL KUPPERMAN

P art of the doctrine of the logical separation of "ought" from "is" was that ethical conclusions could not be got from metaphysical claims. G. E. Moore (1903) devoted a whole chapter to refuting such attempts. The disrepute into which metaphysics sank in Anglo-American philosophy during the middle part of the century certainly did not make anyone anxious to revisit this issue. Early arguments against a logical separation of "ought" judgments from all "is" judgments concentrated on basic, widely agreed facts of human flourishing and satisfactory interaction (Foot, 1958–59) and on institutional facts (Searle, 1964).

More recently, attitudes both toward metaphysics, and toward claims that metaphysical judgments can give support to ethical conclusions, have been softening. Three books especially come to mind: Thomas Nagel's *The Possibility of Altruism* (1970, 1978), Derek Parfit's *Reasons and Persons* (1984), and Frank Jackson's *From Metaphysics to Ethics* (1998). The first two of these books make metaphysical claims, principally about the metaphysics of self or personhood, that they suggest have a strong connection to ethical judgments of a certain sort.

The metaphysics in each case seems to me to be clear and interesting. What is less clear—at least to me—is just what the connection between the metaphysics and the ethics is supposed to be. Is it logical, and if so what is the logic in which this plays a part? Nagel speaks (1978, 18) of "the method of metaphysical ethics: moral and other practical requirements are grounded in a metaphysics of action, and finally in a metaphysics of the person." (What does "grounded" mean here?) Parfit argues for a "reductionist" view of personal identity, which he says "supports claims about both rationality and morality" (Parfit 1984, 445). (Is "supports" a logical relation?) Jackson, as I read him, is not suggesting logical connections between metaphysics and ethics. The supervenience of the ethical on the descriptive, in his view (1998, 128), is "*prior* to metaphysics." Nevertheless, he too holds that philosophical analysis makes a case for a certain sort of ethics, which gives his book at least some family resemblance to Nagel's and Parfit's.

My primary concern in what follows will not be exegesis. It would be tempting to try to work out plausible reconstructions of what Nagel, Parfit, and Jackson think—or might think—the connections are between their accounts of metaphysics and ethics. Certainly their books offer useful models of how metaphysical claims plausibly could be held to be linked to ethical conclusions. Keeping these models as reference points, I will try to work out my own account of how there can be a logical connection between metaphysical claims (principally claims about self or personhood) and ethical conclusions. Other useful models will be drawn from classical Indian philosophy, especially the *Bhagavad Gita* and early Buddhist texts, because there a metaphysics of self (or nonself) clearly is intended to yield ethical conclusions. The starkest cases, especially for Derek Parfit and in classical Indian philosophy, concern issues of life, putatively continued existence, and death.

FACTS AND VALUES

We may begin by examining what might be thought to be the two poles of an "is"/"ought" dichotomy: facts and values. The word "values" can be used, for present purposes, for all normative determinations, including those of morality as well as those (which correspond to a narrower, axiological sense of "value") of what is worth pursuing or avoiding in life. The word "facts" is at home in cases of features of the world that can be determined by the sciences, or by observation or introspection.

Judgment can be suspended on whether there are "moral facts" or metaphysical facts. If there are moral truths and metaphysical truths, perhaps that might seem enough to establish that there are moral facts and metaphysical facts. If it is not enough, then it may not be easy to specify just what is at issue if we ask whether there are such kinds of "facts."

When we ask what "facts" are, two very different kinds of associations may be evoked. First there are those that go with what happens when a television detective or lawyer says, "Just stick to the facts," or when someone suggests, "Let's look at the facts." Secondly, there are associations with things out there, vague shapes on the metaphysical screen, so that some philosophers might think of facts as "furniture of the universe."

To stick to the facts is, on the face of it, to eschew interpretations or inferences. Similarly, looking at the facts suggests an activity of looking at a baseline of what is indisputable, postponing (again) inference or interpretation. Like our talk of sunrises, though, this may represent thinking that is based on out-of-date "knowledge." Few recent philosophers have supported the idea of an edifice of knowledge built on a baseline of what is indisputable. Do what we call facts involve no element of inference or interpretation? If we see people walking about—although, because there is a fence in the way, we see only their heads—does our agreement that it is a fact that people are walking about involve no element of inference? At least one major philosopher, P. F. Strawson, has argued that facts in general involve interpretative constructs of the world, what he calls a "type of word-world-relating discourse" (Strawson 1950, 141). He dramatizes the point by insisting that facts are not "in the world" (1950, 135).

If we look more closely at the discourse of historians, sociologists, and scientists, it becomes clear that the use of "facts" is tilted toward mention of small-scale, seemingly isolated claims. Dates, population sizes, and electoral results are examples, as is the fact that the temperature in this room is 20 degrees centigrade. A scientific theory, even if there is wide agreement among competent scientists that it is acceptable, will be spoken of as telling us a "fact" only as it were by courtesy. Something like this is true also of the "fact" that a major cause of the American Revolution was distrust of the imperial presumptions of the British government, even if competent historians agree on it.

In both these scientific and historical cases, we are marginally willing to speak of "facts" because of the presumed general link between what is "true" and what is a "fact." But the paradigm cases of facts will remain the details, such as dates and temperatures. And as theories or explanations become more and more complex, there will be increasing discomfort with speaking of them as representing "facts." If Einstein's theory of relativity is true, is that a fact?

The temptation to regard facts as like "furniture of the universe" surely has much to do with a naive empiricism, to which the idea of unmediated contact with facts (bumping into them, as it were) is enormously appealing. If Strawson's arguments on truth are accepted, this rests on an indefensible philosophical position. But even if we put these arguments to the side and merely look at examples of the sort of thing we are willing to label a fact, the "furniture of the universe" model proves highly misleading. An example of Bede Rundle's, the fact that the rate of inflation has fallen, is telling in this regard (1993, 10). It is telling in other regards also: many people are willing to speak of the fact that the rate of inflation has fallen even when there is some disagreement among economists about what a reasonable measure of this is.

All of this suggests that talk of "moral facts" or of "metaphysical facts," or debate over whether such exist, surrounds something like a semantic black hole. It is exceedingly difficult to figure out what we might be talking about. Some good philosophers have felt comfortable in such discussions, perhaps because the "furniture of the universe" model has lulled their critical senses, preempting careful examination of what facts are.

The issues may look slightly less confused if we are willing to equate a fact with what makes something true, but considerable problems still would remain. The word "true," much like "fact," is most at home in cases in which we are considering, so to speak, bite-sized objects of knowledge, such as dates, temperatures, and the like. There may well be hesitation in speaking of a large scientific theory, which clearly calls for a web of belief, as "true." "Acceptable" seems more idiomatic, as does "correct." Are philosophical conclusions ever "true"? The issues of whether there is anything in ethics or in metaphysics that we should be willing to call "truth" have well-known difficulties of their own, above and beyond these.

THE DESCRIPTIVE AND THE NORMATIVE

Once we see the obscurities, and also the complexities, surrounding words such as "fact" and "true," we may be tempted to formulate the "is"/"ought" dichotomy in terms instead of descriptive and normative sentences. This does not avoid all philosophical difficulties or sources of possible confusion. Frank Jackson, for example, denies that there "is a sharp *semantic* divide between ethical and descriptive terms" (Jackson 1998, 120). Although this makes clear sense in the context of Jackson's general account, it is natural to ask what then is the difference (if any) between ethical (or normative) and descriptive terms.

One straightforward answer, which is identified most closely with the philosophy of R. M. Hare, is that ethical or normative terms or sentences have a prescriptive element, which is absent from descriptive terms or sentences. What Hare actually says is that moral judgments are "typically" prescriptive (1963, 16). The focus on moral judgments is significant, as is the word "typically."

Hare's claim suggests the question of whether other kinds of normative or ethical judgments share whatever prescriptivity moral judgments may have. This is a large and interesting issue. For the purposes of this paper I will assume merely that *if* moral judgments are typically prescriptive then other kinds of ethical or normative judgments also are (but perhaps not in the same way).

The word "typically," though, is immediately relevant to the argument to follow. If Hare had said that *all* moral (or all normative) judgments are prescriptive, then some tastefully arranged counterexamples would refute his position. He didn't, which makes the debate more complex. Hare's caution, it should be noted, has been echoed by some later writers. Jackson and Philip Pettit, for example, observe that to have beliefs about fairness in a way connected with motivation is the "canonical way" (Jackson and Pettit 1995, 37). This leaves the door open for noncanonical cases.

What connection if any is there between the normative and the prescriptive? It is well known that there are statements normally classified as descriptive that can have prescriptive functions. Examples are "What you are about to drink is poison" and "That will add years to your life." Conversely, normative statements sometimes have no connection with the motivation of someone who regards them as correct and occasionally have a connection the opposite of what one would normally expect. Kurt Baier gives the example of a case in which someone says to a spouse, in all apparent sincerity, "I know that we should save this money for Jack's college expenses, but let's use it to go to Bermuda" (1967, 142). One is intended to imagine that this could be carried through without any guilt or regret: thus distinguishing the case from one we would consider to be *akrasia*, and suggesting that the normative judgment carried no motivational baggage at all. There is no weakness of will, if one imagines that there simply is no will to save the money for Jack's college expenses.

Baier's characterization of his example is convincing, but what follows? He appears to assume that *either* there is a logical connection between moral judgment and motivation that is manifest in all cases, *or* there is no connection in any case. This mistake is repeated by the majority of writers on internalism versus externalism (or prescriptivism versus antiprescriptivism). When Baier shows that there are cases in which there appears to be no connection between moral judgment and motivation, he thinks that he has shown internalism (or prescriptivism) to be totally false.

That this conclusion is premature is actually indicated by the odd cases in which there appears to be a negative connection between moral judgment and motivation. The classic assertion of negative connection is the resolve of John Milton's Satan, "Evil Be Thou My Good." Satan is announcing that, if he has a clear idea of what ought not to be done, he will do it. This is unintelligible unless one assumes that Satan's philosophical position is different from Kurt Baier's: it is important to Satan that judgments of what is evil normally have motivational force (instead of simply being, so to speak, matter of fact). If doing what was evil were simply like saying that the world is flat or that two plus two equals five, there would be no fun in it. Perfectly ordinary people in perverse moods can experience a comparable joy of transgression, sometimes in things so minor as eating or drinking what they know they shouldn't, that would be spoiled and flat if whatever it was did not *feel* like a transgression.

A plausible account of the relation between accepting a normative judgment and being motivated to act accordingly will avoid the all-or-none dichotomy and will look for what is characteristic as opposed to cases that deviate from what is characteristic but may be parasitic on the characteristic uses. The simplest, most banal thing to say is that the vocabulary of "good," "evil," "right," "wrong" exists because of its functions in guiding people (including speakers who use this vocabulary) in their behavior. To have a function, as we all know, is not necessarily to fulfill it, or even to have a good chance of fulfilling it. Thus Baier's argument is rather like finding knives that no one would expect to cut anything, and arguing from this that there is no connection between being a knife and the function of cutting.

A complication—to continue the analogy—is that some things other than knives may be good at cutting. We cannot assume that prescriptivity is restricted to the normative. Consider the difference between "Drinking that would be a bad mistake," on one hand, and "What you are about to drink is poison," on the other, or between "What you are about to do to that complete stranger is extremely cruel and very wrong" and "What you are about to do to her will make her suffer for the rest of her life." In each case the first of the two utterances would normally be considered normative (in the first case prudential, in the second moral) and the second utterance would be considered descriptive (in a broad sense that includes predictions). Yet the likely motivation of someone who heard and accepted the descriptive utterance might well be about the same as that of someone who heard and accepted the normative utterance.

Many philosophers would want to establish a difference between the descriptive and the normative versions by pointing out that additional assumptions are needed to get from the descriptive to the normative. You can infer, from the fact that this is poison, that it would be a bad mistake to drink it, if you add the premise that you do not want immediately to die. You can infer, from the fact that it would make her suffer for the rest of her life, that it would be cruel and wrong to do that to the stranger, if you add the premise that inflicting that kind of suffering is cruel and wrong.

There is nothing wrong with this, and it certainly is neat. But a simpler way of saying much the same thing is this. There is the familiar vocabulary that includes words like "mistake," "cruel," and the like—not to mention the basic general tools of "good," "right," "wrong," etc.—that normally signals that an utterance is intended to have a motivational pull. To say that it is intended to have it, of course, does not guarantee that it will have it, and that it normally will be intended to have it does not guarantee that this speaker right now intends it to have it. Sometimes the vocabulary is used jokingly or ironically, in which case everyone may understand that the motivational pull is not to be expected. But typically, use of the vocabulary is enough to create the presumption that a motivational pull is intended. This presumption can be created equally well, though, without using the vocabulary by utterances that refer to possible events (such as death, dismemberment, and the like) with regard to which definite preferences can be presumed.

In short, although normative utterances normally are linked to the expectation of motivational pull, this is not always the case, and normative utterances have no monopoly on motivational pull. Part of what is distinctive about the normative, as opposed to the descriptive, on my account is that normative judgments do have the normal function of prescriptivity. Sometimes descriptive judgments have characteristics of prescriptivity, but this is by no means a normal function of descriptive judgments.

Do descriptive utterances (whatever we turn out to mean by these) have a monopoly on characterizing the world? It is clear that normative utterances that center on words like "cruel" or "kind and helpful" characterize what they are about: we certainly have a general idea of what to expect those actions or persons to be like. But it will be said that these are "thick" normative concepts, and that "thin" concepts like "good" and "evil" are different. Perhaps, though, the difference is very much one of degree of clarity and specifiability. If someone is described as evil, we normally know not to expect this to be a little old person who has never tried to cause pain or suffering for anyone. A "good" action, in normal conversational contexts, is not likely to be one that cripples half of the population. Beyond this kind of thing, of course, there is a range of possibilities. Thin normative concepts are designed, it has to be said, to be much better at exerting motivational pulls than at characterizing in much detail what they are about. Indeed in many cases more detail might risk some of the motivational pull. We may immediately feel a tug of approval for someone who is described as a good man, but when the speaker goes on to praise his admirable strength in never putting up with an insult or a slight, the tug of approval may quite go away. (In much the same way, we may feel an initial inclination to hear music that a friend describes as wonderful and moving, but when the friend goes on to praise the artistic way in which the composer weaves together pop tunes in syncopated rhythm, contingencies of taste kick in.)

My suggestion is that all normative utterances characterize the world, but that the characterization is rarely at all specific and often is extremely indeterminate. Often it amounts to, as it were, putting a rosy glow around something. The details and the source of the rosy glow are to be specified later. This position, as far as I can see, does not conflict with Hare's. Nor do I think it conflicts with Frank Jackson's. Indeed it looks close to common sense.

If two people disagree in their moral assessment of an action, one calling it good and the other evil, it is highly possible that many of the details of their descriptive statements about it will be the same. It is even logically possible that all of the details will be the same, and that they will agree to what they both consider a complete description, but that one will take a positive view (of what is described) and the other a negative view. Even then, the order of the details, and the points of emphasis, almost certainly would be different, making the case an analog of the duck-rabbit, of which two experiences can differ even if all of the details remain the same.

It may help, in puzzling through all this, to think of ranges of specific cases. We would normally expect two historical or journalistic narratives of a set of events to differ if one writer had a positive view of what occurred and the other had a negative view. The difference might be one of whether certain specific descriptive claims were part of the narrative or not. But equally well, the difference could be in what was treated as salient, or in the coloration of the descriptive language used.

In this way, normative differences will be linked (I think typically) to differences in how what is evaluated is viewed or interpreted. It is as if one person saw the duck-rabbit as a duck and thought "evil" and another saw it as a rabbit and thought "good." Cases in which there are normative differences even though all of the descriptions we can elicit entirely agree in every detail cannot be ruled out, but they surely are rare. We normally assume that the normative differences have more than a casual connection with the differences in description, although what the connection might be remains to be examined.

The discussion thus far has suggested that a general difference between what we term normative statements and what we term descriptive statements is that the former usually center on terms whose normal function is to be prescriptive. The latter usually will lack such terms, although it should be added that there is the alternative that such terms will occur, but in a way (e.g., within quotation marks) that disarms their normal prescriptive function.

There may be other characteristic differences between the two classes of statements. Here is one. Even if Strawson is right that all statements have what amounts to an interpretative element, this element is very often more noticeable in normative statements than in descriptive statements. Obviously there are exceptions on both sides of this contrast. Descriptions offered by proponents of two opposing scientific theories that rely on language and methods that are not shared will have a conspicuous interpretative element. When G. E. M. Anscombe (1958a, see also Anscombe 1958b) reports that she owes her grocer money for potatoes that, at her request, he had delivered, the interpretative element is hardly noticeable at all. The point of view is one that we all share, which is how Anscombe plausibly can maintain that her normative judgment represents a "brute fact."

Indeed it needs to be said that this contrast—between descriptive judgments whose interpretative framework often is able to be taken for granted, and normative judgments whose interpretative framework usually cannot be taken for granted—is highly contingent. We can imagine communities in which there is great consensus in normative interpretations, so that virtually everyone simply "sees" such matters in the same way. In our familiar world, what at one point has seemed conspicuously interpretative can come to have its interpretative elements seem almost invisible. (For extended discussion of this, see Kupperman, in press a.)

JUSTIFYING INTERPRETATIONS

It may be said that the preceding account has left out a major and fundamental difference between normative and descriptive statements, namely that the latter can be tested against the world in a way in which the former cannot be. How plausible is this? A first response might be to look at cases like Anscombe's and to insist that Anscombe's normative claim could be tested against the record of transactions between her and her grocer. One reply to this might be that Anscombe's case is atypical (which is why it is such a clever example) and that very often we don't seem to get far in testing normative claims against the world. This is linked to a second possible reply, which is that what needs to be tested against the world is not the judgment we might agree on (if we share the interpretative take on the world that it assumes) but rather the interpretative take itself. How can we establish that people who have ordered potatoes, which then have been delivered, owe money for them?

The ways in which experience might be held to justify normative judgments are a complicated subject, and what makes it especially complicated is that patterns of justification vary from one sort to another sort of normative judgment. People sometimes have the sense that specific experiences justify a change in moral judgment, enabling them (say) to see as cruel and wrong instances of what they previously had thought perfectly acceptable. (Some first-hand experiences of what slavery was like were taken in this way.) However, the justification of moral judgments often is keyed to general considerations, and to patterns of argument that appeal to general considerations, in a way that is less common in relation to judgments of value in the narrow, axiological sense. I have argued at length (1999a) that generalizations can have only a negligible role in axiology and that experience can put one in a better position to make judgments of what has (axiological) value (although such judgments are never incorrigible). The argument is also that in many cases there is what amounts to an emotional awareness of value, keyed to immediate experience.

Let us concentrate, though, on the ways in which experience can justify interpretative takes on the world that underlie normative judgments. Two comments are immediately in order. One is that the interpretative take on the world that underlies a set of normative judgments might proceed by stages and that an initial stage might involve purely descriptive judgments—say, metaphysical judgments. This may be a key to the relation between metaphysics and ethics and will be taken up later in this paper.

The second comment is that the problem of justifying interpretations connects our investigation to hermeneutics. But hermeneutics concerns texts. These themselves contain indications and direction markers that can be referred to in justification of ways of reading them.

The case for an interpretation of a text can be strengthened by reference to the ways in which key words or phrases are generally used in texts of the period or by the literary context or polemical matrix into which the work was introduced. Sometimes evidence of what the author may have intended can count, especially if the other evidence leaves open a range of possible interpretations and the evidence of intention points clearly to one of these. Usually, however, appeal is made to what is in the text, viewed in the light of the then-existing conventions. On this basis we are often able to determine that some interpretations are much better than others, even though—if the text is one of some complexity—we cannot expect to arrive at what can be considered a definitive interpretation to end all further need of interpretation. A classic example, which comes from I. A. Richards, is that we can dismiss the interpretation of *Hamlet* that regards Claudius as the innocent victim of his crazy nephew. To say this leaves open a range of possible interpretations of *Hamlet* that we cannot readily dismiss.

When we approach the world there is no text. An obvious first thought is that then we have nothing to ground interpretations in, no standards or routes of appeal. Perhaps asking what is the correct interpretation of the world (or of some feature of the world, such as the human self) resembles Wittgenstein's mock question, "What time is it on the sun?"

Responding to this in any full way would require revisiting a number of philosophical battlegrounds. These include the one that centered on whether the sciences can be viewed as merely collecting facts (scientists thus resembling the television detective who says "Just the facts, ma'am") and explaining them by means of theories that also predict new facts. Since the 1960s many have argued that this was drastically oversimple, that scientific theories indeed structure and interpret the facts that they rely on or predict.

The most sophisticated view of this sort is Kuhn's; and it is always worth repeating that, in his concluding contribution to the Lakatos and Musgrave collection (Kuhn 1970), he made it clear that he was neither a relativist nor an advocate of a coherence theory of truth. The world, he insisted, cannot be packed into an arbitrary set of conceptual boxes. Nevertheless, the sciences in his view emerge as forms of "seeing as." His acknowledgement that of course there is scientific progress strongly suggests that some interpretations of the world are better than others. Interpretations can be compared and evaluated even absent a text.

Even if one agrees that scientists in effect argue for interpretations of the world, this is of course not all that they do. Further, excellence of interpretation has a good deal to do with excellence in the primary activities of explanation and prediction. Professional standards of scientific work reflect this. If we look at historical or journalistic interpretations, it might seem that there is a factor of explanation, especially in the former. Clearly, though, it is in practice not quite like scientific explanation. Some philosophers, like Carl Hempel, have wanted to subsume all explanation under a single model. But it is noticeable that historical explanations rarely do appeal, even implicitly, to an overarching generalization of which what happened in this particular case is merely one instance. W. B. Gallie (1959) offers a convincing characterization of what historical explanation more usually amounts to: a thickening of narrative so that the factors that contribute to the eventual outcome are called to the attention of the reader, who comes to expect it or at least is not surprised by it.

If Gallie is right, this suggests that one historical interpretation can be superior to others in its perspicaciousness—picking out details that the reader becomes convinced mattered to what ultimately happened—and in its coherence. Indeed there are established criteria attached to the discipline that point toward this. This gives us another instance (besides that which connects scientific interpretation with explanation) of standards for interpretation absent a text. Can we point to something at all comparable in the case of a normative take on the world?

The answer surely is "Yes." Take the case of *X*, who lies on the floor crying and moaning. In version 1, we are told that *X* has sustained a terrible wound: this suggests the normative judgment that we ought to call an ambulance. In version 2, we are told that X has become exceedingly fond of marzipan but hasn't had any for weeks. This might suggest the normative judgment that we ought to run out and get some marzipan for X. The latter normative judgment perhaps in some cases ought not entirely to be scorned, but it is arguably built into the standards of normative discourse (see Scanlon 1975) that in general appeals based on needs trump those based on nonneeds. That is, to see situations like the one described in such a way that unfulfilled needs are salient is justified by standards internal to normative discourse. Any argument here would have to include the ways in which we learn to participate in normative discourse and the characteristic roles that matters of life, health, and bodily integrity play in its patterns.

To learn normative discourse arguably is to learn respect for basic needs, but it involves many other ways in which normative questions will come to seem— to someone who has mastered the rules of the game—not entirely open. Take Anscombe's example. She has ordered potatoes from her grocer. They have been delivered. It is, she concludes, a brute fact that she owes money (i.e., ought to pay money) for the potatoes. Is there a logical entailment here? It would be hard to argue this. For one thing there might be parts of the story that Anscombe leaves out that could make us think that this particular delivery of potatoes ought to have been free. For another, someone with radical social views, say an admirer of Prudhon who remains convinced that property is theft, could argue that the common sense that makes Anscombe and most of us take it as obvious that she owes money for the pota-toes is actually an example of superstitious property worship (or superstitious obliga-tion-centered thinking). The alternative suggested might be that it would be *nice* if Anscombe gives her grocer the money, if she has it, but that she has no obligation to do this. I am not saying that this is a plausible view, merely that it is one that can be argued, and that hence the obligation is not entailed by any ordinary description of the case. Nevertheless there is a case for saying that Anscombe's having ordered the potatoes and their having been delivered does create—given current entrenched understandings of the meanings of her actions and of the grocer's actions—a strong presumption (not easily defeated) that she owes the money. Even someone who thinks that our culture of property relations should be changed might grant that, given our present structure of meanings. To learn to engage in normative discourse is, among other things, to pick up on that. Even an anthropologist from another planet, where they do things very differently, might cite as "local knowledge" that on Earth when you order potatoes and they deliver them, you owe money for them.

Where does metaphysics fit into this picture of justifying interpretations with-out a text? One thought is that a metaphysics that changes how we describe the world can—to borrow Gallie's term—thicken a narrative of the world in a way that makes a normative interpretation less surprising, less arbitrary seeming. The metaphysics does not so much argue for the normative conclusion as it does nudge the reader in its direction.

METAPHYSICS AND ETHICS

In the concluding section of this paper I will elaborate on this line of thought, with particular attention to issues of life and death. We need to look more closely at connections between metaphysical and normative accounts. In particular we need to consider whether there are logical connections between metaphysical and normative claims.

This examination can be appreciated against the background of views of the self and of normative judgments that are so widely assumed that they might count as common sense. Let me lump these under the headings of "metaphysical individualism" and "normative individualism." Despite the large philosophical literature of the last forty years undermining metaphysical individualism, it is probably true that the average person thinks of herself or himself as remaining the same person throughout life in a strict and philosophical sense and regards the boundaries between persons as being very sharp and clear indeed. This mindset affects philosophical ethics to the point at which very good philosophers writing on morality have assumed that any viable normative system must meet standards of self-interest, thus in effect treating "What's in it for me?" as a fundamental question.

Any philosopher who starts from, or at least does not challenge, metaphysical individualism, and then argues for altruism, has a difficult job to do. There will be a perceived discontinuity: the normative superstructure will seem incongruous given the metaphysical base. The job is not impossible. Hare, for example, in *Moral Thinking*, argues that an ideal morality requires ideal information, which must include what it is like to be any of the beings affected by one's actions; it then might seem plausible that this ideal morality will have to be altruistic. But Hare has to allow the possibility that someone will simply decide not to think morally, thus escaping the pressures of altruism. In effect the "Why be moral?" individualist response is allowed scope.

A less direct (but perhaps more secure) route toward challenging normative individualism involves the rejection of metaphysical individualism. After all, our normative judgments of cases are in relation to explicit or implicit descriptions of the cases. In the philosophy of Kant this point is made by the insistence that what is morally evaluated is a maxim (which in effect includes an interpretation of the case in a language recognizable by the moral software that the theory provides). Other writers (cf. McDowell 1979) have spoken of the role of salience in appreciation of what is judged normatively. Descriptions of cases that are tinged by the rejection of metaphysical individualism can be expected to lend themselves to normative judgments that eschew normative individualism.

The most elaborate and detailed examples of this move are in classical Indian philosophy. They center on rival rejections of metaphysical individualism. That of Hindu philosophy starts from the intuitive assumption of most people that they have a self that remains the same, whatever the changes may be in personality, allegiances, or bodily characteristics. The argument is that this makes sense only if what we think of as the self is a kind of psychic core that does not include anything that pertains to personality or particular thoughts and feelings. But this core, called *atman*, then logically has to be indistinguishable from one being to the next. Hence the individual self is an illusion. We are all like drops of water in a cosmic ocean. (For a somewhat fuller account of this argument, see Kupperman 1999b, 57–58; in press b, chap. 1.)

Buddha's rejection of metaphysical individualism begins by rejecting the Hindu rejection, putting forward instead the idea of *anatman* (no *atman*). There is not adequate experiential evidence, in his view, for an *atman*. When the *Dhammapada* begins, "[The mental] natures are the result of what we have thought, are chieftained by our thoughts, are made up of our thoughts," it means this literally. There is no self underlying or behind psychology. What we think of as a self is not an item of what we are, but rather the systematic interrelationship of occurrent items and of subsystems associated with our bodies and psychologies.

Elaborate arguments are provided for this view in *The Questions of King Milinda* (see especially vol. 1, 63–65). Buddha's view of the self thus is not entirely unlike that, according to scholars like Annette Baier (cf. Baier 1979), developed by Hume in Book II of the *Treatise*. Given the contingent nature of the details of connections among subsystems, as well as of the items that enter our psychologies and bodily makeup, this makes the boundaries between selves far less sharp (and far more subject to ongoing contingencies) than the average person might want to think.

It is significant that the Buddhist analysis of self just cited occurs in the context of a question that is related to reincarnation. Doctrines of reincarnation certainly were embedded in folk Hinduism and also then in folk Buddhism. But anyone who regarded the self as philosophically problematic had to be struck by the question of how one could meaningfully claim that the self of one life was in some sense the self of a previous life. Admittedly there can be similar concerns about how the self at one stage of life is the same self as at a later stage, after there have been personality changes, etc. But in the intralife case there is at least the factor of bodily continuity, so that one could imagine tracking a person through the entire series of changes. This factor is lacking in putative cases of reincarnation.

One way of making sense of Hindu philosophical complacency about reincarnation is to think of an *atman* as a token of whatever all the *atmans* share. This token can occur in the sheathing of a human psychology for a lifetime, and then perhaps later in the sheathing of a frog psychology. A Buddhist philosopher does not have this way out.

When King Milinda asks the philosopher Nagasena (*Questions of King Milinda*, vol. 1, 63), "He who is born . . . does he remain the same or become another?" the answer at first is "Neither the same nor another." But Nagasena goes on to agree that there is a sense in which as a mature adult one is the same person one was as a baby "for all these states are included in one by means of this body." The analogy to continuity of self is what we have when the flame on a lamp burns through the night. By implication, the question "Is it the same flame?" takes on a different character when what happens is that one lamp is used to light another lamp. If there is (as Buddhists hold) some causal connection between one life and another life that is putatively the reincarnation of the first, then the fact that we hardly know whether to say that the flame on the second lamp is the same as the flame that was used to start it suggests a similar guardedness in relation to reincarnation. If the Buddhist view of the self at various stages of life is that it is "neither the same nor another," then this answer applies in spades to putative cases of reincarnation.

Clearly reincarnation might make a difference to moral questions. The case for condemning killing may weaken if one assumes that the person (or animal) killed will simply be reborn and start up a new life. (In much the same way, someone who has a firm and engrossing conviction that *X* has extremely good chances of going to heaven might have a less robust view of the harm of killing X than would someone who lacked this degree of conviction.) The *Bhagavad Gita*, which is a part of a great Hindu war epic, opens with the question of whether the hero should overcome his reluctance to fight against and kill relatives in the other army. The god Krishna points out that killing his relatives will make no significant difference: they will simply be reincarnated (and anyway, in the most sophisticated metaphysical picture the individual self is an illusion). In a world in which nothing makes any significant difference, the default position is caste obligation. The hero is of the warrior caste and therefore should fight.

No Buddhist philosopher would be happy with this answer. The cosmic unity at the heart of Hindu metaphysics is replaced in Buddhism by a flux of particulars, including the elements of what is popularly taken to be self. These include the suffering that might be yours in the future or mine or someone else's. Given the conventional (constructed) nature of what we think of as the self, and the sheer contingency of which bundle it is to which the suffering attaches, we may well be inclined to judge that suffering has negative value, period: it does not matter whose it is. If killing in general involves suffering, for the victim or for others, then one should never take life.

Derek Parfit is right, I think, to see strong similarities between his metaphysics of personhood and that of early Buddhism (see Parfit 1984, appendix J). There is similarity also in the suggestion that accepting such a metaphysics is an agent of personal transformation. Parfit (451) remarks that his analysis of personhood and personal identity has made him care less about the fact that he will die.

It is uncontroversial and unsurprising that a metaphysics, especially one of personhood, can change personal attitudes. What is more controversial is that it gives logical support to ethical conclusions of a certain sort. There are two complicated issues related to this. One concerns the variety of words and concepts related to reason. The other concerns the map of logic itself.

Paradigmatic uses of reason include deductive and inductive inference. There is a great temptation to suppose that the role of reason in ethics must somehow center on these, especially, of course, on deductive inference. But minimal reflection on classic texts should disabuse anyone of this idea. How much deductive inference is involved, for example, in Kant's account of the role of reason in ethics? Insofar as judgments relying on the categorical imperative are held to exemplify rationality, the rationality involved is that of thinking that fulfills the special requirements of moral thought (conceived of—like the aesthetic judgment investigated in the third critique, and like general human thinking as investigated in the first critique—as having preconditions whose validity can be known a priori). Moral thought requires that the maxims one endorses could be willed to be a universal law and is part of what would govern a "realm of ends"; it also dictates respect for persons. Moral rationality hence, in Kant's view, falls along these lines.

Being rational also, in the common view of things, involves not being swept away by emotions of the moment. Conversely, it is not ruled out that some mild emotional responses that any reasonable person would consider appropriate (such as sympathy for an innocent victim) could exemplify what we would judge to be a reasonable response to the world. This is recognized in the judicious complexity of

Hume's account of reason in ethics. There is a narrow sense of "reason," allied to deductive logic, in which "'Tis not contrary to reason to prefer the destruction of the whole world to the scratching of my finger," he observes (Hume 1739/1978, 416). But Hume also says that what is "vulgarly call'd . . . reason" is the calmer passions (419). It is abundantly clear that reason in this colloquial and broader sense has a major role in his ethics.

Do we conceive of what is truly reason as consisting mainly of the capacities for, and operation of, deductive and inductive inference? Is this the essence of reason? Or should we instead take an antiessentialist, Wittgensteinian view of reason, regarding it as a family of capacities and cognitive achievements? There is not space for a full treatment of this issue, but it should be clear that I take the antiessentialist view.

Similarly I would like to suggest a latitudinarian account of the scope and shape of logic. It is very tempting to assume that the only concern of logic, apart from the special subject of inductive inferences, is with entailment. This has the advantage of bringing logic into line with the traditions of mathematical reasoning.

Nevertheless, my suggestion is that if holding X makes it more reasonable to hold Y as well, even though X does not entail Y, it makes sense to recognize this as a logical relation between X and Y. One might symbolize it as "X r Y." Parfit cautiously speaks of his metaphysics of personhood as supporting ethical conclusions of a certain sort. Abandoning this caution, I would like to speak of the relation as logical support.

Why not? The main obstacle would seem to be a kind of traditional essentialism regarding logic. But if it is more rational/reasonable to hold Y if X is included in the basis for Y, this relationship of support surely has enough of a family resemblance to the general subject matter of logic that it can be regarded as logical. Thus I would want to read Nagel (whether or not he would want to read himself in this way) as suggesting that some policy of altruism is logically supported by the metaphysics he provides.

Very probably Nagel would not—or did not—wish to be read in this way: his argument, he says, "does not offer a justification for being moral, but it attempts to explain why typically moral justifications are capable of persuading us" (1978, 143). But if the persuasion is rational, or reasonable, why can't this count as a weak (certainly weaker than entailment) form of logical support? Similarly, if Jackson is right about the supervenience of the ethical on the descriptive, and also that moral functionalism gives "the meaning of moral vocabulary" (1998, 129, 144), then this gives at least a weak form of logical support to the ethical conclusion (157) that what "confers value on a property ultimately comes down to facts about desires" (the word "desire" clearly being used in an extremely broad sense).

CONCLUSION

There are many examples, both in recent (Western) philosophy and in classical Indian philosophy, of arguments that move from metaphysics of personhood—especially as related to matters of death and continued life—to ethical conclusions of various sorts. If we simply think of metaphysics as part of the description of the world, and ethics as well outside of this, this philosophical move is extremely puzzling. My suggestion first has been that all claims about the world—scientific, commonsensical, metaphysical, or ethical—have to be seen as having an interpretative element. If ethical judgments look distinctive, it is that they typically employ vocabulary whose normal function is prescriptive; and also there is the highly contingent fact that the interpretative element in ethical judgments usually (but not always) is more conspicuous and obviously contestable than that in most (but not all) nonethical judgments.

The suggestion, then, is that a metaphysical account, especially one that goes against most people's received views of the world, can move the interpretative take on the world in a direction that an associated ethical account continues. Is this merely a relation of harmonious continuity between some kinds of metaphysics and associated ethical views? My final suggestion is that it can be seen also as a logical relation, weaker than entailment, but still closely linked with the normal range of meanings of such terms as "rational" or "reasonable."

REFERENCES

Anscombe, G. E. M. (1958a) "Modern Moral Philosophy." *Philosophy* 33: 1–10.
_____. (1958b) "On Brute Facts." *Analysis* 18: 69–72.
Baier, Annette (1979) "Hume on Heaps and Bundles." *American Philosophical Quarterly* 16: 285–95.
Baier, Kurt (1967) "Fact, Value, and Norm in Stevenson's Ethics." *Nous* 1: 139–60.
Bhagavad Gita (ca. 1st c. CE/1986) Trans. Barbara Stoler Miller. New York: Bantam Books.
Dhammapada (ca. 3rd c. BCE/1954) Trans. S. Radhakrishnan. London: Oxford University Press.
Foot, Philippa (1958–59) "Moral Beliefs." *Proceedings of the Aristotelian Society* 59: 83–104.
Gallie, W. B. (1959) "Explanations in History and the Genetic Sciences." In *Theories of History*, ed. Patrick Gardiner, 386–402. Glencoe, Ill.: The Free Press.
Hare, R. M. (1963) *Freedom and Reason*. Oxford: Clarendon Press.
_____. (1981) *Moral Thinking*. Oxford: Clarendon Press.
Hume, David (1739/1978) *Treatise of Human Nature*, ed. L. A. Selby-Bigge, rev. P. H. Nidditch. Oxford: Clarendon Press.
Jackson, Frank (1998) *From Metaphysics to Ethics*. Oxford: Clarendon Press.
Jackson, Frank, and Philip Pettit (1995) "Moral Functionalism and Moral Motivation." *Philosophical Quarterly* 45: 20–40.
Kuhn, Thomas S. (1970) "Reflections on My Critics." In *Criticism and the Growth of Knowledge*, ed. Imre Lakatos and Alan Musgrave, 231–78. Cambridge: Cambridge University Press.
Kupperman, Joel J. (1999a) *Value . . . and What Follows*. New York: Oxford University Press.
_____. (1999b) *Learning from Asian Philosophy*. New York: Oxford University Press.
_____. (In press a) "How Values Congeal into Facts." *Ratio*.
_____. (In press b) *Classic Asian Philosophy: A Guide to the Essential Texts*. New York: Oxford University Press.
McDowell, John (1979) "Virtue and Reason." *Monist* 62: 331–48.
Moore, G. E. (1903) *Principia Ethica*. Cambridge: Cambridge University Press.
Nagel, Thomas (1970, 1978) *The Possibility of Altruism*. Oxford: Clarendon Press, 1970; Princeton: Princeton University Press, 1978.
Parfit, Derek (1984) *Reasons and Persons*. Oxford: Clarendon Press.
The Questions of King Milinda (ca. 2nd c. CE/1963) Trans. T. W. Rhys Davids. 2 vols. New York: Dover Books.
Rundle, Bede (1993) *Facts*. London: Duckworth.

Scanlon, T. M. (1975) "Preference and Urgency." *Journal of Philosophy* 72: 655–69.
Searle, John (1964) "How to Derive Ought from Is." *Philosophical Review* 73: 43–58.
Strawson, P. F. (1950) "Truth." *Supplementary Proceedings of the Aristotelian Society* 24: 129–56.

Midwest Studies in Philosophy, XXIV (2000)

The Meaning of Life

JOHN KEKES

I

Most of our lives are spent in routine activities. We sleep, wash, dress, eat; go to work, work, shop, relax; balance the checkbook, clean house, do the laundry, have the car serviced; chat, pay bills, worry about this or that, take small pleasure in small things. We do all this in the intervals between familiar milestones: we are born, mature, age, and die; we have children and lose our parents; we graduate, find a job, get married, divorce, fall in and out of love, set up house; succeed at some things, fail at others; make friends and have fights; move house, change jobs, get fired or promoted, fall ill and recover, save for retirement and retire. So life goes for me, you, and just about everyone, allowing for small individual and cultural variations that affect the form but not the fact of routine. These activities constitute everyday life. Everyday life is what life mostly is. Keeping it going, however, involves constant struggle. From a birth we did not choose to a death we rarely desire, we have to cope with endless problems. If we fail, we suffer. And what do we gain from success? No more than some pleasure, a brief sense of triumph, perhaps a little peace of mind. But these are only interludes of well-being, because our difficulties do not cease. It is natural to ask then why we should continue on this treadmill. After all, we could stop.

The tough-minded answer is that the question falsely suggests that we need reasons for continuing to live. The truth is that our nature impels us to carry on. We have wants and the capacity to satisfy them, and instinct and training dictate that we do so. We live as long as we can, as well as we can, and we do so because we are the kind of organisms we are. It is our nature to struggle. To look for reasons beyond this is to misuse the respite we occasionally enjoy from the difficult business of living.

This bleak view correctly depicts the past and present condition of the majority of humanity. People struggle because they are hungry, cold, and threatened, and they want comfort. One should have compassion for the multitudes living in this way. The fact is, however, that many of us, living in civilized societies, no longer face such unrelenting adversity. For us, fortunate ones, the primitive struggle is over. We enjoy the comforts for which the less favored billions yearn. The point of the struggle in primitive conditions is to overcome obstacles to living. But what should we live for once the obstacles are overcome? What should we do with our comfortable lives? Having a comfortable life does not mean that the struggle is over, only that it takes less deadly forms. The threat is to income, prestige, status, self-esteem; the dangers are social and psychological. Nonetheless, these we also want to avoid. Why should we not say then that in primitive conditions our aim is to attain comfort, whereas in civilized conditions it is to protect and enhance the comfort we already have? We struggle to win such prizes as our society affords and to avoid being adversely judged by the prevailing standards.

This is a superficial view. No doubt, in civilized societies many are motivated in this way, but we also have some freedom and opportunity to stand back and reflect. Much of this reflection needs to be concentrated on the strategy and tactics of the daily struggle. Yet we often have some time and energy left to ponder life and our own lives, to ask why we should live in whatever happen to be the socially accredited ways. We know the standards by which success is judged and the rewards and costs of failure. If we are honest, we admit that we care about success and want to avoid failure, at least in the projects that matter to us. Reflection, however, may prompt us to ask whether they should matter. It may seem to us that the whole business we are caught up in is bogus. We see that children are indoctrinated, adolescents are goaded and guided, and adults are rewarded by the vast, impersonal, ubiquitous molds into which civilized societies press their members. And we may ask why we should put up with it. Why should we care about the emblems of success and the stigma of failure? What does it really matter to us in the dark hours of a sleepless night what our neighbors, acquaintances, or colleagues think about us? They employ standards and judge according to them, but we have come to question the standards. Life will seem hollow if we reflect in this way and we shall rightly ask what meaning it has.

Maybe it has none. Maybe evolution has brought it about that we have a capacity to ask questions about our condition, and in civilized societies some even have the opportunity to employ their capacity. But it is folly to suppose that just because we can ask a question there is going to be an answer to it that we like. There are plenty of useless things in nature, and perhaps this capacity is one of them. Maybe life just is, as black holes, electrons, and hurricanes are. Each has an explanation in terms of the laws of nature and antecedent conditions, but there is no meaning beyond that.

One may meet this answer with despair or cynicism. Both are injurious. They poison the enjoyment there is in life by corrupting the innocent connection between a want and its satisfaction. There intrudes the gnawing question about the point of it all. Despair and cynicism cleave us into a natural self and a preying, harping, jeering, or self-pitying reflective self. We are thus turned against ourselves. Reflection sabotages our own projects. If this is the truth, then the human prospect is dim. Maybe a capacity has evolved in us, and it will undo us.

It is not surprising, therefore, that many people of sturdy common sense simply ignore the question. They go on with the business of living, do as well as they can, enjoy the comforts they may, and prudently keep out of deep waters. This evasion, however, is likely to be possible only for those who are succeeding in navigating life's treacherous waters. The young who are about to start tend to ask why they should follow their elders' mode of life. The old who look back may wonder about whether it was worth it. And the sick, poor, unlucky, and untalented may well ask, with various degrees of resentment, about the point of the enterprise in which they have not done well. It is not possible to ignore the question because it is persistently asked.

Nor is it reasonable to avoid putting the question to ourselves, quite independently of external challenges. It is demeaning to participate in all manner of activities, expending great effort, giving and getting hard knocks, obeying rules we have not made, chasing goals said by others to be rewarding, without asking why we should do all this. Is it not the very opposite of prudence and common sense to invest our lives in projects whose value we have not ascertained? Furthermore, there are exceptionally few lives uninterrupted by serious crises. Grief, ill health, social cataclysms, injustice, setbacks, lack of merited appreciation, being in the power of those who abuse it, and many similar adversities are likely to interfere with even the most prudently lived lives. The questions such adversities raise in us can be answered, if at all, only by reminding ourselves of the point of facing them. Doing that, however, requires having thought about the meaning of our lives.

II

In chapter 5 of his *Autobiography*,[1] John Stuart Mill makes wonderfully concrete what it is like for one's life to have meaning and then to lack it. He writes:

> I had what might truly be called an object in life: to be a reformer of the world. My conception of my own happiness was entirely identified with this object. The personal sympathies I wished for were those of my fellow labourers in this enterprise. . . . [A]s a serious and permanent personal satisfaction . . . my whole reliance was placed on this; and I was accustomed to felicitate myself on the certainty of a happy life which I enjoyed, through placing my happiness in something durable and distant, in which some progress might always be making, while it could never be exhausted by complete attainment. This did very well for several years, during which the general improvement going on in the world and the idea of myself as engaged with others in struggling to promote it, seemed enough to fill up an interesting and animated existence.

Mill lived in this manner until "the time came when I was awakened from this as from a dream. . . . [I]t occurred to me to put the question directly to myself: 'Suppose that all your objects in life were realized; that all the changes in institutions and opinions which you are looking forward to, could be completely effected at this very instant: would this be a great joy and happiness to you?' And an irrepressible self-consciousness answered: 'No!' At this my heart sank within me: the whole foundation on which my life was constructed fell down. . . . The end has ceased to charm, and how could there ever again be any interest in the means? I seemed to have nothing left to live for."

Reflecting on what has gone wrong, Mill offers the following diagnosis:

> All those to whom I looked up, were of the opinion that the pleasure of sympathy with human beings, and the feelings which made the good of others . . . the objects of existence, were the greatest and surest sources of happiness. Of the truth of this I was convinced, but to know that a feeling would make me happy if I had it, did not give me the feeling. My education, I thought, had failed to create these feelings in sufficient strength to resist the dissolving influence of analysis, while the whole course of my intellectual cultivation had made . . . analysis the inveterate habit of my mind. I was thus left stranded . . . without any desire for the ends which I had been so carefully fitted out to work for: no delight in virtue, or the general good, but also as little in anything else.

Mill's explanation of what has deprived his life of meaning is convincing, but we can go beyond it. He became indifferent to his projects and ceased to care about the goals he used to pursue because he became disengaged from them. The circumstances of his disengagement and the nature of his projects are peculiar to Mill, and so is the extraordinary education that was partly responsible for both his achievements and his life's lost meaning. But we can abstract from these peculiarities and recognize Mill's case as typical of many lives whose meaning has been lost. The precipitating experience is that we awaken, as if from a dream, and realize that what mattered before no longer does. Loss of religious faith, the death of a deeply loved person, the recognition that our decisive choices were based on self-deception, the realization that we have devoted our lives to pursuing a hollow goal, the discovery that our passionate commitment is to an irremediably tainted cause are such experiences. The result is disillusion, and life becomes a tedious burden.

These experiences may bring us to regard our activities as worthless. We see ourselves as engaged in the endless drudgery of some soul-destroying job. We do what we do, not to attain some positive good, but to avoid poverty or starvation. Yet some intrinsically worthless activities may have a point if they lead to goals we value. If, however, chores lacking in either intrinsic or instrumental value dominate in our lives, such as tightening screws day in, day out, as in Chaplin's *Modern Times*, then we can rightly judge them meaningless because they are pointless. In other cases, the activities that dominate our lives may have a point, and yet our lives may still be meaningless, because our goals are destructive, like having enough drugs to support an addiction. Lives of this sort are misdirected. Other lives are meaningless because their goals are trivial, like keeping our childhood toys in working order. There are also lives directed at goals impossible even of approximation, like communicating with the dead. These lives are futile.

It will deepen our understanding of what it would be like for our lives to have meaning if we see that it is not enough to avoid these defects. Mill reasonably judged his life meaningless, yet it had worth, for it was dedicated to a good cause; it aimed at the important goal of bettering the condition of humanity, thus it was not pointless, misdirected, destructive, or trivial; and it was not futile either, for the amelioration of misery and the increase of general happiness are feasible goals. Mill recognized that his project in life had these meaning-conferring attributes, yet they were insufficient to give it meaning.

One element that Mill's life lacked was his wanting to continue to be engaged in his project. Before his crisis, he identified himself with it, he actively wanted to pursue it; after it, he did not. There appeared a break between Mill and the worthwhile, purposeful, well-directed, important, and possible project of improving the condition of humanity. The connecting link is Mill's identification with his project, and that is what has come to an end. Mill's case shows that it is a mistake to suppose that there are some types of lives in which meaning is inherent, so that if we live them, we cannot fail to find them meaningful. Meaningful lives must have the features just described, but we must also identify with them, we must want to engage in them. Our motivation is as essential as the intrinsic features of the lives.

The fact is, however, that the combination of the intrinsic features and our motivation is still not sufficient for meaning. We may come to think that reflection excludes the possibility of meaning because it brings home to us the absurdity of even the most reasonable projects. Thomas Nagel gives an account of the philosophical sense of absurdity that "must arise from the perception of something universal—some respect in which pretension and reality inevitably clash for all of us."[2] What is this clash? "Two inevitable standpoints collide in us, and that is what makes life absurd." One is that we "cannot live lives without energy and attention, nor without making choices which show that we take some things more seriously than others. . . . Think of how an ordinary individual sweats over his appearance, his health, his sex life, his emotional honesty, his social utility, his self-knowledge, the quality of his ties with family, colleagues, and friends, how well he does his job, whether he understands the world and what is going on in it." The other viewpoint is that "humans have the capacity to stand back and survey themselves, and the lives to which they are committed, with that detached amazement which comes from watching an ant struggle up a heap of sand. Without developing the illusion that they are able to escape from their specific and idiosyncratic position, they can view it *sub specie aeternitatis*. . . . Yet when we take this view . . . it does not disengage us from life, and there lies our absurdity: not in the fact that such an external view can be taken of us, but in the fact that we ourselves take it, without ceasing to be the persons whose ultimate concerns are so coolly regarded."[3]

This is a perceptive analysis of the philosophical sense of absurdity, but it does not help to understand the kind of meaninglessness that overtook Mill. It is true that we have a capacity to view ourselves from an impersonal cosmic perspective, but the fact is that few of us do so and those who do are by no means uniformly assailed by a sense of meaninglessness. Plato, Spinoza, and Kant among philosophers, Sophocles and Wordsworth among poets, Einstein among scientists come to mind as combining a cosmic view with an intense concern with human welfare. The truths that in the long run we shall all be dead and that from Alpha Centauri we seem like ants lead many reflective people to a heightened appreciation of the importance of human concerns. Nor do people find their lives meaningless, as Mill did, because of a philosophical sense of absurdity. Mill's trouble was not that from a cosmic perspective it appeared absurd to care about his project. What bothered him was that he lost the capacity to "sweat over his appearance, his health, his sex life . . . whether he understands the world and what is going on in it." His life became desultory because he stopped caring, not because his caring appeared to be absurd from a nonhuman point of view.

The experience we need to understand is the break that sometimes occurs in everyday life between us and our projects. The projects used to matter, but they no longer do. This may happen because our projects are worthless, pointless, misdirected, trivial, destructive, or futile. Or it may happen because although our projects have none of these defects, they may still lack meaning because of our attitude toward them. Our attitudes may sometimes be sapped by a sense of absurdity, but they are more often sapped by a disengagement of our will and emotions that has nothing to do with absurdity. It must also be allowed that people may find their lives meaningless because they are meaningless. But not all lives are. The question is: what is it that engages our will and emotions, gives meaning to our lives, given that our projects are not defective and we do not suffer from a sense of absurdity? There are two types of answers: the religious and the moral, and we shall examine them in turn.

III

The religious approach to the question is pithily expressed by Wittgenstein: "The sense of the world must lie outside the world. In the world everything is as it is, and everything happens as it does happen: *in* it no value exists. . . . If there is any value . . . it must lie outside the whole sphere of what happens and is the case."[4] The world is the natural world, and it is a world of facts, not of values. If anything in the natural world has meaning or value, it must come from the outside of it. And it is on the outside that the religious answer concentrates. As Wittgenstein puts it, "Ethics is transcendental,"[5] and he means that "Ethics is the enquiry into what is valuable, or, into what is really important, or . . . into the meaning of life, or into what makes life worth living, or into the right way of living."[6]

We know then the direction in which to look for the religious answer, but before we can look an obstacle needs to be overcome. Religious answers vary greatly in scope, ranging from the very general to the quite specific. Specific religious answers are given by Christianity, Buddhism, Islam, and so forth. The general religious answer is based on the belief that there is a cosmic order that is the ultimate source of meaning. Specific religious answers, then, are interpretations of this supposed cosmic order in terms of revelation, religious experience, miracles, sacred books, the deliverances of prophets, sages, mystics, and various gnostics. In trying to understand the religious answer, it is best to begin with the general one, leaving aside the respective merits of different specific interpretations of it.

Part of the general answer is then that there is a cosmic order in reality. The natural world in which we live is a part of reality and it reflects that order. Through science we may discover some aspects of this order, but there are large and deep questions to which there can be no scientific answers. Why is there a natural world? How did it come into being? Why does it have the order it has? Why is it that of the countless alternative possibilities in the natural world it is self-conscious human beings that have been realized? What is the human significance of the cosmic order?

Scientific theories about the big bang and evolution do not even begin to answer these questions because the questions can easily accommodate the scientific answers and go beyond them. What was there before the big bang? Why was there one? Why were there natural entities that could evolve? Why were the conditions that shaped the direction of evolution as they were? Science asks and answers questions internal to the natural world. Religion, if it is reasonable, accepts these answers, asks questions external to the natural world, and endeavors to answer them. That some specific religious answers are myths tells no more against the general religious answer than alchemy, astrology, and phrenology tell against science.

Let us suppose for a moment that there is a cosmic order and that the natural world that science aims to understand is but a part of it. Why, if that were so, would it have anything to do with the meaning of life? A Stoic parable will help here. Take a dog tied to a cart drawn by a horse. The dog's position is unenviable, but it can still be made better or worse depending on what the dog does. It can understand its position and act accordingly: move when the cart moves, rest when the cart does. Or, it can try to resist, in which case it will be dragged, and the going will be much rougher than it needs to be. And so it is for us. We can try to understand and live according to the cosmic order, or we can ignorantly or unreasonably pit ourselves against it. The meaning of human lives is given by our place in the cosmic order, and our lives will go well or badly, depending on how well we understand and conform to it.

The Stoics did not think that human beings have a special place in the cosmic order, or that if we live reasonably, then we shall somehow free ourselves from the necessity it imposes on us. They thought that the only freedom we can have is to understand the necessity to which we are subject. Platonists, Jews, Christians, and a host of philosophers and theologians go beyond this and take the more optimistic view that the cosmic order is not just necessary, but also good. If our lives are governed by understanding it, then we shall not only avoid unnecessary suffering, but enjoy positive benefits. This is called salvation, and the hope that its possibility creates is the dominant tradition in religious thought. Ethics is transcendental because whatever has meaning in the natural world has it as a result of being in harmony with the good cosmic order. Meaning is not made, but found, and it is found outside of the natural world. The key to meaningful lives thus is to cultivate our understanding of the necessary and good cosmic order and to bring our projects in harmony with what we have thus understood.

One problem with the religious answer becomes apparent if we reflect on the mythical fate of Sisyphus, as Albert Camus did in *The Myth of Sisyphus*.[7] Sisyphus revealed divine secrets to humanity, and for this he was condemned by the gods to roll a heavy rock uphill to the crest of a mountain until it rolls down, then to roll it up again and again after it rolls down, and to do this for all eternity. Sisyphus's life is the epitome of meaninglessness. Camus's suggestion is that our time-bound lives are like Sisyphus's, albeit on a less heroic scale. The religious answer needs to show that this is not true.

Richard Taylor offers an interesting suggestion that bears on this.[8] He says:

Let us suppose that the gods, while condemning Sisyphus . . . at the same time, as an afterthought, waxed perversely merciful by implanting in him . . . a compulsive impulse to roll stones. . . . I call this perverse, because from our point of view there is clearly no reason why anyone should have a persistent and insatiable desire to do something as pointless as that. Nevertheless, suppose that is Sisyphus' condition. He has but one obsession, which is to roll stones. . . . Now it can be seen why this little afterthought of the gods . . . was . . . merciful. For they have by this device managed to give Sisyphus precisely what he wants—by making him want precisely what they inflict on him. . . . Sisyphus' . . . life is now filled with mission and meaning, and he seems to himself to have been given an entry to heaven.[9]

Taylor's suggestion provokes a doubt. Sisyphus's belief that his life has meaning is false. He believes that his meaningless life has meaning only because the gods have manipulated him. We may wonder, however, whether meaning can be based on false beliefs. But let us set this doubt aside for the moment and observe that, whatever we may think of Taylor's suggestion, it is not the religious one. Taylor suggests that the meaning of life comes from living the way we want to live, whereas the religious answer is that meaning comes from living according to the cosmic order. A further twist to the myth of Sisyphus, however, will show how it might give rise to the religious answer.

Suppose that Sisyphus's fate remains as before, but when he reaches the crest, the rocks are incorporated into a gigantic monument glorifying the gods. Sisyphus's life then is no longer pointless or futile. He is part of a larger scheme, and his activities, difficult as they are, have a purpose. It may be further supposed that Sisyphus understands this purpose because the gods have explained it to him. This, of course, is the religious answer to the question about the meaning of our own lives as we face the endless struggles our various projects involve. The cosmic order is God's self-designed monument, and the ultimate purpose of all reasonable projects is to enact the small role assigned to us in this monumental scheme. We know that there is such a scheme, and we know that it is good, even if its details remain obscure to our limited intellects, because it has been revealed to us by a sacred book, by prophets, or by our own interpretations of our experiences.

IV

The religious answer is unpersuasive. In the first place, it is impossible to adduce any evidence in its favor because all evidence available to human beings comes from the natural world. There can thus be no evidence of what may be the case beyond the reach of evidence. Sacred texts and prophets, of course, make various claims about what there is beyond the natural world, but there can be no reason to believe their claims because the authors of the texts and the prophets are human beings who, like us, have access only to the natural world. There undoubtedly are events and experiences that have, at least at present, no natural explanation. But to call the events miracles or the experiences religious is once again to go beyond what the evidence permits. To acknowledge that there are events and experiences in the natural world that we cannot explain lends no support whatsoever for explaining them in terms of a cosmic order. If there is a cosmic order, we cannot know anything about it: not *that* it exists, and even less *what* form it takes. The questions that religion asks about what there is external to the natural world have no rationally defensible answers. This does not make the questions uninteresting or illegitimate, but it does make all answers to them arbitrary. Arbitrary answers can be accepted on faith, but that does not make them less arbitrary. If the meaning of life depends on understanding and being motivated to live according to a cosmic order, then life has no meaning because we cannot understand the cosmic order and consequently cannot be motivated by it.

Assume, however, that these doubts about the religious answer are misplaced. Assume that the natural world points toward a cosmic order. That would still be insufficient to give life meaning. To know that there is a cosmic order is not to know what it is. But assume further that we can extrapolate from features of the natural world and form some views about what the cosmic order is because the natural world reflects the cosmic order. Knowing some things about the cosmic order, however, is still not enough for meaning, as the last twist to the myth of Sisyphus makes it obvious. Why would it make Sisyphus's life meaningful if he knew that the rocks he is rolling help to construct a monument for the glory of the gods? He knows that he is part of a plan, that his endless drudgery has a purpose, but neither the plan nor the purpose is his own. He is, in effect, enslaved by the gods. Having a part in monument building gives no more meaning to Sisyphus's life than having had a part in pyramid building gave to the slaves of the Egyptians. Of course, neither Sisyphus nor the real slaves had a choice in the matter; they both had to do what they had to do—just like the dog tied to the cart. They may resign themselves to it; they may accept the inevitable; but why would that make their lives meaningful? Meaningful lives require more than understanding the uselessness of opposing the immense force that coerces us to do its bidding.

What would have to be added to the cosmic order to make our lives meaningful is that it is not merely necessary, but also good. If we understood this about it, it would motivate us to live according to it. We would then see its necessity as the key to living a good life, and this, of course, is just what the dominant tradition in Western religious thought claims. But is this a reasonable claim? Why should we think that the cosmic order is good? Perhaps it is indifferent; perhaps it is not good, but bad; or perhaps it is a mixture of good, bad, and indifferent. What reason is there for accepting one of these possibilities, rather than the others?

In trying to answer this question, we need to remember the assumption we have accepted for the sake of argument: that it is reasonable to derive inferences from the natural world about the cosmic order. What features of the natural world, then, imply that the cosmic order is good? These features, it might be said, are that the natural world sustains life and the human form of life; that many human beings live happy and beneficial lives; that there are many acts of honor, decency, and self-sacrifice; and that people often strive to be kind and just. In general, we can read back our moral successes into the cosmic order.

This approach, however, is fundamentally flawed. For any form of life that the natural world sustains, there are numerous others that have perished in the struggle for survival. Alongside happy and beneficial human lives there are at least as many that are unhappy and destructive, and, probably more than either, lives that sometimes go one way and sometimes the other. Selfishness, cruelty, greed, aggression, envy, and malice also motivate people and often lead them to cause serious unjustified harm to others. If we extrapolate from how things are in the natural world to what the cosmic order must be like, then we cannot just concentrate on the good and ignore what is bad and indifferent. If the natural world reflects a cosmic order, then there is much that is bad and indifferent in the cosmic order, in addition to what may be good.

If the cosmic order has to be good in order to endow our lives with meaning, then we have no reason to believe that our lives have meaning. For understanding the cosmic order will not then motivate us to try to live according to it, but to try to avoid its malignity or indifference. If Sisyphus had remained reasonable in the midst of what the gods forced him to endure, he would not have concluded that the monument the gods were building to glorify themselves was good or that his enforced contribution to it gave meaning to his drudgery.

There is then no reason to accept the religious answer to the question of whether our lives have meaning, because we have no reason to believe that there is a cosmic order; because if there is one, we have no reason to believe anything about what it is; and because if we hold beliefs about what it is on the basis of what the natural world implies, then reason prompts the belief that the cosmic order is a mixture of good, bad, and indifferent elements.

V

Let us, then, turn from the religious to the moral approach to the meaning of life. The distinction between the two approaches has been broached by Plato in *Euthyphro*.[10] The subject there is piety or holiness, but it has become customary to pose the question Socrates puts to Euthyphro in more general terms to be about the source of the good. Assuming that there is a God, what is the relation between God and the good? Does God make the good good or does God's will reflect the good that exists independently of it? The religious answer is the first, the moral answer is the second. Because morality is about the good, regardless of whether there is a God whose will could or would reflect the good, the concern of morality is not with God, but with what God's will might reflect.

According to the moral approach, Wittgenstein was wrong to think that "[e]thics is transcendental."[11] It is revealing, however, to bear in mind Wittgenstein's reason for thinking as he did. Commenting on Schlick's view about "two conceptions of the essence of the Good," Wittgenstein says that "according to the superficial interpretation, the Good is good because God wills it; according to the deeper interpretation, God wills the Good because it is good." Wittgenstein, then, goes on: "I think that the first conception is the deeper one: Good is what God orders. For this cuts off the path to any and every explanation of 'why' it is good, while the second conception is precisely the superficial, the rationalistic one, which proceeds as if what is good could still be given some foundation."[12] The moral approach to the meaning of life assumes, for reasons given in the preceding section, the failure of what Wittgenstein thinks of as the deeper conception. Wittgenstein is wrong to regard the moral approach as "the superficial, the rationalistic one," precisely because it recognizes the obligation that Wittgenstein spurns of giving reasons for claims about what the good is, if its pursuit is to endow life with meaning. It is a further feature of the moral approach that it looks for these reasons within the natural world, rather than outside of it.

Before we can address the question of where in the natural world these reasons could be found, clarity requires distinguishing between a wide and a narrow sense of morality. In the narrow sense, the concern of morality is with what is right. In this sense, morality is about the formulation of impersonal, impartial, disinterested rules that ought to govern human interactions. In the wide sense, the concern of morality is not merely with what is right, but also with what is good. In this sense, morality is not only about rules, actions, and obligations, but also about ideals, virtues, conceptions of a good life, personal aspirations, intimate relationships, private projects, supererogation, and so forth. The moral approach to the meaning of life is moral in the wide sense: what gives meaning to life is the pursuit of good projects. Doing what is right is an important part of that, but it is only a part. Right actions are impersonal conditions of a moral life, whereas the meaningfulness of moral lives derives from the personal sphere in which there are great individual variations. (A technical expression of this point is that the meaning of life is to be found in the aretaic/eudaimonist, rather than in the deontological, aspect of morality.)

We can once again begin by returning to the earlier suggestion of Richard Taylor about where in the wide sense of morality (or in the aretaic/eudaimonist aspect of it) the source of meaning may be found. Taylor thought that Sisyphus's life would have meaning if he wanted to pursue the project to which the gods have doomed him. According to Taylor, the crux is the wanting, not the nature of the projects or how we came to have them. Meaning thus comes from us, not from our projects. We confer meaning on them. On this view, meaning is subjective.

The distinction between "subjective" and "objective" can be drawn in a number of different ways, and there is much confusion about the whole question. It is important, therefore, to make it clear that what is meant by the meaning of life being subjective is that its meaning depends wholly on how the agents regard their lives. According to this view, a life has meaning if the agent sincerely thinks so, and it lacks meaning if the agent sincerely denies it. The objective view, then, is that the agents' thinking that their lives have meaning is the necessary and sufficient condition for their lives having meaning. The objective view, by contrast, grants that the agents' attribution of meaning to their lives is necessary for their lives' having meaning, but it denies that it is sufficient. According to the objective view, lives may lack meaning even if their agents think otherwise, for they may be mistaken.

There are three reasons for rejecting the subjective view and accepting the objective one. The first emerges if we recall the doubt we ignored earlier. We may want to pursue a project only because we have been manipulated, just as Sisyphus was by the gods in the last twist to the myth. It seems clear, however, that there is a difference between wanting to pursue a project because of indoctrination or artificial stimulation of the cortex and wanting to pursue it as a result of having reflected and discovered that it makes our lives meaningful. If meaning were subjective, if it were created merely by our wants and beliefs, it would make no difference to meaning whether our wanting to pursue a project is genuine or manipulated. And it would be inexplicable how the discovery of manipulation could lead us to regard as meaningless a project that we regarded as meaningful before the discovery. Wanting to pursue a project is certainly connected with the meaning of life, but there is more to meaningful lives than that we want to pursue some project.

The second reason grows out of the first. Suppose that we genuinely want to pursue a project, so that we have not been manipulated. Suppose that Sisyphus just found himself wanting to roll rocks. That this is not sufficient for meaning is shown by the fact that the bare having of a want is not enough to move us to try satisfy it. The satisfaction of a want has to matter to us. And its mattering depends on its fitting into the overall causal nexus that connects that want to our other wants, and to our hopes, plans, goals, ambitions, and memories. If we all of a sudden discovered in ourselves an urge to roll rocks, we would not automatically act on it. We would ask ourselves why we want to do that and how it would affect our lives and projects if we did it. There is an explanation that we would want to give ourselves, especially since the want in question is assumed not to be trivial, like scratching one's nose, but a meaning-conferring one, like deciding to make rock rolling one's project in life.

It might be thought, however, that excluding manipulation and having an explanation of why the satisfaction of a want is important to us are requirements that the subjective view can meet. But this is not so. To ascertain whether we have been manipulated, or to explain why something is important to us, inevitably involves reference to objective considerations that exist independently of what we think. Manipulation is interference from the outside by people, the media, the gods, or whatever. To exclude it requires having reasons to believe that we have not been unduly influenced in these ways. And the explanation of why something matters to us must have to do with the influence on us of our upbringing, education, family, society, and so forth. The nature and strength of these influences are independent of what we think about them.

The third reason against the subjective view emerges from the recognition that we want to pursue a project because we believe that it would make our lives better than other available alternatives. But whether this is true depends on whether its pursuit would actually make our lives better. After all, we may pursue a project because we mistakenly believe that it would make our lives better, we may discover that we are mistaken, and we may change our minds about the meaningfulness of the project. If the mere belief that a project is better than the alternatives were sufficient to make the project meaningful, this change of mind could not occur.

It may be said in defense of the subjective view—that the sincere belief that our lives have meaning is necessary and sufficient for our lives' having meaning—that what these three objections show is that the truth of our beliefs may affect how good our projects are, but it will not affect our sense that our lives are meaningful, if we believe them to be so. This is partly right and partly wrong. It is right that we may find our projects meaningful even if, unbeknownst to us, our wants are manipulated and our beliefs in the importance and goodness of our projects are false. But it is wrong to conclude from this that the subjective view that meaning depends merely on our beliefs is correct. The very recognition that meaning requires both that we should fail to know that our wants are being manipulated and that we should fail to realize that our beliefs are false implies the relevance of objective considerations. For the knowledge that our wants are manipulated and beliefs false would destroy our belief in the meaningfulness of our projects. That we may be ignorant of the objective conditions of our projects' having meaning does not show that those conditions are irrelevant to their meaning. It shows that we may be mistaken in believing that our projects have meaning. If we realize that we are mistaken, that our wants are manipulated, or that our beliefs in the importance or goodness of our projects are false, then we would be the first to think that the projects we regarded as meaningful were in fact meaningless. This is just what would happen to Sisyphus if he knew the facts.

We are justified in concluding, therefore, that, in addition to the relevant wants and beliefs, there are objective conditions that must be met by meaningful lives. One of these conditions is that the wants must be genuine; and the other is that the beliefs must be true. Consequently, meaning depends on both subjective and objective conditions. To think otherwise, as Taylor does, is not to suppose that meaning depends on what God wills, as the religious approach claims, but that it depends on what the agent wills. As the religious approach relativizes meaning to God's will, so the subjective moral approach relativizes it to the agent's will. Both leave it unexplained how the subjective state of willing, whether it be God's or human agents', could be sufficient to establish what it is that makes lives meaningful.

The strongest case for the moral approach to the meaning of life will therefore recognize that meaning depends on both the subjective and the objective conditions. The subjective condition requires us to be in the appropriate psychological states of wanting and believing. The objective condition requires that our projects actually make our lives better. Meaning then depends on the coincidence of these two conditions: on our psychological states' being successfully directed toward the appropriate objects. As David Wiggins puts it: "psychological states and their objects [are] equal and reciprocal partners. . . . It can be true both that we desire x because we think x good, and that x is good because we desire x. . . . The quality by which the thing qualifies as good and the desire *for* the thing are equals and 'made for one another.'"[13]

It need not be supposed that this presupposes commitment to a cosmic order. It is not surprising that in the course of evolution there has emerged something like a correlation between what we want and what is good for us. We would be extinct if it were otherwise. Yet the correlation is less than perfect. Objective conditions both shape and constrain our wants, but within the limits they impose on our projects, there is much scope for experiments in living. Evolutionary success has not freed us from necessity, but it has opened numerous possibilities that we may pursue within the limits of necessity.

We may conclude, then, that according to the moral approach our lives have meaning if the following conditions are met: first, they are not worthless, pointless, misdirected, trivial, or futile; second, we have not succumbed to the view that all human projects are absurd; third, we have identified with projects that we genuinely want to pursue; and fourth, our belief that successful engagement in our projects will make our lives good or better is true.

VI

The problems of the moral answer begin to emerge if we recognize that the fourth condition of meaningful lives is ambiguous. It may mean that successful engagement in our projects will make our lives *morally* better or that it will make them better in *nonmoral* ways. This ambiguity derives from the ambiguity of the "good" in good lives. Our lives may be good because they conform to the requirements of morality, or they may be good because we find them satisfying. Satisfaction in this context should not be identified either with pleasure or with the feeling that results from having met one's own physiological or psychological needs. To be sure, meeting them is an example of satisfaction, but satisfaction may also be derived from doing our duty at considerable cost to ourselves, imposing hard discipline on ourselves, beholding the success of others that does not reflect on us at all, or seeing that justice is done even though we do not benefit from it. These two constituents of good lives may coincide, or they may not. Morally good lives may not be satisfying, and satisfying lives may not be morally good. It is a moral ideal dating back at least to Socrates that our satisfactions should derive from living in conformity to the requirements of morality. If the ideal holds, the ambiguity of the "good" will disappear. The projects we pursue then will be morally good, and our lives will be at once good and meaningful because we will find our engagement in our morally good projects satisfying. This is the ideal that motivates the moral answer to the meaning of life. The ideal, however, is flawed, and the moral answer fails.

There are two different lines of argument that lead to this conclusion. The first is that morally good projects need not be satisfying. What happened to Mill makes this point obvious. Morally good projects may be tedious or painful; they may involve doing our duty at the cost of self-sacrifice, self-denial, the frustration of our desires, and going against our strong feelings. The modicum of satisfaction we may take in doing what we feel we ought to do is often greatly outweighed by the dissatisfactions that are the by-products of having to act contrary to our nonmoral projects.

The second line of argument that leads to the failure of the moral answer is that even if it were true that morally good projects are satisfying, it would not follow that *only* morally good projects are satisfying. There may be satisfying immoral and nonmoral projects, and successful engagement in them may give meaning to our lives. That immoral lives may be meaningful is shown by the countless dedicated Nazi and Communist mass murderers, by those many sincerely committed terrorists who aim to destabilize one society or another through committing outrageous crimes against innocent civilians, and by people whose rage, resentment, greed, ambition, selfishness, sense of superiority or inferiority give purpose to their lives and lead them to inflict grievous unjustified harm on others. Such people may be successfully engaged in their projects, derive great satisfaction from them, and find their lives as scourges of their literal or metaphorical gods very meaningful.

The moral answer, however, is vitiated not only by moral monsters, but also by lives dedicated to the pursuit of nonmoral projects, which may be athletic, aesthetic, horticultural, erotic, or scholarly, or may involve collecting, learning languages, travel, connoisseurship, the invention of ingenious gadgets, and so forth. The lives of many people are given meaning by projects that are neither morally good nor immoral, but morally indifferent. People engaged in them may by and large conform to morality. The meaning of their lives, however, derives from their engagement in nonmoral projects and not from living in conformity with the requirements of morality. It follows from the possibility that immoral and nonmoral projects may give meaning to lives that the moral answer is mistaken in regarding successful engagement in morally good projects as a necessary condition of meaningful lives.

In sum, the moral answer that meaning derives from living good lives founders because of the ambiguity of the "good." If the "good" is taken to be "morally good," then the claim is false because morally good lives may not be meaningful and meaningful lives may not be morally good. If, on the other hand, the "good" is interpreted as "nonmoral good," then the answer ceases to be moral, since it allows that meaningful lives may be immoral or nonmoral. The moral answer, therefore, turns out to be either false or not moral. Its defenders, of course, normally intend it to be interpreted in the moral sense, so the likely charge they have to contend with is that their answer is false.

VII

There are, then, strong and independent reasons that show that neither religion nor morality provides a satisfactory approach to the meaning of life. But there is yet another and deeper reason why they both fail: they seek a general answer. Their basic assumption is that finding meaning depends on finding something that applies equally to all lives. The religious approach looks for that something to a cosmic order; the moral approach seeks it in morality. They recognize individual differences, but they treat them as mere variations on the same basic theme. Individual differences matter to them only because they compel us to do different things to conform to the same general meaning-conferring requirement. Given our characters and circumstances, we may have to serve the will of God in different ways, you as an artist, I as a soldier, or we may have to apply the categorical imperative in different situations or pursue the common good by means of different actions. But they both assume that, for all of us, meaning is derived from the same source, be it the will of God or some moral principle. It is this assumption that makes it impossible for both approaches to recognize the possibility that different individuals may derive meaning for their lives from radically different sources. This is the assumption that prevents them from acknowledging that individual differences have a fundamental influence not only on what we must do to pursue a meaning-conferring project, but also on which of many meaning-conferring projects we should aim to pursue. It is the assumption that all meaning-conferring projects must ultimately be variations of some one or few patterns that is responsible for the mistaken view that the phrase "the meaning of life is . . ." can be completed by some general formula that will make the resulting sentence hold true of all lives.

The problem is that if we give up the assumption that there is a general answer to the question of what gives meaning to life, then we seem to be led back to the subjective view that we had three good reasons to reject earlier. But these reasons continue to hold even if no general answer provides the additional necessary and sufficient condition that must be added to the subjective condition. The wants whose satisfaction we seek may be manipulated, self-destructive, trivial, inconsistent, or otherwise detrimental and thus fail to make our lives meaningful. And the beliefs we hold about the kind of life that would be meaningful may be false. Conformity to the subjective condition is necessary, but insufficient, for meaningful lives, and conformity to the objective by searching for a general answer exacts the unacceptable cost of denying that different lives may be made meaningful by conformity to different meaning-conferring requirements.

It is in this way that answering the question: Does life have a meaning? has become a perennial philosophical problem. The problem originates in a disruption of everyday life. Because we are unsuccessful, bored, poor, tired, unlucky, sick, grief-stricken, victims of injustice, or readers of subversive books, we start reflecting on the point of the routine activities we endlessly perform. Once we embark on this reflection, it is hard to stop. Reflection puts an end to the unreflective innocence with which we have unquestioningly lived in accordance to the prevailing conventions. As we question, so we feel the need for answers, and we turn to religion or morality. But the religious answer fails because no reason can be given for thinking that there is a cosmic order that would confer meaning on lives lived in conformity to it. And the moral answer fails because meaningful lives may be immoral or nonmoral and moral lives may not be meaningful. Defenders of the religious answer insist that the problems of morality can be met only by appealing to a cosmic order that would guarantee the identity of good and meaningful lives. Defenders of the moral answer insist that there must be moral reasons for regarding the cosmic order as good and that these reasons are either unavailable, or, if available, cannot themselves be transcendental. The religious and moral answers to this perennial problem agree in seeking a general answer, but they disagree whether it is to be found in the transcendental or in the natural world.

VIII

The way out of this impasse is to give up the search for a general answer. That brings us to an approach to the meaning of life that is free of the defects of the religious and moral answers. Let us call this approach "pluralistic." Its description is now a simple matter, because it involves no more than assembling the conclusions that have been reached by the preceding arguments. These conclusions may be formulated as conditions of meaningful lives. According to the pluralistic approach, then, lives have meaning if they meet the following conditions:

1. They are not dominated by worthless, pointless, misdirected, trivial, or futile activities.
2. They are not vitiated by the belief that all human projects are absurd.
3. They involve the pursuit of projects with which the agents have genuinely identified; they thus exclude all forms of manipulation.
4. Their agents' genuine identification with their projects is based on their true belief that successful engagement in them will make their lives better by providing the satisfactions they seek; they thus exclude all projects in which the agents' subjective identification is not correlated with objective conditions.
5. Their objective conditions are located in the natural world, not outside of it; they thus exclude the religious answer.

6. Their agents' subjective identifications are based on the pursuit of projects that yield either morally good, or immoral, or nonmoral satisfactions; they thus exclude the moral answer.

7. Their agents' subjective identifications with their projects reflect individual differences; they thus exclude all general answers.

These conditions are individually necessary and jointly sufficient to make lives meaningful. The main purpose of all the preceding arguments has been to attempt to explain and justify them.

The argument has been meant also to make it evident that the proposed approach is pluralistic, not in the trivial sense that there are many conditions that meaningful lives must meet, but in the important sense that meaningful lives may take a wide plurality of forms. The plurality of meaningful lives reflects, in addition to individual differences in our characters and circumstances, also individual differences in the type of projects that we pursue. These projects may be religious or moral, but they may also be scientific, aesthetic, athletic, scholarly, horticultural, military, commercial, political, poetic, and so on. The pluralistic approach recognizes that any project may contribute to making a life meaningful, provided it meets the conditions listed above. Meeting these conditions excludes many possibilities, but for present purposes, the most important among them is the possibility of a general answer to the question of what project or what type of project would make all lives meaningful. The basic difference between the pluralistic approach, on the one hand, and the religious and moral modes of reflection, on the other, is that the first denies and the second assert that there is a general answer.

It remains to point out that this difference constitutes a radical break between the pluralistic approach and traditional philosophical and religious thinking about the meaning of life. For one central claim of the pluralistic approach is that individuals must make their lives meaningful by genuinely identifying themselves with their projects and that doing so must reflect the differences of their capacities, interests, and preferences. It is because of these differences that there can be no acceptable general answers to questions about the meaning of life. A general answer must apply to all human lives, but if meaningful lives must reflect individual differences, then general answers, by their very nature, are doomed.

Part of the reason why the pluralistic approach constitutes a radical break with traditional philosophical and religious ways of thinking about the meaning of life is that all these ways aim to provide a general answer. This is what all the major religions, metaphysical systems, and moral theories aim to do. For Jews, it is the Covenant; for Christians, it is the life of Christ; for Buddhists, it is the Karma; for Moslems, it is the law as laid down in the Koran; for Platonists, it is the Form of the Good; for Stoics, it is natural necessity; for Hegelians, it is the dialectic; for utilitarians, it is the maximization of general happiness; and so on. If the pluralistic approach is right, then all these, and other, general answers are fundamentally misguided because they are essentially committed to denying individual differences in what lives can be meaningful. The pluralistic approach is an attempt to proceed in a different way.

Another central claim of the pluralistic approach is that meaningful lives may not be morally good and morally good lives may not be meaningful. The fundamental reason for this is that meaningful lives often depend on engagement in nonmoral projects. Such projects may be crucial to making lives meaningful, but engagement in them may violate or be indifferent to the requirements of morality. This claim is also contrary to the traditional ways of thinking about meaningful lives because the traditional assumption is that only morally good projects could make lives meaningful.

The assumption that underlies this tradition is that the scheme of things is such that ultimately only morally good lives will be satisfying and immoral or nonmoral lives cannot be. The pluralistic approach rejects this assumption as groundless. Immoral or nonmoral lives could have sufficient satisfactions to make them meaningful. This is hard to accept because it outrages our moral sensibility, which is deeply influenced by this tradition. Accepting it, however, has the virtue of doing justice to the plain fact that many evil and morally unconcerned people live meaningful lives. It also explains what this tradition has great difficulty with explaining, namely, why so many people live lives in which immoral and nonmoral satisfactions dominate moral ones. The explanation is that such satisfactions may make their lives meaningful. It is thus a consequence of the pluralistic approach that the questions of what makes lives meaningful and what makes them morally good are distinct and should not be conflated as it is traditionally done.

NOTES

This paper has been much improved by the criticisms and suggestions of Graeme Hunter, Joel Kupperman, Jonathan Mandle, Wallace Matson, and especially Rachel Cohon. Their help is gratefully acknowledged.

1. John Stuart Mill, *Autobiography* (New York: Columbia University Press, 1924).

2. Thomas Nagel, "The Absurd" in his *Mortal Questions* (Cambridge: Cambridge University Press, 1979), pp. 11–23; quoted passage on p. 13.

3. Nagel, "The Absurd," pp. 14–15.

4. Ludwig Wittgenstein, *Tractatus Logico-Philosophicus*, trans. D. F. Pears and B. F. McGuinness (London: Routledge, 1961), 6.41.

5. Wittgenstein, *Tractatus*, 6.421.

6. Ludwig Wittgenstein, "A Lecture on Ethics," *Philosophical Review*, 74 (1965), pp. 3–12; quoted passage on p. 5.

7. Albert Camus, *The Myth of Sisyphus*, trans. Justin O'Brien (London: Hamish Hamilton, 1955).

8. Richard Taylor, *Good and Evil* (New York: Macmillan, 1970).

9. Taylor, *Good and Evil*, p. 259.

10. Plato, *Euthyphro*, trans. Lane Cooper, in *Plato: The Collected Dialogues*, ed. Edith Hamilton and Huntington Cairns (Princeton: Princeton University Press, 1961).

11. Wittgenstein, *Tractatus*, 6.421.

12. Friedrich Waismann, "Notes on Talks with Wittgenstein," *Philosophical Review*, 74 (1965), pp. 15–16; quoted passage on p. 15.

13. David Wiggins, "Truth, Invention, and the Meaning of Life," *Proceedings of the British Academy*, 62 (1976), pp. 331–378; quoted passage on pp. 348–49.

Midwest Studies in Philosophy, XXIV (2000)

In Defense of a Common Ideal for a Human Life

E. M. ADAMS

VALUE SUBJECTIVISM AND CULTURAL RELATIVISM

Value subjectivism and moral relativism are common currency in Western societies. One prominent strand is modern naturalism, based on the modern scientific approach to reality that depends on sensory experience as our only data-gathering mode of epistemic encounter with the world. It claims that moral and other normative or value judgments are not grounded through our semantic and knowledge-yielding powers to objective normative structures and value features of reality. So disagreements in value judgments that are not based on disagreements about the facts, it is said, cannot be resolved by search for the truth of the matter, for there is no truth of the matter. This kind of value subjectivism is especially pernicious in a culture in which commitment to individualism is strong, for it tends toward atomization and dissolution of the social order, which leads to politicization of the culture and efforts by the power structure to control the culture.

Some humanistic critics of eighteenth-century Enlightenment cosmopolitan ideals of humanity and society, following the lead of Vico and Herder, agree with the scientific naturalists that there is no common transcultural ideal of what a human being or a society should be and that therefore there is no common morality by which people or social institutions of different cultures or times can be judged. But they are different from the modern naturalists in that their cultural relativism does not stem from a narrow sensory empiricism, but is, nonetheless, a reaction to the undermining of the humanistic dimension of the culture by the skepticism and subjectivism grounded in modern naturalism. From their humanistic way of studying human phenomena, they conclude that a historically evolved culture is a form of life that defines human identity, the ideals and norms of the people, and their social institutions and ways of categorizing the world; furthermore, they claim that there is no independent or objective reality with respect to which these may be held accountable and judged correct or incorrect. They maintain that the ideals and the worldview of a cultural community may be valid although incompatible with equally valid ideals and views of other historical communities. The incompatibility, however, cannot be a logical inconsistency, for that would indicate a transcending truth or reality with respect to which they could be judged. It can be only the impossibility of integration. They claim an internal objectivity and truth for some value judgments and factual beliefs and falsity for others; that is, they acknowledge that internal to a form of life some value judgments and factual beliefs are true and some are false in relation to the world as constituted by the cultural categories of the form of life in question. But they embrace cultural relativism, for they claim that each communal form of life has a world of its own and there is no transcendent or external reality to which it can be held epistemically accountable. They are, indeed, genuine communitarians, what we may call "deep" communitarians.

A community, they contend, is constituted by a shared, historically evolved form of life that embraces the culture and the social order. Although this position would tend toward fission of a pluralistic society into ethnic groups, it would not lead to atomization and dissolution of a culturally homogeneous society, as naturalistic subjectivism with individualism tends to do.

The value subjectivism of the naturalists actually undermines claims to knowledge in any area of the culture, for the justification of truth claims in any field requires objective and correct value judgments about the grounds or reasons for the truth claims at issue. And of course the grounds and reasons are justificatory; they show the truth claims they support to be worthy, or at least more worthy, of belief. The cultural relativism of the humanistic communitarians leaves us with either cultural idealism, according to which each culture posits or projects its own world, without any independent reality to which it is accountable, or with a pliable independent reality in itself that lends itself to multiple valid ways of being culturally delineated. There are difficulties with either alternative. One common difficulty is how people of different cultures could communicate, understand, and interact with one another without a shared world present to them with much the same form. However, both naturalistic value subjectivism and communitarian cultural relativism would be without excuse or reason if realistic humanism should prove to be true. Rather than dwelling on the difficulties with value subjectivism and cultural relativism, I shall present a case, based on realistic humanism, for a universal ideal for a human life—an ideal that would be valid, and could be recognized as such, by human beings in any civilization.

REALISTIC HUMANISM AND RATIONAL AGENCY

Realistic humanism holds that lived experience and rational agency, even rational thinking, presupposes that at least some subject matters, especially human phenomena, have inherent normative and meaning structures in addition to the factual dimension recognized by modern science and that discourse that involves normative, value, and meaning concepts is of or about these structures and may be objectively true or false in terms of them. The position claims that emotive (affective and conative) experience in which normative and value concepts are grounded and that perceptual understanding and reflection based on self-awareness, which give rise to the language of meaning, are knowledge-yielding under critical assessment. The case for the epistemic character of these modes of experience turns on philosophical analysis of the language we use to report such experiences and what it is meaningful to say and not meaningful to say about them.

Because it makes sense, as I have contended in other works,[1] to speak of emotive experiences as expressible in language, as having logical form and logical relationships, as illusory, as hallucinatory, as correct or incorrect, as rational or as irrational, we may conclude that they have a semantic dimension and are knowledge-yielding. Similar considerations of what it is meaningful to say about the modes of experience in which the language of meaning is grounded, namely, reflection on our own subjectivity and what we may call "expression perception" and "perceptual understanding" of others and their behavior, support the claim that these too are knowledge-yielding. On this basis, realistic humanism claims that what is known through these modes of experience and what we grasp through meaning concepts are unique and irreducible structures of meaning inherent in the subject matter in question.

So realistic humanism holds that lived experience reveals through its presuppositions that at least some subject matters, especially human phenomena, have inherent normative, value, and meaning dimensions as well as the factual structures on which science focuses with its reliance on sensory experience as our only knowledge-yielding, data-gathering mode of encounter with reality. It holds also that all of these dimensions have a role in causation and that subject matters with these categorial dimensions require a world with an equally complex structure for its intelligibility.[2]

Human beings, in any civilization, are, at least to some extent, rational agents and thinkers, for civilization requires rational action in cooperative endeavors, rational action requires some measure of success in decision making and in knowledge seeking, and success in decision making and knowledge seeking requires rational thinking. Rational thinking presupposes the basic principles of normative logic. So the basic principles of normative logic are neither subjective nor culturally relative, for they are embedded in the normative constitution of a thinking mind and presupposed in rational thinking, regardless of whether they are ever articulated or reflected on. They are common to all cultures, and every thinking person is vulnerable to criticism in terms of them, for everyone with somewhat mature human powers is under an inner imperative, as part of one's inherent normative constitution, to be consistent and correct in one's experiences, thoughts, and beliefs and justified in one's decisions and actions. We experience an inconsistency in our experiences, beliefs, and decisions as trouble and try to locate and correct the error. This is what drives and guides fruitful thinking and cultural progress. It is what keeps us in touch with the real world and makes for success in human enterprises.

Human beings are not subject only to the principles of logical criticism. As rational agents, in rational decisions and actions, we presuppose the principles by virtue of which they are rational, and we are subject to appraisal in terms of them; they are the fundamental principles of life criticism. Agents with knowledge-yielding powers act on reasons, and they have an inner requirement that their reasons be good ones, that they justify their actions and projects, even their self-organization and the life they are living.

Enlightened rational thinkers are not content to take a single truth claim as true regardless of how apparent it may be; they demand that it fit into and cohere with a wider web of truths in order to be acceptable, ultimately that it fit into a comprehensive view of the world. In a similar manner, a rational agent cannot be satisfied with the apparent justification and meaningfulness of an action simply in terms of its success in achieving its immediate intent. We look for its justification and meaning in terms of its bearing on a wider complex of purposes or requirements. We ask about how the action in question fits in with some larger project in which we are engaged or to which we are committed; and we ask of this project or some still more inclusive project how it fits into and will bear on the life we are living; we ask of the life we are living how it fits into and bears on the communal, social, and historical context of our existence; and, if we have the conceptual room for it, we ask how our life project and human history fit in with the normative structure and dynamics of the universe, or, as some religious people would say, how our life and human history fit in with the will of God. We seek the ever broader context because both the ultimate value and the meaningfulness of our actions, projects, and lives depend on it.

Of course we do not go through this whole sequence of questions in considering the justification or meaningfulnes of most of our actions. The point is that the next question in the sequence is always pertinent regardless of whether it is ever considered. Justification of an action is manifestly incomplete at any point short of the limit imposed by the meaninglessness of a further question. This line of questions is parallel with the sequence of "Why?"s asked in the search for the understanding of phenomena. At any point, a further "Why?" is always pertinent, and rational thinkers are vulnerable to it so long as it is a meaningful question. Rational beings seek justificatory reasons for their beliefs and actions and explanatory reasons for what they take to be real, for without them their beliefs and actions would be unreliable. And furthermore, their inner normative constitution requires it of them. Failure to do so is a failure in self-fulfillment. Only a life based on rational thought and decision and subject to rational approval under critical assessment is worthy of rational agents, for rational agents are not agents who are in fact rational but beings who ought to be rational.

HUMAN BEINGS AND THE OFFICE OF PERSONHOOD

So far we have talked about rationality, but our primary concern is with morality and the principles of ethical criticism. Ethical criticism is the area of rational criticism that is concerned with the appropriateness or worthiness of an action, project, or life for a human being under the circumstances and conditions of one's existence. Just as medical criticism of the decisions and actions of physicians in treating their patients reflects on them as physicians, moral criticism of the decisions, actions, and lives of people is rational criticism that reflects on them as human beings, as persons.

The concept of a person is an office concept. Some concepts are of things in terms of selected or essential features or properties exemplified in them: "mica," for example. We may call these "factual" concepts, for they pertain to the factual constitution of the things they denote. Some concepts are of things in terms of what they are for—in terms of their function, what they exist or are structured to do: "pump," for instance. The concept applies to something in terms of its normative structure. These are functional concepts. Office concepts involve yet another dimension. They apply on the basis of responsibilities—functions that have to be known in order to be had and that can be fulfilled only under the guidance of knowledge and critical judgment.

Although most offices are formed by a division of responsibilities in cooperative endeavors, personhood is a natural office, one to which human beings are born. Human beings who do not have the requisite powers for the responsibilities inherent in personhood are either immature or impaired in some way. But just as a pump that will not pump is still a pump, but a defective one, human beings who are more or less mature biologically but lack the powers to fulfill the responsibilities of personhood are still persons, but impaired ones.

Although all the persons we know are human beings and it may be that only human beings are persons, we know nothing that rules out the possibility of other kinds of beings having the office of personhood. What is essential is not our biological nature, but our capacity for experience, knowledge, critical judgment, and rational living. Even if a biological nature is essential, it may be possible for other biological species to have the requisite powers and normative constitution for personhood.

The defining responsibility of personhood for a human being is to define and to live a life of one's own that would be worthy of one both as a human being and as the individual one is in the circumstances of one's existence—that is, a life that would be justified and approved under rational and moral criticism. One can do no greater wrong to people with somewhat normal and mature human powers than to deny them the opportunity to have a life of their own and to live it by the exercise of their own knowledge-yielding and critical powers so long as they are more or less responsible, so long as the life they live and their actions are more or less justified as appraised under rational and moral criticism.

Of course, communitarians are right in claiming that human beings are culturally and socially generated. When we reach the point of critical reflective consciousness, we find ourselves a project already in progress, one that has been formed from inherent drives, instincts, inclinations, desires, social and cultural influences, and commands and directives of others. With critical self-consciousness, one begins to take charge of one's self and the life one is living and may modify or even radically redefine one's identity and the life one is living. One may reconstruct one's normative self-concept and the life plan that one developed under conditioning and the direction of others. Of course one has to have a fairly well-developed self and a store of cultural capital in order to gain a critical perspective on one's defining self-concept and life plan and to gain some degree of mastery over them.

One of the primary objectives of a liberal education is to develop the requisite powers and to gain mastery of one's self and the life one is living. This means liberation, insofar as possible, from the cultural and social forces that formed one's early selfhood and direction. Liberation by enlightenment and critical self-examination is not so much a matter of shucking off one's initial identity and abandoning the life project one finds in progress at the dawn of one's critical self-consciousness. Although it may involve corrections and modifications and sometimes even a radical change, it is primarily a matter of exploring and coming to understand the "commitments" involved and the justificatory grounds or reasons for them. Even if none are abandoned or modified, the critical process converts them from effects or uncritical acceptances to genuine commitments and thus makes them one's own. This is an enlightenment that frees one from cultural slavery; it is an enlightenment that lifts one out of the causal dynamics of one's natural and social environment into the realm of rationality and freedom, even with regard to one's identity and life enterprise. It makes one more fully human, with a deeper level of involvement in the constitution of one's self and in one's life. But we can never bring under reflective review all of the complex organization of the semantic dispositions, states, acts, and their presuppositions that make us up and completely reconstruct ourselves. It is always a matter of degree.

Nevertheless, as rational agents, we are under an inner constitutional imperative, one that is taken up in our normative self-concept when we get it right, to develop the requisite powers and to define and to live a life of our own. This requires that we have an identity of our own as well; we cannot have a life of our own without it. Insofar as one is a product of natural, social, and cultural causal conditions or the manipulations of others, one is more a thing than a person, and the life one lives is a product of forces and decisions from outside oneself. Only an authentic self can have an authentic life of one's own.

The imperative to be rational in thought and action and to define one's self and a life that would be worthy of one, one that would be approved under rational and moral criticism, is not simply an inclination, a want, or a desire; it is a responsibility, grounded in our nature as human beings. This responsibility defines our natural office of personhood. It is the basis of human rights.

The extent to which one lives by and fulfills the constitutional requirements of personhood is a basis for evaluating one both as a human being and as a person. If one lacks the requisite powers for fulfilling the normative requirements involved, one is either immature or impaired; if one has the necessary powers and yet fails to live by one's normative constitution, one is morally at fault. Developing the requisite powers and living by them in the circumstances of one's existence under the constraints and requirements of one's governing constitution is the primary way to perfect one's being.

So a worthy life for a human being must be an authentic life of one's own. This means that it would have to be constituted by one's own commitments and be such that it would be approved under one's own rational and moral criticism. Of course one's own rational and moral criticism of oneself should square with the rational and moral criticism that other informed people would make of one, for such criticisms, regardless of who makes them, are either correct or incorrect; according to realistic humanism, there is a truth of the matter. But if one's life did not have one's own approval, it would not be authentically one's own life, for one would not fully embrace it and identify with it. Indeed, one would not be an integrated self; one would disapprove of one's life while living it and disapprove of oneself for living it. It would be self-destructive.

No one, unless one is too immature or one's powers are not functioning normally, is indifferent to rational and moral criticism, whether one's own or that of well-informed people whom one respects. This is because as knower/agents we are under an inner imperative, a normative requirement embedded in our governing constitution, to be rational in the way we organize our selves and our lives. In other words, we are rational beings; by our nature, we ought to think and act on the basis of reasons. We are not, or should not be, the product of blind naturalistic or social causes. As persons, we are knowledge-based beings, and as such we are responsible for both who we are and what we think and do. There is no way that we can live successfully and fulfill our being without thinking and living in accordance with the requirements of rationality and morality.

The imperatives of our normative constitution have to be known in order to become responsibilities and fully effective in our lives. We form a normative concept of ourselves as human beings, first under social influence and direction, but with the development of our own powers of reflection and criticism, we take charge and more or less convert this socially formed normative image of ourselves into personal self-images for which we are responsible. It is our ideal of a human life. It is our inner compass and censor. We feel guilty when we are swayed by passion or desire or influence to violate it. It is the basis of our moral approval or disapproval of our own actions and those of others.

Naturalistic subjectivists and communitarian relativists reject the view that we have an inherent normative constitution that is grasped in our normative self-concept. The subjectivists hold that our normative self-concept is the product of social conditioning, noncognitive feelings, or self-constituting decisions. In any case, they say, on the basis of their naturalistic metaphysics, that there is no normative structure in us to which it can be held accountable and with respect to which it can be judged correct or incorrect. Communitarian cultural relativists claim that our normative self-concept, and thus our moral judgments, are products of our communal form of life. They admit that our moral judgments are true or false according to whether they conform to the communal ideal of a human life, but the ideal of life itself has no objective ground in human nature that transcends the particular culture, although it may be judged internally in terms of how well it fits in with the whole communal form of life.

According to realistic humanism, a social/cultural context is required for human beings to develop their inherent nature, just as an ecological context is necessary for them to develop their nature and mature as biological beings. And in forming a conception of oneself as a rational agent, as a person, one can get a false or distorted conception that will pervert and systematically mislead one in one's moral judgments and decisions and wreck one's life. If one has a perverted normative self-concept, one may judge what is right, wrong and what is wrong, right. Even though such people may have integrity and a strong moral will, they are the kind of people Aristotle considered wicked in contrast with those who act unethically from a weak will that yields to strong desires or passions or influences and yet feel guilty for doing so.

THE UNIVERSAL IDEAL OF A HUMAN LIFE

So what can we say, on the basis of realistic humanism, about a universal, transcultural ideal of a human life? We have already concluded that the universal ideal of a human life, the archetype by which the life of anyone anywhere is subject to being judged and for which all human beings have a constitutional responsibility and motivation to strive, is an authentic life of one's own that is worthy of one's humanity and individuality in the circumstances of one's existence. But what does this involve?

A human life is quite different from that of any other animal. Whereas all animals have biological lives, a human life, although grounded in and deriving its energy from a biological organism, is knowledge-based and constituted by a web of states, acts, and projects defined by structures of meaning that are melded together by logical relationships, normative requirements, critical judgment, and a life plan—an intentional structure that holds the whole complex together and gives it direction in much the way the plot of a novel integrates various experiences and episodes in the lives of the characters and gives the work unity and focus. Our identity as persons and the constitution of our lives lift us, at least partially, out of the causal grips of nature into the realm of rationality and freedom. Of course our thoughts and actions are not arbitrary or uncaused; they have a different kind of causation. Reasons are causes in the internal dynamics of the self, and the self as an organized whole is moved to act for reasons settled on by the resolution of its internal dynamics.

Our identity as persons and the singular nature of our lives gave rise to the ancient belief, still very much alive in some circles, that we are immaterial substances with our own energy source and that we will in the end make a complete break with nature and escape its entropy and seal of death. But we have no rational basis for such a belief. It seems to turn on the mistaken assumption or theory that the concept of a person is a substance concept rather than an office concept and that as persons we are immaterial substances with mental or spiritual energy. Some ancient Greek philosophers thought that reflection and rational thought, contrary to somatic sensations, sensory perceptions, and emotions, neither engage nor depend on bodily states and processes. But everything we know indicates that we have no energy source other than our bodies and that we are inescapably tied to and dependent on them. In fact, every mental or spiritual state or act has a physical dimension. However much we may rise above or transcend it and become creators in our own right, we remain anchored in and subject to nature. But since nature has brought us forth and we are so intimately interwoven with it, we may be forced to change our modern conception of nature as purely factually constituted in order to make our existence intelligible. It may have to be categorially richer than the sciences acknowledge.

Our concern, however, is with what constitutes a worthy life for human persons, persons who have to deal with all the biological drives, impulses, weaknesses, disabilities, limitations, diseases, aging, and death connected with their bodies. No one can live a life that is worthy of one without good life morale, without positive life attitudes. One needs an appropriate framework of belief that grounds and sustains these attitudes and provides one with a compass and guidance. That is what character is. Recent efforts toward character education in public schools concentrate on trying to instill a list of noncontroversial character traits in children and teenagers such as honesty, truthfulness, respect for others, tolerance for differences, and the like, without any conceptual or belief system that would validate and stabilize these sentiments and behaviors. One needs a framework that includes not only a normative self-concept, but a view of what it is to be a human being, a conception of the normative structure of society, a worldview, and a view of how oneself and human beings in general fit into the social order and the world.

Life morale is much like job morale. One cannot have good job morale without believing that one's job is important, that there is a supporting environment, that it matters greatly how well one performs it, and that one is doing well in it. In a similar manner, good life morale requires that one take personhood to be a highly important office, indeed, the most important office a human being can have, even that the universe is reaching a higher level of fulfillment in the personhood of human beings; that the responsibilities of personhood override all others; that great issues are at stake in living a human life; that there are forces allied with and supportive of one; and that one is fulfilling the responsibilities of the office reasonably well. Religions usually provide some such framework. That is why religion is considered important for morality and for life in general.

The defining responsibility of the office of personhood, as previously observed, is the ground of human rights, what we must be free to do and have the means to do if we are to have an opportunity to have and to live a life of our own. The freedom rights of an office are not simply areas in which the office holder is at liberty to make decisions at his or her discretion; they impose normative limits and requirements on others. To violate or to ignore the human rights of others is to treat them as though they were not persons; it is to base one's actions on a false view of reality. The personhood of others not only imposes normative limits on us but requires us, if we are in a position to help, to come to their assistance when their rights are in jeopardy or when they have compelling needs that threaten their ability to live a worthy life. Furthermore, the defining responsibility of our personhood requires us to join with others in providing effective protective and supportive social structures and institutions that give all members of society the opportunity, insofar as they are able, to have a life worthy of their humanity and individuality. So in living one's life one should respect especially the human rights of others and be responsive to their essential needs insofar as one is in a position to help.

According to realistic humanism, it is not just human beings and the social order that have an inherent normative dimension. Much, if not all, of the environment does, even the whole world. It is most striking and undeniable in the biological and ecological realms, but this rich categorial oasis would not be intelligible in an otherwise purely factually structured world. There are normative requirements that impinge on us from this wider world. We know some of these normative requirements, according to the epistemology of realistic humanism, through our critically assessed emotive experiences, others from theory construction. A person's normative constitution requires him or her to take account of these requirements as well as the ones emanating from himself or herself, other people, and the social order and to give them their proper weight in the total complex. It is simply a matter of knowing and living in response to reality, which is a requirement of rationality.

A necessary condition of life morale, and thus a requirement of rationality, is that one's relationships, experiences, actions, and life as a whole be meaningful. This means that one must find self-expression and fulfillment in them, which requires that one's life have integrity, that it be a coherent whole integrated by a life plan. Lack of unity in one's life, as lack of unity in one's worldview, disrupts or fragments the self and impairs one's identity. And a fragmented life robs the fragments of their meaningfulness and the disjunctive life as well. Furthermore, one's life needs to be integrated into a wider context of meaning in order to be meaningful. This may be in terms of family, community, nation, human history, or even in a relationship to the ultimate powers of the universe as interpreted in many religions. Fragmentariness in one's life or world threatens meaningfulness at any point where there is a break.

Self-fulfillment and happiness are not the goals of a worthy life, but one should pursue ends in which one can find self-fulfillment and happiness. Happiness is the experience of self-fulfillment and functioning well in living a life that is right for one both as a human being and as the particular individual one is in the circumstances of one's existence. There are goals that are not right for any human being and there are goals that are right for all human beings. Every more or less normal human being should seek to develop his or her human powers, to live a rational life beyond moral reproach, and to be a productive and constructive force in society by pursuing values that utilize his or her abilities to the fullest and make for social betterment and continuing personal growth.

What we have roughly sketched, I submit, is a universal ideal for a human life. It is abstract, to be sure, but it is sufficient to provide the basis for a common morality that transcends cultural differences. This is not to say that everyone will readily embrace it. The contention is that a valid ad hominem argument can be made on its behalf to rational agents in whatever culture in terms of their organizing and governing constitution.

We find the common ideal of a life, not in the various kinds of identities, actions, and lives that are in fact approved and celebrated in the multiple cultures of the world, but in the presuppositions of rational thought, rational living, and rational and moral appraisals of human beings and their actions, regardless of the forms they may take in various cultures. They provide us with an unavoidable framework of commitments for living a worthy life.

PHILOSOPHY AND CULTURAL CRITICISM

All culturally approved identities, actions, and lives in any society are subject to critical review by appeal to the presupposed constitutional principles of rational thought and agency, which must not be confused with what we may call "the cultural mind," the widely shared and culturally promoted assumptions, beliefs, or theories about the normative constitution of human thought and agency and its implications for the culture's way of life, social order, and worldview. The cultural mind of a society may be in error in ways that systematically pervert the identity of people, corrupt their morals, distort or undermine the social order, give rise to an erroneous worldview, and generate a pathological way of life in general. The principal task of philosophy is to excavate and to clarify the inherent normative constitution of rational thought and agency and to expose and to offer corrections for errors in the cultural mind.

Many moral philosophers seem to think that they can specialize in ethics without having to give attention to other areas of philosophy. In a similar manner, many working in epistemology and metaphysics seem to think that they can ignore the whole normative realm of the culture, including ethics. But all of these are interdependent and must be done in concert. Philosophy is a systematic discipline. An error or mistaken assumption in one area may mislead one in other areas.

The conservative attack on individualism springs from the belief that individuals have no basis for morality other than divine revelation in a sacred book or communal traditions and ways of life. So they think that liberals who believe in the autonomy of the individual, the belief that individuals should define their own identity and life, have nothing to direct and to guide them but their own desires, preferences, and feelings, which they regard as simply noncognitive psychological effects of biological conditions or comprehended facts. So they fear that liberals, with their emphasis on individualism, will undermine our institutions and dissolve the social order, leaving us with a mass of warring individuals guided only by self-interest and the limits of their power.

Individualism with moral subjectivism would, indeed, tend toward dissolution of the social order or domination by a power structure. On the basis of realistic humanism, however, individualism and a healthy free society are compatible. Such a realistic humanism holds that, in terms of the inherent nature of human beings and the world and the full spectrum of our knowledge-yielding and critical powers, morality is grounded in knowledge and reality and that individuals have an inner moral compass and governing constitution. Thus the people of a society have a sound basis in a critically formed moral consensus for reforming the cultural/social form of life that their historical community has developed.

NOTES

1. See the works cited in note 2.
2. For a full discussion of realistic humanism and its implications for life, culture and society, see my *Philosophy and the Modern Mind: A Philosophical Critique of Modern Western Civilization* (Chapel Hill: University of North Carolina Press, 1975, 1985), *Metaphysics of Self and World: Toward a Humanistic Philosophy* (Philadelphia: Temple University Press, 1991), and *A Society Fit for Human Beings* (Albany: State University of New York Press, 1997).

Can the Dead Really Be Buried?[1]

PALLE YOURGRAU

Though grave-diggers' toil is long,
Sharp their spades, their muscles strong,
They but thrust the buried men
Back in the human mind again.

—W. B. Yeats, "Under Ben Bulben"

A NEGLECTED SYLLOGISM FROM SOCRATES

What happens to you when you die? Most people, no doubt, including most philosophers, believe that in normal circumstances you will be buried. That is, you will be placed in a casket and the casket in turn introduced back into the womb of what Plato called your 'real' mother[2]—Mother Earth. Call this proposition (1): The dead are buried. Many people, however, including many philosophers, of a religious stripe believe that at death our immortal souls flee this vale of tears to take up residence in a happier realm (or in an even sadder realm, if this be their fate).[3] Call this proposition (2): The (souls of the) dead go to heaven (or to hell). Finally, many people, including most philosophers, believe that when you die you simply cease to be—having been *something*, you become *nothing*. You simply disappear. (In the words the chief utters to Dustin Hoffman in "Little Big Man," "You are rubbed out.") The more tender hearted try to sweeten this doctrine by adding that if you are lucky, or famous, you will survive as a memory. Let us call this proposition (3): When you die, you become nothing—or nothing but a memory.

Now which if any of these propositions is true? The second, concerning our immortal souls, is beyond the scope of the present paper, but I would like to address the first and the third proposals. I believe firmly not only that these common perceptions are mistaken but that the fact that they are mistaken was first pointed out over

2,000 years ago, in Plato's *Phaedo*.[4] Philosophers, however, are sometimes rather slow on the uptake, and 2,000 years have proved insufficient time for Plato's insights to be appreciated. Yet Plato has already shown that propositions (1) and (3) are deeply misguided. When asked by Crito how he should be buried, Socrates replies, rightly, that this question presupposes that he will remain with his friends after he has died. Crito, however, in company with almost all philosophers who have taken up this question in the two millenia following Socrates' death, proves blind to the logic of Plato's reasoning. Socrates, I suggest, has implicitly constructed the following syllogism: (a) You can bury something only if it exists; (b) When one dies, one ceases to exist;[5] ergo, (c) The dead cannot be buried. This argument is not only valid but also sound.

Now apart from Plato I have never encountered another human being who appears to have noticed the fact that Socrates' syllogism is sound. "How extraordinary," comments Wittgenstein, sarcastically, "that Plato could have got even as far as he did! Or that he could not get any further! Was it because Plato was so *extremely* clever!"[6] I am inclined to answer, "Yes!" Or rather, it is not that he was extremely "clever" but rather that Plato was extremely unbiased, unfettered by the chains of prejudice that, he tells us in *The Republic*, bind most of us, preventing us from attaining the correct perspective from which to view the physical world. "How extraordinary," says Wittgenstein, that Plato alone managed to break free from these chains. Well, how extraordinary, I reply, that Bach alone managed to write the *St. Matthew Passion*.

Now the reader, no doubt, will wish to try his or her hand at disputing Socrates' little syllogism. Where, however, should it be attacked? The argument is unquestionably *valid*. What remains then is to question its *soundness*. If it is not sound, then at least one of its premises must be false. But which one? Does the reader really believe that one can bury something that doesn't exist? Can he find a spade sharp enough to bury Santa Claus? Or is the reader inclined to cast doubt on the second premise? If you really believe, however, that after death you survive (in your embodied form), then I strongly urge you *not* to allow yourself to be buried! No, sad to say, it is only the living who can be buried.

What about proposition (3), however, that at death you become nothing, or nothing but a memory? Here, too, Plato has introduced light into the darkness. What was something, he makes clear, cannot become nothing. Indeed, he also makes the reverse point: what was nothing cannot, magically, become something. That is why Socrates insists that the living have come from "the dead"[7] no less than the dead from the living. Now it is a *fact* concerning Socrates that after he takes the poison and dies he will no longer exist. But there cannot exist a fact about *x* if there is in no sense an *x* for this fact to be a fact *about*. Similarly, before Socrates was born or was conceived, it was already a *fact*—albeit a fact that no one could have *grasped*—that he did not exist. If the reader is inclined to deny that this is a fact then he or she must believe that *before* Socrates was born (or conceived) he *already existed*! But who now is the crazy one: Plato or my dear reader?

The philosophically sophisticated, however, may attempt a more subtle dodge, exploiting the resources of modern philosophical logic. Thus Alvin Plantinga, in *The Nature of Necessity*,[8] acknowledges the fact that there are possible worlds in which

Socrates does not exist but rejects the suggestion that in such worlds there are "singular propositions" denying existence to Socrates. A singular proposition, he says, is "one that is about some specific object . . . and either predicates or denies some property of that object" (136). According to Plantinga, then, the nonsingular, "impredicative" proposition, (a) Socrates *does not* have the property of existing, is true in some possible worlds, whereas the singular proposition, (b) Socrates *has* the property of nonexistence, "is true in no possible worlds whatever" (151). By Plantinga's lights, "if there *were* a world in which (b) is true, then certainly in that world Socrates would *be* but not *exist*" (151). We will address the latter claim shortly, but for now I simply leave it to the reader to judge for him- or herself how much light is shed on our question, whether or not it is a fact that Socrates did not exist before he was born, by Plantinga's invocation, in a modal context, of "singular propositions."

TO THE MEMORY OF MY FATHER

Now Plato's whole discussion clearly turns on the recognition of what would later be called (following Aristotle) the distinction between *essence* and *existence* (adumbrated already in *The Phaedo*). Roughly speaking, your essence tells us *what* you are, whereas your existence concerns the question of *whether* you are. More precisely, one can divide your essence into two parts: first, those properties you cannot exist without; second, those properties you can never lose, whether or not you exist. Death, then, Plato seems to be saying, involves a change in your state of *existence*, not a change in your *essence* (from which, like a metaphysical shadow, you cannot be separated). In a word, when you die you cease to *exist*; you do not become a different *kind* of being. When you die, you cease being a live person and become a dead person. Death does not transform you magically from being a *person* into a being, say, a *memory*—nor into being a concept, nor a corpse, nor into being nothing at all—any more than it transforms you into a prime number (although most philosophers, amazingly, believe that at death you do in fact metamorphize into at least one of these categories of being, with the possible exception of the last). Nor, when you are born, do you cease being a mere concept—or being a mere twinkle in your parents' eyes, or being nothing at all—and suddenly become a person, a human being. Birth and death do indeed involve metamorphoses—but a metamorphosis from being a *possible person* into being an *actual person* (or the reverse).

Lest it be thought that I am fighting a mere straw man here, consider the important essay by Hidé Ishiguro, "Possibility."[9] According to Ishiguro, "possible worlds and possible objects are constructs of thought, they are not the kinds of things to which actual beings can stand in any relation" (85). (Possible objects include, clearly, possible persons.) Further, "I do not hold that the actual world is one among the possible worlds" (85) [presumably, the same holds for possible persons: for Ishiguro, an actual person, is not one among possible persons]. Finally, "it is *the concept* of a possible object which is such that anything that instantiates it differs *at least* in these and those specified features from the actual objects in question" (85, emphasis in original). It would seem then that the only approach left open for Ishiguro is that when I am born, a certain *concept*, or a certain *ideal construct*—but not a certain *possible person*—has been magically transformed into an *actual person*! Now birth is indeed, as we are told, a miracle, but it is simply too miraculous for belief that a *concept* can be transformed into a *person*.

Concerning our supposed magical transformation, upon death, into memories, you are invited to look at the dedication of most any book on your shelf. Reaching, then, for my own shelf, my hand chances upon a volume where on opening it I read: "To my mother and to the memory of my father." Now a dedication like this, let us suppose, is intended to give public expression to one's love for and/or gratitude to the person(s) named. This makes sense of the author's reference to his mother. His mention of his father, however, along these lines, misses the mark. I understand his problem. His father no longer existing, he feels he cannot simply refer to him, as he can to his mother. There seems to be no one there to refer to. Surely, however, he does not really intend to express his love of and/or gratitude to the *memory* of his father. It is his father he misses, not the memories; the father to whom he may owe a debt, not the memories; the father, not the memories, who has departed. Nothing, in short, could be more different than your *father* himself, now dead, than the *memories* of your father. To be sure, the memories may indeed put you in mind of your father—but then a similar purpose is served by your favorite *photograph* of your father. Can one imagine, however, dedicating a book: "To my mother and to my favorite photograph of my father"?[10] But it is no more nonsensical to dedicate a book to a photograph than to a memory.

BEYOND EXISTENCE AND NONEXISTENCE

With considerations like these in mind one would think that the literature on the logic and metaphysics of death would be replete with discussion of time, existence and quantification, in particular, with analyses of reference to and quantification over *the nonexistent*. Quite the contrary, however, is the case. In the recent collection of readings *The Metaphysics of Death*,[11] assembled by John Fischer, there is, apart from my own contribution, "The Dead" (1987), almost no discussion of the problem of reference to or quantification over (the dead as) *nonexistent objects*, and this despite the fact that almost every author in the collection declares up front that *death implies nonexistence!* The index, for example, contains seven entries under "nonexistent objects," all without exception to my own essay. In that work I argued that the crucial metaphysical fact about the dead that is that *they do not exist*.[12] Experience has taught me that most people feel immediately compelled to add that the dead *used to exist*. This is true but irrelevant. If, for example, I point out that your glass is now *empty*, you have hardly illuminated its present condition, vis à vis emptiness, by insisting —with a significant look in your eyes—that it *used to be full*.

The metaphysical picture I was appealing to can be made explicit as follows. Consider the various facts about Socrates that obtain in the course of time, from time (t_1) to time (t_4):

(t_1) Socrates does not exist.
(t_2) Socrates is born (i.e., comes to exist).
(t_3) Socrates flourishes.
(t_4) Socrates dies (i.e., ceases to exist).

It is striking that Socrates 'occurs in', or is 'present in', all four facts just given. This truth, however, is puzzling, since in the facts that obtain at (t_1) and at (t_4) Socrates after all does not exist. How, then, can there be a fact, a truth, concerning Socrates, if there is no Socrates for there to be a fact, a truth, *about*? This constitutes, I believe, *the fundamental metaphysical problem* concerning birth and death. (Plato, in *The Phaedo*, was the first philosopher to appreciate, clearly, the force of this fundamental problem, and also the first to offer a powerful solution.)

If it is true that the dead do not exist[13] one must face up to the fact that we are now somehow succeeding in referring to objects that do not exist—that is, we are referring to the nonexistent. Further, we must face up to the fact that before and after your life you were *in a state of nonexistence*—that, therefore, you were and will again be a *being* who endures the state of nonexistence. One cannot make sense of these facts, however—which imply 'ontological travel', as it were, to and from existence—without recognizing an existential category beyond both existence and nonexistence, a category that like a bridge spans both existence and nonexistence and admits traffic between them. We need to acknowledge, then, some sort of distinction between 'being' and existence—that is, between *an object itself* (which can enter and exit the state of existence) and *the state of existence* (or of nonexistence) of that self-same object. Now nothing crucial, of course, hinges on my choice of terms here. The essential point is my distinguishing between being-Socrates or the being-of-Socrates (or, if you wish, the very *possibility* of Socrates), and the *existence* (or *actuality*) of Socrates. I argued that although upon death Socrates ceased to exist, he did not thereby "become nothing"; there did not cease being such a person as Socrates (i.e., such a possible being). Your death eliminates your existence, not your 'being'; even death cannot erase *the possibility* of your coming to exist (nothing can).

Now, I did not intend thereby to invoke spooky entities or the ghosts of departed persons, nor to introduce discussion of our 'immortal souls'. The latter, of course, should they exist at all, could never, qua immortal, go out of existence. I 'bracketed' the whole issue of our possible immortality and proceeded on the assumption that upon death we take leave of existence. I was attempting to draw attention to the fact that whereas Socrates' state of *existence* changes when he dies, his state-of-'being'-Socrates does not. Socrates is a *man*, whereas the existence-of-Socrates is a '*state*'. The man, Socrates, changes over time, from enjoying a state of existence to suffering the state of nonexistence. We can refer to, then, or quantify over, the dead because the (unfortunately named) 'existential quantifier' expresses, in truth, not existence (as W. V. Quine has insisted)[14] but rather *being*—that is, being-what-there-is-(to-come-to-exist, or to-go-out-of-existence). Existence per se is best expressed by a primitive predicate, say "E!" One thus concludes from "Socrates is dead" that "Socrates does not exist," and from the principle of Existential Generalization (EG) that "($\exists x$ (x = Socrates & ~E!(x))," that is, "There is such a being as Socrates and he fails to exist."

It is a mistake, then, naively to assume with Quine that classical first-order predicate logic or quantification theory, as developed by Frege, suffices to articulate the truths of ontology. Sadly, however, this has been the legacy of the influential Plato scholar Gregory Vlastos with respect to Plato's ontology. Clearly, however, for Plato existence and nonexistence do not exhaust the categories of ontology, and existence itself, if Plato is right, is not captured by the "existential quantifier." One should also question Vlastos's naïve critique, in "Metaphysical Paradox,"[15] of the "degrees of reality doctrine" often attributed to Plato. John Martin, for one, in "Existence, Negation, and Abstraction in the Neoplatonic Hierarchy,"[16] has offered a sympathetic account of Plato's supposed doctrine using, more imaginatively, the resources of an expanded formal logic. Indeed, in "What Is Frege's Relativity Argument?"[17] I have argued that even in the foundations of arithmetic it would be a serious mistake to assume that Plato has nothing to teach Frege. One should not, then, attempt to simplify and distort Plato's ontological insights, in effect to emasculate them, by dressing them up in the most naïve fashion in the clothing of modern logic; one should seek rather to use the fullest resources of modern philosophical logic to offer an imaginative reconstruction of what Plato really meant to say.

Note, by the way, that in classical logic one cannot even express the obvious truth that Socrates is dead. If one says, for example, $\sim\exists x\,(x = \text{Socrates})$, then one has said something either false or truth-valueless, since in classical Fregean logic every term in a truth-valuable statement must refer (i.e., refer to something that exists), but since Socrates is dead, he no longer exists, and so there is no (existent) object for "Socrates" to refer to. And if one says, instead, $\exists x\,(x = \text{Socrates and } x \text{ is dead})$, then once again one has said something either false or truth-valueless, for given that Socrates is dead, hence nonexistent, it cannot be true that $\exists x\,(x = \text{Socrates})$.

Now in "The Dead" I alluded to the recent development by Terence Parsons and others of the (nonclassical) logic of nonexistent objects (inappropriately, for my purposes, known as 'Meinongian' logic), an extended modern development curiously neglected by all other contributors to *The Metaphysics of Death* (and indeed, to my knowledge, in the field as a whole). I suggested that discourse about the dead, as opposed to (the prevalent) discussion of fiction, is the appropriate field of application of this new branch of logic. With the distinction 'being' versus existence in hand, we are well positioned to resolve other traditional puzzles connected with death, such as (a) who the subject of the harm of death is (since at death the subject ceases to exist), (b) when that harm occurs (during life seems too early, after death too late), and (c) whether the unborn also suffer the harm of (here, prenatal) nonexistence. In a later work,[18] I proposed the thesis presented above, that the dead cannot be buried. It emerged, further, on my account, that the birth and death of Socrates are *changes* he undergoes—changes in his state of existence.

Now this modest proposal has met with a not entirely happy reception. Some aproaches, however, are in harmony with mine. In "The Dead" I maintained that besides the harm of death itself the dead can suffer various other harms—including and especially the calumny of their successors—in spite of the fact that they will obviously be unaware of these harms. Experience has taught me that many people strongly reject this thesis. A notable exception is Anne Sayre in her sober, clear-headed study *Rosalind Franklin and DNA*.[19] Sayre protests the injustice done to Franklin by James Watson in his (in)famous account of "the race for DNA," *The Double Helix*.[20] "Rosalind," Sayre writes—not "the memory of Rosalind"!—"has been robbed, little by little; it is a robbery against which I protest" (190). She speaks of "an injustice to one individual now dead" (195) and adds that "what Rosalind has been deprived of she is unaware of" (195). "Living people," according to Sayre, "have means of defending themselves which are denied to the dead" (194). Finally, Sayre writes that "there seems to me almost no way in which a good and greatly gifted person—Rosalind Franklin, now dead—can be used for wrong and embittering purposes that she has not been put to" (196). Clearly, Sayre's thoughts are in harmony with those of Simone Weil.[21]

It is also true that, along independent lines, Stanley Rosen has argued in his recent book, *The Question of Being: A Reversal of Heidegger*,[22] that "Plato and Heidegger existed at one time, but now that they are dead or no longer exist they may be said to 'be,'" (115), and this is encouraging. Nevertheless, it is also true (a) that Rosen concludes the above sentence with the words, "in the sense that we may encounter the consequences of their former existence," and (b) that he adds on the same page that "Sherlock Holmes and Commander Data do not exist and never have existed, and, as far as we know, never will exist. But they may be said to 'be' in the sense that they are characters in a work of fiction which has effects on our existence." Concerning (a) I would suggest that the 'being' of Plato is in no way dependent on our ability to "encounter consequences of [his] former existence," but results merely from the fact that *there is such a person as Plato*, a fact *revealed* to us by (the consequences of) his former existence, in the past, and undestroyed by his nonexistence after death. Concerning (b) I would recommend the commonsensical view that in fiction we do not use proper names to refer to *beings* of any (peculiar) kind, but rather *pretend* to make reference to perfectly ordinary objects. That is indeed why Saul Kripke changed his mind from his seminal "Semantical Considerations on Modal Logic,"[23] in which he wrote that "in worlds other than the real one . . . new individuals, like Pegasus, may appear" (65), to *Naming and Necessity*,[24] in which he asserted that "it is said that though we have all found out that there are no unicorns, of course there *might* have been unicorns. . . . [T]his is an example of something I think is not the case" (24).[25] That is why, as Socrates indicates in *The Phaedo*, it is in principle possible for Socrates to come back from death. Nonexistent people, like the dead, are not 'fictions'. There is, even after his death, such a being as Socrates. Contrariwise, as Kripke points out, unicorns are mere creatures of fiction. There are no genuine *beings* there to *come* to exist in the future or in some other possible world.

Also encouraging are some comments of David Kaplan's in his essay "Afterthoughts":[26] "*Past individuals* are also, in my view, *nonexistent*" (147, emphasis added), and "[I]t would then be natural to add a narrow existence predicate to distinguish the *robust being* of true *local existents*, like you and me, from the *more attenuated being* of the *nonexistents*" (151, emphasis added). Equally encouraging is Thomas Nagel's espousing a metaphysical thesis, closely related to the one I proposed in "The Dead" (138), that most people will never exist.[27] Nagel writes thus in *The View from Nowhere*:[28] "Almost every possible person has not been born and never will be and it is a sheer accident that I am one of few who actually made it" (211). Those writers on the metaphysics of (birth and) death, however, who have explicitly referred to my account do not give me cause for optimism. David Heyd, for example, in *Genethics*,[29] writes that "Palle Yourgrau believes against Nagel that inexistence [i.e., presumably, nonexistence] before and after life are ontologically symmetrical,[30] and that the only difference between the two is psychological and epistemological (not knowing in advance the identity of the not-yet-conceived person)" (246, note 31).

He adds, however, that "Yourgrau's suggestion . . . is based on a mysterious distinction between being and existence (both the dead and the unconceived have being, although they do not exist anymore or yet, respectively)" (246–7).[31] "Mysterious" or not, however, something like the distinction I wish to make is hardly new to the history of philosophy. There are clear intimations of it in the thought of Parmenides and Plato as well as in the medievals, and it is also not unknown in the modern period. Thus in *Being and Some Philosophers*,[32] in a section entitled "Existence versus Being," Etienne Gilson cites Kant's older contemporary, Christian Wolff: "Being is what *can* exist. . . . In other words, what is *possible* is a being: *Quod possible est, ens est*" (114). Further, "possibility is the very root of existence, and this is why the possibles are commonly called beings. . . . [W]e commonly speak of beings past and future, that is of beings that *no longer exist* or that *do not yet exist*. . . . [T]heir being has nothing to do with *actual existence*; it is though a merely possible being, yet a being" (115, emphasis added).

Now Fred Feldman, too, in his contribution to *The Metaphysics of Death*, "Some Puzzles about the Evil of Death" (1991), is unconvinced by my approach. In company with Heyd, he writes that "[s]ome commentators suppose that we stop existing when we die but we do not stop 'being' [and that this] helps solve the problem of the evil of death. . . . See Palle Yourgrau's, 'The Dead.' In this paper I have made no such distinction" (392). Heyd's issue concerning the unborn I will address below, but it is worth noting straight off that although Feldman and Heyd reject the distinction "being versus existence," as "mysterious" or useless,[33] they continue in their own essays to help themselves to copious and unapologetic reference to and quantification over the dead, while simultaneously continuing to affirm that at death one ceases to exist—quantifying thereby by their own accounts over *what isn't*.[34] Rather than focusing on their discussions at this point, however, let us begin at the beginning and address the original sinner, Thomas Nagel, whose seminal essay, "Death" (1970), his contribution to *The Metaphysics of Death*, is the source of most of the recent discussions of the issues now before us.

THE ORIGINAL SINNER

In his essay Nagel assumes that "death is the unequivocal and permanent end of our existence" (61),[35] but goes on to affirm (correctly in my view) that the true subject of the harm of death is nevertheless the person himself who has died. In "The Dead" I took Nagel to task for not addressing the dilemma raised by his own conclusion: that although the departed Smith is the subject of the harm of death, by Nagel's own account Smith has ceased to exist. Indeed, in her reply to Nagel at a meeting of the American Philosophical Association in 1970,[36] Mary Mothersill raised just such an objection: "Here there seems to be a contradiction. . . . 'Smith is dead at time *t*' entails 'There is no time *t* + *n* subsequent to *t* such that at *t* + *n* there exists an *x* and *x* = Smith.'. . . [But] the sentence '*F* of *a*' . . . implies 'There exists an *x* such that *F* of *x* and *x* = *a*.' Nagel's thesis, then, commits him to the following oddity: 'There is a time, *t*, such that at *t* Smith is unfortunate and there exists no such person as Smith'" (373). In point of fact, Nagel's position is even more problematic than this, for he explicitly adds that "that fact [that his life is over] rather than his past or present condition constitutes his misfortune. . . . Nevertheless if there is a loss, *someone* must suffer it, and *he must have existence*" ("Death," 67, emphasis added). Thus Nagel is simultaneously affirming that (1) Socrates suffers the harm of death; (2) Socrates, as dead, *has ceased to exist*, and (3) the subject of the harm of death (Socrates) *must have existence*!

THE HARM DONE BY WITTGENSTEIN

Mothersill, then, has put her finger on a contradiction in Nagel's account of the harm of death, but, as Frege has said elsewhere, "this spark of sound sense is no sooner lit than extinguished," for rather than going beyond Nagel and settling his metaphysical accounts, she backslides, makes no headway in logic and metaphysics, and ends up abandoning the sound intuition that Nagel himself was unable to defend. To begin with, Mothersill, although apparently accepting that death implies nonexistence, continues, herself, to *refer* to the dead. Indeed, in an obvious echo of Wittgenstein (in the *Philosophical Investigations*) she writes, "The name Smith [*sic*] does not drop from circulation when its bearer dies. Whatever was ever true of Smith remains true" (374). What has become, then, of her own comment, against Nagel, that, by the principle EG, from "'*Fa*' is true" it follows that "$(\exists x)(Fx \& x = a)$"? She may have rejected Nagel's view that it is Socrates himself who is harmed by his death, but insofar as she continues to use the name "Socrates" to refer to the dead, hence nonexistent, Socrates and to make true statements about him, she is subject to the very same dilemma she has adduced for Nagel. Worse, she goes on to reject the very intuition to which Nagel had called attention—that death harms the one who dies. "[Smith's] death," she writes, "is an event in *our* lives and perhaps a misfortune *for us*. It is not a misfortune *for Smith*, since it is not an event for Smith. Death, as Wittgenstein observes [in the *Tractatus*] is not an event of life, since death is not lived through" (375, emphasis added).

Now Wittgenstein himself feared that his philosophy may in the end do more harm than good, and sad to say Mothersill's invocation of his early doctrine goes some way toward confirming his fears. Philosophy, however, as F. P. Ramsey said, *must be of some use and we must take it seriously*. We are in danger of losing our grip on the gravity of our topic. There is after all a sense in which not only does one's death constitute an event in one's life, it constitutes one of its major chapters. Indeed, this is precisely how one's death is viewed by Ronald Dworkin, Thomas Nagel, Robert Nozick, John Rawls, Thomas Scanlon, and Judith Jarvis Thomson in their "Assisted Suicide: The Philosopher's Brief,"[37] an amicus curiae brief submitted to the Supreme Court. The authors cite a previous ruling in which the Court recognizes the right of people to make for themselves decisions "involving the most intimate and personal choices a person may make in a lifetime, choices central to personal dignity and autonomy."[38] According to the authors, "most of us see death—whatever we think will follow it—as the final act in life's drama, and we want that last act to reflect our own convictions, those we have tried to live by, not the convictions of others forced on us in our most vulnerable moment" (44).

Again, consider Mothersill's drawing the conclusion from Wittgenstein's clever remark in the *Tractatus* that your death, not being an event in your life, cannot harm you.[39] The moral she has drawn from Wittgenstein's text, if taken seriously, would make a mockery of the crimes committed at Auschwitz. This will serve to indicate what is at stake in our discussion. Is it not enough, then, that millions of innocents died at death camps like Auschwitz? Must we add to their fate by claiming, with Mothersill, that their deaths were not after all a misfortune *for them*, but at most for *us*, the *living*? Are those who weep at the mere name "Auschwitz" weeping *for themselves*? Is the *killing* of millions of Jews in the death camps to be *removed* from the list of Hitler's crimes—since their deaths, not being "*events in their lives*," cannot, if Mothersill is to be believed, be taken to have *harmed* the victims?

What shall we make, then, of Wittgenstein's remark? Obviously, there is a sense in which Socrates' death did not take place 'during' the course of his *life*, just as his marriage to Xanthippe was not an event 'in' his *bachelorhood. The 'limits' or 'endpoints' of a series need not be a part of that series.* Thus, it is true of the (continuous) series of real numbers but not of the (dense) series of rational numbers that every subset bounded above, or 'limited', has a least upper bound that is a member of the series. Should we conclude then, in the spirit of Mothersill, concerning the series of events in the life of Socrates, that Socrates the bachelor *never got married*,[37] or that the event of his marriage was not something that involved Socrates himself? Obviously this would be at best a bad joke. Exactly when, one might ask, did Xanthippe marry her husband? If she married the-bachelor-Socrates she was never really married at all. But if she married the-married-Socrates her husband was a bigamist. And so on. The phenonemon of limits or end points of series, moreover, is widespread. The end of a race, it might be said, is not 'part of' the race itself. Nevertheless, the winner himself does actually cross the finish line. Again, the end of a movie, one might say, is not 'part of' the movie itself. In spite of this, movies do, indeed, come to an end. And so on. Concerning, then, the limit or endpoint in question with Mothersill and Wittgenstein, we need to distinguish Socrates, *the man* (a 'substance', as Aristotle would put it), from the-bachelor-Socrates, which is not a man but a 'state' of a man, and it is the man, not the 'state'-of-the-man, that marries. Similarly, we must distinguish Socrates, the man, from the-existent-Socrates, which is, again, not a man but a 'state' of a man, and it is Socrates, the man, not the-existent-Socrates, the 'state', who dies and thereby ceases to exist. Socrates' death, then, like his birth, insofar as it constitutes a 'limit point' in his life, is in one sense not an event *in* his life, but *it remains for all that something that befalls Socrates himself*. Now of course Mothersill might well protest at this point that whereas his marriage involves a change in Socrates, if his death be viewed as a change, where will we find the needed 'substance' to underlie this change (since on dying Socrates ceases to exist)? For as Aristotle says, "there must be a *substrate* underlying all processes of becoming and changing" (*Physics*, E2, 226a11). Just here, however, is where the misconception lies. The 'substrate' needed to underlie the change involved in Socrates' dying is precisely Socrates himself, *the man*, whose '*being*' (-Socrates) remains unaffected even as his '*state*' of *existence* is replaced by that of *nonexistence*.

A COMEDY OF ERRORS (OR THE NIGHT OF THE LIVING DEAD)

Lacking the distinction between 'being' (or possible existence) and existence (or actuality), Mothersill lets Nagel's insight about the subject of the harm of death slip through her fingers. Her lack of the appropriate conceptual tools emerges clearly when she comments that "Nagel speaks a good deal about the dead as 'the objects of our pity.' Does he think that as such they 'exist' in some intentional domain?" (374). Unable to distinguish Socrates from the-existent-Socrates, Mothersill can only understand our pity for Socrates himself as an invocation of some mental or 'intentional' mode of existence (much as, as we saw earlier, some authors are led to dedicate their books not to their deceased parents but rather to the *memory* of their late parents). An entire universe separates Mothersill here from Simone Weil, the 'Platonist': "Piety with regard to the dead: to do everything for what does not exist. . . . To love purely is to consent to distance. . . . [T]he love we devote to the dead is perfectly pure. . . . We desire that the dead man should have existed, and he has existed" (*Gravity and Grace*, 19, 58, 59). Indeed, "love needs reality. . . . [D]eath does not prevent the beloved from having lived" (57).

The failure of the ontological imagination of Mothersill and others has brought forth a veritable menagerie of monstrous thoughts as philosophers have struggled to avoid the conclusion that Nagel embraced: that it is the dead themselves who are harmed by death. Thus George Pitcher, in "The Misfortunes of the Dead" (1984) (in *The Metaphysics of Death*), in an effort to flee from Nagel's position, adopts, amazingly, the view that it is the *living*-Socrates who is 'harmed' after death by those who tell lies about him! "Although both ante-mortem and post-mortem persons can be described after their death," writes Pitcher, "only *ante-mortem* persons can be wronged *after* their deaths" (161, emphasis added). Let us, however, strip off the Latin clothing that covers Pitcher's amazing metaphysics. In plain English, then, what Pitcher is saying is that only the *living*-dead can be harmed after their death! For "it is impossible to wrong a post-mortem person. Post-mortem persons, we said, are if anything, just so much dust; and *dust cannot be wronged*" (161, emphasis added). As we observed earlier, however, at death, or 'post mortem', Socrates does not "become so much dust." Dust *exists* and can be buried; the dead *no longer exist* and thus cannot be buried. Pitcher, it seems, like Mothersill before him, cannot distinguish the man, Socrates, from the 'state', ante-mortem-Socrates or post-mortem-Socrates. He twists his thought, therefore, into the teratological expression "the *ante*-mortem Socrates *after* death"—that is, in plain speech, "the *living*-dead Socrates," which is to designate the subject of harm after Socrates' death. What Pitcher is in need of, however, is clearly not the monstrous *state*, "the-living-dead-Socrates," but rather the perfectly ordinary *substance*, the man, Socrates, who enjoys life, when alive (ante mortem), but must suffer the harm of death upon dying (post mortem).

Now one would think that mere contemplation of the ontological knots Pitcher has tied himself into would be a sobering inducement to seek an alternative path. This is not, however, how events have transpired. For Joel Feinberg, in "Harm to Others" (1984), his contribution to *The Metaphysics of Death*, to contemplate Pitcher's account of harm after death is to embrace it. "All *ante*-mortem-persons," he writes, "are subject . . . to being harmed *after* their deaths, by betrayals, [etc.] . . . but no 'post-mortem-person' can be wronged at all. *How could one break a promise to a corpse?*" (183, emphasis added). And how about the harm brought about by death itself? "We should now say that it is the *living* person *ante-mortem* who is (usually) harmed directly by his own *death*" (186, emphasis added). So once again there is an invocation of the 'living-dead' Socrates. But wait: things get even worse. When exactly is Socrates harmed by his death? Surely, when he dies (and forever after). Not so, for Feinberg: "[T]he harmed condition began at the moment he first acquired the interests that death defeats" (186). Indeed, "if it was going to happen that he would die at time *t*, he must have been in a harmed condition *for almost all of his life*" (186–7, emphasis added). Thus, in sum, for Feinberg death does harm Socrates —only it harms 'the living-dead-Socrates,' and harms him "for almost all of his life"![41] Surely it is time for those who do not wish to employ the distinction "'being' versus existence" to rethink their position. Indeed, this becomes even more apparent when we consider the nonexistence not just of the dead but of the unborn (or unconceived).

A MORASS OF QUANTIFICATION AND MORALS

Heyd, as we saw earlier, in *Genethics* faults me for observing an ontological symmetry between the nonexistence of the unborn and that of the dead. Why, however, would anyone want to deny that before your birth (or, if you wish, your conception) you are every bit as nonexistent as you are after your death? Why, indeed? The fear here would seem to be that to recognize this ontological symmetry would inevitably force one to adopt two controversial positions: (4a) that birth and death are *changes* in the selfsame individual (substance), and (4b) that it is unreasonable to deny that there are many unborn who never do come to enjoy the benefit of existence and who therefore suffer the 'harm' of nonexistence. Heyd, however (like Mothersill), has no truck with (4a), and he is at one with Nagel, in "Death," in rejecting (4b). According to Nagel, "[I]t cannot be said that not to be born is a misfortune" (67). Heyd, for his part, urges that "we owe gratitude to one who saves our life; we do not owe our parents such gratitude (for having been saved from the limbo of nonexistence)" (*Genethics*, 123). It is not, however, as if Heyd rejects all talk of the nonexistent. "The subjects of genesis choices," he says, "are, by definition, persons who do not exist. . . . [They] are persons who are possible, that is . . . they might exist but they might equally well not come into existence" (97). He distinguishes among the nonexistent those whose existence is dependent on human choices (the merely "potential") from those not so dependent (the "actual"). "This means," he says, "that actual people do not necessarily actually exist! That is to say, actual people may be either those who exist now . . . or those who will exist in the future. . . . Most future actual people are not known to us; nevertheless they enjoy a moral status" (98). With other nonexistent persons, however, the merely "potential," whose conception or birth is still a matter of human choice, he is less generous: "the question of discrimination against potential people cannot even arise as they have *no moral status of any kind*" (99, emphasis added).

Now, what is obvious from the start is that Heyd is blithely quantifying over what isn't, since on his own admission even "actual" people "do not necessarily exist." Worse, to *some nonexistent persons* he accords a moral status, to *others* not. Further, he permits himself to refer to the future itself as logically fixed ("the future existence of 120 million Mexicans in the twenty-first century is [by economists] taken as a given fact; these are actual people, though they do not yet exist," 98), while simultaneously acknowledging its openness to human choice. Quine's position here, by contrast, is more consistent: "People who will be born are real people, tenselessly speaking, and their interests are to be respected. . . . People, who, thanks to birth control, will not be born, are a *figment, there are no such people*. . . . [T]he four dimensional view affords a place in the sun to all future actualities, however unpredictable."[42] We have gained, then, a fourth dimension, but we have lost the unborn. Even if we were to accept, however, the spatialization of time Quine proposes via four-dimensional "space-time," it hardly follows that we should eschew all reference to merely possible people, who, if things had gone differently, *would* have joined the ranks of the living. Even on its own terms, moreover, Quine's view is suspect. Why, for example, does he speak of birth control? Do we really need condoms to prevent the unwanted birth of "figments"?

Heyd's position, as we have seen, is more unstable than Quine's. He allows the moral status of a nonexistent person to vacillate back and forth according to the whims of its (potential) parents: "As long as you have not decided whether to bring a child into this world, I too cannot relate to it as actual. Once you decide to have it . . . I cannot but take its future interests into account. . . . [But] [t]his does not mean that for *you* the child has at the same moment become actual. For you can still change your mind and decide not to bring it about" (102). This position puts one in mind of Warren Quinn's approach in his highly regarded study "Abortion: Identity and Loss."[43] According to Quinn, "that we can refer to a possible but as yet nonexistent being who, if he comes to exist, will have some significant relation to that which the fetus will become, is not, I think, enough to make abortion seriously problematic. For while it seems possible now to harm the interests of an as yet nonexistent human being who will in fact come to exist, I do not believe that one can in any way affect the interests of a merely possible human being who does not now and never will in fact exist—*even by the very act that prevents it from ever existing*" (22, emphasis added).

Now, in "The Dead" I pointed out that preventing someone from coming to exist is of course a different kind of harm from killing the living, but on what possible basis can one claim, with Quinn, that the former does not constitute any kind of harm whatsoever? For Quinn, unlike Quine, acknowledges that there is a possible being whom one has prevented from enjoying the benefits of joining the living. Quinn, one might say, has been careless. He has acknowledged the existence of just enough metaphysical rope to hang himself. James Sterba, by contrast, is less careless. In "Abortion, Future Peoples, and Distant Generations"[44] he asserts that in certain circumstances one has a right to be born, or a right not to be born, but he also maintains, paradoxically, that "neither [right] entails any metaphysical commitment to possible persons . . . as bearers of rights . . . who 'are' whether they exist or not" (437). I leave it to the reader to make sense of Sterba's position, or Quinn's, or Quine's, or Heyd's. For my part, I do not see any profit in pursuing Heyd and company any further into this morass of quantification and morals but propose instead to examine a related discussion by Ruth Barcan Marcus, a seminal figure in quantified modal logic from whom one expects some enlightenment on the ontological status of possible people.

THE SINS OF MODAL LOGIC

It will be noted that propositions (4a) and (4b) commit one, in effect, to the thesis that actual persons become actual having been, before, merely possible (as well as that actual persons constitute a proper subset of those that are possible). Let us make this thesis explicit: (5) Nothing can become *actual* without having been, previously, *possible*. One would think that this metaphysical thesis is, in Plato's words, "safe"—yet it has been in effect rejected by one of the foremost authorities on modal logic. Not, however, by Saul Kripke. Our propositions are in effect part of the semantic/ ontological framework adopted by Kripke in his early "Semantical Considerations on Modal Logic." As we saw earlier, he says in that work that "intuitively, in worlds other than the real one, some actually existing individuals may be absent, while new individuals, like Pegasus, may appear" (65). Now, quantified modal logic (QML) has had some distinguished opponents, including, of course, Quine, but what is surprising is that one of its original proponents, Marcus, whose contributions antedate Kripke's, is herself quite hostile to the idea that we may be permitted to refer to or quantify over all possible individuals, if these are taken to include more than the actual ones. In a recent essay, "Possibilia and Possible Worlds" (1985/86),[45] she argues forcefully against Kripke's importation of (merely) possible individuals into QML. "The semantics for Kripke's theory," she writes, "appears to be symmetric as between referring to actual objects and referring to possible objects. . . . No special problem is noted about assigning possible objects to individual variables serving as individual constants" (206).

Now although it is true, as we have seen, that Kripke did in "Semantical Considerations on Modal Logic" incautiously speak as if he were in a position to name, and so to refer to, individual (merely) possible objects like Pegasus, it is also true that in *Naming and Necessity* he recanted on this point, denying that a proper name from myth or fiction can be used to refer to a particular possible but nonactual object. Still, as he put the matter in a 1971 Addendum to his "Semantical Considerations on Modal Logic," "I could no longer write, 'Holmes does not exist, but in other states of affairs, he would have existed.' Such a fictional name as 'Sherlock Holmes' no longer seems to me to name some particular possible-though-nonexistent entity. . . . This change affects my view of the linguistic status of fictional names in ordinary language but does not affect the model-theoretic issue involved in the text, namely . . . some of the entities which actually exist might not have existed, and there might have been entities other than those which actually exist" (172).[46] He thus proposes a domain of possible (not all actual) individuals to quantify over in the semantics of QML, but does not purport (any more) to be able to *name* particular possible individuals. Nor does he derive his belief in such a domain from contemplation of particular possibilia given to us by proper names (like "Pegasus").

Now, in my last sentence, I nearly wrote, "nor does he derive his belief in the *existence* of possible individuals from. . . ," but I had to check myself, since "existence," here, means "actual existence," and Kripke of course does not believe in the *actual* existence of merely *possible* people. Once again, I would suggest, we are in need of the distinction "'being' versus existence," where our quantifiers range over all 'beings'—here, all possible people. Kripke's failure to introduce this distinction, coupled with his excessive focus on, and early lack of caution with, proper names, may have conspired to help put Marcus off the track. In any event, she appears to conclude from the fact that various *proper names* lack referents (she cites "meinongian examples of possibilia," as well as proper names scientists might devise for planets that fail to materialize)—hence that they fail to point to particular possible but nonactual individuals—that '*there are*' no possible objects to quantify over. She does not appear to address Kripke's *general* intuition that "there might have been entities other than those that actually exist." What she does say concerning an imagined attempt to name a particular possible individual is, however, worthy of close attention. She appears to be addressing time as well as modality: "Suppose I say of a given terrain, 'There might have been a mountain here.' I might even purport to give it a name, 'Mt. White.'. . . Suppose there is then an eruption and a mountain forms. Could I claim that *a possible individual, Mt. White, has become actual*? Of course not. To be a material object the object must have had a unique and traceable history in a material order of things. *It isn't a thing waiting in the wings to take its place among the actuals when called.* There was at the time of 'naming' no history of a definite, albeit only possible, mountain, such that the very possible mountain that I claimed to name 'Mt. White' was propelled onto the stage of the actual world" (206–7, emphasis added).[47] The second italicized sentence reminds one strongly of Heyd's assertion that "we do not owe our parents gratitude for having been saved from the limbo of nonexistence," and I daresay her reasoning here is in line with his, as with that of many thinkers in the field. What can be said, then, in response to this line of thinking?

To begin with let us grant, for the sake of argument, Marcus' thesis about proper names: Mt. White not being presently available to attach the proper name "Mt. White" to, I cannot fix the name to a specific merely possible mountain and so refer to it. In point of fact, I believe this assumption about proper names to be faulty, but let it pass for now. Let us assume with Marcus, further, that "there is an eruption and a mountain forms" (207). Now, it seems, she will let us name it. To prevent confusion I will baptize it "Mt. Black." Mt. Black, then, came into existence, or 'was born', at time t. "This is . . . a case," as she puts it, "of a thing in the actual world having its inception at a particular time and place" (207). It is equally true, however, and can hardly be denied by Marcus (or Heyd) that at some earlier time, $t - n$, Mt. Black did *not* exist. If we accept Marcus' account of proper names then perhaps *we* could not *know* at $t - n$ that this was true. It may seem awkward that there are facts or truths that we (at a given time, or in a given possible world [recall Plantinga]) cannot grasp, but there is certainly nothing incoherent in this supposition. Kripke, too, has entertained this possibility, in a modal context. In contemplating a possible world where Moses does not exist, for example, he notes that "we can say that that's a world in which Moses doesn't exist, though *they* can't say it."[48]

For all that Marcus says, then, it remains that at $t - n$ it was a *fact* that Mt. Black did not exist. This fact, moreover, concerns the (*then*) *nonexistent object* Mt. Black.

That '*there is*', already at $t - n$, such a *possible*-object to come to exist is shown by the actual course of events: at t it *in fact came* to exist. To deny this, Marcus must in effect claim that Mt. Black became *actual* without ever having been *possible* (a truly immaculate conception)! Can one really, however, deny the metaphysical thesis *Nothing can become actual without having previously been possible*? Pace Marcus and Heyd, then, it seems we are driven inescapably by the force of logic alone to acknowledge that, in Marcus' words (almost), 'a possible individual, Mt. Black, has become actual' and that Mt. Black *was* after all, in her evocative phrase, "a thing waiting in the wings to take its place among the actuals when called." Otherwise put: the inception or 'birth' of Mt. Black may be the cause or source of its *existence*, but it cannot be the cause or source of the *possibility* of its existence—of the fact that 'there is such a being' as Mt. Black *to come to exist*.

ON CREATION: HUMAN AND DIVINE

It follows from this line of thought as well, in accord with our earlier reasoning, that the birth and death of Mt. Black are *changes* in the selfsame mountain, whose 'being' *underlies* the changes in its existence, since it is *true-of* Mt. Black at $t - n$ that *it* (that very mountain) lacks existence, true-of it at t that it (*the very mountain* that formerly lacked existence) has existence, and true-of it, yet again, at some time $t + m$, that it once again lacks existence. I see no way, therefore, to save Peter Geach's assertion in *God and the Soul*,[49] following Aquinas, that "in creation, the thing created does *not* undergo change" (83, emphasis added). How, then, does he understand creation? "God's creating an individual c would be expressed by a proposition of this sort: There is just one A; and God brought it about that $(\exists x)(x$ is an $A)$ [e.g., x is a human soul in body b]; and for no x did God bring it about that that x is an A; and c is an A" (83). I think I see what Geach has in mind here. The issue at stake, however, is a general ontological one about what it means to come into existence for any kind of being—whether human, or living, or not.

When I'm finished baking a loaf of bread, then, I'll have before me *an actual loaf*, a particular loaf of bread that previously did not exist. Call it "Peter." Now it may seem that in baking that loaf of bread I was not relating to that very individual, Peter, formerly a merely possible loaf of bread, but now an actual loaf.[50] I mixed and baked actual ingredients—had my hands on them—and as a result of that activity involving flour and yeast and water, and so on, that particular individual, Peter, came to exist. If my reasoning has been sound, however, this picture of things is ontologically deceptive. For any individual, x, whether person or loaf, can Geach really *deny* any of the following? (a) Individual x *came into existence* at time t; (b) at time $t - n$, x *did not yet exist*; (c) at time $t - n$, there already *was* such a being as x to *come to* exist (i.e., x was *possible*); (d) x's actual *birth* at t is not itself responsible for proposition (c) being true (your *birth* does not make your existence *possible*, but rather the reverse is true; obviously, your birth makes you *actual*, not *possible*); and, finally, (e) propositions (a) and (b) together show that individual x underwent a *change* (in existential status) from $t - n$ to t. Geach, like Marcus, seems to be attributing to each of us a conception that is more than immaculate, miraculously achieving *actuality* without ever having endured *possibility*!

Now Geach claims in his discussion to be following the great Aquinas, and I believe he is indeed being faithful to the master. St. Thomas writes, for example, that "everything that has *being* subsequent to *non-being* is *changed* from non-being to being"[51] (70, emphasis added). Here St. Thomas clearly signifies by the term "being" what I have called "existence"; he does not invoke "being," in the special sense I have introduced, at all, and I will henceforth use "exist" and "existence" to translate his doctrines. Let us see, then, how far even a mind as great as Aquinas' can get without the benefit of our distinction. "If created things," he writes, "such as heaven and earth and the like, did not exist from eternity, but began to exist after they had not existed, we *must admit* that they were *changed* from nonexistence to existence" (70, emphasis added). "But all change," he goes on, "requires some sort of subject. . . . However, *the subject* of the change whereby a thing is brought into existence *is not the thing itself* that is produced because this thing is the *terminus* of the motion, and the terminus and the subject of motion are not the same. Rather, the subject of the change is that from which the thing is produced, and this is called matter. Accordingly, if things are brought into existence after a state of nonexistence, it seems that matter had to exist prior to them" (70, emphasis added). Here I would object that the *subject* of the change from nonexistence to existence *is* 'the thing itself', whereas the *terminus* of this 'motion' or change is not 'the thing itself' but rather the *existence* of the thing. Lacking this distinction Aquinas retreats further and further into darkness. He objects to his seeming conclusion, above, that "matter must have existed always, even if the world did not exist always" (71), that "the arguments just reviewed do *not* compel us to postulate the eternity of matter, for the production of things in their totality *cannot* properly be called *change*. In no change is the subject of the change produced by the change" (71, emphasis added). For God creates everything, according to Aquinas, matter included: "[S]ince the total production of things by God, which is known as creation, extends to *all the reality that is found in a thing*, production of this kind *cannot* properly verify the idea of *change*, *even though* the things created are brought into existence subsequently to nonexistence. Existence that succeeds to nonexistence does *not* suffice to constitute *real* change" (71, emphasis added). Here, not only does Aquinas contradict his own earlier pronouncement on change, he sins against logic itself. For how can we possibly deny that *x changes* when it proceeds from *one* state (nonexistence) to *the contrary* state (existence)? That is exactly what change *is*!

To avoid this obvious conclusion, St. Thomas must torture his thought: "[C]reation . . . is not a true change, but is rather *a certain relation* of the created thing, as a being that is dependent on the Creator for its existence and that connotes *succession to previous nonexistence*" (71, emphasis added). Yet, whatever this "certain relation to the Creator" may be, is not coming to exist as "succession to previous nonexistence" *by definition change*? Pursued by the very force of logic, Aquinas tries to keep one step ahead: "In every change," he argues, "there must be something that *remains the same* although it undergoes alteration in *its manner of existence*" (71, emphasis added). Just so. As I have insisted, it is Socrates himself, the selfsame 'being', who undergoes alteration in his state of *existence* when he is born or, if you wish, is 'created by God'. But this, for Aquinas, would mean that God does *not* create "*all* the reality that is found in the thing." His creation, on my account, produces only Socrates' *existence*, whereas Socrates' *'being'* is "coeternal with God." Aquinas, apparently, believes this to be a violation of Catholic doctrine: "Catholic faith acknowledges nothing to be coeternal with God" (72). On my account, however, although Socrates' *'being'* may indeed be "coeternal with God," his *existence* is not. Only in the case of divine being does 'being' imply existence. This is of course the essence of the ontological argument, but then Aquinas was no friend of this famous argument.

Rejecting the ontological distinction between 'being' and existence, Aquinas is, sadly, prepared in effect to jettison logic itself, for he now claims that "[i]n Creation this [change of some one thing from nonexistence to existence] does *not* take place *in objective reality*, but only *in our imagination*. That is, we *imagine* that one and the same thing previously did not exist and later existed" (71–72, emphasis added). St. Thomas, then, is now simply *denying* that in "objective reality" Socrates himself came to exist, having previously not existed. We merely "imagine" that this is so. This, however, is surely nothing less than a reductio ad absurdum of Aquinas' whole account.

It would seem then, contra Marcus, that all of us have after all been "saved [by birth] from the limbo of nonexistence." Moreover, unless we are so arrogant or so chauvinistic as to assume that we (present or actual people) are the only human beings who *could* have been or *could* ever be born, it follows also that 'there are' unborn human beings who will forever be "things waiting in the wings to take their place among the actuals when called," even if we grant to Marcus our inability to refer *by name* to a single merely possible individual. If this seems altogether too much metaphysics to bear, one should recollect that it is logic itself that has led us to this position. Indeed, Geach himself has written that "logic is not partisan, and knows nothing but to strike straight; but the sword is invincible, bearing the Maker's name" (*God and the Soul*, 85). One need only add that those who live by the sword must be prepared to die by it.

APPENDIX I

Tractatus Ontologico-Philosophicus

1. Death implies nonexistence.
    1.1   The dead can't be buried.
    1.2   Reference to the dead involves reference to nonexistent objects.
2. If a fact about *x* exists or obtains, there must in some sense 'be' such a thing as *x*.
    2.1   Before your birth and after your death it is a fact that you don't exist.
    2.2   Your death eliminates your *existence*. It does not erase your *'being'* or the *possibility* of your existence. (Nothing can.)
3. Nothing can become *actual* without having previously been *possible*.
    3.1   Birth and death affect the *actuality* of your existence, not its *possibility*.
    3.2   Birth and death represent *changes* in your state of *existence*.

3.21 Birth and death do *not* represent changes in your *essence*. They concern *whether* you exist, not *what* (kind of being) you are.

4. The dead and the unborn are just like you and me. They are the same *kinds* of being, with the misfortune not to *exist*.

4.1 The dead and the unborn are *people*, not memories, or concepts, or intellectual constructs, or nothing at all.

4.11 What was a *concept* cannot become a *person*.

4.111 An expectant couple is expecting to have a *baby*, not a *concept* of a baby.

4.2 *Actual* people represent those among *possible* people who happen to *exist*.

4.21 The realm of the possible does not wax and wane over time.

4.22 Most (possible) people will never exist.

4.221 The aborted have suffered a double harm: they have been denied admission to the realm of the living, and moreover had the abortion not intervened they *would have* joined the living. (They had their bags packed, metaphysically speaking, with no place to go.)

5. It is possible in principle to return from death.

5.1 Everyone born has already returned from, or 'survived', the nonexistence of 'death'—that is, prenatal nonexistence (cf. *Phaedo*).

5.2 To make sense of 'existential travel'—namely, birth and death—it is necessary to recognize *a third ontological category* that like a bridge spans existence and nonexistence. We may call this possibility or 'being'.

5.21 Only for divine beings do existence and 'being' coincide. This is one of the lessons of the ontological argument.

APPENDIX II

Some Metaphysical Theses Espoused by My Opponents

1. Socrates himself is harmed by his death and this harm consists in suffering *nonexistence*. But whoever suffers this harm must have *existence*. (Nagel)
2. Socrates himself is *unharmed* by his death since his death is *not an event in his life*. (Mothersill)
3. Socrates continues to *exist* after his death, only he is *no longer alive*. (Feldman)
4. Socrates can be *harmed* after he dies, but it is the *living*-dead Socrates (i.e., the "ante mortem Socrates, *after his death*") who suffers these harms. (Pitcher, Feinberg)
5. *When* is Socrates harmed by his death?
   a.   *Eternally*. (Feldman)
   b.   Not at the moment of his death (that is when he ceased to be). Rather, *at the first moment* (*in his life*) *he first acquired the interests* that death defeats. (Feinberg)
   c.   *Never*. (Mothersill, Rorty)

6. To be born is a good, but if your 'parents' decide to *abort* you, your interests are *unharmed*. (Nagel, Quinn, Heyd)

   a.   If your parents decide *not* to abort you, then they *can harm* your interests, even *before* you exist. (Quinn, Heyd)

7. In certain circumstances there is a right to be born or not to be born, but neither right entails any metaphysical commitment to possible persons as bearers of rights who 'are' whether they exist or not. (Sterba)

8. If your 'parents' decide to abort 'you', then you were never more than a '*figment*'. (Quine)

9. Your nonexistence *before your birth* cannot be compared with your nonexistence *after death*. (Heyd)

10. *Actual* people are *real* people, like you and me. Merely *possible* people are mere *concepts*, or *intellectual constructs*, or '*figments*'. (Ishiguro, Marcus, Quine)

11. You can dedicate a book to your *living* mother but not to your *dead* father. You can only dedicate a book to your late father's *memory*. (Nearly universal belief. [Check your bookshelf.])

12. When you die you cease to exist, but although we can refer to the dead this does *not* imply reference to, hence quantification over, *nonexistent objects*. (Nearly universal belief.)

13. When your parents, or God, 'create you' or bring about your birth, this does *not* imply *a genuine relationship* between you and them before and during your birth or creation. (Ishiguro, Geach, Aquinas)

14. You become an *actual* being without ever having been a merely *possible* being "waiting in the wings." (Marcus)

15. Although there are possible worlds in which *Socrates doesn't exist*, that *doesn't* imply that there are in those worlds true 'singular propositions' involving *Socrates* himself stating that *Socrates doesn't exist*. (Plantinga)

NOTES

1. An ancestor of this paper was presented at colloquia at Boston University and Wellesley College. Thanks to Eli Hirsch for comments on the earlier version.

2. Plato makes this claim, of course, in *The Republic*. He makes it clear, however, that this proposition is not a metaphysical thesis he wishes to propose but rather a "noble lie," necessary for the just state to flourish. That the ceremony of the consecration of the burial of the dead can indeed serve a powerful, unifying national purpose is made abundantly clear by Lincoln's *Gettysburg Address*. See Gary Wills, *Lincoln at Gettysburg* (Simon and Schuster, New York, 1992), for a thoughtful discussion of what exactly Lincoln thought he was doing in giving this address.

3. For many, the thought of their deceased beloved lying underground, food for worms, is too painful to be borne. If in addition the beloved is thought to be in some sense divine, the thought becomes not just painful but impossible, as Wittgenstein brings out in a remarkable passage: "What inclines even me to believe in Christ's Resurrection? It is as though I play with the thought.—If he did not rise from the dead, then he decomposed in the grave like any other man. *He is dead and decomposed*. In that case he is a teacher like any other and can no longer *help*; and once more we

are orphaned and alone" (*Culture and Value*, trans. P. Winch, University of Chicago Press, 1980, 33e). Compare, however, what Simone Weil has written: "The idea that that which does not exist any more may be a good is painful and we thrust it aside. That is submission to the Great Beast" (*Gravity and Grace*, Routledge, London, 1963, 148).

4. In point of fact, Plato has fun in *The Phaedo* conflating, to serve his own purposes, the fact that at death even though you cease to exist you remain something—i.e., do not become nothing—with the (alleged) fact that at death your immortal *soul* continues to *exist*. Socrates is after all at pains in the dialogue to make clear that among other things he is telling a "bedtime story" to alleviate the nighttime fears of his disciples, and the thought of one's immortal soul surviving one's bodily death is surely far more soothing than the abstract ontological insight that even death cannot erase the fact that "there is," in some sense, such a being as Socrates. (Recall Wittgenstein's moving comments above.)

5. At least in one's embodied form.

6. *Culture and Value*, 15e.

7. I put scare quotes around this term because, as Plato is clearly aware, there is no term in natural langue used to designate the prenatal nonexistents. Calling them "the dead" is nevertheless permissible in this context, since, as Plato in effect is insisting, the prenatal nonexistents are no less nonexistent—or 'dead'—than are the dead.

8. Clarendon Press, Oxford, 1974.

9. Proceedings of the Aristotelian Society (supp. vol.), 54, 1980, 73–87.

10. One must distinguish dedicating a book *to* one's mother and *to* the memory of one's father from dedicating a book *in memory* of one's father. Nothing I have said above speaks against the rationality of the latter.

11. Stanford University Press, Stanford, 1993.

12. It is really a shocking fact that it this (obvious) thesis that has encountered the most resistance.

13. If, by contrast, you wish to deny this, then you in turn must face the dilemma of explaining how it can be that the dead *exist*. (As Woody Allen says, at a minimum you must admit that your death will have a bad effect on your golf game.) See below for attempts, like Quine's, to "spatialize" time, via modern physics, in order to sidestep the issue of making sense of the nonexistence of the dead. To paraphrase the old saying, if Einstein had not existed, Quine would have had to invent him.

14. "Existence and Quantification," in *Ontological Relativity and Other Essays*, Columbia University Press, New York, 1969, 97.

15. *Platonic Studies*, Princeton University Press, Princeton, N.J., 1973.

16. *History and Philosophy of Logic*, 16, 1995.

17. *Canadian Journal of Philosophy*, 27, no. 2, June 1997.

18. *The Disappearance of Time: Kurt Gödel and the Idealistic Tradition in Philosophy*, Cambridge University Press, Cambridge, 1991, 146–152. Open Court Publishing Company has just brought out a new, expanded edition of this book, entitled *Gödel Meets Einstein: Time Travel in the Gödel Universe*.

19. W. Norton and Co., New York, 1975.

20. Atheneium, New York, 1968.

21. See note 3 and also below.

22. Yale University Press, New Haven, Conn., 1993.

23. 1963; reprinted in L. Linsky, ed., *Reference and Modality*, Oxford University Press, Oxford, 1977, 63–72.

24. 1972. Reprinted in book form, 1980, Harvard University Press, Cambridge, 1980.

25. I have not seen Kripke's (unpublished) John Locke Lectures, but apparently he adopts there a third position on fictional discourse.

26. In J. Almog et al., eds., *Themes from Kaplan*, Oxford University Press, New York, 1989.

27. The idea being that among all possible persons surely the vast majority will never be born.

28. Oxford University Press, New York, 1986.

29. University of California Press, Berkeley and Los Angeles, 1992.

30. Presumably, Heyd himself rejects my suggestion (with Plato) that there is an ontological symmetry between prenatal and posthumous nonexistence. But where does this leave him? Suppose, for example, that he wishes to build a new summer cottage in Nantucket. Does he think this cottage already exists? Presumably not. Now suppose he goes ahead and has his cottage built, but that, alas, a storm destroys it soon after it is built. After its destruction surely Heyd will agree that it no longer exists. It is my turn, then, to ask Heyd: "How exactly does the nonexistence of the cottage *before* it was built *differ* from its nonexistence *after* its destruction by the storm?" Who is it, then, who is really invoking mysterious distinctions here?

31. In point of fact, my thesis of the ontological symmetry of prenatal and posthumous existence does not rest on the distinction between existence and 'being'. My symmetry thesis is founded simply on the commonsensical belief that if you don't exist you don't exist—whether before your birth or after your death. Heyd, it seems, rejects this commonsense belief.

32. Pontifical Institute of Mediaeval Studies, Toronto, 1952.

33. Other critics have not been so gentle. Indeed, my assertion in my paper that merely possible people should not be dismissed as ontological fictions simply because abortion has deprived them of actual existence caused a referee for a distinguished publishing house to suspect me of being a toady for the right-to-life movement. "This doctrine," he or she wrote, "is political ideology masquerading as academic philosophy." Metaphysics, however, is not politics. (See, further, my discussion below of Warren Quinn on abortion.)

34. Feldman, it is true, only assumes the nonexistence of the dead for the sake of argument. "In fact," he writes, "I think this assumption is extremely implausible. . . . My own view is that a person is just a living human body. In typical cases, when the body dies, it continues to exist as a corpse. So the thing that formerly was a person still exists, although it is no longer alive (and perhaps no longer a person)" (313). As against this view consider Aristotle's pithy comment from *De Anima*, "For living things, it is living that is existing." Indeed, Feldman seems curiously insensitive to Aristotle's distinctions of *matter* versus *form* and of *accidental* versus *essential* properties. My matter may survive my death, but not so my (human) form. But if any property is essential to my existence it is surely my living human form. Once this has been, as Plato says, 'separated' from me, I, the living human 'substance', cease to exist, though my 'matter' survives, in the 'form', now, of a corpse. I stress this point lest one take my own account to be too 'platonic' or 'unaristotelian'.

Note, further, that similar remarks apply to all living beings. Pace Feldman, it is not true that "no one would dream of saying that when a tree dies, it goes out of existence" (313). Aristotle, for one, would. The reason why so little attention is paid, in ordinary life, to this ontological fact about trees is no doubt that for many the corpse of a dead tree, if I may put it thus, contains what for them is *important* about a tree—namely, its *matter*, that is, the wood. In general, the greater the 'dominance' of the material over the formal element in a substance, the less our concern with the ontological distinction between a substance and its 'corpse'. For human-being, surely, the distinction between form (hence substance) and matter, has maximum importance.

35. One way to avoid Nagel's assumption is to treat time as a kind of fourth (quasi-)*spatial* dimension, in effect to 'spatialize' time. This is the approach favored by Harry Silverstein in his contribution to *The Metaphysics of Death*, "The Evil of Death" (1980). In this he follows W. V. Quine, who continues to maintain this view in the sections of *Quiddities* (The Belknap Press of Harvard University Press, Cambridge, 1987) entitled "Future," and "Space-Time." If time is a kind of 'space', then position in time, as in space, carries no ontological implications. This is a consistent and coherent view, and I cannot seriously evaluate it here. Suffice it to say that (a) this approach does violence to our most basic intuitions about time, (b) yet *seems* to be supported by relativity theory, although the issue is subject to much dispute among experts, and (c) leads to a serious problem about whether 'spatialized time', since it in no sense 'passes', deserves the name "time" at all. Gödel thought it didn't. Which, then, is the more radical proposal, that the dead are nonexistent objects, or (in an effort to avoid this conclusion) that *time* itself is nonexistent? Finally, (d) relativity theory is after all an *empirical* theory. If it had not been true, how then could we have resolved the puzzles about past nonexistents like the dead? For a full discussion of the relationship of relativity theory to the metaphysics of time see my book *Gödel Meets Einstein: Time Travel in The Gödel Universe* (1999), cited earlier.

36. Published in J. Rachels, ed., *Moral Problems: A Collection of Philosophical Essays*, Harper and Row, New York, 1971, 2nd ed. 1975, 372–383.

37. Reprinted in the *New York Review of Books*, March 27, 1997, 41–47.

38. *Planned Parenthood v. Casey*, 505 U.S. 833, 851 (1992).

39. Mothersill, of course, is hardly alone in claiming that your death cannot harm you. Amelie Rorty, for example, in "Fearing Death" (in *Mind in Action*, Beacon Press, Boston, 1991) asserts that "a harm must be a harm-to-someone; but if the dead are by definition extinct, they cannot be harmed by not existing" (197).

40. Curiously, Graham Nerlich, in his review of (the first edition of) my book *The Disappearance of Time* (*Philosophical Quarterly*, 46, no. 183, April 1996), accuses me of making just this mistake! Indeed, throughout his review, Nerlich manages to get things exactly backward. "There is a long discussion of personhood," he writes (259), "based on the premise that necessarily the dead are not persons." My text, however, insisted that since we are essentially living beings—in particular, persons—at death we cease to exist but we do *not* cease to be *persons*; a dead person is after all still a *person*. Nerlich, however, continues: "The consequences drawn from the plausible claim that persons are essentially living beings seem perverse, comparable to claiming that because, necessarily, bachelors are unmarried then they are never married at weddings" (260). As should be clear from our discussion above, he is here foisting on me precisely the mistake made not by me but by my opponents. Nerlich seems to belong to that category of soldier who is good at shooting, but not so good at choosing the right person to shoot at.

41. Feldman's answer to this question of when exactly death harms the dead is, if anything, even more bizarre than Feinberg's. In "Some Puzzles about the Evil of Death," he writes that "[there is] a question about when her death is a misfortune for her. . . . [T]he answer to this question must be '*eternally*.' For . . . we are really expressing a complex fact about the relative values of two possible worlds [namely, the actual world where she dies and the 'closest' possible world where she doesn't]" (321, emphasis added).

42. *Quiddities*, 75, emphasis added. Note that even on Quine's account the dead cannot be buried, for as Quine would have it the dead occupy a spatiotemporal position that, short of time travel, we in 'the present' have no access to. No access, no shoveling underground.

43. *Morality and Action*, Cambridge University Press, Cambridge, 1993.

44. *Journal of Philosophy*, 77, no. 7, July 1980.

45. Reprinted in *Modalities*, Oxford University Press, New York, 1993.

46. Addendum in Linsky, *Reference and Modality*.

47. She repeats this line of reasoning again at 207: "Could I say, on discovering Neptune, that the possible planet I referred to is now actual?"

48. "Second General Discussion," *Synthese*, 27, 1974, 509–510.

49. Schocken Books, New York, 1969.

50. Recall Ishiguro's doctrine in "Possibility," that "possible objects are not the kinds of things to which actual objects can stand in any relation."

51. *Compendium Theologiae*, part 1, chap. 99: "Controversy on the Eternity of Matter," in St. Thomas Aquinas, Siger of Braberd, St. Bonaventure, *On the Eternity of the World*, trans. C. Vollert et al., Marquette University Press, Milwaukee, Wisc., 1964, 70–72.

Midwest Studies in Philosophy, XXIV (2000)

Later Death/Earlier Birth

CHRISTOPHER BELSHAW

A ssume life is good and more of it is better. There seem to be two ways in which it might be extended. I could die later, or I could have been born earlier. But our attitudes to the periods of nonexistence which bound our lives differ. Dying later appeals, whereas being born earlier does not. Our attitudes are thus asymmetrical. Should they be? Lucretius, as is well known, rejects this asymmetry and counsels against despair. Why fear, or worry about, or regret the inevitability of death, when its counterpart, the void at the beginning of life, elicits little or no concern? Such, if we accept it, is the balm. But Lucretius' strategy invites two further responses. His argument may backfire and make things worse. We are concerned about the later nonexistence. So we ought, in consistency, to be concerned about the earlier. Or the basis for his counsel may be rejected. Though, on the face of it, these periods of nonexistence should be of similar concern, it may be thought that the surface here doesn't run deep, and that there are, after all, reasons to regret the one and yet not the other. Before birth and after death there is, equally, nothing, but just where these nothings stand in relation to our lives itself warrants a difference in attitude. A later death is desirable, whereas an earlier birth is not.

This, in brief, is the account of the asymmetry that I want here to defend. Post mortem nonexistence is bad (if at all) because it deprives us of good experiences that we would otherwise have had. I could die later. But prenatal nonexistence is not bad for similar reasons. For I could not have been born earlier. Though someone could have been born earlier, that person would not have been me. I realize this, and hence, or more or less, the asymmetry in attitude.

Yet this account has been ably and oftentimes resisted by Anthony Brueckner and John Fischer. They agree that our attitudes are asymmetrical. But they offer a different explanation. On their version a very widespread disposition to focus on the future, rather than the past, is itself adequate to explain the asymmetry.[1] And appeal to a difference in possibilities is inadequate just because, or so they argue, this second asymmetry does not exist. I could die later. But equally I could have been born earlier. The authors have urged this before, in relation to an earlier paper.[2] And this component within their overall argument is now more finely honed in response to Frederick Kaufman,[3] who has also insisted that the time of birth plays a critical role in establishing identity.

Both parties to this discussion get things wrong. Though for my money on the side of the angels, Kaufman's argument is not always clear, his terminology sometimes ill chosen, and concessions to alternative accounts serve only to weaken his case. Not altogether surprisingly, Brueckner and Fischer appear to misunderstand him at times, and are led, via that misunderstanding, into some avoidable complications. More important, however, the various protagonists all look to subscribe to views, first, about the relation between what is desired and what is possible and, second, about the 'metaphysics of personal identity'[4] which now strike me as standing in need of further clarification. Though the faults here are particular, the moral to be drawn from them is general.

I'll try to draw that moral and at the same time defend a modified version of my original account. I couldn't have been born earlier. But there are two important caveats. First, the relation between this claim and any observations about our asymmetrical desires needs careful explication. Second, the sense in which an earlier birth is impossible is, on my telling, less robust than might at first be assumed. It is, however, or so I'll argue, quite robust enough.

PSYCHOLOGICAL CONTINUITY I

My life hangs together. I anticipate events in the future and remember events in the past. Future events, when past, will be remembered and further events anticipated. Unanticipated events are, once experienced, themselves remembered, whereas distant events, now forgotten, were remembered for a time. My life doesn't hang together in such a way that every part is accessible from now, but it hangs together nevertheless. There are not discrete chunks of activity, periods of ordinary goings on, which I must learn about only as I learn of the lives of others. And it hangs together in another way. Some past events are now forgotten. Many others were never experienced. But events of both kinds continue to influence me today. What I am like now depends on what I was like, and what happened, earlier. Thus is my present psychology a function of the past. Obviously it is not a function of the future, even if my anticipation of future events helps shape my psychology today. This is not surprising. We mostly believe causation works in a certain direction.

There is space here for an explanation of our asymmetrical attitude to nonexistence. Suppose life is good. And imagine I die five years later than I actually do, leaving the actual time of birth as it is. There'd be extra years of good experience. These would be added to my life but would leave my earlier and present life intact. But now imagine instead that I am born earlier, here leaving the time of death as in fact it is.[5] Again, there'd be extra years of good experience. These would be added to my life but would make a difference to my earlier and present life. If I'd been born five years earlier, almost everything would be different. I would, for example, have been ten when in fact I was five. So I wouldn't have been to the school, had the friends, sung the songs which have in fact helped shape my life. The particular psychology which actually characterizes my life would not have obtained.[6] Suppose I am reasonably happy with, fond of, resigned to my present lot. A later death will appeal. But an earlier birth will not. And as this concern with a particular psychology may well be legitimate, so the asymmetry of desire can be justified.

This explanation is, in essence, good enough. Kaufman makes a similar claim but puts the point very slightly differently, emphasizing the importance of psychological continuity in a fairly general sense and making less of the particular psychology which is associated with a particular life.[7] And this leaves a loophole. For consider Mary. Suppose, as Brueckner and Fischer suggest,[8] that she is a life-long New Jersey resident. And call, as they suggest, the actual sequence of person stages that make up her life history, running from t_1 to t_2, "M." The psychological states within M are causally connected with one another. But the psychological states within M are not causally connected with any merely possible psychological states. There aren't connections running from the actual to any possible world. Are there here the makings of an objection to the asymmetry thesis? Brueckner and Fischer believe that there are, and claim that Kaufman, in his appeal to psychological continuity, has "mixed up actuality and possibility in a certain way."[9]

For imagine, if you can, Mary's being born earlier than t_1, in Majorca. This is, as the authors say, to imagine a possible world. None of the psychological states within it are causally connected with any states in the actual world. So Mary's purported earlier experiences are not causally connected with her actual experiences. Psychological continuity is lost. But

> [e]xactly parallel points hold regarding a thought experiment in which we imagine Mary dying ten years later than t2. We imagine a possible world distinct from the actual world in which, say, Mary has ten years worth of post-t2 New Jersey–based psychological states. None of these merely possible non-actual psychological states is psychologically continuous with any actually existing state. . . . None of them, for example, is a memory of Mary's actual experience of her 5th birthday party. . . . Thus it is hard to see how Kaufman's consideration of the notion of psychological continuity might show that one could not have been born earlier (though one could have died later).[10]

At least some defenders of the asymmetry thesis argue that though we might die later (and so regret our actual time of death), we cannot be born earlier (and so we do not regret our actual time of birth).[11] This argument is ill served by appeal to considerations which, when unpacked, appear to rule out both an earlier birth *and* a later death. But to posit either is to posit additional psychological states which, as they are not actual, are equally detached from the connected series of actual states which make up our lives. If Kaufman overlooks the symmetry here and conflates actuality and possibility in the way Brueckner and Fischer suggest, then so much the worse for his argument. But not, I think, so much the worse for his conclusion. And Brueckner and Fischer, in phrases here omitted, themselves allude to a securer claim. For though no merely possible psychological state *is* continuous with any actual psychological state, many such states "*might have been* continuous with an actually existing state."

No merely possible state *is* a memory of Mary's fifth birthday party, but some such state "*might have been* such a memory."[12]

This concession is doubly puzzling. First, it seems itself to lead to a queer view about possibility. Merely possible states are not in fact connected to actual states but might have been. Doesn't this suggest that it's a contingent truth that the merely possible and the actual are in this way separate? And isn't that odd? What Brueckner and Fischer are trying to get at here could, at the least, have been more perspicuously expressed.[13] More important, it gives too much away. For it reintroduces an asymmetry, and moreover the one which, I'm confident, Kaufman was after all along. There are merely possible states, under the supposition of a later death, that might have been continuous with the actual states in *M*. But we cannot so readily make sense of this for merely possible earlier states. If there had been earlier states, then virtually all later states would have been qualitatively different. Neither *M*, nor anything like it, would have occurred. If Mary were to die later, her birthday memories would last longer. But if she had been born earlier, her fifth birthday would have been different, with different guests and different food. And so neither her present memory, nor anything like it, would have survived. Or consider a real person. If James Dean had died later, he'd probably have made more films and have been less of a cult figure today. But if he'd been born earlier he wouldn't have made any of the films he actually made. He would have led a completely different life.

So the point is not that psychological continuity is wholly lost under the supposition of an earlier birth. It is that a given continuity is replaced by another. Brueckner and Fischer will say the same for a later death. But there is still an asymmetry. Even if, in considering an original life and two seemingly possible extensions, we allow that we are here faced with three numerically different series, it remains the case that a qualitatively identical counterpart of the original life will be replicated (and then of course extended) under the supposition of a later death, whereas no part of this life will be qualitatively the same under the alternative supposition of an earlier birth.

We might care to have lived the life we've actually lived and to have made the films we've actually made. We might realize that living this (or even a qualitatively very similar) life would have been impossible had we been born earlier. Thus our interest in and desire for an earlier birth, supposing they ever exist, might disappear. The loophole can be closed.

TWO ASYMMETRIES

Yet all of this has been, in a certain respect, imprecise. I may seem to have assumed that an earlier birth is impossible. Given a wholly different psychology, we have a different person. I want to be me. So I don't desire that, a consequence of which would be that I never existed. Certainly Brueckner and Fischer interpret Kaufman as though making such a claim.[14] But is the claim true? And where do the various writers stand in relation to it? Both questions need to be addressed.

Start with asymmetry. Much of the literature refers both to our asymmetrical attitudes[15] and to something called the asymmetry thesis. The terms are useful, but distinctions need to be made. There is, first, an asymmetry of desire. I want to die later but not to have been born earlier. As well as desires, there are beliefs. Not a few will say that I could die later but couldn't have been born earlier. So there is a belief in an asymmetry of possibility. Now whereas it is uncontroversial to claim that such desires and such beliefs exist, other claims are controversial. One is that the asymmetry of desire is justified. Another is that belief in the asymmetry of possibility is true. A third relates these, maintaining that the asymmetry of possibility justifies the asymmetry of desire. Because an earlier birth is impossible, it is not something I want. Each of these controversial claims might be described as an asymmetry thesis. But which are true? And how are they related?

It may be tempting to assume that the asymmetry of desire can be explained only by recourse to the asymmetry of possibility. That would be a mistake. For the questions of why we don't want an earlier birth, and whether such a birth is possible, remain distinct. Clearly, to begin with, I may be hostile to something that is possible. I don't want to be victim to a terrorist attack when traveling abroad. But such things happen. So appeal to the second asymmetry isn't obviously necessary to explain differences in desire. It may be that the consequences of an earlier birth are, with good reason, unwelcome. Also, though perhaps less clearly, such an appeal is also insufficient to explain our attitudes. First, I may want something that is in fact impossible. Perhaps it is impossible, by chemical and alchemical means, to turn lead into gold. This did not prevent many, Newton included, from desiring it. Second, something may even be logically impossible and still desired. Perhaps time travel is in this sense impossible. This will not prevent my wanting to go back and have conversations, in Paris or on Elba, with Napoleon. Third, something may be known (or believed) to be logically impossible and still desired. I am persuaded of the logical impossibility of time travel. But I still want to talk to Napoleon. An objection can be deflected. The objection is that we cannot genuinely desire something which we know to be logically impossible. But we can say that it at least *seems* to us that we desire this. Our desires, or at least our apparent desires, are not easily restrained.

Suppose an earlier birth is impossible. We don't need to know or believe this in order to justify our not wanting an earlier birth. It is surely reasonable to decide against a radically different psychology, a very different kind of life, even before deciding whether the procedure which will make for that difference will threaten my very identity. So I can explain and justify the asymmetry of desire before deciding whether or not further asymmetries hold. Further, we need more than to know or believe that an earlier birth is impossible in order to justify our attitude. Desires can persist. And though persuaded of its impossibility, I could still want to have been born earlier. The absence of particular desires is perhaps best explained by reference to further, higher-order desires, rather than simply to an awareness of what is possible. In this case, then, our desire to preserve the overall character of our life will help obliterate the desire for an earlier birth, should it unthinkingly be formed.

The two asymmetries are, then, strictly independent of one another. But of course this is not to say that the second asymmetry is utterly irrelevant here. It may continue to play some contributory role in explaining the asymmetry of desire or to be linked with that asymmetry in some other way.[16] And certainly it is widely assumed to play some such role. Moreover, the question of whether I might have been born earlier is clearly of independent interest. For these several reasons, then, it can legitimately be pursued.

METAPHYSICAL IDENTITY

Is it possible for someone to be born earlier than in fact they are? A current orthodoxy might seem first to suggest that it is not. But then a standard amendment to that orthodoxy will, in turn, suggest that it is. Many people will accept, that is, some (roughly) Kripkean claim about the necessity of origin, holding that if a given person is the issue of certain parents, and more particularly of a certain sperm and egg, then that person is necessarily the child of those parents and develops necessarily from that sperm and egg. Allowing for certain biological facts, this strongly suggests that a given person is necessarily born at, or very close to, a particular time. Suppose Mary is born in 1949, lives, and dies in 2009. This very person could have died earlier or later. But this very person could not have been born earlier or later, even if someone both physically and psychologically very similar could have been born earlier or later. Thus the orthodoxy. But it is often now observed that an important consideration is so far neglected. The sperm and egg could be frozen, stored, and then united at a later date. Or the zygote which develops after the sperm and egg unite could be frozen, its development arrested, and restarted later. So although it may be necessary that Mary has her origins at a certain time, it is not similarly necessary that she be born at a certain time. Her whole life, from fetus to death, might have been lived in a later century. And thus the amendment.[17]

Brueckner and Fischer refer to and accept this orthodoxy.[18] Kaufman vacillates. For consider the claim "I could have been born earlier." Kaufman sometimes seems to think that this is true but not what concerns us. At other times he suggests the claim is ambiguous and true in one sense but false in another, while yet at other times he maintains that it is false.[19] The first view is, for a while, in the ascendance. He mentions but rejects Nagel's claim that it is impossible for someone to be born earlier, conceding to Kripke that an individual is identified across possible worlds by reference to his or her genetic constitution and citing various writers who have made the point that the genetic material from which a person develops could have had various different temporal as well as spatial histories.[20] But all this, he says, is irrelevant to the matter under discussion. What we are concerned about are not questions of "metaphysical personal identity," the question of whether the same individual could have been born at some different time. Rather we are concerned with psychological personhood, with the preservation of our psychological selves, and what disturbs us is the thought of psychological extinction.

Brueckner and Fischer are somewhat insensitive to the confusions and shifts in Kaufman's position. Not unreasonably, they fasten on to these remarks about irrelevance of metaphysical personal identity. And again, not unreasonably, they think he is just wrong. For

> in comparing Mary's earlier birth with her later death, we need to consider possible worlds distinct from the actual world, ones that contain Mary and various merely possible, non-actual psychological states that differ from her actual ones (that might have existed, but never did in fact exist). This takes us straight *into* 'metaphysical personal identity' territory.[21]

This complaint against Kaufman follows, obviously enough, upon the earlier claim that he confuses actuality and possibility. On Brueckner and Fischer's account, to reject metaphysics is to turn away from any serious consideration of what might or might not have happened to Mary, of what is possible for her, and of the nonactual worlds in which she might be located. If Kaufman wants genuinely to pursue the questions of whether and to what extent an individual's life having a different shape is possible, then there is no option but to take seriously metaphysical questions like these.

This is all a muddle. And it's a muddle that comes about, in part, just because talk of metaphysics is here, as so often elsewhere, woefully vague. Obviously, Kaufman has to consider what different lives are possible for an individual, has to consider (if you prefer the formulation) in which possible worlds a given individual can be found. If (as Brueckner and Fischer suggest) that's where metaphysics resides, he will have no argument with it.[22] Almost as obviously, we can have legitimate concerns about our histories beyond concerns for our bodies. If (as Kaufman seems to think) much that is licensed by "metaphysical personal identity" overlooks these concerns, then, as presumably Brueckner and Fischer will agree, an important lacuna has been noted. Thus there isn't here a disagreement about a matter of substance. Rather there are just different assumptions about how a term of art is used.

There are cross purposes here, then. But to note those is not yet to respond to the central question: is it possible for a given individual to have been born earlier than he or she was actually born? I think a fair sketch of a worthwhile answer can be provided. Start with some sort of grasp of the physical facts. We can construe the Kripkean point as establishing at least that a human being made of, or deriving from, such and such material could have come into existence at different times. This is uncontroversial.[23] It's similarly uncontroversial to maintain that alteration to the time of birth, as it normally makes for considerable differences in experience, will generate considerable differences in psychology. A not wholly implausible view here can be put crudely, but forcefully: physiology is a function of genes, and psychology a function of environment. Refine this if you will, but note first that there will remain a core of truth within the distinction, and note second that refinements depend upon closer attention to the scientific facts of the case: we may find, for example, that many dispositions are inherited. So far there is nothing of philosophical interest. And so there is still nothing about which Kaufman on the one hand, and Brueckner and Fischer on the other, should disagree.

This can change. For the neutral description is consonant with three views about identity. The first involves denial. One could maintain that having explained when, how, and why physiology and psychology can vary, there is simply no more to say. There are myriad facts about the various different aspects of a person, but there is no single fact, either additional to or deriving from those facts, as to whether a person could be born at a different time. The question, could I (as opposed to my body) have been born earlier? will just not get an answer,[24] and its apparent straightforwardness and coherence will be said merely to mislead.

The second and third views both allow for identity claims but then differently locate them. It could be maintained that identity is tied to the body. If and only if that is the same, then the person is the same. This roughly Kripkean view is not hopelessly straightforward. Having demanded the same body, there are still questions about how many changes a body can undergo and yet remain, in essence, the same. There are further questions about whether continuity of the one body is required. But on this view there is clearly space for the claim that the same person could be born earlier. Alternatively, one could hold that identity connects with the mind. If and only if the same mind, or character, or personality is present are two people one and the same. Again this skeletal view needs flesh. It can be provided in many different ways. But on this view it is, given the sensitivity of character to environment, at least hard to see how the same person could be born earlier.

We can ask, which view is Kaufman's? And we can also ask, which view is correct? Kaufman opts most often for the second. He seems prepared, as I've already suggested, to allow that identity goes with physiology but wants nevertheless to insist that psychological continuity is our legitimate and paramount concern. Strictly, I could be born earlier but, with good reason, do not want to be.

This is not an inconsistent position. Nevertheless, it invites criticism. To concede that the very same person could have been born at a different time is at least to encourage questions as to why this is of so little interest. As I've said, the psychological havoc that would be brought about by an earlier birth is enough to explain its overall undesirability, but further issues still need to be addressed. Imagine someone close to you suffers some abrupt and irreversible psychological trauma. You may continue to care.[25] But suppose he is altogether different from the outset. There seems to be some pressure on you to explain your complete lack of interest in someone who is, after all, the very same person. The more the absence of concern seems to be unproblematic, the less plausible it is, surely, to maintain that identity nevertheless obtains.

A better account (and certainly an ally of the one that Kaufman might have insisted on all along) is simpler. We should adopt the third view and hold that identity involves psychology. Profound and wholesale differences here result in a different person.[26] Other people could have developed from the physical stuff from which, in fact, I developed. Someone who, from the start, is psychologically wholly dissimilar just wouldn't have been me. And someone developing from this stuff and then being born at a substantially different time would be, in this respect, wholly dissimilar. Thus although a later death is possible, an earlier birth, at least within readily imaginable circumstances, is not.

Am I here adopting a certain position on "metaphysical personal identity"? Remember, the meaning of that phrase isn't altogether clear, but at least on one widespread interpretation, the answer is no. I am making a claim about what is and what is not possible for a person. My body could have been frozen, then thawed and developed at a later time. But in that case I would never have existed. So I assert. This is not, however, to pretend to a deep truth, to some special philosophical or metaphysical insight. It is not offered as a position on how things really are and so as a rival to some alternative metaphysical picture. Rather it is intended merely to reflect, and perhaps in part to anticipate,[27] how in fact we speak. We tend to care more about minds than bodies and identify people, ourselves and others, with their psychologies. We say she no longer exists when deep in the grip of Alzheimer's but not when physically incapacitated. We feel more strongly the pull of fictions in which someone is trapped in another's body than those in which the shell is occupied by a different mind.[28] And so on. Thus criticism of the second view and the advocacy of the third is in one way soft: to favor my account over its rival is to do no more, I think, than agree that between this account and our everyday goings on there is a natural resonance. And so if the view is, as I claim, correct, then this is in virtue of that resonance, and not because of some independent and deeper conditions which antecedently demand it.

Objections are of two kinds. First, I am just wrong about our everyday concerns and the respective weightings we give to the body and the mind. This objection is not, I think, serious or substantial. For it appears to concede my central claim, that whether or not we can be born earlier is not a distinct metaphysical puzzle but a function of, or component in, a larger and often everyday discourse. The second objection makes no such concession. It insists that nothing of interest follows from our speaking one way rather than the other: it could be that we say such and such things, but are simply wrong. This second objection does raise a matter of substance. But I reject it. Though I agree we might be wrong about certain physical facts—we might falsely believe, for example, that some medical conditions are irreversible or, and here more importantly, grossly underestimate the extent to which character and personality are inherited—this is still to hinge what we should say on some extraphilosophical concerns. What I don't see is that we could be wrong about the nature of ultimate reality beyond this concatenation of physical facts. What I don't see, that is, is that there could be a metaphysical truth about identity which is anterior to and independent of the familiar mix of ordinary concerns.

I want to emphasize these last points. There is no proscription here on mystery. Ultimate reality may be very different from how we imagine it. And it may be that the philosophical enterprise has some important role to play in uncovering it. It might, in identifying possibilities, point to fertile ground. But it is unclear how this ultimate reality can affect a quotidian notion such as that of "same person" unless, in the end, it affects it in gross and—to us—pertinent ways. Consider souls. It may be that there is in each of us some single, indivisible, immutable, and immaterial core which will, on some accounts, be described as a soul. But unless it turns out that this makes for some physiological and/or psychological differences, and differences, to boot, that we care about, then there will be no reason to ally the soul to the person. Perhaps a person having my soul could have come into existence earlier. But why should I think, in virtue of that, that such a person would be me? And what sense could be made of the suggestion that, irrespective of what I and others think, anyone with this soul *really is* me?[29]

SOME REFINEMENTS

This claim, that I cannot be born earlier, needs still to be qualified. Because it is supposed to derive from our ordinary ways of going on, and because those ways depend on various garden-level facts as we encounter them, the claim does not purport to express a necessary truth. Being born earlier is now, in fact, impossible. But this isn't to say that it's thoroughly impossible, ruled out for everyone at all times.

Suppose, first, that our concerns are different. Different also are some of the facts of biology. Suppose we care more about our character and dispositions than we do about actual experiences and memories, and it turns out that these are inherited, rather than shaped by our encounters with the world. Then, certainly, because of freezing, I might agree that I could have been born later. Shifting from here to the idea of an earlier birth is harder, but if our concerns are in this way different, and if there are people whose birth is arrested through freezing, then it will be possible for those people to be born earlier.

Suppose now that though our concerns are the same, the attendant physical facts are more thoroughly different from those which now obtain. Freezing is not an option only for those unborn but can be applied indiscriminately to all of us. All our activity on the surface of the world could have been frozen and brought to a halt in 1984. Time passes, but not much happens for a decade. People already alive are stopped in their tracks. Those in the womb remain. My brother, born that year, would instead be born later. Although he wouldn't be virtually the same today as in fact he is, still today's characteristics would all, after an interval, be displayed. For nearly all the events which in fact have shaped his psychology would still unfold, but at the later time. Here again, a later birth is possible. Suppose the world is such that periods of global freezing regularly and naturally occur. Then a technique is developed for avoiding the freezing. People like my brother might say, "If this technique had been around before, then I could have been born earlier."[30]

Suppose, again, that there is evidence in favor of reincarnation. We live ordinary lives. But then some among us seem to acquire memories of previous lives and in compelling detail. It's as if we were born earlier, lived and died, and then were reborn with temporary amnesia, and so unaware of our prior existence. And so the earlier birth leaves, until its recall, our present lives untouched. Those without such memories may discover that they too would like to have been born earlier.

I could go on. But it should be clear that my main purpose here is not to defend the suggestion that an earlier birth is possible, but rather to indicate the limitations on my claim that it is not. That claim is supposed to engage with the world we inhabit; it is not intended to range over the fantastical and arcane.

PSYCHOLOGICAL CONTINUITY II

Set bizarre circumstances to one side. Then I claim that we cannot be born earlier. And I connect that claim with our everyday descriptions of a range of actual and possible events. We are not disposed to recognize bodily identity, displaced across time, as sufficient for personal identity. It can be objected, however, that I here fail to acknowledge the full complexity of our reactions to some even quite normal situations. Dying later will change nothing of my present self. Being born earlier will change everything. Can we desire to change some things? One thought is that we can. Brueckner and Fischer have this thought. And then, in the further defense of the possibility of an earlier birth, they attempt to capitalize upon it:

> It seems that there is no bar to imagining a genuinely possible world containing Mary (or a counterpart thereof) equipped with psychological states *other than*

those in M (or other than counterparts of those in *M*). Surely she could have had New Jersey–based experiences during the period t1–t2 that differ from those in *M*, say, in virtue of changing her place of residence. In imagining Mary's possibilities we are not constrained to hold fixed the psychological states in *M* (or not constrained to consider counterparts of those states). If there is a possible world in which Mary has psychological states differing from those in *M* during the period t1–t2 (or differing from their counterparts) then it seems reasonable to hold that there is a possible world in which Mary has states differing from those in *M prior to* that period (or differing from their counterparts).[31]

Against Kaufman, then, and also against the position I have so far been defending, there is here the express claim that a particular psychological continuity isn't necessary for personal identity. My life begins at a certain time and then develops in a certain way. It has a particular content. But it could have begun earlier and then gone differently. And the warrant for this derives from concessions we will naturally make.

There are some things right and some things wrong in this. What is right is plain enough. Think about the future. A range of things can happen to my body, and I will still survive. And my psychology can develop in various ways yet carry me along with it. Similarly for the past. Just as someone could have had a partially different body at an earlier stage—he might have been scarred or lost a finger or a limb as result of a bicycle accident—so too someone's psychological states could have been to some degree different, even though the very same person survived. We can call the actual series of states that makes up Mary's life *M*, but if some of those states had not existed, such that *M* had not existed, Mary herself would have continued to be. If, with his emphasis on the possibility of a later death, Kaufman suggests we can imagine subsequent additions but no internal alterations to *M*, he makes a mistake.

Still, it isn't clear where we might go from here. Suppose we agree that Mary's life could have had a partially different content. Should we then agree that her life could have had (as the supposition of an earlier birth requires it to have had) a wholly different content? The argument is uncompelling. We will not agree that if I can survive while a small part of me is destroyed or replaced by plastic, then I can survive if every part of me is destroyed or replaced by plastic. Nor will we agree that if I could have got through life with fewer people to talk to I could have got through life with no one to talk to. So we can readily concede that things in the past might have been to some degree different without its following they could be as radically different as the hypothesis of an earlier birth will require. Where to draw the line? We can properly say that there is no precise answer to this question.

There is, though, a further point. Remember that Brueckner and Fischer earlier invite us to imagine Mary's being born not at t_1, in New Jersey, but earlier, in Majorca. This fancied birth differs in respect to both space and time from the actual. But there's an asymmetry here. I've said that we don't want the earlier birth, for we recognize its consequences are such as to deny to us existence. It will lead to an unimaginable overhaul of all our experiences, and so in an ordinary sense, of who we are. Yet shouldn't the same be said of a different location? If Mary had been born, even at the same time, in Majorca, virtually everything—her friends, her language, her education, her politics—would have been immeasurably different. Again, or so it seems, Mary would not have existed. But the asymmetry comes about just because we are often willing to consider, and sometimes even to desire, these sorts of differences. My parents thought of emigrating to Australia in the months before I was born. I am glad they didn't, not because I fear that in such a case I wouldn't have existed, but because I suspect my life would have been so much the worse. The parents of a friend moved to Ulster. She regrets this and thinks her life would have been better had they stayed in Surrey.

I claim here no more than that such attitudes, which appear to countenance widescale and *ab ovo* variation in psychological content, do quite commonly occur. What now to make of them? One view is that they demolish my argument and make clear the sufficiency of a bodily criterion. Another is that they bear witness to a genuine distinction. A shift in time annihilates us, whereas a shift in space does not. But I think the better view insists on both the symmetry and the cogency of the argument so far. I could not have been born at a (substantially) earlier time. Nor could I have been born in a (radically) different place. That our thinking is more often consonant with the former than with the latter claim has a straightforward explanation. People do move, and expected children find new homes. We are accustomed to this. But it is not as though when imagining this sort of continental dislocation we have a clear idea of the sorts of changes that would be involved but believe that in spite of these, we would still have existed. Rather, we seriously underestimate the scale of change. If we were to get that right, then, I suspect, we'd be more inclined to see how existence is threatened. But people do not plan for children and then somehow contrive to have them born at different times. The very idea is alien. Because it is alien we are not inclined to have sloppy thoughts about it.

This last point connects, of course, with an earlier claim. The argument is not based around what, indiscriminately, we do say. It takes into account what we would say when apprised of the facts, suitably reflective, and aiming to be consistent.

SUMMARY

I've made various claims, and then qualified those claims in various ways. Some will find this unsatisfying. But remember what is at issue here. The question is, why do we have the attitudes we do? How are they to be justified or explained? We need, first, to say what those attitudes are. As people differ, so do their attitudes. An account which glossed over these differences and avoided qualification would be impoverished. Still, there are worthwhile generalizations. Most of us are somewhat anxious about death. Few would like to have had an earlier birth. This asymmetry of desire is, then, widespread. But we should not expect it to be universal. We are caused by our different experiences to want different things. We are caused, too, to have different beliefs. As is evident, people have different beliefs about whether they might have been born at a different time. Even so, one aspect of the asymmetry of possibility may appear to be clear and straightforward. It is, we might say, either true or false that we can be born earlier.

Is it true or false? One of my more central aims has been both modest and plain. I've wanted simply to defend, in the broadest terms, Kaufman's (sometime) claim that we cannot be born earlier from the contention of Bruckner and Fischer that we can. But that has involved two activities of some complexity. First, I've tried to disentangle some of the uncertainties within Kaufman's account. His position on whether an earlier birth is possible is, to say the least, wavering. Second, connected with this, but more general and more important, I've wanted further to explore the status of this claim about an earlier birth, and in particular its relation to questions of science, psychology, and metaphysics. This exploration bears upon my answer. I've claimed that we cannot be born earlier. But at the same time I've tried to give this claim an unelevated status. In particular, I've wanted to deny that I am here accessing the metaphysical realm. Rather, that claim is one that best latches on to and makes sense of various small-scale and everyday concerns.

Perhaps this can be put in a different way. In explaining our attitudes, claims about the asymmetry of possibility will appear to play a critical role. If you think an earlier birth is possible, the puzzle about why, in general, this is undesired can seem real. If you believe it isn't possible, this question might look to be easily answered. I've wanted, of course, to deny that there need be any tight fit here. But I've also wanted in some way to invert the argument. The claim about possibility is just not, at least as I've construed it, a prior datum, a hard metaphysical fact which might be supposed to inform our attitudes. Rather the claim I've wanted to defend, that an earlier birth is not possible, is subsequent to and derives its truth from those various attitudes.

And perhaps the point can be made in a third way. I considered, toward the middle of the paper, three distinct views. The first suggests there is just no fact of the matter as to whether someone might be born earlier, whereas the second and third suggest, in different and contrasting ways, that there is. Of these, I favored the latter. But that can leave things appearing too stark and implying that contrary positions might admit of a decisive refutation. What in the end is needed here, I suspect, is to see that there is just no fact of the matter as to whether there's a fact of the matter.

NOTES

1. Anthony Brueckner and John Martin Fischer, "Why Is Death Bad?" *Philosophical Studies* 50 (1986), pp. 213–221; "The Asymmetry of Early Birth and Late Death," *Philosophical Studies* 71 (1993), pp. 327–331; "Death's Badness," *Pacific Philosophical Quarterly* 74 (1993), pp. 37–45.

2. Christopher Belshaw, "Asymmetry and Non-Existence," *Philosophical Studies* 70 (1993), pp. 103–116.

3. Frederick Kaufman, "Death and Deprivation; or, Why Lucretius' Symmetry Argument Fails," *Australasian Journal of Philosophy* 74 (1996), pp. 305–312. Brueckner and Fischer reply in "Being Born Earlier," *Australasian Journal of Philosophy* 76 (1998), pp. 110–114.

4. Though not this phrase exactly, both Kaufman and Brueckner and Fischer refer repeatedly to "metaphyical personal identity" and various cognates.

5. An initial response to Lucretius' problem alleges that the wish to be born earlier involves merely a relocation and not a genuine extension of life. A later death, in contrast, does offer an extension. Thus asymmetry. It is true that many thoughts are like this. But there is no solution here, even if there is encouragement to a more precise formulation.

6. Here I make explicit that the discussion concerns substantial differences in the time of birth and/or death. And this is to be assumed throughout. There is usually neither an interest in, nor problems with, shifting things by a couple of days.

7. See, in particular, pp. 307–308.

8. Brueckner and Fischer (1998), p. 3.

9. Brueckner and Fischer (1998), p. 111.

10. Brueckner and Fischer (1998), p. 112.

11. At least some defenders, that is, will appeal to the asymmetry of possibility. And Brueckner and Fischer interpret Kaufman this way. But their objection holds even if a weaker claim is made, to the effect that we are rational in desiring later states, but not earlier states. They can say the additional states are equally impossible, and so (on the face of it) equally suspect as objects of desire. But of course my counter to their objection also still holds.

12. Brueckner and Fischer (1998), p. 112.

13. In certain footnotes and at various places in the text the authors indicate that the same points could be expressed in some counterpart-theoretic way. It might be argued that so expressed the points are clearer. But I shall not consider these alternative formulations.

14. For example, "Kaufman holds that whereas Mary could have died later, she could not have been born earlier." Brueckner and Fischer (1998), p. 113.

15. See, for further examples, Stephen Rosenbaum, "The Symmetry Argument: Lucretius against the Fear of Death," *Philosophy and Phenomenological Research* 50 (1989), pp. 353–371; Ishtiyaque Haji, "Pre-Vital and Post-Vital Times," *Pacific Philosophical Quarterly* 72 (1991), pp. 171–180; Belshaw (1993).

16. It might be suggested, for example, that a weak asymmetry will be entailed. For it might be said that though I can desire something believed to be impossible, I cannot desire it as much, or as strongly, as a very similar thing that I believe to be possible. More important, and as I shall go on to explain, it might be suggested that our notions of what is possible here will in part derive from, rather than precede, the overall shape of our desires.

17. What sorts of possibilities are at issue here? Suppose the technology for freezing is developed and made available. Then for those born subsequently, freezing, and thus a later birth, is physically possible. But it's logically possible for the technology to have been developed earlier. So those born hundreds of years ago could have been born later. Does this technology allow for a possible earlier birth? Suppose someone is frozen, and later born. This person could have been born earlier. But that is a special case. It is not at all clear how the freezing hypothesis opens the possibility of some being born earlier, if in fact they are born in the normal way.

18. See Brueckner and Fischer (1998), p. 110. And, as there suggested, see also Brueckner and Fischer (1986), p. 215, and Brueckner and Fischer (1993), note 2.

19. Thus, "[g]iven the possibility of my genetic constitution or bodily configuration existing earlier, it seems I therefore could have existed earlier. We can concede Kripke's point about metaphysical personal identity, but remain unmoved about the questions that here concern us" (p. 308). But earlier, "[s]ometimes 'person' refers to a biological entity . . . and at other times it refers to an ongoing centre of self-awareness" (p. 307). And then later, "I have argued that a person cannot exist earlier than in fact he or she did" (p. 311).

20. For example, Rosenbaum (1989), p. 362, and also Fred Feldman, "Some Puzzles about the Evil of Death," *The Philosophical Review* 100 (1991), p. 222.

21. Brueckner and Fischer (1998), pp. 112–113.

22. Though there's room for one qualification. Possible worlds are many. Kaufman could think that we need to consider the different physically possible worlds, whereas we don't need to consider the merely logically or metaphysically possible worlds, in which Mary can be found.

23. I may seem to be assuming that being born and beginning to exist are (for us) one and the same thing. But I make no such assumption. What I do assume, however, is that my coming into existence is not one and the same thing as the coming into existence of the material from which I derive. It is this gap that may by various means be prolonged.

24. See here Derek Parfit's very relevant discussion of reductionism, indeterminacy, and empty questions, in Part III of *Reasons and Persons* (Oxford: The Clarendon Press, 1984).

25. Though again, you may not. This kind of case, familiar from many discussions of personal identity, raises enough problems of its own. And I don't want to suggest the persistence of concern in such cases would clearly be rational. It would, however, surely be natural, and at least in that sense can be distinguished from the more artificial cases we need to consider in thinking about a possible earlier birth.

26. "Wholesale" is intended to be vague. Someone might ask what degree of change is compatible with preserving identity, what degree incompatible. There is no answer to such a question. My point is only that some massive change will destroy identity. But here again, the point is not at all deep.

27. For technological developments will soon make certain questions real. And it is unreasonable to suppose that we can have as yet no idea as to how we will answer them.

28. Thus Ovid. But some will argue that this concern for the mind betrays a too intellectual perspective. Not so. A dancer, say, may be so damaged by an accident or disease that we are tempted to say she no longer exists. But this will be, I think, in virtue of her psychological reaction to incapacity, rather than to the incapacity itself.

29. Certain of Parfit's views, especially as they occur in Sections 81 and 82 of *Reasons and Persons*, will be recognizable here.

30. An earlier birth might not only be possible, but also desirable. Imagine the world will soon collide with an asteroid. It will be destroyed. So lives will be cut short. But if they'd started earlier these lives would not have been cut short.

31. Brueckner and Fischer (1998), p. 114.

Midwest Studies in Philosophy, XXIV (2000)

Death and the Psychological Conception of Personal Identity

JOHN MARTIN FISCHER AND DANIEL SPEAK

She was born in spring,
But I was born too late.
Blame it on a simple twist of fate.

—"A Simple Twist of Fate" (*Blood on the Tracks*), Bob Dylan

I. THE PROBLEM: OUR ASYMMETRIC ATTITUDES

It is frequently claimed in the literature on the metaphysics of death that human beings have asymmetric attitudes toward death and prenatal nonexistence. The claim is that we tend to consider the prospects of our future deaths as bad or unfortunate for us, whereas we do not regret the fact that we were born when we actually were born, rather than earlier. This is not to say that we would think of *any* future death as bad; if we are asked to consider that we might be in the end stages of a very painful, debilitating, and terminal disease, we might well look at death in such circumstances as a welcome relief. However, when it is assumed that life is still good, we tend to consider death (but not failure to be born earlier) a bad thing for the individual in question.

This alleged datum—the assymetry in our attitudes toward prenatal and post-humous nonexistence—poses a problem for an appealing account of death's badness. On the assumption that death is a period of nonexistence that is an experiential blank, then it is tempting to say that death is bad for the individual who dies insofar as it deprives the individual of the goods (whatever they are thought to be) of life. We find this "deprivation account" of death's badness highly plausible.[1] But if the deprivation account of death's badness is correct, then it would appear to imply that we should also consider the fact that we were born when we actually were, rather than earlier, a bad thing. It seems that the time of our birth deprives us of time during which we could enjoy the goods of life in just the way in which the time of our death deprives us of such goods.

One could of course address this apparent problem in various ways. One approach would be to stick with the deprivation account and accept the conclusion that we should indeed have symmetric attitudes toward prenatal and posthumous non-existence. There are various different versions of this approach. One possibility would be to contend that we should regret *both* the fact that we do not die later and the fact that we are not born earlier. Another possibility would be to regret *neither* fact.

An alternative way of responding to the problem is to continue to embrace the deprivation account of death's badness but to argue that (despite the initial appearance) it does not entail that we should have symmetric attitudes toward prenatal and posthumous nonexistence. A salient version of this strategy contends that whereas a person could live longer than he actually lives, he *could not* have been born earlier than he actually was born. Thus, since deprivation requires the relevant possibility, death can deprive the person of the goods of life, but the time of his birth—the fact that he was born when he actually was born—cannot deprive him of such goods.

Thomas Nagel presented this way of defending the deprivation account in "Death," although he confessed to some doubts about its adequacy.[2] Why exactly is it not possible for an individual person to have been born considerably earlier than he actually was born? It is not clear why this would be impossible (in some broad metaphysical sense). If it is suggested that it is a necessary condition of an individual's being the individual he actually is that he come from a particular sperm and egg, then why is it impossible that that sperm and egg have existed considerably earlier than they actually existed? Of course, the particular sperm and egg came from the individual's parents, but why exactly is it impossible (in some appropriately broad metaphysical sense) for the parents to have lived considerably earlier?[3]

II. THE PSYCHOLOGICAL CONCEPTION OF THE PERSON

Recently Frederik Kaufman has proposed a different way of arguing that an individual could not have been born earlier.[4] In brief, Kaufman argues that when an individual is concerned about his own death, he is concerned about the death of a "psychologically thick" person—an individual with a particular history and thus a particular set of memories, desires, beliefs, values, personality traits, and so forth. But, Kaufman argues, such an individual could not have existed earlier; an individual existing (considerably earlier) would necessarily have been some other particular individual (construed in the "thick" way). Thus the deprivation account can be defended.

It is not clear to us that it is impossible (in the relevant way—in some broadly metaphysical sense) for the same thick individual to have been born considerably earlier than he actually was born. But we grant that this sort of possibility is at best very far-fetched; it would appear to require wholesale changes in the past: various persons existing and events taking place considerably earlier than they actually do. About this Kaufman says:

> So even if it is not logically impossible for me, thickly conceived, to have existed slightly earlier, it is so extremely unlikely that an earlier existing person would turn out to be qualitatively identical (or even similar) to me as I currently am as to make it virtually impossible that I could have existed earlier.[5]

We will grant, then, for the sake of the argument, that human persons, thickly conceived, could not (in the relevant sense) have been born much earlier than they actually were.[6]

It will be helpful to lay out Kaufman's reasoning in some detail. Kaufman is concerned to distinguish between thick and thin conceptions of personhood. The thin conception involves nothing more than "metaphysical essences." Kaufman says:

> A person, on this view, is simply a particular essence, and that person exists in all possible worlds which contain that essence. The details of one's actual life are wholly contingent features of an individual. On this understanding of 'person,' since the features of one's actual life are not in any way constitutive of the person one is, it is possible for one to be shorn of all the attributes of one's actual life and remain the same person throughout the changes.[7]

Kaufman concedes that one's metaphysical essence could have been born earlier— could have been associated with a different thick self. But he considers this irrelevant to the issues about death and earlier birth. He says:

> [I]nsofar as concern about death is driven by concerns that one's conscious personal existence will be extinguished forever, the fact that one's metaphysical essence might occur in different times and places seems beside the point. This is why certain possible occurrences that leave my metaphysical essence intact but which nevertheless extinguish my subjective sense of myself as myself are things which, like death, I could not survive; such as brain zaps, philosophical amnesia, permanent coma, some versions of reincarnation, or 'merging with the infinite.'[8]

In defending his view, Kaufman presents the following intriguing example:

> My metaphysical essence—whatever it is—might have led a very different life. I could have lived as an Eskimo, for example, had my parents given 'me' to an Eskimo tribe upon my birth. I would speak Aleut, live in igloos and hunt seals. That person—metaphysically me—would be otherwise unrecognizable to the person I currently am, the one who grew up in middle-class America. The conscious personal life of the Eskimo 'me' would consist of completely different memories, projects, beliefs and commitments. Whatever point of view the Eskimo 'me' would have on his life and circumstance, it will be vastly different from my current subjective awareness. . . . Were the 'thin'

metaphysical me to be raised by an Eskimo tribe, the conscious personal entity that I currently am would regard him as a complete stranger. I wish him well, but I am no more concerned about his death than I am about the death of any other stranger.[9]

Thus, on Kaufman's view, it is important to distinguish between the thin person (the metaphysical essence) and the thick person (the person with a particular set of memories, histories, projects under way, beliefs, and values). Kaufman holds that what we worry about, when we consider our own deaths, is the elimination of the thick person. But this sort of person cannot have been born earlier than he or she actually was born, and thus the time of one's birth cannot deprive the thick person of goods he or she otherwise would have had. Thus, the deprivation account of death's badness is perfectly compatible with our asymmetric attitudes toward prenatal and posthumous nonexistence.

III. CRITIQUE OF KAUFMAN

We are willing to concede the actual time of one's birth cannot deprive the thick person of goods he or she otherwise would have had. But why exactly should this be the *only* relevant issue? That is, why should we agree with Kaufman's contention that it is irrelevant that the thin person—the metaphysical essence—could indeed have been born earlier (and thus could have been associated with a different thick person)? We will contend that persons often make judgments that presuppose that it is coherent to care—and perhaps care deeply—about which thick person one's metaphysical essence is, as it were, attached to. (For the purposes of this discussion, we will adopt Kaufman's terminology.)

Imagine that you read in the newspaper that a certain hospital has had various problems with "baby-switching" cases: babies have been mixed up in the maternity ward, and couples have been given babies who are not biologically theirs to take home. Assuming that you had a generally pleasant and favorable set of childhood experiences, you might say to yourself, "I'm relieved that sort of thing did not happen to me! I'm glad that my biological parents brought me home from the hospital and raised me." This seems to be a perfectly natural and not uncommon kind of thought, and it seems to presuppose that one can coherently make judgments about which thick person one's thin self is attached to. If one's family life was particularly pleasant, one might explicitly contrast, in one's mind, one's early childhood experiences with (as one would naturally assume) the experiences one would have had, had one gone home from the hospital with another couple.

Suppose, however, that one's early childhood experiences were particularly horrid, involving significant poverty and physical and psychological abuse. Under such circumstances, it would not at all be unreasonable, upon reading the newspaper article, to wish that one had in fact gone home from the hospital with another family. One might wistfully think about having gone home with a happy, loving, and financially secure family; it would be natural to say to oneself, "My life would have been very different. . . ." Again, these sorts of judgments appear to presuppose precisely the coherence of stepping outside one's thick self in a certain way, contrary to Kaufman's supposition.

Return to Kaufman's Eskimo example. Recall that Kaufman concludes, "Were the 'thin' metaphysical me to be raised by an Eskimo tribe, the conscious personal entity that I currently am would regard him as a complete stranger. I wish him well, but I am no more concerned about his death than I am about the death of any other stranger."[10] But let us now fill in the details of the story a bit differently. Imagine that you were adopted when you were very young, so that you have never known who your biological parents are. It happens that you have been raised in a middle-class community in Anchorage, Alaska. One day—when you are (say) forty years old —you get a telephone call from an elderly couple who explain that they are your biological parents. They would like to see you, and you arrange to meet them at a restaurant in Anchorage. When they arrive at the restaurant, you are surprised to learn that they are from an Eskimo tribe who live some distance from the city. They apologize profusely for having had to give you up for adoption at birth, but they already had eight children, and they just could not manage another. They are a lovely, warm, generous couple who have learned to speak English in their later years, in anticipation of this meeting with you.

The meeting is very emotional, and your feelings and thoughts are chaotic for some time afterward. But as you think about your biological parents and the story they told, you develop a strong feeling of sadness that you were not in fact raised by them in the Eskimo tribal community. You do love your adoptive parents, and you are grateful for all the love they have given you. But you can't help wondering what your life would have been like had you been raised by your biological parents among your biological brothers and sisters in the Eskimo community. You wonder about it constantly, and although you know there is nothing now that can be done to change the fact that you were raised in a middle-class community in Anchorage, you nevertheless wish that it had been different.

Of course, the story need not be told in this manner; upon meeting your biological parents, you might have little or no regrets about not having been raised by them. But the point is that the story *can* be told in this way. It seems perfectly natural for human beings to prefer to have been raised by their biological parents, even when they have had relatively favorable circumstances. It would seem even more reasonable to have such a preference, if the adoptive circumstances are unpleasant and difficult.

When Kaufman concludes that the "conscious personal entity that I currently am" would regard the individual raised by the Eskimos as a "complete stranger" and that he would be no more concerned about this individual's death than about that of any other stranger, this is a compex and puzzling claim. But it is interesting to ask why Kaufman focuses on whether the individual as raised in the middle-class community would be concerned about the *death* of the already-mature individual raised in the Eskimo community. This does not seem to be the relevant question. Rather, the question would appear to be whether the individual raised in the middle-class community could coherently form preferences about having been raised in the Eskimo community. If it is possible for the middle-class individual to prefer having been raised in the Eskimo community, then his not having been so raised could deprive him of significant goods. That is all that is required; the middle-class individual's alleged attitudes toward the death of the already-mature Eskimo individual seem beside the point.

If the judgments and preferences in the cases discussed above are coherent, then it is plausible that we can in general form judgments and preferences about which thick persons our metaphysical essences—or thin selves—are associated with. Put in simpler language, it seems plausible that we can make judgments and form preferences about which lives to lead, where the possibilities include lives with very different beginnings from those of our actual lives. It is not an uncommon thought experiment to wonder what it would be like actually to be someone else; one might wonder whether one would like to switch places with another person. Of course, some versions of the thought experiments are perfectly compatible with Kaufman's view. For example, it is compatible with Kaufman's view that a thick individual can imagine himself in some other person's job or life circumstances now. But what does appear to be incompatible with Kaufman's view is the possibility of imagining that one has led another individual's life from the beginning. And yet it does not seem incoherent to form the preference for having led another individual's life from the beginning or to be relieved that one has not.

Regrettably, we do not have a decisive argument that the judgments and preferences discussed above are possible. It is in fact hard to see how to argue for their possibility. We do, however, wish to point to a possible source of confusion in the considerations Kaufman adduces on behalf of the contention that such judgments and preferences are without any basis and thus irrelevant. Recall Kaufman's claim:

> This is why certain possible occurrences that leave my metaphysical essence intact but which nevertheless extinguish my subjective sense of myself as myself are things which, like death, I could not survive; such as brain zaps, philosophical amnesia, permanent coma, some versions of reincarnation, or 'merging with the infinite.' And, like death, I regard these possibilities as bad insofar as they deprive me of the goods of life. Knowing that my essence might continue on without me, as it were, is no comfort.[11]

Suppose a person is subject to a "brain zap" that significantly changes one's "quasi-memories," preferences, values, and beliefs. As a result of this direct electronic stimulation of the brain, the individual has a very different personality from the one he had prior to the stimulation. We agree with Kaufman that this would be tantamount to death for the original individual. Once we have begun our lives and formed our personalities—our "thick selves," as it were—we have a strong interest in not having these personalities (the total configuration of memories, beliefs, preferences, values, and so forth) radically altered in certain ways. When such alterations take place, we consider this tantamount to death.

But there is a difference between an alteration of this sort and a hypothetical case in which one's life circumstances would have been different from the beginning (thus allowing for the development of a different personality or thick self). An alteration of the sort in question involves a radical *discontinuity* (to which one does not consent voluntarily). That is, one's metaphysical essence is associated with *one* thick self, and then this association is severed and *another* thick self becomes attached to the same metaphysical essence; we have strong negative reactions to these sorts of cases. We do not want our lives to be *discontinuous* in this sort of way, and thus we have a strong negative reaction when we contemplate such possibilities.

But Kaufman appears to infer from this sort of negative reaction to the "alteration" cases a conclusion about hypothetical cases in which one's circumstances are different *from the beginning* (thus allowing for the gradual and continuous development of a very different kind of personality or thick self). This kind of inference is problematic, because one's aversion to alteration and thus discontinuity (of certain sorts) is irrelevant to contexts that are different from the actual circumstances *from the beginning*. That an individual of course would object to being subject to an involuntary brain zap that would significantly alter his personality does *not* show that he could not reasonably prefer that he had been raised in very different circumstances from the actual ones.

Apart from the invocation of intuitions about cases of alternation and thus discontinuity, we do not see that there is any sort of *argument* in Kaufman's article that would establish that the judgments and preferences discussed above about leading entirely different lives are necessarily incoherent, mysterious, or without any basis. Although this kind of argument is not explicit in Kaufman's work, we suppose someone might argue as follows. The thick individual has a point of view or perspective—a set of experiences, memories, desires, and values—by reference to which he can coherently form preferences about leading various kinds of lives. But a thin person by definition does not have such a point of view and thus cannot coherently be thought to form preferences about different lives. After all, where would such preferences come from? What would they be based on?

But this argument rests on a mistake. It supposes that the preference for leading one total life (a life from the beginning) as opposed to another must be generated from the perspective of the thin self or metaphysical essence. This is admittedly impossible, but it is also unnecessary. On the picture we are suggesting, it is possible for us, construed as thick persons (with the appropriately rich perspective of a thick person) to make judgments and form preferences about various scenarios in which our metaphysical essences are associated with different thick selves. So the preferences about such scenarios are generated from the perspective of our thick selves, even though they are about the possibility of our thin selves being associated with other thick selves. There is nothing incoherent in this picture, as far as we can see.

We have pointed to a number of contexts in which human beings naturally make judgments and form preferences about leading very different lives (from the beginning). We have not sought to dispute Kaufman's claim that thick persons could not have been born much ealier than they were actually born. We have instead raised questions about Kaufman's claim that thick personhood is the *only* notion of personhood relevant to concerns about the dates of our death and birth. If it is coherent to prefer that one had been raised in very different circumstances from the beginning, then there is no bar to saying that it would be coherent to prefer that one had been born considerably earlier. In Kaufman's terms, one would be exhibiting a preference that one's metaphysical essence be associated with a different thick person.

It is of course possible to insist that the sorts of judgments and preferences we have claimed are coherent are at a deeper level simply incoherent or without any basis. But it is important to see that one would thereby be calling into question some fairly common kinds of practices (of making certain judgments and forming certain preferences).[12] Further, we do not see a strong *argument* in Kaufman's article (or elsewhere) to convince us that we *should* abandon these practices. When he seeks to argue for his conclusion, Kaufman appears to go from considerations pertaining to radical discontinuity and disruption to those pertaining to alternative circumstances that are different from the beginning (but involve no such alteration or disruption).

IV. BELSHAW'S "CONSERVATION CLAIM"

In his recent paper, "Death, Pain, and Time," Christopher Belshaw presents an approach that is very similar to that of Kaufman. As we understand Belshaw's argument, he wishes to start with the assumption that almost everyone does indeed have an asymmetric attitude toward prenatal and posthumous nonexistence. That is, the vast majority of people, if not everyone, will consider that the time of their death can deprive them of goods but will not think of the time of their birth as similarly depriving them of goods. He then wishes to offer an explanation for this asymmetry. Belshaw says:

> We want, most of us, for the past to be as it is, and so are neither indifferent to its shape, nor interested in amending it. Older people can, on occasion, express a wish to be younger. Historians sometimes, and unthinkingly, say they'd like to be older than they are. The rest of us generally do not. We recognise that our being born at a certain time is, in large part, responsible for who we are today. Someone born at a different time just wouldn't, in an everyday sense, be me. And so we want neither to reduce prenatal nonexistence, making ourselves older, nor, as a means of regaining youth, to increase it. Nor are we simply indifferent to past nonexistence, caring neither one way nor the other when we were born. Rather, our concern is with *conservation*, with keeping the facts of prenatal nonexistence just as they are. For many of us recognise, and many more can easily be brought to recognise, that a concern for the present to be as it is, and for us to be who we are, implies a concern that the past be as it was, and thus that we be born when in fact we were. . . . Indeed, the point can be put more dramatically: to want to be born at a different time is, in effect, to want not to exist, and for someone else to exist in your place. It's not surprising that this is something only a very few of us want.[13]

Belshaw's view is presumably similar to Kaufman's in that he is suggesting that to want to be born at a different time is to want to be a different thick person (in Kaufman's terminology) and that very few persons would want this. According to Belshaw, we do not want to have been born earlier because we recognize (or could easily be brought to recognize) that if we had been born earlier, our personalities would have been significantly different. The key assumption is that we would not want our personalities to be significantly different (from the beginning, as it were).

But this assumption has problems that are similar to those that plagued Kaufman. Belshaw is seeking to explain what he takes to be a very prevalent and almost universal attitude toward birth. His crucial supposition is that almost everyone would not prefer to have had a different personality from the beginning. But this does seem to be a *very* conservative principle, and it is not at all clear that it is true. Surely many individuals would not want to have had a different personality from the beginning. These individuals—perhaps they are a majority (even a large majority)—have led basically good lives under generally favorable circumstances. Even many people who have struggled considerably will no doubt prefer not to have had a different personality from the beginning (where they do not have control over the nature or features of this other personality).

But surely there are many deeply unhappy persons—persons who grew up under conditions of horrible poverty or terrible physical or emotional abuse. Many of these individuals suffer from the emotional scars of their troubled early childhoods, and quite a few of them lead very unhappy lives. Why wouldn't these people be willing to take the risks involved in having a different personality? And of course it is not only individuals from disadvantaged or troubled backgrounds who suffer from deep, persistent, and unpleasant emotional and mental problems; chronic depression and schizophrenia are not reserved for those who have grown up in poverty or suffered abuse. Why is it so obvious that *almost everyone* would want to keep the past as it is because they want desperately to keep the basic features of their personality as they are? This would seem to be conservative in the extreme and to be based on an unwarranted assumption that almost everyone is sufficiently satisfied with their personalities that they would be unwilling to take the risks associated with having a very different personality.

Now we want to emphasize that it does seem reasonable that *most* people would not prefer to have been "someone else" (in the sense of having a very different personality, and—importantly—not being able to select the nature and features of this personality). But this is not enough for Belshaw's stated purpose, because he believes that the desire to hold fixed the time of one's birth is almost universal. At the beginning of "Death, Pain, and Time," Belshaw states the point starkly: "We wish to die later. But we don't wish to have been born earlier. Our future nonexistence matters to us in a way that past nonexistence does not."[14] Later he criticizes approaches that seek to explain our assymetrical attitudes toward prenatal and posthumous nonexistence in terms of our attitudes toward pain and pleasure, saying "our asymmetrical attitude regarding pleasures and pains is, I shall maintain, complex and untidy, while that concerning nonexistence is more straightforward, and relatively easy to understand."[15]

But the considerations discussed above indicate that it is not plausible to assume that there is an almost universal desire to maintain one's personality as it is (and not risk assuming another personality, over the features of which one has no control). The situation here is more "complex and untidy" than Belshaw supposes. If this is so, and if there is indeed an almost universal lack of a wish to have been born earlier, then this wish (and the attendant asymmetry in our attitudes toward prenatal and posthumous nonexistence) cannot be explained in terms of Belshaw's "conservation claim."[16]

NOTES

1. Thomas Nagel defends the deprivation account in "Death," reprinted in *Mortal Questions* (Cambridge: Cambridge University Press, 1979). For developments of this approach, see, for example, Anthony Brueckner and John Martin Fischer, "Why Is Death Bad?" *Philosophical Studies* 71 (1993), pp. 213–221; and F. M. Kamm, "Why Is Death Bad and Worse than Pre-Natal Non-Existence?" *Pacific Philosophical Quarterly* 69 (1988), pp. 168–174; and *Morality, Mortality: Volume I* (New York and Oxford: Oxford University Press, 1993), esp. pp. 13–71.

2. Nagel, 1979, pp. 8–9.

3. For a discussion of these issues, see Brueckner and Fischer, 1993.

4. Frederik Kaufman, "Pre-Vital and Post-Mortem Non-Existence," *American Philosophical Quarterly* 36 (1999), pp. 1–19.

5. Kaufman, 1999, p. 14.

6. It is not clear that Kaufman needs so strong a conclusion as that it is *impossible* for an individual to have been born significantly earlier than he actually was born. It would seem to be sufficient, for Kaufman's purposes, that certain *counterfactuals* would be true (whether or not the impossibility claim is true). So it would seem to be sufficient that it is true that anyone born considerably earlier would not be identical to the individual in question. And this could be true compatibly with the (perhaps remote) possibility that the individual in question could have been born considerably earlier. The counterfactuals and the possibility claims correspond to different modalities, and strictly speaking, what appears to be relevant to Kaufman's argument are merely the counterfactuals. For a discussion of the logic of arguments involving these two importantly different kinds of modalities, see John Martin Fischer, *The Metaphysics of Free Will* (Oxford and Cambridge, Mass.: Blackwell Publishers, 1994), esp. pp. 87–110.

7. Kaufman, 1999, p. 11.

8. Kaufman, 1999, p. 11.

9. Kaufman, 1999, p. 12.

10. Kaufman, 1999, p. 12.

11. Kaufman, 1999, p. 12.

12. Consider the following parable, which we owe to Glenn Pettigrove. Odysseus, on his long journey home from Troy, is paid a visit by Zeus one Mediterranean afternoon. Zeus informs Odysseus that the gods have been contemplating human attitudes toward life and death. Not surprisingly, a heated dispute has arisen on Mount Olympus. In order to resolve the dispute, Zeus has proposed that they perform a little experiment. Because of his reputation for craft and cunning, Odysseus has been selected as the subject of the experiment. The experiment is simple, requiring nothing more from Odysseus than a single choice between two options: (1) complete, eternal annihilation, effective tomorrow, or (2) to be born fifty years earlier than he had been and live to the ripe age of one hundred (twice as long as his lifetime under option 1), at which time he would be completely and eternally annihilated.

After securing from Zeus the assurance that the life under option (2) would contain at least as much honor as his current life, it seems likely that the cunning Odysseus would choose an earlier birth over an immediate death. And it seems that many, if not most, of us would choose similarly. Of course, in Kaufman's terminology the choice would be for our metaphysical essence to have been associated with a different thick person. Perhaps Kaufman would contend that upon careful reflection most persons would not make the choice for earlier birth, but it is not at all clear that this is so. Our attitudes toward the time of our birth—and thus the possibility of having a different thick self—are more complex and ambivalent than Kaufman supposes.

13. Christopher Belshaw, "Death, Pain, and Time," in *Philosophical Studies* 97 (2000), pp. 317–341, esp. pp. 324–325.

14. Belshaw, 2000, p. 317.

15. Belshaw, 2000, p. 317.

16. We are grateful to Dominick Sklenar for helpful conversations about the topics of this paper, and to Frederik Kaufman and Glenn Pettigrove for generous comments on a previous version.

Thick and Thin Selves:
Reply to Fischer and Speak

FREDERIK KAUFMAN

O n the assumption that one's death is the permanent extinction of conscious personal existence, death is bad, when it is bad, because it deprives one of the goods of life that otherwise would have been enjoyed. This is the answer many have given to Epicurus' challenge regarding the badness of death.[1] However, the "deprivation account" for the badness of death leads straightaway to a problem: if death is bad because it deprives one of goods that otherwise would have been enjoyed, then birth is bad too for the very same reason, for being born when one was apparently also deprives one of goods that could have been enjoyed had one been born earlier. First articulated by Lucretius, the "symmetry argument" threatens to undermine the deprivation account for the badness of death.[2]

The alleged symmetry between prevital and post mortem nonexistence can be broken, I believe, by developing a line of thought found in Thomas Nagel's now classic article on death.[3] Nagel suggested that whereas a particular person could have died later than in fact he or she did, that same person could not have existed earlier, for an earlier existing person would be someone else. Offering no defense or elaboration of this claim, Nagel has been severely criticized for supposing that personal identity is disrupted by earlier existence.[4] But distinguishing between "thick" and "thin" accounts of persons will allow us to see why a person could die later but not be born earlier, making it possible for death to deprive, whereas earlier existence, being impossible (in some suitably broad sense), cannot.

"Thick" persons are biographical persons, persons in the sense of having a full complement of psychological states, memories, beliefs, ongoing projects, values, aspirations, and commitments. You are such a person. If you think it would be bad for you to die, it will be bad precisely because the conscious personal entity that you are—an entity with a particular history, particular loved ones, and particular projects under way—will be deprived of goods that longer life would allow you to enjoy. Your death would deprive you of all that makes your life valuable to you. "Thin" persons, by contrast, are shorn of their thick traits such that all that remains is one's metaphysical essence, whatever that is. The conscious biographical self that loves life and can be deprived by death is associated with a particular thin person but is not identical to it, since changes in one's metaphysical essence need not affect one's conscious personal self-awareness. Similarly, one's metaphysical essence might continue on without a particular first-person awareness as, for example, on some theories of reincarnation. Therefore, your personal conscious awareness of yourself—the thick self—is not the same as the metaphysical essence with which it is associated.

Thin selves can exist earlier than they in fact do, with no ill effects, as it were. My metaphysical essence (a particular body, genetic constitution, brain, Cartesian soul, or whatever) could have existed 200 years ago. That thin self would remain metaphysically me. However, the thick self associated with that essence would be very different than the self that I currently am. The thick self that I currently am is constituted by a particular biography, a life history filled with specific events, loved ones, memories, beliefs, desires, choices, and so forth. Imaginatively trying to picture the thick self that I currently am existing 200 years earlier than I in fact do disrupts my currently established biography, since I would remember, say, both fighting in the Civil War and watching my favorite television shows as a child. The self that would exist in my place, that is, be associated with my essence were it to exist 200 years ago would have a radically different biography. It would, in short, be a different (thick) person.

It seems, then, that whereas thin selves can exist earlier than they in fact do, thick selves cannot. Moving one's metaphysical essence back in time disrupts the current thick self associated with a particular essence. Therefore, the current thick self cannot be deprived by not existing earlier, since the thick self associated with an earlier existing essence would have a different biography and thus be a different (thick) person. However, the currently existing thick self could be deprived by death, since additional experiences can constitute an extension of one's biography, not its disorganization. A particular person could have died later than in fact he or she did and remain the same biographic person, since the appropriate psychological connections can hold between a current thick self and a later existing one, whereas appropriate psychological connections cannot hold between the current thick self and one that came into existence earlier than in fact it did. Thus can we argue that the deprivation account for the badness of death does not commit us to thinking that we are deprived by coming into existence when we do, if we think that our going out of existence when we do is an evil that befalls us.

In "Death and the Psychological Conception of Personal Identity," John Martin Fischer and Daniel Speak grant, "for the sake of the argument, that human persons, thickly conceived, could not (in the relevant sense) have been born much earlier than they actually were."[5] But they deny that is the only relevant issue: "We will contend that persons often make judgments that presuppose that it is coherent to care—and perhaps care deeply—about which thick person one's metaphysical essence is, as it were, attached to."[6] They adduce several examples that show how the current thick self can form judgments regarding alternate biographies that could have ensued had one's metaphysical essence been situated differently. For example, the thick self that I currently am might wish that my metaphysical essence had been raised among the Eskimos, thus giving rise to a very different thick self, that is, a different constellation of beliefs, memories, desires, commitments, and so forth.

Fischer and Speak apparently think that the fact that we can form judgments about alternate lives shows that those other lives were genuine possibilities for us, and hence that we can be deprived by not having led those lives: "If it is possible for the middle-class individual to prefer having been raised in the Eskimo community, then his not having been so raised could deprive him of significant goods."[7] However, mere preference cannot be sufficient for deprivation, since I might prefer many things of which I have not been deprived. I strongly prefer to be rich, but I have not been deprived of a fortune. But more importantly, we cannot move from judgments (preferences, desires, wishes, and the like) about different lives to their possibility. Derik Parfit observes, "When they learnt that the square root of two was not a rational number, the Pythagoreans regretted this. We can regret truths even when it is logically impossible that these truths be false." And Dostovesky's Underground Man rails against the fact that twice two is four—what if he just doesn't like it?[8] These are genuine judgments even though they are judgments about the logically impossible. Fischer and Speak might say they are not coherent judgments—they often qualify judgments about alternate lives this way—but making possibility necessary for judgments is question begging. What is at issue is whether it is possible for (thick) me to have lived a very different life; the fact that I can form a judgment about a different life doesn't show that I could have lived it.

Although the thick self that I currently am can form judgments about the lives of other thick selves that could have been associated with my essence (I might wish that my essence had been raised by the Eskimos), this thick self cannot actually have been a different thick self. The lump of metal that forms a statue could be formed into a different statue, but a particular statue cannot be a different statue. So if the thick self that I actually am cannot have been a different thick self, then I cannot be deprived by not being a different (thick) person, irrespective of how much I might want to be someone else.

What about the thin self: can it be deprived by not having a different thick self associated with it? As Fischer and Speak realize, thin selves have no perspective and can form no preferences. But they argue that a preference can be formed by the thick self that the thin self have a different thick self associated with it—thick me can wish that there were a different thick self connected to my essence. However, this does not show that the thin self could be deprived by not having had a different thick self connected to it. Your essence would not be deprived were I to have preferences that a different thick person exist in your stead, so why should it be any different with my view of my own essence? Because they can form no preferences, thin selves cannot be deprived of anything (preference being a necessary, not a sufficient, condition for deprivation).

In response to Fischer and Speak, then, I conclude that thick me cannot be deprived by there not being a different thick self in its stead, because thick me cannot be a different self, irrespective of how much I might wish it to be so; and since thin me has no preferences, it too cannot be deprived by not having had a different thick self attached to it. Moreover, Fischer and Speak's discussion does not directly engage the central question at issue, namely, must a defender of the deprivation account for the evil of death have symmetrical attitudes about prevital and post mortem nonexistence? I have argued that distinguishing between thick and thin persons makes it clear why death can deprive, whereas not existing earlier cannot, so our asymmetrical attitudes are justified. Fischer and Speak argue that because I can form preferences about alternate lives—presumably including earlier lives—those lives are possible, and if possible, then I can be deprived of them. So on their view, I could be deprived by not existing earlier; hence asymmetrical attitudes about the time before we exist and the time after we die are unjustified. But since neither preference nor possibility is sufficient for deprivation, their argument is no threat to my solution for the symmetry problem.

NOTES

1. Epicurus' challenge to those who think death is an evil, and hence that it is rational to fear one's own death, appears in his *Letter to Meneoecus*: "Accustom yourself to the belief that death is of no concern to us, since all good and evil lie in sensation and sensation ends with death. So death, the most terrifying of ills, is nothing to us, since so long as we exist, death is not with us; but when death comes, then we do not exist. It does not then concern either the living or the dead, since for the former it is not, and the latter are no more." *Epicurus*, trans. Russell Geer (Indianapolis, Ind.: Bobbs-Merrill, 1964), p. 54. It is clear that Epicurus is talking about being dead, not dying, which can be awful and hence something of rational concern. The "deprivation response," in one form or another, is put forward by virtually everyone who considers Epicurus' argument, philosopher and nonphilosopher alike. For some sample philosophers, see Fred Feldman, "Some Puzzles about the Evil of Death," *The Philosophical Review* 100 (1991), pp. 205–227, and Anthony Brueckner and John Martin Fischer, "Why Is Death Bad?" *Philosophical Studies* 71 (1993), pp. 213–221.

2. Lucretius, *On the Nature of Things*, trans. C. Bailey (Oxford: Oxford University Press, 1920), III. 927: "Look back again to see how the past ages of everlasting time, before we are born, have been as naught to us. These then nature holds up to us as a mirror of the time that is to come, when we are dead and gone. Is there aught that looks terrible in this, aught that seems gloomy?" Our equanimity regarding our past nonexistence is supposed to show that our concerns regarding future nonexistence are unwarranted, but perhaps we should lament our past nonexistence as well as our future nonexistence, if symmetrical attitudes are warranted at all.

3. Thomas Nagel, "Death," reprinted in *Mortal Questions* (Cambridge University Press, 1979), pp. 1–10. Nagel expresses reservations about his proposal.

4. See Brueckner and Fischer, "Why Is Death Bad?"; Feldman, "Some Puzzles about the Evil of Death," pp. 223–224; Richard Sorabji, *Time, Creation, and the Continuum* (Ithaca, N.Y.: Cornell University Press, 1983), pp. 228–229.

5. John Martin Fischer and Daniel Speak, "Death and the Psychological Conception of Personal Identity," *Midwest Studies in Philosophy* 24 (2000), p. 86.

6. Fischer and Speak, "Death and the Psychological Conception of Personal Identity," p. 87.

7. Fischer and Speak, "Death and the Psychological Conception of Personal Identity" p. 88.

8. Derik Parfit, *Reasons and Persons* (Oxford: Oxford University Press, 1984), p. 175. Fyodor Dostoevsky, *Notes from Underground*, reprinted in Walter Kaufmann, *Existentialism from Dostoevsky to Sartre* (Cleveland, Ohio: Meridan Books 1956). The Underground Man says (p. 61), "Merciful Heavens! But what do I care for the laws of nature and arithmetic, when, for some reason, I dislike those laws and the fact that twice two makes four? Of course I cannot break through the wall by battering my head against it if I really have not the strength to knock it down, but I am not going to be reconciled to it simply because it is a stone wall and I have not the strength."

Midwest Studies in Philosophy, XXIV (2000)

The Termination Thesis

FRED FELDMAN

1. HISTORICAL BACKGROUND

The Termination Thesis (or "TT") is the view that people go out of existence when they die. Lots of philosophers seem to believe it. Epicurus, for example, apparently makes use of TT in his efforts to show that it is irrational to fear death. He says, "as long as we exist, death is not with us; but when death comes, then we do not exist."[1] Lucretius says pretty much the same thing, but in many more words and more poetically: "Death therefore to us is nothing, concerns us not a jot, since the nature of the mind is proved to be mortal; . . . when we shall be no more, when there shall have been a separation of body and soul, out of both of which we are each formed into a single being, to us, you may be sure, who then shall be no more, nothing whatever can happen to excite sensation."[2]

A considerably clearer and more economical statement of TT can be found in L. W. Sumner's "A Matter of Life and Death." Sumner says, "The death of a person is the end of that person; before death he *is* and after death he *is not*. To die is therefore to cease to exist."[3]

In John Martin Fischer's recent anthology of papers on the metaphysics of death, there are many passages in which philosophers seem to endorse TT. The philosophers in question appeal to it for a variety of purposes and often do not agree about its significance. One fairly good example is Thomas Nagel, who puts it in the antecedent of a conditional in the first sentence of his essay, though I think he provisionally endorses it elsewhere: "If death is the unequivocal and permanent end of our existence, then the question arises whether it is a bad thing to die."[4] Other "terminators" in the Fischer anthology include Harry Silverstein,[5] Stephen Rosenbaum,[6] Palle Yourgrau,[7] Steven Luper-Foy,[8] and Joel Feinberg.[9]

In his book *Thinking Clearly about Death*, Jay Rosenberg presents a vigorous endorsement of TT. This comes out in a preliminary way in his discussion of Aunt

Ethel and her corpse. Rosenberg seems to want to say that when she dies, Aunt Ethel goes out of existence, and her corpse comes into existence.[10] Rosenberg devotes several chapters to an argument designed to show that "we cannot make coherent sense of the supposed possibility that a person's history might continue beyond that person's death."[11] I believe that this is Rosenberg's way of expressing an idea equivalent to TT.

2. THE IMPORTANCE OF TT

It's interesting to note that TT has been invoked on both sides of the debate about the evil of death. Epicurus, Lucretius, Rosenbaum, and others maintain that it is irrational to fear death. They claim that death cannot harm us. They make use of TT in their arguments. They claim (approximately) that since we cease to exist when we die, and nothing can harm us when we don't exist, death cannot harm us. Thus, it is irrational to fear death. So TT is sometimes brought in as part of an argument intended to show that death is not to be feared.

But the very same metaphysical principle is sometimes employed in the effort to explain the horror of death. Luper-Foy, for example, insists emphatically that death can be a great evil, especially if it comes prematurely. Part of the evil of death as he sees it is that when we die, we are "annihilated." We go utterly out of existence. When we no longer exist, we are incapable of pursuing the projects that give meaning to our lives. Thus, death harms us.[12]

TT occupies a central position in a number of other more purely metaphysical issues concerning death. There is, for example, the question whether psychological connectedness is the mark of personal identity. It has been suggested that if people continue to exist without psychology after they die, then a person might be identical to some later thing (a corpse) with which the person is psychologically unconnected. Another question is whether we can live again after we have died. TT seems relevant. For if we go out of existence when we die, then a return to life would seem to involve a return to existence after a period of nonexistence. Some metaphysicians find this sort of "gappy" existence intolerable. There is also a question about the relation between a person and his "remains." Is this relation identity, or is it rather a relation that holds between an entity and another entity into which the former has "substantially changed"?[13] If we accept TT, we seem committed to saying that no one is identical to his remains. There is also a familiar line of argument against a form of materialism: "people go out of existence when they die; their bodies often survive. Therefore, people cannot be identified with their bodies." The appeal to TT in the first premise should be obvious.

In any case, it should be clear that TT plays some role in a variety of important metaphysical debates.

3. POSSIBLE MISUNDERSTANDINGS OF TT

A

It's easy to mistake TT for the view that when a person dies, he or she ceases to exist "as a person." If we understand the concept of a person in such a way that in order to be a person at some time, something must be alive or self-conscious, or morally responsible for his or her own actions at that time, then materialists will be in general agreement that *people cease to exist as persons when they die*. This doctrine follows immediately from the assumption about the concept of personality and the fact that people cease to be alive or self-conscious when they die. So the doctrine that people cease to exist as persons (in any such sense) when they die is relatively uncontroversial.[14] But this view is distinct from TT, for TT is not the view that people cease to exist "as people" when they die. It is the view that they cease to exist *simpliciter* when they die.

Let's say that something ceases to exist *simpliciter* at a time if it simply goes out of existence at that time. In the typical case, a thing ceases to exist *simpliciter* at a time if it exists for a while up to that time, but exists no longer after that time. On the other hand, in the typical case we can say that something ceases to exist *as a person* at a time if it was a person for a while up to that time but stopped being a person then. Making use of these expressions, we can formulate a pair of principles:

TTs: When a person dies, he or she ceases to exist *simpliciter*.
TTp: When a person dies, he or she ceases to exist as a person.

When I speak here of the Termination Thesis, I mean something like TTs, not something like TTp.[15]

B

It's also easy to confuse TT with the view that when a person dies, he or she ceases to have any sort of moral or psychological importance. Someone might say that he hates the thought of his own death because he hates the thought of ceasing to be of any moral importance—ceasing to be "morally considerable." Another might say that he hates the thought of his own death because being dead will be, from his own perspective, as empty and as meaningless as not existing at all. Such a person might take himself to be endorsing TT.

However, TT is not a doctrine directly about moral or psychological or other importance. It is not any claim of this sort:

TTi: When a person dies, he or she ceases to have any moral or other significance; being dead is as meaningless as not existing at all.

Rather, TT is the view that people simply stop existing when they die. It's not the claim that being dead is as meaningless as not existing; it's the claim that when you are dead, you don't exist at all. If not being there makes you meaningless, then death will make you meaningless. But TT does not say that. It just says that you won't be there.

C

I have heard people say things like this: "When I die, I will no longer exist. I will just be a corpse." Such a remark seems self-contradictory. If the speaker will exist as a corpse after his death, then he will exist. So he shouldn't say both (a) that he won't exist and (b) that he will be a corpse. Perhaps the thought can be expressed more clearly in this way: "When I die, I will no longer exist *as the same sort of thing I am now*. Instead, I will exist merely as a corpse." It may seem that someone who says this means to be endorsing a version of the Termination Thesis.

However, the quoted remark is not a formulation of TT. The quoted remark is inconsistent with TT. For in the first place, TT is not the view that when people die, they cease existing *as the same kind of thing they formerly were*. TT says nothing about "existence as a kind of thing." Rather, TT implies that when a person dies, he or she ceases existing as any kind of thing, since he or she ceases existing altogether. And in the second place, if a person goes on existing as a corpse after death, then he or she most certainly does go on existing. If you exist as a corpse, then you exist. In that case, TT is false, since TT implies that when people die they don't go on existing as anything.

4. WHY I THINK TT IS FALSE

I have many reasons for thinking that TT is false. I want to mention some of these. It may appear that I am here presenting *arguments* against TT. But that's not my aim. I know that those who accept TT (the "terminators") will not be moved by my remarks. I know that they will have TT-consistent redescriptions of the phenomena that I describe. I mention these reasons in an effort to remind the reader of the extent to which our ordinary talk and thought about death seem to presuppose that people go on existing (though perhaps not as people anymore) after they die.

A

In a field behind my house there stands a huge old elm tree. It has been dead for many years. I suppose it was a victim of the so-called Dutch Elm Disease. I also suppose that the tree was well over fifty years old at the time of its death. I doubt that anyone would want to say that the large arboreal object currently in the field never lived or that it came into existence just a few years ago when the elm tree died. Virtually everyone would agree, I think, that this now-dead tree is more than fifty years old and that it previously lived. Careful study of the annual rings might seem to confirm these estimates of age and former life. If this is right, and people would say the same thing about other dead trees, then virtually everyone would agree that trees don't go out of existence when they die.

It seems to me that what's true of trees is true of every other sort of organism. In every case, if an organism dies, but its remains remain, then it remains. The transition from being alive to being dead is a transition that happens to *some persisting object*. If we assume that people are organisms too, then these thoughts provide reason to suppose that TT is false. For if all other organisms have the capacity to continue in existence past their deaths, then why should people be different?

B

I sometimes wander through graveyards. I see many gravestones. On these stones I often see the words "Here lies" followed by the name of the deceased. I believe that in many cases the claim inscribed on the gravestone is true. The deceased does indeed lie (dead) in the grave. Of course, if it is a very old grave there is a good chance that the deceased no longer lies there. Perhaps he has rotted away and returned to the dust whence he came. The fact that so many of these inscriptions seem plausible demonstrates the pervasiveness of the idea that people do not go out of existence when they die. For if people went out of existence when they died, there would never be a case in which some formerly living person lies dead in his grave. Every "Here lies" would be a lie.

C

I believe in a sort of straightforward materialism about people. I think we are our bodies. If this sort of materialism is true, then I am my body. In that case, I must have the same history as my body. Since my body will go on existing for a while after I die (unless I die in a remarkably violent way), I will go on existing after I die. Of course, I will then be dead. I will not be conscious. Perhaps I will not even be a person any more. But I will be there. You can't get rid of me so easily. So TT seems to me to be false.

D

In some cases there is reason to wonder about why a person died. Perhaps there is a suspicion of foul play. Perhaps there is doubt about the nature of some illness or injury. In these cases, a medical examiner might perform an autopsy. By looking closely at details of the corpse, the examiner hopes to learn more about what happened to the person who died. I can imagine a medical examiner uncovering a long-embedded bullet and saying, "This is the bullet that struck him twenty years ago. It lodged here near his heart, and the surgeons felt at the time that it would be safer just to let it stay put. It has remained here in the same place for all these years. He died of a stroke."

The remarks of this imaginary medical examiner seem perfectly acceptable to me. I can readily imagine that there might be a person who is hit by a bullet on one occasion and then later dies as a result of a stroke. I can readily imagine that an autopsy might be performed on this dead person and that the medical examiner might then remove the long-embedded bullet. The object that formerly was a living person still exists—now as a corpse—and still contains the bullet. If such a thing could happen, then TT is false.

E

A friend of mine lived with her elderly mother. One morning, my friend found her mother sitting in her accustomed chair, apparently resting. My friend spoke to her mother, encouraging her to have some breakfast. The mother did not respond. Eventually my friend became concerned and checked more closely. She found that her mother had been dead all the while.

My description of this example implies that TT is false. For if TT were true, my friend could not have spoken to her mother and could not have encouraged her mother to have some breakfast. Nor could she have discovered that her mother was dead. For if TT were true, the object in the chair that morning was not my friend's mother. My friend's mother would have gone out of existence sometime during the night, only to be replaced by some strange entity never before seen by my friend. Yet my description of the case seems perfectly natural and appropriate.

F

Imagine a case in which a person was dressed in a tight-fitting, hard-to-button suit at the time of death. The corpse is discovered dressed in the same outfit. It might seem that none of the buttons has been undone. The zippers are untouched. No alien fingerprints are found on the clothing. How did the person get out of the suit without unbuttoning the buttons and unzipping the zippers? How did the corpse get in there? If TT is true, these things must have happened. I find it far more reasonable to suppose that there were no entrances and exits in this case. I find it far more reasonable to suppose that the person died in the tight-fitting suit and then later the very same object (no longer living and perhaps no longer a person, but still the same object) was found in the suit. Thus, I find it more reasonable to deny TT.

5. SOME ARGUMENTS FOR THE TERMINATION THESIS

Why would anyone think that TT is true? Some apparently have thought that the very concept of death itself entails that TT is true. Suppose someone thought that the concept of death is the concept of *the annihilation of a living organism*.[16] Then there would be a quick argument to the conclusion that people go out of existence when they die:

> 1. x dies at $t = df$. x is a living organism up to t & x is annihilated at t.
> 2. If (1) is true, then people go out of existence when they die.
> 3. Therefore, people go out of existence when they die.

The argument is valid. The conclusion is TT. But surely no one should be impressed by the argument. The proposed definition of "x dies at t" clearly presupposes the very doctrine that is here under debate. Antiterminators will simply reject it. In any case, the proposed definition is independently implausible.[17]

Other lines of argument for TT depend more heavily on alleged features of the concept of *being a person* or what I will call "*personality.*" It might be claimed that in order for something to be a person it must have the first-person perspective,[18] or that in order for something to be a person it must have rationality, intentionality, the capacity to treat others as persons, the capacity to engage in verbal communication, and consciousness.[19] Other claims about personality might be made, but I will let this list suffice. They provide a basis for another argument for TT:

> 1. When a person dies, he or she ceases to be a person.
> 2. When a person ceases to be a person, he or she ceases to exist.
> 3. Therefore, when a person dies, he or she ceases to exist.

In this argument, the alleged necessary conditions of personality provide the basis for the first premise. It is widely agreed (especially among materialists) that people lose their first-person perspectives, their rationality, their ability to engage in verbal communication, and so on when they die. Thus, if these are necessary conditions of personality, then death robs us of our personalities. We cease being persons (in this sense) when we die.

The second premise is more problematic. Why should we think that people cease to exist when they cease to be people? Someone might take note of the fact that "person" is a sortal predicate.[20] They might think that where *F* is a sortal predicate, statements of this form are all true:

S: When an *F* ceases to be an *F*, it ceases to exist.

For this reason, they might argue, the second premise of the argument has to be true.

However, the general line of reasoning here is flawed. There are many sortals for which S is wrong. Consider, for example, "student," "virgin," "ABD," "recruit," "child." Each of these is a sortal (according to typical criteria of sortality), and none of them supports S. Surely no one will want to say that virgins go out of existence when they lose their virginity! So the mere fact that "person" is a sortal (if indeed it is) does not guarantee that persons go out of existence when they lose their personality.

David Wiggins has provided a useful distinction between "substance sortals" and "phase sortals."[21] Roughly, the distinction is just that substance sortals are ones that verify S; phase sortals are the rest. "Virgin" is just a phase sortal. That explains why virgins can survive the loss of their virginity. But "person" is supposed to be a substance sortal. Thus, line (2) is true (it might be argued).

Although the argument would be bolstered if it could be shown that "person" is a substance sortal, the bare claim seems to stand in need of defense. Surely we have to *show* that "person" is a substance sortal first. And this requires showing first that persons go out of existence when they cease being persons. Some will want to insist that "person" is a phase sortal. They will claim that in some cases it is literally true that some human body formerly was a person but now is reduced to a mere parcel of moldering flesh.

Furthermore, it's not so clear that people do stop being people when they die. We certainly speak of "dead people," as for example when we say that dozens of dead people were found in the rubble after the earthquake.[22] Thus, it's not clear that line (1) is true either. This version of the argument from personality fails.

In his recent book, *The Human Animal*, Eric Olson defends his form of "animalism." According to this view, each of us is fundamentally an animal—a living human organism. Olson shows (persuasively, in my opinion) that animalism is incompatible with the view that personal identity is to be explained in terms of psychological connectedness. For in the first place an animal pretty clearly can persist through dramatic and irreversible psychological disruptions. And in the second place, in transplant and teleportation cases there would be psychological connection, but there would be no identity of animals. If we are animals, there would be no identity of us.

In a typical case, a person is temporally flanked by items of questionable personality. Prior to the time at which someone is clearly a person, there is a fetus. Without begging any question about identity, we can say that the fetus "develops into the person." At the other end of life, again without begging any questions, we can say that the person "degenerates into a corpse." Olson's form of animalism involves the view that the person is strictly identical to the fetus but strictly diverse from the corpse. Thus, although Olson seems happy to say that the very same entity can be a nonpsychological non-"personal" bundle of immature cells at one time and a thriving person at a later time, he seems unwilling to say that the very same entity can be a thriving person at one time and a fresh corpse at another.

This combination of views seems strange. If I am an animal, and I can exist without psychology as a fetus, why can't I exist without life as a corpse? Surely there are plenty of dead animals. Doesn't this mean that there are plenty of items that formerly were living animals and that now are still animals but dead? Olson rejects this suggestion and hints at an argument for TT. Olson says this:

> The changes that go on in an animal when it dies are really quite dramatic. All of that frenetic, highly organized, and extremely complex biochemical activity that was going on throughout the organism comes to a rather sudden end, and the chemical machinery begins immediately to decay. If it looks like there isn't all that much difference between a living animal and fresh corpse, that is because the most striking changes take place at the microscopic level and below. Think of it this way: If there is such a thing as your body, it must cease to exist at *some* point (or during some vague period) between now and a millions years from now, when there will be nothing left of you but dust. The most salient and most dramatic change that takes place during that history would seem to be your death. Everything that happens between death and dust (assuming that your remains rest peacefully) is only slow, gradual decay. So whatever objects there may be that your atoms now compose, it is plausible to suppose that they cease to exist no later than your death. There is no obvious reason to suppose that any 150-pound object persists through that change.[23]

This is an astonishing passage. Surely in every case in which a 150-pound person dies and leaves a 150-pound corpse, there are plenty of obvious reasons to suppose that a certain 150-pound object persists through the change from being alive to being dead. I mentioned several of these earlier. I can mention one more: suppose a terminally ill 150-pound person is resting on a sensitive scale when he dies. Suppose he dies peacefully, so that the needle of the scale does not move. It pointed to "150" before he died, and it continued to point to "150" when and after he died. It did not even quiver at the moment of death. It would have been hard to remove the person and replace him with an equally heavy corpse. It would have been nearly impossible to do this without causing the needle on the scale to move. Since the needle did not move, there is at least some prima facie reason to suppose that some 150-pound object persisted through the change.[24]

The passage from Olson contains hints of two lines of argument for TT. One of these concerns what we may call without further explanation "big changes." Following Olson, we can imagine some case in which a 150-pound person dies. The body gradually rots away. After a hundred years, there is just a skin and bones; the flesh has been removed by maggots. After a thousand years, there is just a dry skeleton; after ten thousand years there is just some scattered dust. Olson's remarks suggest an argument according to which the thing that was the person did exist when the person was alive but does not exist at all after ten thousand years; there must have been a time when that object went out of existence. The big changes all took place at the moment of death. Therefore, the thing that was the person went out of existence at the moment of death.

I see no reason to agree that the object in question goes out of existence at the moment of those "big changes." For all Olson has said, it might be that the object *dies* at the moment of "big changes" but continues *existing* as a corpse for several thousand years. No particular reason is given to suppose that there is a link between those "big changes" and the termination of existence.

The passage from Olson suggests a slightly different line of thought. It may be difficult to pin down the precise moment when the corpse ceases to exist. Perhaps the best we can say in such cases is that the corpse ceases to exist (as Olson puts it) "during some vague period." The notion that a person might go out of existence "during some vague period" may be unsettling. We may feel that it would be tidier if there were some well-defined first moment of nonexistence for people. Perhaps this gives us some reason to look around for a more salient moment to identify as the moment when the person ceases to exist. The moment of death suggests itself as salient. Big changes occur then. It's relatively easy to identify. At least, it's easier to identify than the "moment" when the corpse goes out of existence. Thus we may be inclined to say that the things that are people go out of existence when they die.

But the corpse is a genuine thing; it exists for a while and then ceases to exist at or during some time.[25] So there must be some time (or vague period) when the corpse goes out of existence. If it was metaphysically untidy to have persons with vague terminations, it will be equally untidy to have corpses with vague terminations. Yet we have them. Nothing Olson says prohibits our saying that this is the time (or vague period) when the thing that formerly was the person finally ceases to exist.[26]

Another line of argument for TT is based on the idea that certain essential properties are lost at death. If the property of *being alive*, for example, were an essential property of the things that have it, then it would follow that something goes out of existence whenever something loses its life. Different philosophers have appealed to different properties in a similar way. Thus, for example, Lynne Baker claims that *having a first-person perspective* is an essential property of each person.[27] She thinks (reasonably, in my opinion) that people lose their first-person perspectives when they die; from this she infers that people go out of existence when they die.

Baker's view is that each thing that really is a person is such that it is metaphysically impossible for that thing to exist at any time without having a first-person perspective. I cannot believe this. I think most little babies gradually come to have the first-person perspective. In the standard case, the baby exists for a while without the first-person perspective, and then the very same item—the thing that was the baby—comes to have a first-person perspective. If this happens, then Baker's essentialist claim is false.[28] Similarly, if someone falls off his motorcycle and strikes his head on the pavement, he may lose his first-person perspective for a while. It's hard to see why this would mean the end of his existence, especially if he later recovers and regains his first-person perspective.

Someone (though not Baker) might confuse her thesis with the less controversial claim that it is metaphysically impossible for a thing to be a person at a time without having a first-person perspective at that time.[29] Those who reject TT can happily accept this view. They can say that when people die, they lose their first-person perspectives; they can agree that it follows that they then also lose the property of *being people*. But they can say that the very things that formerly had a first-person perspective and that were people continue to exist after ceasing to be people and ceasing to have a first-person perspective. (For those who see things that way, "person" is a phase sortal.)

My own view is that even this benign thesis is open to objection. I think there are plenty of people who do not have the first-person perspective. I cite my nephew Douglas as an example. Douglas was very seriously injured in an automobile accident and now lies nearly motionless in a nursing home. Though it is hard to tell for sure, it seems very likely that Douglas has lost his first-person perspective. He seems to be in a deep coma. Yet he's still a person—a comatose person, to be sure, but a person nevertheless. (How could he be my nephew if he were not a person? Why would the insurance company keep paying his bills if he were not a person? Why would my sister visit and talk to him if he were not a person?)[30]

Let me draw a general conclusion about essential properties and TT. Suppose some philosopher identifies some property, C, that healthy living people typically have but lose at death. (Any of a number of psychological properties will do.) She then claims that C is essential to people. On this basis she concludes that people go out of existence when they die.

The problem with any such argument, as I see it, is that the central premise is question-begging. Since I assume that people are their bodies, and I already know that C is lost at death, I will be disinclined to accept the notion that C is essential to persons. I will of course admit that people typically have C while they are living people. I may even grant the truth of some modal claim such as the claim that it is necessary that if something is a person at a time, then it has C at that time. But I will deny that each person, x, is such that necessarily x has C at every time that x exists. For I will think that some things that are people go on existing as corpses without C. The argument from essential properties gets us nowhere.

6. PERSONAL TEMPORAL SEGMENTS

A philosopher might try to construct a metaphysical scheme that will force TT to come out true. He could start by adopting a metaphysical principle:

TP: If a physical object lasts through a stretch of time, then for every substretch of that time, it has a temporal segment that lasts precisely through that substretch.

Consider some human body. Suppose it lasts for a hundred years. Suppose it is fetal for the first few months, then infantile, then adolescent, then mature, then elderly, and then dead for a while. We could say that for each of these phases, there is a temporal segment of the body that lasts just through that phase. So in addition to the body, there are (a) the fetus-segment, (b) the infant-segment, (c) the adolescent-segment, (d) the mature-segment, (e) the elderly-segment, and finally (f) the dead-segment.

None of these temporal segments is strictly identical to the body. Their diversity follows from their differences in temporal extent. But of course it would be somewhat misleading to say, for example, that the mature-segment is a "completely different thing" from the body. It would be overly contentious and a bit silly to pretend to be astonished by the fact that when you put the body and the mature-segment on a scale, the scale does not indicate some weight many times greater than the weight of the body. After all, each of these items is a proper (temporal) part of the body. They have a lot in common with the body, and they bear important metaphysical relations to it. Just as a scale does not indicate the sum of your weight and the weights of all your spatial parts at a time, so it should not indicate the sum of your weight and the weights of all your temporal parts at a time.

Our imagined philosopher might then introduce some argumentation designed to show that some property is crucial to personality. He might claim, for example, that *having the first-person perspective* is such a property. He might say that something is a person at a time if and only if it has the first-person perspective at that time. As I have indicated, I am dubious about this choice of "person-making property." In order to move forward, let us agree to speak more abstractly here of the feature in virtue of which something is a person at a time. Let us assume that some psychological feature has been selected. This may be *having the first-person perspective*; it might be *being capable of engaging in voluntary action*; it might be something else. In any case, some allegedly person-making feature has been chosen. Then our philosopher might ask us to focus on a certain type of temporal segment. Specifically, she asks us to focus on a temporal segment of the body that lasts throughout the period during which the person-making feature is exemplified. The metaphysical principle cited above ensures that there is such a segment. Any such segment is a temporal segment of a human body, but it differs from other such segments in virtue of the fact that it is alleged to be a person throughout its existence.

In the case of each human body, the selected temporal segment has some interesting features. For one thing, it has the person-making feature at every moment of its existence. For another, it comes into existence when the person-making property arises, and it goes out of existence when the person-making feature terminates. Clearly, if such a segment dies at some time, it will lose its person-making feature at that time. It will then terminate when it dies. This temporal segment may appear to be precisely the sort of "person" some have imagined—an entity with the person-making feature, an entity that goes out of existence when it dies, but nevertheless an entity that is a purely material object made of human cells, tissues, and organs.

If the philosopher wants to expand on his view, he can go on to offer some commentary on the data mentioned above. He can say that of course there are "dead people." But on his view all talk of dead people is slightly loose, for as he sees it, it would be more accurate to say that there are dead human bodies former segments of which were people. He can say that there is an obvious truth to the claim that we perform an autopsy on a corpse to find out why it died, even though the corpse itself was never living. The underlying truth, in his view, is that we perform an autopsy on a body at a time when it is dead (when else?) in order to find out why it died. When we do this, we inevitably do it at a time when the corpse is also present and at a time when the person is no longer present. But there is no mystery here. The person is an earlier, no-longer-present segment of the body. The corpse is a later, not-previously-present segment of the body. The coroner's interest is in what happened to the body.

The view just described may seem to ensure that something like the Termination Thesis is true. However, the situation is somewhat more complex. The view does not have the implication it may seem to have.

One problem that affects the described view is that it implies that we are never alone; wherever there is a person, there are many clones. First, note that as the view was described, there are as many distinct temporal parts of a human body as there are distinct stretches of time during which that body exists. Given that many of these stretches overlap, it follows that at any moment during the history of a body, there will be indefinitely many distinct but overlapping temporal segments present.

As I described the imagined view above, it involves the notion that some psychological property such as *having a first-person perspective* is sufficient for personality. I called this "the person-making property." Anything that has the person-making feature at a time is a person at that time. This was supposed to explain why the selected segment—the one that ends at death—was supposed to be a person at every moment of its existence. Yet if this is sufficient to make something a person at a time, then it surely follows that many of the overlapping temporal segments are also persons during various stretches of their existence.

In order to see this more clearly, let us consider a certain temporal part of a human body that definitely *does not* go out of existence at death. For this purpose, we may consider a temporal part that starts at conception and continues to exist until the body disintegrates into a disorganized array of dust particles. Call this part "B" (for "body"). In addition, consider the temporal part that starts existing at the moment when the person-making feature initially arises and terminates at death, when the person-making feature ceases. Call this part "P" (for "person"). Now consider the long period of time during which both B and P seem to be present.

Throughout this period of time, B and P are atom-for-atom duplicates. At each moment during this time, B and P are exactly alike with respect to all intrinsic properties. Most importantly, they are exactly alike with respect to brain structure and activity. Every brain cell in P's brain is also a brain cell in B's brain; every neuronal firing in P's brain is a neuronal firing in B's brain. I assume that P has the person-making feature in virtue of things that are going on P's brain. It has a certain structure. Certain events occur in that brain. Other things are dispositional: P's brain is such that if it were affected in such-and-such ways, it would react in such-and-such ways. Given these physical facts about P's brain (and the relevant laws of neuropsychology), it follows that P has the person-making feature.

But since B is an atom-for-atom duplicate of P, it then also follows that B has the person-making feature at every moment that P has it. Given the assumption that the mental supervenes on the physical and the fact that B is physically indiscernible from P, they cannot differ with respect to the possession of the person-making feature. In this case, at every moment at which they both exist, B is just as much a person as P is (given the assumption that the possession of a person-making feature makes something a person at a time).

The upshot of all this is that the proposed metaphysical scheme implies that some persons (temporal segments relevantly like P) go out of existence when they die. "Person" acts like a substance sortal for such things. But the same scheme also implies that other things that are persons during some parts of their existence do not go out of existence when they die. Things such as B are persons for long stretches of time (throughout the time that P exists), but these things do not go out of existence when they die. For them, "person" acts like a phase sortal. As a result, the imagined metaphysical scheme does not serve to establish TT. Some persons continue to exist after they die; they just stop being persons and start being dead human bodies.

7. A MORE RADICAL APPROACH

Another philosopher might take a more radical approach.[31] He might say that as he uses the term "person," it correctly applies to a thing only if that thing has the person-making property *throughout its existence*. Furthermore, he might insist that nothing is properly called a person unless it is "maximal" in this sense: it is not a proper temporal part of any larger segment that has the person-making property throughout its existence. Thus, from the fact that B has the person-making property for ninety years, nothing follows about the personality of B. B's problem, on this view, is that it lacked the person-making property during some fetal stretches prior to the ninety-year stretch and also during some post mortem stretches after the ninety-year stretch. So on the present view, although B had the person-making property steadily for ninety years, B was not a person. P was a person, however, because P had the person-making property at every moment during which P existed and is not a proper part of any larger such thing. No temporal segment of P is a person because each such segment is part of a larger segment that has the person-making property throughout its existence.[32]

There is a complexity, however. The radical philosopher will probably want to distinguish between two sorts of personality. One is the "absolute" property of *being a person*. The other is a time-relativized variant: the property of *being a person at a time*. On the view in question, P is the only absolute person in the story. B is not an absolute person. On the other hand, at every time at which B has the person-making property, B has the time-relativized property. For all such times *t*, B is a person-at-*t*.

This more radical view does ensure that something like TT is true. On this view each absolute person has the person-making feature at every moment of its existence; it is not a proper temporal part of any larger such thing. When an absolute person dies, he or she loses the person-making feature. He or she therefore ceases to exist. A form of TT is true. This form of TT may be understood in this way:

TTa: When an absolute person dies, he or she ceases to exist.

It is important to take note of the fact that, according to this view, whenever an absolute person is present, many other items are also present. This follows from the metaphysical principle TP: If an object exists during a stretch of time, then a temporal part of that object precisely occupies every substretch of that time. This is the principle that guarantees that there is a temporal part that begins when the person-making feature begins and ends when it ends. As a result, the view is committed to the notion that whenever a human body is present, infinitely many temporal segments of that body are also present. These segments are alike in having a component that exists just at the moment; they differ in their temporal extents. Some started earlier; some started later; some will end earlier; some will end later.

On the radical view, the absolute person himself is just one of these temporal segments of his body. It is the unique segment that begins to exist when the person-making property begins to be instantiated in the body and ends when that property ceases being instantiated. The body as a whole is not an absolute person. No other segment is an absolute person. At best, such other segments overlap a person.[33] They are things that are persons-at-times but not absolute persons.

Since many of these persons-at-times go on existing after death, another version of the Termination Thesis turns out to be false on this view:

TTtr: When something that has been a person-at-some-times dies, he or she ceases to exist.

This version of TT is false because, for example, in a typical case a person's body is a person-at-many-times during the life of the person and does not cease to exist when the person dies. So it turns out that even this radical conception of persons does not make TT come out unequivocally true.

I think it's interesting to see that the radical view does not guarantee the truth of a certain further version of TT.

On the present metaphysical scheme, there are many items passing through this location where I am. Among these are the many temporal segments currently coinciding with me. Some are items of tiny temporal extent, such as the instantaneous current temporal stage of my body. Others are items of greater temporal extent, such as the stage that began on my thirteenth birthday and will terminate when I die. Another is my body, which began to exist when I was conceived and which (let us assume) will continue to exist until some vague period long after my death when it disintegrates.

Now I want to tell you a little about myself. I think I am my body. I think I formerly was a fetus. I think someday I will be dead—just a corpse. When I refer to myself, I mean to be referring to *this human body*—the one that is writing this essay; the one with these memories and hopes and self-awareness. I do not mean to be referring to some mere temporal segment of (what I take to be) myself. As in the case in which I refer to something with a demonstrative, such as "that," I think I have a certain amount of power to determine what I am referring to when I refer to something with "I." Since I mean to be referring to my body when I say "I," I think it is correct for me to say that I am this body.

My sense of myself is not utterly off the wall. I have discussed this point with friends. I am convinced that many others use the word "I" in a relevantly similar way.

When they refer to themselves, they take themselves to be referring to their currently living human bodies. Like me, these friends think that they formerly were fetuses and will someday be corpses. They see nothing odd in imagining times in the past when they lacked the person-making feature—indeed, times when they lacked all psychological properties. They also see nothing odd in imagining times in the future when they will exist but again will lack all psychological properties. These are times when they will be dead.

The radical view grants that the thing I call "me" exists. Advocates of the radical view may call such things "human bodies." But the radical view insists that these entities are not absolute persons. They are temporally larger items that contain absolute persons as proper temporal segments. The radical view implies that many of my human friends are not absolute people. It implies that when we refer to ourselves by saying such things as "I am thinking of death," we are self-referring to things that are not absolute people. We are referring and ascribing the thought, according to the theory, to things that are "too big to be absolute people."

I am willing to grant that there might be some people who think of themselves otherwise. Perhaps when one of them uses the word "I" to refer to himself, he means to refer to an entity that will go out of existence at death. I have no way to prove that they cannot be doing this. If they do this, they are thinking of themselves as things that are, on my view, mere parts of things like me and my friends. But I won't impose my conceptual scheme on them. If that's what they take themselves to be, then so be it. (Perhaps they should be called "short people.") And I grant that the objects to which these people refer when they use "I" will go out of existence when they die. But I beg them to be equally tolerant of me and my friends. They should grant us the right to refer to what we take to be ourselves when we use the word "I." And if they grant us this privilege, then they have to admit that yet another version of the Termination Thesis is false: This is the version that says that *things like us go out of existence when they die*. This version is false because my friends and I are things like us, and we won't go out of existence when we die.[34]

NOTES

1. Epicurus (1940): 31.
2. Lucretius (1940): 131.
3. Sumner (1976): 153.
4. Nagel (1979): 61.
5. Silverstein (1980): 100.
6. Rosenbaum (1986): 120.
7. Yourgrau (1987): 137.
8. Luper-Foy (1987): 270.
9. Feinberg (1984): 171.
10. Rosenberg (1983): 27.
11. Rosenberg (1983): 96.
12. Luper-Foy (1987): 289.
13. There are more options. Some are discussed below.
14. I think the doctrine is multiply ambiguous. On some readings it seems to me to be true; on others false. I discuss its various senses in "Death and Personality," pp. 118–123 of my (1992).

15. Some philosophers claim that personality is an essential property of each person. If personality is an essential property of persons, then persons would go out of existence when they stop being persons. Thus, we have a possible argument from TTp to TTs. I discuss some versions of this idea below.

16. Roy Perrett says something quite like this on p. 14 of his (1987).

17. In (1992) I explained why I take the proposed definition to be implausible. I mentioned a careful butterfly collector who captures, kills, and mounts her butterflies without damaging so much as a microscopic scale. I said that the butterflies in her collection have all died, but none has been annihilated. See my (1992): 59.

18. Lynne Baker presents an extended account of the first-person perspective in her (1998): 327–348. In (1999b) she says, "A first-person perspective is the defining characteristic of all persons, human or not" (p. 3).

19. Daniel Dennett says all of these things (and one more) in his (1976): 177–178.

20. The concept of sortal has been around for a long time, but in modern history, Wiggins is often cited as responsible for reviving interest. He in turn credits Aristotle, Locke, and Strawson for introducing and developing the concept. See his (1980): 7–8. For detailed discussion of some attempts to explain the concept of a sortal predicate, see my (1973): 268–282.

21. See Wiggins (1980): 24–27. In fact, Wiggins uses the term "phased sortal," but I think my usage has by now become more familiar.

22. Judith Thomson makes essentially this point in her (1997). She asks (p. 202) why there is anything wrong with supposing that there are dead cats and dead people in a house after the roof falls in. I also mentioned dead people (and compared them with dead cats discovered after a natural disaster) in my (1992), p. 104.

23. Olson (1997): 151–152. In fairness to Olson, I should point out that he is not explicitly discussing the argument of which I find hints in the passage. Olson seems to be engaged in trying to show that there is no such thing as "my body."

24. I say that this is "at least a prima facie reason" to say that something persisted; I do not say that it is conclusive proof. But in light of such facts as the fact about the needle (and facts like the ones mentioned earlier) I think there is a substantial burden of proof on anyone who maintains that *no 150 pound object persists through the changes.*

25. It's not clear to me that Olson believes that the corpse is a genuine thing. Perhaps he follows Peter van Inwagen in supposing that the only genuine material things are living. But in this case, it is odd that he mentioned in his example that "the remains" of the deceased rested peacefully. For if the remains rest peacefully for a while, then those remains must exist for a while. Eventually they will go out of existence. Why can't we say that the thing that was the person goes out of existence when the remains go out of existence?

26. My view, therefore, is that David Mackie (an animalist of a different stripe) has a more plausible view on this question. See his (1999): 219–242.

27. "If [a person] ceased to be a person (i.e., ceased to have a first-person perspective), however, she would cease to exist altogether." Baker (1999b): 2.

28. She would say that when the baby gains the first-person perspective, a new object comes into existence—this is the person. Thus, on her view (as I understand it) it's not strictly correct to say that the person formerly was a baby.

29. In (1992) I suggested that there is a concept of personality for which this sort of claim might be true. I called it "the psychological concept of personality." See pp. 103–104.

30. I wrote to Neil Busis, who is the director of a website called "Neuroguide: Neurosciences on the Internet." He is a specialist in neurological disorders. I asked him whether there is any neurological disorder in which the victim loses the first-person perspective. My thought (perhaps overly influenced by too much Oliver Sachs) was that there must be some neurological basis for the possession of the first-person perspective. Surely, if there is such a basis, it could be lost through disease or injury. Then we would have a person without the first-person perspective. Busis wrote back and told me that some stroke victims suffer from something quite like the condition Baker describes as "loss of the first-person perspective." He called it "anosognosia," and he said that people suffering from it lose the ability to distinguish between themselves and other items in their environments. He described it as "confusion between figure and ground." It is not clear to me that

anosognosia is as pervasive as loss of the first-person perspective. But the point is that it would con-
ceivable that a person could undergo some neurological damage that would bring about such a loss.
The person would then be (as Baker sees it) psychologically more like an intelligent dog. In my
view, such an unfortunate would be an unfortunate *person*. Baker (if I understand her correctly)
would say that such a stroke would make the person go out of existence, though his body would still
be there, walking and talking somewhat as before. See her (1998).

31. It might be interesting to compare the view of Hud Hudson in his (1999) to the view of this
imaginary philosopher.

32. It might seem that the mere statement of the view is sufficient to refute it. The view has
some strange implications. One is this: in the example cited, there are two items, B and P. They are
atom-for-atom duplicates for ninety years. Each has the person-making property steadily throughout this period. Yet one of them—P—is a person, and the other—B—is not a person. This seems
very strange. What strikes me as being even stranger is that what bars B from personality is that it
existed at an earlier time when it was just a fetus and will exist at a later time when it will be a
corpse. It seems odd that this highly personal object should be denied personality on the basis of
these facts. As I see it, fetuses normally develop into adult persons; persons deteriorate into
corpses. But the imagined view implies that these familiar facts have to undergo a certain amount
of redescription.

33. Although his conceptual scheme is different, Hudson introduces some interesting concepts that have correspondents here. A "maximal person" would be a person that is not a proper
temporal part of a person; a "temporary person" would be something that has a maximal person as a
proper temporal part; a "person-part" would be a proper temporal part of some maximal person.
(For the actual definitions, see Hudson (1999), p. 304.)

34. I am grateful to several friends for comments and encouragement. After seeing his stu-
dents struggling with some passages in *Confrontations with the Reaper*, Owen McLeod suggested
that I might do well to try to clarify my thoughts about the Termination Thesis. Ted Sider, Clay
Splawn, and Kris McDaniel read earlier drafts of this paper and provided knowledgeable and
insightful criticism and suggestions. Their generous help is especially appreciated, since, so far as I
know, none of them is inclined to agree with my main points in this paper. Conversations with
Lynne Rudder Baker and Richard Feldman have also been very helpful. I have benefitted from
studying Carter (1999), Mackie (1999), and Olson (1997). Each of these works contains doctrines
or arguments similar to ones I have presented here.

REFERENCES

Baker, Lynne Rudder (1997) "Why Constitution Is Not Identity," *The Journal of Philosophy* 94,
no. 12 (December): 599–621.
Baker, Lynne Rudder (1998) "The First-Person Perspective: A Test for Naturalism," *American
Philosophical Quarterly* 35, no. 4 (October): 327–348.
Baker, Lynne Rudder (1999a) "What Am I?" *Philosophy and Phenomenological Research* 59, no.
1 (March): 151–159.
Baker, Lynne Rudder (1999b) "Materialism with a Human Face," unpublished manuscript.
Carter, W. R. (1999) "Will I Be a Dead Person?" *Philosophy and Phenomenological Research* 59,
no. 1 (March): 167–171.
Dancy, Jonathan, ed. (1997) *Reading Parfit* (Oxford: Blackwell Publishers, 1997).
Dennett, Daniel (1976) "Conditions of Personhood," in Rorty (1976): 175–196.
Epicurus (1940) "Letter to Menoeceus," in Oates (1940): 30–34.
Feinberg, Joel (1984) Selection from *Harm to Others* (Oxford: Oxford University Press, 1984),
reprinted in Fischer (1993): 171–190.
Feldman, Fred (1973) "Sortal Predicates," *Noûs* (September): 268–282.
Feldman, Fred (1991) "Some Puzzles about the Evil of Death," *The Philosophical Review* 100,
no. 2 (April), reprinted in Fischer (1993): 307–326.

Feldman, Fred (1992) *Confrontations with the Reaper: A Philosophical Study of the Nature and Value of Death* (New York: Oxford University Press, 1992).

Fischer, John Martin, ed. (1993) *The Metaphysics of Death* (Stanford: Stanford University Press, 1993).

Hudson, Hud (1999) "Temporal Parts and Moral Personhood," *Philosophical Studies* 93, no. 3 (March): 299–316.

Lucretius (1940) *On the Nature of Things*, in Oates (1940): 69–219.

Luper-Foy, Steven (1987) "Annihilation," *The Philosophical Quarterly* 37, no. 148 (July): 233–252, reprinted in Fischer (1993): 269–290.

Mackie, David (1999) "Personal Identity and Dead People," *Philosophical Studies* 95, no. 3 (September): 219–242.

Nagel, Thomas (1979) "Death," in Thomas Nagel, *Mortal Questions* (Cambridge: Cambridge University Press, 1979), reprinted in Fischer (1993): 61–69.

Oates, Whitney J., ed. (1940) *The Stoic and Epicurean Philosophers* (New York: Random House, 1940).

Olson, Eric (1997) *The Human Animal* (New York and Oxford: Oxford University Press, 1997).

Perrett, Roy (1987) *Death and Immortality* (Dordrecht, the Netherlands: Martinus Nijhoff Publishers, 1987).

Rorty, Amelie Oksenberg, ed. (1976) *The Identities of Persons* (Berkeley and Los Angeles: The University of California Press, 1976).

Rosenbaum, Stephen (1986) "How to Be Dead and Not Care," *American Philosophical Quarterly* 23, no. 2 (April), reprinted in Fisher (1993): 119–134.

Rosenberg, Jay (1983) *Thinking Clearly about Death* (Englewood Cliffs, N.J.: Prentice-Hall, 1983).

Sider, Ted (1999) "Four Dimensionalism" (unpublished manuscript).

Silverstein, Harry (1980) "The Evil of Death," *The Journal of Philosophy* 77 no. 7 (July), reprinted in Fischer (1993): 95–116.

Sumner, L. W. (1976) "A Matter of Life and Death," *Noûs* 10 (May): 145–171.

Thomson, Judith Jarvis (1997) "People and Their Bodies," in Dancy (1997): 202–229.

Wiggins, David (1980) *Sameness and Substance* (Oxford: Basil Blackwell, 1980).

Yourgrau, Palle (1987) "The Dead," *The Journal of Philosophy* 86, no. 2 (February), reprinted in Fischer (1993): 137–156.

The Evil of Death Revisited[1]

HARRY S. SILVERSTEIN

I n "The Evil of Death"[2] I attempted to refute the "Epicurean view" (henceforth EV)—the view that death cannot intelligibly be regarded as an evil for the person who dies because the alleged evil occurs only when its "recipient" no longer exists. Epicurus himself articulated EV's basic argument quite eloquently in the following passage from the *Letter to Menoeceus*:

> [S]o death, the most terrifying of ills, is nothing to us, since so long as we exist, death is not with us; but when death comes, then we do not exist. It does not concern either the living or the dead, since for the former it is not, and the latter are no more.

In short, one who is still alive has not suffered the evil of death; but after one has died one no longer exists to be the recipient of goods or evils. Hence, according to EV, the contention that death is an evil for the person who dies is essentially incoherent.

EV could plausibly be dismissed fairly quickly if we could claim that something can be good or evil for a person, A, even if it can make no difference, positive or negative, to A's experience—that is, if we could reject what I called the "Values Connect with Feelings" view, or VCF (ED, pp. 107ff.). For if "A-relative" goods and evils need have no possible connection with A's experience, then there would seem to be no obstacles (or at least no obstacles other than the "merely technical" obstacles involved in making sense of posthumous reference and predication—see ED, pp. 106–107 and 112 ff) to the claim that such goods and evils may entirely postdate A. Similarly, EV could be dismissed fairly quickly if we could accept what I called the "Standard Argument" (henceforth SA). In brief, SA contends that we can get around EV by focusing not on the evil of death but on the goodness of life, a focus that not only avoids the confusion of supposing that death is an actively evil state that we somehow exist to suffer from but allows us to view the evil of death as an ordinary evil of deprivation. There is no difficulty, so SA contends, with the following claim:

C_L. A's continued life is good for A.

For if A continues living, then he obviously continues to be a possible value recipient. But if A's continued life can intelligibly be regarded as good for A, then its loss can intelligibly be regarded as bad for A; hence, EV is refuted.

However, neither of these lines, I contended, is ultimately successful. Even weak versions of VCF—versions that, for example, do not require that there be an actual, but merely that there be a possible, connection between an A-relative evil and A's suffering—appear to rule out posthumous goods and evils; yet rejecting all versions of VCF, even such weak versions, seems quite implausible. And the problem with SA, I argued (ED, pp. 98–102), is that it requires an illegitimate comparison between the value for A of A's (continued) life and the value for A of A's death. Briefly, if C_L—the apparently unproblematic claim to which SA appeals—is to be relevant to EV, it must be interpreted as "life-death" comparative rather than "life-life" comparative. That is, it cannot be interpreted as asserting, for example, that A's actual continued life is better than an "average" continued life, or is better than a continued life of total sensory deprivation (a continued life that might be regarded as "similar" to death), or the like; for while such assertions are unproblematically intelligible, they do nothing to show that life as such can intelligibly be said to be better for A than death, or, therefore, that A's death can intelligibly be regarded as an evil for him. Rather, C_L must be interpreted as asserting in part:

C_{LD}. A's continued life is better for A than A's death is [good] for A.

But from the point of view of EV, C_{LD} is unintelligible for the same reason that the simple claim that A's death is an evil for A is unintelligible. If the fact that A does not exist when he is dead means that A's death cannot intelligibly be ascribed any A-relative value (i.e., that A's death cannot intelligibly be said to be good, bad, or indifferent for A), then it also means that A's death has no A-relative value to which the A-relative value of A's life can intelligibly be compared.

Thus, there is no quick fix available to those of us who wish to reject EV; refuting it requires serious argument. My attempt at such an argument included two key claims involving the interpretation of VCF: first, that the relevant connection between an A-relative evil, x, and A's negative feelings is not that x does (or can) *cause* those feelings but that x is (or can be) the *object* of those feelings; and second, that future events (states, etc.) can, in the required sense, be objects of such feelings. And the second of these claims required the adoption of what was perhaps the most controversial component of "The Evil of Death," namely, a four-dimensional framework, a la Quine, according to which objects and events from different times, like objects and events from different places, are viewed as coexisting. In sum (ED, pp. 111–112):

[T]he four-dimensional framework allows, indeed requires, us to view posthumous objects and events, like spatially distant objects and events, as existing —in Quine's words, it views objects, events, etc. from all places and times (or better, from all place-times) "as coexisting in an eternal or timeless sense of the word." Thus, we seem to have solved our problem. By adopting the four-dimensional framework we can say . . . that posthumous events exist; . . . that posthumous events can therefore be objects of appropriate feeling in the sense required by VCF; . . . and, hence, . . . that the Epicurean view can justifiably be rejected. In brief, A's death coexists with A ("in an eternal or timeless sense of the word"), and is therefore a possible object of A's suffering, and is therefore an intelligible A-relative evil.

In the nearly twenty years since its original publication "The Evil of Death" has been the subject of a number of criticisms, explicit and implied, both in the published literature and in private conversation and correspondence. It remains my view, however, that its central claims are correct. My purpose in this paper will be to defend those claims against the main criticisms that have been raised against them. In the first section I will defend the view that we cannot circumvent EV by regarding death as an ordinary evil of deprivation—in short, I will defend my opposition to SA —against the views of Warren Quinn and Fred Feldman.[3] In the second section I will defend the first of the two "key claims" mentioned above—namely, that to be an A-relative good or evil x need only be a (possible) *object*, not a *cause*, of A's relevant feelings—against the criticisms of Stephen Rosenbaum. And in the third and final section I will defend and clarify my conception of the required four-dimensional framework against the criticisms and (in my view) confusions of Barbara Levenbook and Palle Yourgrau.

I. DEATH AND DEPRIVATION

After making the claim that "to the extent that having a human life is a good, abortion can be, it would seem, a bad thing or *loss* for the fetus" (Quinn 1984, p. 37)—a claim that clearly applies SA to abortions—Warren Quinn responds to my objections to SA as follows (Quinn 1984, p. 37, note 19, emphasis added):

> Harry Silverstein argues that "loss" in the literal sense implies subsequent existence in a deprived condition. It is clear, on the other hand, that those who with me speak of "loss" of life through, for example, accident or illness mean to call attention to *the difference for the worse from the point of view of the subject* that the accident or illness makes by causing it to be true that *he will not have the life he would otherwise have had*, and do not mean to imply that the subject will subsist in some existentially deprived state. *Since it seems perfectly intelligible, it is perhaps not important to establish whether this usage constitutes a metaphor or an ordinary sense.*

I did indeed contend, as Quinn claims, that a literal loss "implies subsequent existence in a deprived condition." But although I still believe that this contention is defensible, I shall not defend it here. For whether or not we can legitimately claim that we are using "loss" in its literal sense when we say that "A has lost his life," the crucial, substantive, problem remains—the problem, namely, that we cannot in any event simply *assume* that the "loss" of life is the sort of loss that can intelligibly be regarded as an evil for the loser.[4] For to make such an assumption is obviously to beg precisely the questions at issue, the questions raised by EV and by my objections to SA. Yet in speaking of "the difference for the worse from the point of view of the subject" that, "by causing it to be true that he will not have the life he would otherwise have had," the loss of life allegedly brings about, Quinn appears to be making precisely this assumption, an assumption against which the Epicurean counter-arguments, and thus my objections to SA, still apply. In this context, "not hav[ing] the life he would otherwise have had" does not, of course, mean "having a continued life that is less fulfilling than the continued life he would otherwise have had" but rather "not having any continued life at all." And A's "not having any continued life at all" can intelligibly be viewed as a "difference for the worse" for A in comparison with "having a continued life" only if "not having any continued life at all" can intelligibly be given an A-relative value. And that is precisely what EV denies.

It would appear, therefore, that Quinn fails to revive SA. There is, however, another possible interpretation of the above passage. Perhaps what Quinn has in mind is not a comparison between the value for A of A's continued life and the value for A of the lack, or "loss," of A's continued life (i.e., A's death)—the comparison that EV condemns as unintelligible—but rather a comparison between the value for A of a longer life (the life he will have if he continues living) *viewed as a temporal whole* and the value for A of a shorter life (the life he will have if he dies now) *viewed as a temporal whole*—a "life-life" comparison of a different kind from that which I rejected as irrelevant to EV, a comparison that thus seems unscathed by my objections to SA. Moreover, whether or not this is a plausible interpretation of Quinn's view, it clearly is the sort of view propounded by Fred Feldman. Feldman explicitly disavows the problematic "life-death" comparison and summarizes his version of the view that death is an evil of deprivation (he calls this the "Deprivation Approach"—Feldman 1991, p. 308) as follows (Feldman 1991, p. 320; a similar passage appears in Feldman 1992, p. 153):

> I am not proposing that we compare a person's welfare level during life to his welfare level during death. . . . [T]he [proper] comparison is a comparison between one's welfare level (calculated by appeal to what happens to one during his life) at one possible world with his welfare level (also calculated by appeal to what happens to him during his life) at another possible world. . . .
>
> In effect, then, my proposal presupposes what Silverstein calls a "life-life comparison." To see how this works, consider again the example concerning my imagined death en route to Europe. My proposal requires us to compare the values for me of two lives—the life I would lead if I were to die on the plane trip and the life I would lead if I were not to die on the plane trip. Since (according to our assumptions) the shorter life is less good for me, my death on that trip would be correspondingly bad for me.

Now I agree that by pursuing this sort of approach we can indeed get around EV. But this is so only because this approach, by requiring that alternative possible lives be compared, and thus viewed, as wholes—and hence as temporal wholes—involves at least the implicit adoption of precisely the four-dimensional framework that is the controversial centerpiece of my proposal. (To view a life as a temporal whole is to view the entire life, from beginning to end, as "there"—and, thus, as "existing" in the four-dimensional framework's atemporal sense—to be analyzed, compared to other actual or possible life-wholes, etc.)[5] Indeed, the concluding sentence of "The Evil of Death" has obvious parallels with the above passage from Feldman (ED, p. 116, emphasis added):

> [I]t is the "four-dimensional" ability to understand life in durational terms, to view one's life *as a temporal whole* and to make *evaluative comparisons between it and alternative possible life-wholes*, which ultimately accounts for the fact that statements of the form "*A*'s death is an evil for *A*" are commonly regarded as not merely intelligible, but true.

And the crucial point here is that no "four-dimensional" account, including Feldman's, can ultimately maintain the view that death is an ordinary evil of deprivation—and thus no such account, including Feldman's, truly revives SA. This point as it applies to Feldman's account becomes clear if we consider his answer to the question "*When* is death an evil for the person who dies?" For standard evils of deprivation, the question "When is the deprivation an evil for its recipient?" poses no difficulty; the time at, or during which, the deprivation is an evil for its recipient is simply the time at, or during which, its recipient exists in a deprived state. But this simple answer does not, of course, work for death. The answer Feldman applies to the death case is the following (Feldman 1991, pp. 320–321):

> Suppose a certain girl died in her youth. . . . If Lindsay is the girl, and *d* is the state of affairs of *Lindsay dying on December 7, 1987*, then the question is this: "Precisely when is *d* bad for Lindsay?" I have proposed . . . that . . . when we say that *d* is bad for Lindsay, we mean that the value for her of the nearest world where *d* occurs is lower than the value for her of the nearest in which *d* does not occur. So our question comes to this: "Precisely *when* is it the case that the value for Lindsay of the nearest world in which *d* occurs is lower than the value for her of the nearest world in which *d* does not occur?"
> It seems clear to me that the answer to this question must be "eternally." For when we say that her death is bad for her, we are really expressing a complex fact about the relative values of two possible worlds. If these worlds stand in a certain value relation, then (given that they stand in this relation at any time) they stand in that relation not only when Lindsay exists, but at times when she does not.

On a "weak" interpretation of this passage Feldman is simply claiming that the statement "Lindsay's death is bad for her" is "eternally" true. But from the perspective of the four-dimensional framework (a point to which I shall return in section III), (a) *all* statements are, if ever true, always (and thus "eternally") true; and (b) this fact is independent from all relevant temporal questions, including the question Feldman claims to be answering. Suppose, for instance, that a year before her death, Lindsay had lost her leg. From the point of view of the four-dimensional framework, just as "Lindsay's death is bad for Lindsay" is eternally true, so "The loss of her leg is bad for Lindsay" would be eternally true. But this fact does not answer, and indeed is entirely irrelevant to, the question "When is the loss of her leg bad for Lindsay?"—a question the correct answer to which would, of course, remain: "during the final year of her life." Hence, if the above passage is to be construed as providing an answer to the question "When is Lindsay's death bad for Lindsay?" it must be given a "strong" interpretation, an interpretation according to which Feldman is literally claiming that "Lindsay's death is bad for her eternally, that is, at every time." But although this answers the "when" question, it does so at the price of abandoning the "Deprivation Approach." For if some event, x, is bad for A eternally, and thus not merely at times before x itself has occurred but at times before A himself was born, then whatever sort of evil x is, it cannot plausibly be viewed as an ordinary evil of deprivation. To contend that x is an evil of deprivation when x is bad for A not simply before the alleged deprivation (namely, x) itself occurs, but even before there is any subject, A, to be deprived, is surely to stretch the notion of an "evil of deprivation" beyond any reasonable limits.

I conclude, therefore, that the proposal Feldman puts forward does not defend SA against my account but rather incorporates part of my account (namely, the four-dimensional framework) and abandons SA. Furthermore, Feldman's answer to the question "When is death an evil for its recipient?"—namely, "eternally"—is not only counterintuitive but seems plainly question-begging as a response to EV. For an important part of EV's motivation lies in the assumption that, whenever an A-relative evil itself may occur, the only time at which that evil can be bad for A is during A's lifetime—an assumption that allows room for A-relative evils that entirely *predate A* (since such evils may have causal effects that harm A during his life) but appears to rule out A-relative evils that entirely *postdate A*, including A's death. Moreover, since this assumption is based, in my opinion, on VCF (the point being that it is only during A's life that A can experience goods and evils), and since, as I indicated above, I think at least a weak version of VCF must be accepted, I believe that any adequate response to EV must preserve at least some version of this assumption—that is, it must allow us to retain the view that, in some significant sense, the time of A's life has special importance so far as A-relative goods and evils, including posthumous goods and evils, are concerned. And the only way I can see to do this is to adopt *all* of my account—not simply the four-dimensional framework, but also the version of VCF which that framework supports. By saying that the relevant connection between an A-relative evil, x, and A's negative feelings is that x is (or can be) the *object* of those feelings, and that, via the four-dimensional framework, posthumous events (states, etc.) can be such objects, my proposal makes room for posthumous goods and evils while preserving the assumption at issue. For although on my proposal, x, the object of A's negative feelings, can entirely postdate A, the time at which A can have those feelings—feelings whose possibility remains essential to the claim that x is an intelligible A-relative evil—remains restricted, of course, to the time of A's life. And no other proposal I know of allows us thus to reject EV while still according the requisite special status, even with respect to posthumous goods and evils, to the time of A's life.[6]

But of course both my version of VCF and the four-dimensional framework on which it depends have been subjected to challenges, challenges that will be the focus of the next two sections.

II. OBJECTS, CAUSES, AND VCF

I shall not attempt here to provide a general defense of VCF against the counterclaim that x can be an A-relative evil even if x neither does, nor can, make a relevant difference to A's experience[7]—though I would contend that those who reject VCF owe us an explanation of why, for example, the problem of posthumous harm seems to be a "real" problem in the way that the problem of posthumous reference is not. But assuming (as I shall henceforth) that some version of VCF is true—and, hence, that for x to be an evil for A, x must make, or at least be capable of making, a relevant (i.e., a "negative") difference to A's experience—I shall attempt to defend my specific version of it, and in particular the following two claims, both of which, as I indicated earlier, are crucial to my account:

VCF$_1$. The relevant connection between an A-relative evil, x, and A's negative experience—A's feelings of grief, for instance—is not that x does (or can) *cause* those feelings but that x is (or can be) the *object* of those feelings.

VCF$_2$. Future events (states, etc.) can be objects of relevant (negative) experience.

VCF$_2$ stands or falls with the four-dimensional framework, which is the subject of the next section. But VCF$_1$, which I want to discuss here, is itself crucially important. For unless we countenance "backward causation"—which I emphatically do not—future events cannot *cause* present experiences. Hence, unless we can justifiably reject the claim that, for x to be an evil for A, x must be capable of *causing* A to have negative experiences, the attempt to evade EV fails immediately. But just this claim, not surprisingly, is supported by some of my critics, particularly Stephen Rosenbaum. In his words (Rosenbaum 1986, p. 130):

[O]ne of [Silverstein's] basic assumptions goes without support, that assumption, namely, that an event's being an object of feeling, not a cause, is what is important in saying whether posthumous events are bad for a person. It seems to me that unless this hypothesis receives some support, we are free to reject it, especially since I have already argued that a causal relationship between the event and the person is necessary.

So far as I can see the only "argument" Rosenbaum gives in support of the view that a causal relationship is necessary consists in the claim that x cannot be evil for A unless x exists (Rosenbaum 1986, p. 124)—the point being that nothing that does not exist can be a cause of negative feelings. But it is likewise true that nothing that does not exist can be an *object* (in my sense) of negative feelings; hence, this claim does not provide the slightest reason for preferring Rosenbaum's view to mine. Now it is true, to be sure, that Rosenbaum later discusses a concept of "object" according to which "objects" of negative feelings need not exist. In his words (Rosenbaum 1986, p. 130):

[I]t is clear that events which have never occurred and will never occur *can*, in some sense, be *objects* of our psychological attitudes. For example, Britons in the early 1940's feared an invasion of Britain by the Nazis. Yet that event never occurred.

And his subsequent discussion clearly assumes that this is the concept of "object" that is relevant to my argument. But this assumption is simply false. Whereas Rosenbaum here is in effect assuming a *de dicto* conception of the objects of psychological attitudes, my argument employs a *de re* conception. That is, whereas on his conception the claim

FEAR. A Nazi invasion of Britain is the "object" of A's fear

is true provided that the claim

FEAR$_{dd}$. A fears that $(\exists x)$ (x is a Nazi invasion of Britain)

is true, on my conception this claim is true only if the claim

FEAR$_{dr}$. $(\exists x)$ $[(x$ is a Nazi invasion of Britain) & $(A$ fears $x)]$

is true. And of course FEAR$_{dr}$ is not true precisely because there never in fact was a Nazi invasion of Britain.[8]

Hence, until and unless Rosenbaum provides a persuasive argument that my *de re* conception is somehow illegitimate, I think I am justified in concluding that he has failed to provide any persuasive argument against VCF$_1$. I must also concede, however, that "The Evil of Death" provided no real argument in its favor. This omission I shall now attempt to repair. Consider, to begin with, Case 1:

1. Unknown to John, his wife, Ann, is having an affair with his friend Phil.
2. Another friend of John, namely, Jim, learns of the affair by overhearing a conversation between Ann and Phil.
3. After agonizing deliberation Jim concludes, correctly, that John would rather know about the affair than remain in ignorance—and so Jim informs John that Ann is having an affair with Phil.
4. Thus, John shifts immediately from being gloriously happy to being totally miserable.

In this case both Ann's having an affair with Phil and Jim's informing John of Ann's behavior are causal factors in the production of John's misery (if either had not occurred, John would not have become miserable). But only Ann's behavior, we can assume, is the *object* of those feelings, and surely the most plausible view is that only Ann's behavior is an evil for John. (If we ask John himself "Were you harmed by Ann [because of her affair], by Jim [because he told you what Ann was doing], or both?" the natural answer would be "I was harmed by Ann, not by Jim; Jim simply informed me of the harm Ann was doing.") Hence, this case conforms better to my view than to Rosenbaum's.

Now although I think Case 1 does at least raise doubts as to whether the causal connection between Ann's affair and John's misery is the relevant connection, it does not, admittedly, constitute an adequate response to Rosenbaum. For whereas Rosenbaum's central contention is that x's being a causal antecedent of A's negative feelings is a *necessary* condition of x's being an evil for A, Case 1 shows at most that x's being a causal antecedent of A's negative feelings is not a *sufficient* condition of x's being an evil for A. However, I think Case 2, a case that inserts "deviant causation" into Case 1, provides a strong argument against Rosenbaum's necessary-condition claim:

1. A friend of John, namely, Jim, *thinks* that he has learned that John's wife Ann is having an affair with John's friend Phil, for Jim *thinks* that he has overheard a conversation between Ann and Phil discussing their affair. In fact, however, Jim is mistaken; the couple he overheard, a couple with voices similar to Ann's and Phil's (hence Jim's mistake), were actually Jan and Bill.

2. After agonizing deliberation Jim concludes, correctly, that John would rather know about an affair between Ann and Phil than remain in ignorance—and so Jim tells John that John's wife Ann is having an affair with Phil.

3. Moreover, though Jim was mistaken about what he overheard, *it is in fact the case* that John's wife Ann is having an affair with John's friend Phil.

4. When Jim tells his story, John shifts immediately from being gloriously happy to being totally miserable.

In this case the claim that Ann's affair with Phil is the object of John's misery, and, hence, is an evil for John, seems to me to be entirely plausible, indeed unproblematic. But if that is right, then we have undermined Rosenbaum's necessary-condition claim. For though in Case 2 Ann's affair (if I am right) remains the *object*, it is no longer a *causal antecedent*, of John's misery; in Case 2 it is Jan and Bill's affair that, combined with Jim's mistake, *causes* John's misery. Hence, for Ann's affair to be an evil for John it is not even *necessary* that it be a cause of his misery. Nor can one contend that we can regard Ann's affair as an evil for John in Case 2 only by surreptitiously rejecting VCF entirely. For holding that Ann's affair is an evil for John in Case 2 is entirely compatible with holding that it would *not* be an evil for him if it were, for example, an object of positive rather than negative feelings on his part—if, say, his response to Jim's story were "Wow! Ann is having an affair with Phil? Cool! Good for her!" And one final point: These examples have nothing to do with *posthumous* evils and thus do not beg the underlying question.

I conclude that VCF_1 stands unscathed by Rosenbaum's criticism.

III. THE FOUR-DIMENSIONAL FRAMEWORK

I shall not attempt here to enter the debate concerning the comparative merits of the four-dimensional framework in general.[9] Rather, I shall simply attempt to clarify my conception of that framework—the conception that I think is required to combat EV—by eliminating a crucial confusion common to several responses to "The Evil of Death," the confusion, namely, of supposing that the framework has the strongly counterintuitive implication that anything that ever exists always exists. In response to my argument, for example, Palle Yourgrau says (Yourgrau 1987, p.141):

I find it exceedingly difficult to give up my intuition that dead people simply do not exist. . . . And I do not mean merely that the dead do not *now* exist; for objects in time, what does not exist now does not exist at all.

And in this passage Yourgrau is clearly assuming that, on my strange view, dead people continue to exist. Similarly, Barbara Levenbook says (Levenbook 1984, p. 416, note 8):

Silverstein . . . develops a "four-dimensional framework" according to which someone exists atemporally and coexists with all events . . . eternally. Silverstein does not, thereby, provide a solution to the problem of accounting for harm at, or after, death, as it has been understood here, for his view denies that someone's death is the end of his existence (though it permits one to say it is the end of someone's temporal existence).[10]

It is true that "The Evil of Death" endorsed Quine's claim that, on the four-dimensional framework, people from all times coexist "in an eternal or timeless sense of the word," and it also characterized four-dimensional predicate ascriptions as "atemporal" (ED, pp. 113 ff). Nonetheless, the four-dimensional framework, as I construe it, does *not* imply that anything that ever exists "always" exists—at least not in any sense that is at all controversial. The central source of confusion on this point, I suspect, is simply the failure to keep the two frameworks (three-dimensional and four-dimensional) and their correlated "existence" concepts properly distinct. Let us, then, look more closely at these frameworks and concepts.

The four-dimensional framework abstracts from both "here" and "now"; it is, as I shall put it, both spatially and temporally neutral. By contrast, the three-dimensional framework abstracts only from "here" and is thus only spatially neutral; in the three-dimensional framework, a temporal reference to "now" is in effect built into the foundations. And this difference is reflected in their correlated "existence" concepts. To distinguish these concepts, let us dub "exists" as it is used in the four-dimensional framework "exists$_4$" and "exists" as it is used in the three-dimensional framework "exists$_3$." Like their respective frameworks, "exists$_4$" is both spatially and temporally neutral, whereas "exists$_3$" is only spatially neutral. Thus, "x exists$_4$" leaves both the place and the time of x's existence open—that is, as yet unspecified—whereas "x exists$_3$" leaves only the place of x's existence open; that x exists *now* is built into "x exists$_3$." And "now" is similarly built into every claim in the three-dimensional framework that asserts or assumes existence: "Ann is$_3$ asleep" means that Ann is *now* asleep;" Lila Silverstein lives$_3$ in Seattle, whereas Eva Silverstein lives$_3$ in Stanford" means that Lila Silverstein *now* lives in Seattle whereas Eva Silverstein *now* lives in Stanford; and so on. (This is not, of course, to say that it is impossible in the three-dimensional framework to talk about the future and/or the past. But it is true that, because of this framework's built-in "now," the future and the past can be spoken of only from the restrictive, not to say parochial, perspective of the present. Hence, we can speak of past and future only by changing tenses, tenses that all include a reference to "now." Thus, to say "x existed$_3$" is to assert that x existed at some time *before now*; similarly, to say "x will exist$_3$" is to say that x will exist at some time *after now*. Consequently—and I think this is a fact by which we should, in Wittgenstein's sense, be *struck*—when we want, for example, to say that some object's existence extends from the distant past to the distant future, we can do this, in the three-dimensional framework, only by using a cumbersome, tripartite, expression referring to past [*before now*], present [*now*], and future [*after now*]—an expression such as "long has been, was, is now, and long shall be.")

Now the fact that "x exists$_4$" leaves the time as well as the place of x's existence open does mean that this sentence, unlike "x exists$_3$," is true at every time if it is true at any time—just as the fact that both sentences leave the place of x's existence open means that both sentences are true everywhere if they are true anywhere. Hence, "Henry VIII exists$_4$" is true (since there was a time—specifically, from 1491 to 1547—during which Henry VIII was alive), whereas "Henry VIII exists$_3$" is false (since he is not alive *now*). However, while "x exists$_4$" is always true if it is ever true—and thus *in this sense* the four-dimensional framework views anything that ever exists as "always" existing—this is no more controversial than the fact that both "x exists$_4$" and "x exists$_3$" are true everywhere if they are true anywhere—and thus both *in this sense* view anything that exists anywhere as existing "everywhere." For—and this is the crucial point—just as the fact that both "x exists$_4$"and "x exists$_3$" are true everywhere if they are true anywhere does not imply that x's *existence itself* extends throughout all space or lacks spatial boundaries, so the fact that "x exists$_4$" is always true if it is ever true does not imply that x's *existence itself* extends throughout all time or lacks temporal boundaries (and is thus "eternal"). This *would*, of course, be the implication if one claimed that, for a particular x, "x exists$_3$" is true at all times (and this is why I think the criticisms in question in effect conflate "exists$_3$" and "exists$_4$"). For to say that "x exists *now*" (which is what "x exists$_3$"asserts) is true at all times *is* to say that x is an eternal being. But this is not an implication of "x exists$_4$"; just as "Henry VIII exists$_3$" (asserted, let's suppose, in 1540) does not deny that Henry's existence is restricted to a particular human-sized spatial area (though by itself it does not specify that area's size or location), so "Henry VIII exists$_4$" (asserted at any time) does not deny that Henry's existence is restricted to a particular human-sized temporal span (though by itself it does not specify that span's size or location). And, thus, there is nothing at all controversial about the four-dimensional framework's "always true" existence statements.

As a concrete example consider, for instance, "timeline" charts in history texts and encyclopedias, charts that portray time as just another dimension and are thus in effect applications of the four-dimensional framework. Specifically, suppose there is such a chart showing the lives of English monarchs from William the Conqueror to Elizabeth II. A particular person, such as Henry VIII, either appears on the chart or does not. And since Henry VIII does appear, then he appears "always," even long after his death; he does not, for instance, go on the chart when he is born and come off when he dies. For given the meaning of "exists$_4$," *that* would be strange, indeed ludicrous; it would mean that it was true at one time that Henry VIII lived from 1491 to 1547 but false at another time.[11] And the "timeline" provides a good illustration of the way in which the four-dimensional framework incorporates the fact that people come into and then go out of existence—namely, by specifying a temporal beginning point and a temporal end point. For instance, on the monarch chart, Henry VIII's section would start at the point marked 1491 and end at the point marked 1547. (By contrast, if an immortal being, such as God—a being who "exists$_3$ always"—were included in the chart, then no matter how far the chart were extended back into the past or forward into the future, his section would have no beginning point or end point [this might in practice be indicated by a "backward" arrow at the beginning of God's line on the chart and a "forward" arrow at the end of it].)

Further, if it is asked how the four-dimensional framework deals with "now," the brief answer is: the same way the three-dimensional framework deals with "here." Just as the three-dimensional framework can easily handle the spatial indexical "here" despite the fact that this indexical is not built into the three-dimensional framework, so the four-dimensional framework can easily handle the temporal indexical "now" despite the fact that this indexical is not built into the four-dimensional framework. That is, just as we can add a "here" spatial specification in a three-dimensional claim (for example, we can say "Alice is$_3$ asleep here") so we can add a "now" temporal specification in a four-dimensional claim (for example, we can say "Alice is$_4$ asleep now"). Moreover, we can analyze or unpack both indexicals in essentially the same way, the way I suggested in the "The Evil of Death" with respect to "now"—namely, as tied to the place or time of the utterance. Thus, "Alice is$_3$ asleep here" can, I think, be unpacked roughly as "Alice is$_3$ asleep; and the spatial location of Alice's sleep is$_3$ the same as, or at least very close to, the spatial location of this utterance"; and similarly, "Alice is$_4$ asleep now" can be unpacked roughly as "Alice is$_4$ asleep; and the temporal location of Alice's sleep overlaps$_4$ that of this utterance" (compare ED, pp. 113ff). And the timeline chart again provides a useful illustration. We can, for instance, add to the chart an arrow pointing to a particular point on the time line with the caption "this is now," just as we can add an arrow to an ordinary map (a map that reflects, or at least is entirely compatible with, the three-dimensional framework) with the caption "you are here." And such a timeline arrow, if used correctly at the present time, would of course tell us that Elizabeth II is the current English monarch. But just as the "you are here" arrow is not intrinsic to the map, which in and of itself contains no "here"—it is rather an external addition, an addition, moreover, that must constantly be changed as the viewer's spatial location changes—so the "this is now" arrow is not intrinsic to the timeline chart, which in and of itself contains no "now"—it is rather an external addition, an addition, moreover, that must constantly be changed as the viewer's temporal location changes.

Having now explained that, and why, the four-dimensional framework does not have the counterintuitive implications suggested, let us go back to the quotations from Levenbook and Yourgrau and see precisely where they go wrong. Levenbook, to repeat, says:

Silverstein . . . develops a "four-dimensional framework" according to which someone exists atemporally and coexists with all events . . . eternally.

Silverstein does not, thereby, provide a solution to the problem of accounting for harm at, or after, death, as it has been understood here, for his view denies that someone's death is the end of his existence (though it permits one to say it is the end of someone's temporal existence).

And this is simply mistaken, for reasons that should now be clear. Although the four-dimensional *framework* is atemporal in the sense that "now" is not built in, and although the *truth* of claims using "exists₄" could be characterized as "eternal" (if that's just another way of saying that such claims are, if ever true, always true), the four-dimensional framework emphatically does *not* imply that a human being's existence *itself* is either atemporal or eternal, and thus emphatically does not "deny that someone's death is the end of his existence." On the contrary, to repeat: The four-dimensional framework is just as compatible with the claim that a human being's existence has temporal boundaries (and is thus "temporal") as the three-dimensional framework is compatible with the claim that a human being's existence has spatial boundaries (and is thus "spatial"). And when all this is clear, the confusion in Levenbook's final parenthetical clause—"(though it permits one to say it is the end of someone's temporal existence)"—should also be clear. On the four-dimensional framework, as on the three-dimensional framework, the "end of someone's temporal existence" is the end of someone's existence *period*. Contrary to what Levenbook seems to suppose, the four-dimensional framework no more countenances two "modes of existence," temporal and atemporal, one that ends at death whereas the other somehow continues indefinitely onward, than the three-dimensional framework countenances two "modes of existence," spatial and "aspatial," one of which ends at the body's outer limits whereas the other extends indefinitely outward.

Turning to Yourgrau, his first claim, again, is the following:

I find it exceedingly difficult to give up my intuition that dead people simply do not exist.

And the point, once more, is that the four-dimensional framework does not deny that "dead people do not exist" on any standard interpretation of this claim. For although a sentence such as "Henry VIII exists₄" is *true* now, this is entirely compatible with the claim that not only does Henry's existence have temporal boundaries, but the concluding boundary—the end point—of his existence is earlier (indeed, significantly earlier) than the time at which this sentence is uttered.

Moving on to Yourgrau's second claim—namely:

I do not mean merely that the dead do not *now* exist; for objects in time, what does not exist now does not exist at all.

—the obvious question is: What *more* does Yourgrau think is being asserted by "*x* does not exist at all" than is being asserted by "*x* does not exist now"? Compare, for instance, "Henry VIII does not exist *now*" and "Henry VIII does not exist *at all*." If the latter is interpreted to mean that Henry VIII never existed—that there never was a Henry VIII who was a king of England—then it is simply false. The only other way I can think of to try to make sense of this statement is to suppose that Yourgrau, like Levenbook, is assuming that my theory contends that objects have two modes or kinds of existence, temporal and atemporal, and that this statement is then a way of rejecting that contention. But if this supposition is right, then of course my reply to Levenbook serves equally as a reply to Yourgrau.[12]

Since one of the central themes of the above discussion is that the four-dimensional framework's treatment of time is essentially the same as the three-dimensional framework's treatment of space, and, hence, that its implications concerning the relation between existence and time are no more strange or controversial than the three-dimensional framework's implications concerning the relation between existence and space, I think a useful capstone to this discussion is provided by the following thought experiment, an experiment in which we consider a third framework whose relation to the three-dimensional framework parallels the three-dimensional framework's relation to the four-dimensional framework. And I think this thought experiment is useful not only as a way of cementing my reply to claims of the sort made by Yourgrau and Levenbook but also as a way of answering a new question that may have arisen in light of this reply, namely:

> If the four-dimensional framework is as benign and noncontroversial—not to say boringly domesticated!—as Silverstein is now arguing, does it retain the strength necessary to serve the ends it was intended to serve in "The Evil of Death"?

Consider, then, what I shall call the zero-dimensional framework, a framework in which *both* "here" *and* "now" are built into the foundations and which is thus neither spatially nor temporally neutral. Similarly, this framework's "existence" concept—namely, "$exists_0$"—also has both "here" and "now" built in. Thus, "x $exists_0$" is true only if x's existence is both here and now. Hence, whereas (from my perspective) "Harry Silverstein $exists_0$" is true, "Bill Clinton $exists_0$" is not; just as "Henry VIII $exists_3$" is false because Henry's existence is not *now*, so "Bill Clinton $exists_0$" is false because Clinton's existence is not *here*. And just as the three-dimensional framework can deal with times other than now, albeit clumsily, through the use of different tenses, so, we may suppose, the zero-dimensional framework has worked out a way to deal with places other than here, albeit clumsily, through the use of what I shall dub "spenses." Thus, we may suppose, the zero-dimensional framework has two spenses (this is a simple supposition; it could be more complicated), a "here" spense—the spense of "exists" (i.e., of "$exists_0$")—and an "out there" spense, the "exists" form of which is "exouts." Thus, just as in the three-dimensional framework "Henry VIII $existed_3$" is true even though "Henry VIII $exists_3$" is false, so in the zero-dimensional framework "Bill Clinton $exouts_0$" is true even though "Bill Clinton $exists_0$" is false. The zero-dimensional framework, in short, is a framework that seems as restrictive and primitive from the point of view of the three-dimensional framework as the three-dimensional framework itself seems to be from the point of view of the four-dimensional framework.

Suppose, now, that philosophers in a civilization whose primary conceptual framework is the zero-dimensional framework begin to puzzle over the following question: "How can events spatially distant from A intelligibly be claimed to be good or bad for A?" For, they argue, nothing that does not exist can be good or bad for A, and events spatially distant from A do not (from A's perspective) exist. Returning to the case of John and his philandering wife Ann, suppose that Ann's affair is going on in another city: She and John live in Seattle, but she often goes to Spokane on business, and that is where her affair with Phil is taking place. From John's Seattle perspective, then, Ann's affair with Phil does not exist$_0$; that is, "Ann is$_0$ having an affair with Phil" is false. And how, these philosophers ask, can John be harmed by a nonexistent affair? Now imagine that, in response to this puzzle, a philosopher named Silverzero (who is clearly a brilliant and far-seeing philosopher!) suggests that the solution lies in switching to a three-dimensional framework, a framework that does not have "here" built into its foundations and thus allows us to ascribe existence to objects and events *wherever* they may be. "On this framework," Silverzero says triumphantly, "since 'Ann is$_3$ having an affair with Phil' is true somewhere (viz., Spokane), it's true everywhere; hence, it's true where John is, in Seattle; hence, her affair can intelligibly be said to be an evil for John." And suppose further that Silverzero is then criticized by philosophers who fail to see his point. Thus, a critic named Yourzero says:

> I find it exceedingly difficult to give up my intuition that spatially distant objects simply do not exist. . . . And I do not mean merely that they do not exist *here*; for objects in space, what does not exist here does not exist at all.

And a critic named Levenzero says:

> Silverzero . . . develops a "three-dimensional framework" according to which someone exists aspatially and coexists with all objects . . . throughout all of space. Silverzero does not, thereby, provide a solution to the problem of accounting for spatially distant harm, as it has been understood here, for his view denies that the outer surface of a person's body constitutes the limit of his existence (though it permits one to say it is the limit of someone's spatial existence).

I assume we would all say that these criticisms are confused. And I assume we would all also say that Silverzero's obvious response to such criticisms, a response whose central point would be that his theory in no way denies that a human being's existence is spatial (i.e., that it has spatial limits), does not in any way weaken his theory or prevent it from providing a solution to the puzzle of spatially distant harms. Similarly, I think criticisms to my theory of the sort raised by Levenbook and Yourgrau are confused, and my response to those criticisms in no way weakens the theory or prevents it from providing a solution to the puzzle of posthumous harms, including the evil of death.[13]

NOTES

1. I am indebted to my former student Mike Morgan for asking the questions that got me thinking about "evil of death" issues again after many years, and to Mike, Dave Shier, Joe Campbell, and Michael O'Rourke for helpful comments on earlier drafts.

2. Silverstein 1980. Page references to this article will employ the model "ED, pp. x–y."

3. Another writer who in effect defends SA is Barbara Levenbook (Levenbook 1984). But in her case the failure (as I think) to appreciate the problems with viewing death as an ordinary evil of deprivation is complicated, at least as this failure relates to my argument, by related confusions concerning my four-dimensional framework, confusions which will be discussed in section III. Hence, to avoid extraneous complications in defending my opposition to SA, that defense will focus exclusively on Quinn and Feldman.

4. I thought I made this point clear in "The Evil of Death." For example, in considering the claim of L. S. Sumner (Sumner 1976, p. 160) that, though the loss of life is a "peculiar sort" of loss, it is nonetheless a literal loss, I argued (ED, footnote 4, p. 373 [from p. 100]):

> [E]ven if Sumner could adequately defend . . . a literal sense of "loss" according to which his claim were true, that would not, of course, be sufficient to defend the standard argument; he would also have to show, against the Epicurean view, that this "peculiar sort" of loss, like ordinary sorts of loss, can intelligibly be regarded as an evil for the loser.

5. "Timeline" charts in, for example, history texts view historical periods, monarchs' reigns, and the like as temporal wholes in a similar way; and as I discuss in section III, such charts in effect apply the four-dimensional framework.

6. This endorsement of the "special status" of the time of A's life does not contradict the passage in "The Evil of Death" (ED, p. 114) in which I characterized death as an "atemporal" evil. For neither that nor any other passage in "The Evil of Death" was intended to address the question "When is A's death an evil for A?"; its purpose was rather to spotlight the points of contact between my account and Nagel's (see Nagel 1979, esp. pp. 65–67) by distinguishing goods and evils whose ascription to A requires the four-dimensional framework and its correlated atemporal predication (such goods and evils being dubbed "atemporal") from goods and evils whose ascription to A is compatible with the three-dimensional framework.

More importantly, my endorsement of the "special status" of the time of A's life is not intended to imply that my account's answer to the question "When is A's death an evil for A?" must be "during the time of A's life"; I would prefer to say that my account supports the following more complicated view:

1. The time at which the evil itself—namely, A's death—occurs is immediately following A's life.

2. Since ascribing this evil to A requires the four-dimensional framework, it is an "atemporal" evil in the sense defined in "The Evil of Death."

3. The time during which this evil can be an object of A's negative feelings (and its being an intelligible A-relative evil requires that it be capable of being such an object) is the time during which A is alive.

4. (1), (2), and (3) comprise the whole truth about time in this case.

For in this way we retain, via (3), the crucial idea that the time of A's life has special status without being committed to the intuitively odd view that x can be bad for A before x itself exists.

Strictly speaking, of course, this view does not answer, but rather rejects, the question at issue; it holds, in effect, that the question "When is x bad for A?" is inapplicable to posthumous xs. And it should be noted that, on what I called the "weak" interpretation of his response to the "when" question, Feldman might perhaps be construed as expressing a similar view. The question then arises whether *this* sort of view is compatible with the claim that death is an ordinary evil of deprivation. And the answer to this question remains negative; indeed, the view that in the death case the question "When is *x* bad for *A*?" is inapplicable, and thus has no answer at all, seems to me to be even farther removed from the assumptions implicit in the notion of an "evil of deprivation" than the view expressed by the "strong" interpretation of Feldman, the view that in the death case the answer to this question is "eternally."

For a recent exchange on the question when death is bad for the person who dies, see Lamont 1998, Li 1999, and Grey 1999. For a discussion of the more general puzzle as to when persons exemplify "posthumous" properties (properties such as "being eulogized"), see Ruben 1988; I briefly defend my approach against Ruben in note 13.

7. An interesting version of this counterclaim is defended by John Fischer, who argues that by introducing a Frankfurt-style "counterfactual intervener," we can plausibly deny that *x*'s being bad for *A* requires even the *possibility* of *x*'s making a relevant difference to *A*'s experience (Fischer 1997, pp. 344 ff). However, Fischer's "counterfactual intervener" cases—cases in which a "counterfactual intervener" would intervene when and if necessary to prevent a particular *x* (e.g., *A*'s being ridiculed by his friends behind his back) from impinging on *A*'s experience—do not constitute any argument against the view that *x*'s impinging on *A*'s experience must at least be *intelligible*. Indeed, such intelligibility is in effect built into these cases; for these cases are cases where such impingement *could* take place *but for* the intervener's intervention. But this means, in my view, that my sort of proposal remains the only way to combat EV. For if *x*'s impinging on *A*'s experience must at least be intelligible, that means that, where *x* is a posthumous evil, *x* must be an intelligible *object* of *A*'s experience, which in turn requires the adoption of the four-dimensional framework.

8. Rosenbaum's discussion here might be intended, or at any rate interpreted, as an expression of the sort of "phenomenalist" objection I tried to anticipate in the following passage (ED, note 15, p. 375 [from p.111]):

A typical instance of this sort of objection, applied to posthumous events, is the following:

A posthumous event itself, as distinct from one's thoughts about it, can never be an object of joy, suffering, etc. For it is always possible, at least in principle, that one's beliefs, hopes, etc., about the event—beliefs that mediate between it and one's joy, suffering, etc.—will turn out to be false, i.e., that the anticipated posthumous event will never take place. But since one's joy, suffering, etc., will be the same whether these beliefs are true or not, it cannot be the posthumous event itself, even where it actually occurs, which is the object of joy, suffering, etc.

And exactly the same objection can, of course, be applied to spatially distant events. For example, one would suffer from a false report of a spatially separated friend's death in exactly the same way that one would suffer from a true one; hence, by the same argument, one's friend's death cannot itself be the object of one's suffering, even where it actually occurs. Insofar, then, as we can justifiably reject such arguments when they are applied to spatial distance, we can justifiably reject them when they are applied to temporal distance.

Since I think this passage provides a fully satisfactory answer to this sort of objection, I will say no more about it here.

9. I would note, however, that "The Evil of Death" did provide some discussion of the overall merits of this framework (see especially ED, pp. 112ff). For a recent contribution to this debate, see Sider 1997.

10. This issue was perhaps raised most clearly and straightforwardly in e-mail correspondence from Mike Morgan. Mike wrote:

One question I have is how this four-dimensional framework can account for a person ceasing to exist. It seems that on your view, people will always exist in an atemporal sense, and this is strange. For example, you argue that the widow's husband must exist atemporally so that there is something to refer to, but then how do we account for the fact that he really no longer exists (he's dead!)? In other words, on the four-dimensional account, what does it take to say that someone, or even something, does not exist? Or does everything, according to this view, always exist in some atemporal sense?

11. It is true, of course, that, as such charts are used in practice, they stop at the "present" (*now*) and thus are continually revised as the "present" moves forward. However, this is not intrinsic to the chart—and thus does not indicate that such charts really have "now" built in in the way that "exists$_3$" does; we can in principle extend such charts as far as we like into the future, just as we can extend them as far as we like into the past. The reason we typically end such charts at the "present" is simply epistemological: We cannot reliably predict future monarchs (Leibniz's attempts at such prediction notwithstanding), so there is no point in extending the chart into the future. (And in areas where such prediction is possible, e.g., astronomy, we do make charts that extend into the future.)

12. I cannot forbear noting that Yourgrau's views in general are exceedingly strange—far stranger, in my opinion, than any of the views expressed in "The Evil of Death." Specifically, he defends a neo-Meinongian outlook according to which the existential quantifier ranges over "being" rather than "existence," "existence" being just one property among others (though his Meinongianism is a parsimonious one in which some "things"—for example, Pegasus—are not given even the status of "being" [Yourgrau 1987, p. 144]). For example, he claims: "the realm of existence is the merest dot of an 'i' in the vast sea of being" (Yourgrau 1987, p. 147). And an implication he draws is that the unborn (i.e., those who never did and never will exist), like the dead, have "being" or "are," *and thus also, like the dead*, "suffer from the evil of nonexistence" (Yourgrau 1987, p. 148)!

13. I believe that consideration of the zero-dimensional framework also supports my solution to the puzzle as to when persons exemplify posthumous properties—a solution implicit in the discussion of note 5—against the solution proposed by David-Hillel Ruben (Ruben 1988). Suppose that someone now (in 2000) is eulogizing Napoleon (cf. Ruben 1988, p. 212), and consider the question: "*When* does Napoleon exemplify the property of being eulogized?" The puzzle is that (a) since the eulogy is occurring in 2000, the "natural" answer to this question seems to be "in 2000"; yet (b) Napoleon does not exist in 2000—and how can *A* exemplify properties at a time when *A* himself does not exist? Ruben's solution, briefly, is to distinguish between "real" states or changes and "Cambridge" states or changes, and then to argue that (1) the assumption that *A* can exemplify properties only while *A* exists applies only to properties relating to "real" states or changes; (2) posthumous properties relate only to "Cambridge" states or changes; and hence, (3) we can give the "natural" answer to the above question—namely, "in 2000"—without paradox. My solution, by contrast, is in effect to reject the question, to say that the question "When does *A* exemplify property *P*?" is inapplicable where *P* is a posthumous property. Specifically, my response to the question about Napoleon is:

> Napoleon lived from 1769 to 1821; he is being eulogized in 2000; and that's the whole truth about "when" in this case. There *is* no further question as to "when" Napoleon exemplifies the property of being eulogized.

And what consideration of the zero-dimensional framework shows, in my view, is that this solution is at least as "natural" as Ruben's. This can be brought out as follows. Consider again the case of John and his unfaithful wife Ann, and suppose that, although John remains in Seattle throughout, Ann's acts of infidelity always take place in Spokane. From the perspective of the zero-dimensional framework there is a puzzle as to "where" John exemplifies the property of "having an unfaithful wife," a puzzle that exactly parallels Ruben's "when" puzzle. We cannot, it would seem, say that John exemplifies this property in Seattle, for Ann committed no unfaithful acts there; yet it seems equally implausible to say that John exemplifies this property in Spokane, since John himself was never in Spokane. And this puzzle seems to be just as serious from the point of view of the zero-dimensional framework as Ruben's puzzle is from the point of view of the three-dimensional framework. For if Spokane is "here," then John does not exist$_0$ (making "in Spokane" a very implausible answer to the "where" question); and if Seattle is "here," then Ann's infidelities do not exist$_0$ (making "in Seattle" a very implausible answer to the "where" question).

Now the "natural" response to this puzzle from the perspective of the three-dimensional framework—a response that I assume virtually all of us would endorse—is surely the following:

John was in Seattle; Ann's unfaithful acts occurred in Spokane; and that's the whole truth about "where" in this case. There *is* no further question as to "where" John exemplified the property of "having an unfaithful wife."

But this "three-dimensional" response to the zero-dimensional "where" question exactly parallels my "four-dimensional" response to the three-dimensional "when" question. Hence, if we judge the former response to be perfectly natural, indeed unproblematic, I see no reason why we should not make the same judgment about the latter.

REFERENCES

Feldman 1991. Feldman, Fred, "Some Puzzles about the Evil of Death," *The Philosophical Review*, 100: 205–227; reprinted in John Martin Fischer, ed., *The Metaphysics of Death* (Stanford, Calif.: Stanford University Press, 1993), pp. 307–326. References in the text are to the Fischer volume.

Feldman 1992. Feldman, Fred, *Confrontations with the Reaper: A Philosophical Study of the Nature and Value of Death* (Oxford: Oxford University Press, 1992).

Fischer 1997. Fischer, John Martin, "Death, Badness, and the Impossibility of Experience," *Journal of Ethics*, 1: 341–353

Grey 1999. Grey, William, "Epicurus and the Harm of Death," *Australasian Journal of Philosophy*, 77: 358–364.

Lamont 1998. Lamont, Julian, "A Solution to the Puzzle of When Death Harms Its Victims," *Australasian Journal of Philosophy*, 76: 198–212.

Levenbook 1984. Levenbook, Barbara Baum, "Harming Someone after His Death," *Ethics*, 94: 407–419.

Li 1999. Li, Jack, "Commentary on Lamont's 'When Death Harms Its Victims,'" *Australasian Journal of Philosophy*, 77: 349–357.

Nagel 1979. Nagel, Thomas, "Death," in Nagel, *Mortal Questions* (Cambridge: Cambridge University Press, 1979), pp. 1–10; reprinted in John Martin Fischer, ed., *The Metaphysics of Death* (Stanford, Calif.: Stanford University Press, 1993), pp. 61–69. References in the text are to the Fischer volume.

Quinn 1984. Quinn, Warren S., "Abortion: Identity and Loss," *Philosophy & Public Affairs*, 13: 24–54; reprinted in Warren S. Quinn, *Morality and Action* (Cambridge: Cambridge University Press, 1993), pp. 20–51. References in the text are to *Morality and Action*.

Rosenbaum 1986. Rosenbaum, Stephen E., "How to Be Dead and Not Care: A Defense of Epicurus," *American Philosophical Quarterly*, 23: 217–225; reprinted in John Martin Fischer, ed., *The Metaphysics of Death* (Stanford, Calif.: Stanford University Press, 1993), pp. 119–134. References in the text are to the Fischer volume.

Ruben 1988. Ruben, David-Hillel,"A Puzzle about Posthumous Predication," *The Philosophical Review*, 97: 211–236.

Sider 1997. Sider, Theodore, "Four-Dimensionalism," *The Philosophical Review*, 106: 197–231.

Silverstein 1980. Silverstein, Harry S., "The Evil of Death," *The Journal of Philosophy*, 77: 401–424; reprinted in John Martin Fischer, ed., *The Metaphysics of Death* (Stanford, Calif.: Stanford University Press, 1993), pp. 95–116. References in the text are to the Fischer volume.

Sumner 1976. Sumner, L. S., "A Matter of Life and Death," *Noûs*, 10: 145–171.

Yourgrau 1987. Yourgrau, Palle, "The Dead," *The Journal of Philosophy*, 84: 84–101; reprinted in John Martin Fischer, ed., *The Metaphysics of Death* (Stanford: Stanford University Press, 1993), pp. 137–156. References in the text are to the Fischer volume.

Midwest Studies in Philosophy, XXIV (2000)

Death and Asymmetries in Normative Appraisals

ISHTIYAQUE HAJI

1. INTRODUCTION

Many who think that death is bad for the individual who dies think that death is *extrinsically* bad for the deceased, and that it is bad because it deprives the deceased of the goods of life that she would have enjoyed had she not died when she did.[1] Against this way of thinking others, following Epicurus, have argued that death is not, indeed *cannot* be, bad for the one who dies.[2] A crucial plank in central Epicurean arguments for the innocuousness of death for the deceased is, adopting Harry Silverstein's terminology, some "value connects with feelings" (VCF) thesis.[3] And a focal strand running through attractive versions of this thesis is that something is bad for an individual only if it is possible for that individual to have appropriate experiences as a result of that thing. The VCF thesis fuels the following powerful line of argument in favor of the Epicurean: As no one experiences or can experience one's death as bad, or has or can have any unpleasant experiences as a result of one's death, death cannot, it is concluded, be intrinsically or extrinsically bad for the deceased. In this paper, I develop an objection to this vital plank of the Epicurean argument by appealing to examples of what I dub "moral death." The examples help unearth some striking asymmetries in "agency presuppositions" of various sorts of normative appraisal. In particular, they motivate the view that whereas one *cannot* be *morally responsible* for an action that issues from "actional elements" like beliefs and desires that are not "truly one's own," beliefs and desires, for instance, that have been implanted in one against one's will, one *can* do *moral wrong* even if one's action is caused by "unauthentic" beliefs or desires; and, further, that something *can* be *extrinsically bad* for one even if radical manipulation of things like one's values, desires, beliefs, and memories results in the "moral death" of one's prior self. The asymmetries, in turn, pave the way to undermining pertinent versions of the VCF thesis.

2. EPICUREAN PRESUPPOSITIONS

To secure the conclusion that death is not bad for the one who dies, Epicurus seems to have relied on the "termination" thesis—that one ceases per se to exist at the time of one's death—and some version of the VCF thesis.[4] Distinguishing different concepts of personhood casts serious doubt on the former thesis. *Biological persons* are human organisms or members of the species *Homo sapiens*, and unless such persons are at ground zero or some relevantly dramatic situation at the time of their deaths, they usually survive their deaths. *Psychological persons* are entities that instantiate a rich psychological profile. Among other things, such entities are self-conscious and can engage in purposeful action. *Experiential persons* are entities that can have sensations or feelings. Clearly, a human being ceases to exist as a psychological or an experiential person but need not cease to exist per se—that is, cease to exist as a bio-logical person—at the time of her death. The Epicurean argument against death's badness need invoke not the dubious termination thesis but only the sensible alter-native that human beings cease to exist as experiential persons when they die.

As an intuitively reasonable representative of the VCF thesis, consider Silverstein's version. He says:

> [T]here appears to be a conceptual connection . . . between x's having a certain value for A (e.g., x's being an evil for A) and A's having an appropriate experi-ence or feeling (e.g., A's suffering) as a result of x. . . . x can intelligibly be said to have a certain A-relative value provided merely that it be possible, or possi-ble under certain conditions, for A to have the appropriate feeling as a result of x. For A's suffering from, e.g., undetected betrayal is possible in the sense that he may later discover the betrayal and suffer as a result.[5]

This passage suggests the following rendition of the VCF thesis.

> VCF1. A state of affairs, x, is bad for an agent, A, only if it is possible for A to have an unpleasant experience as a result of x.

VCF1 is best construed as specifying a necessary condition of the *extrinsic* badness for a person of some state of affairs. For assuming that values connect with feelings (or experiences or sensations), a reasonable supposition is that versions of VCF theses that delineate required conditions for the intrinsic badness of states of affairs for persons would be versions that imply that state of affairs x is intrinsically bad for agent A only if x is, or can be, an unpleasant experience for A.

The underlying idea of VCF1 is straightforward: Something is extrinsically bad for a person only because it leads to, or can lead to, later unpleasant experiences for that person. The "lead to" here is, presumably, to be understood in a causal sense. We have, then, as clarification of VCF1:

> VCF2. A state of affairs, x, is extrinsically bad for an agent, A, only if either (a) x causes A to have an unpleasant experience, or (b) it is possible that x may cause A to have an unpleasant experience.

So, for example, eating poisoned candy is extrinsically bad for Sweet Tooth for, though she thoroughly enjoys savoring the candy, which she does not suspect is poisoned, the candy will later cause her to feel excruciating pain. Silverstein and Stephen Rosenbaum both suggest that undetected betrayal is bad for some agent like Sweet Tooth because she *can* later discover the betrayal and suffer as a result.[6]

The notion of possibility in clause (b) of VCF2 requires elucidation. John Fischer has plausibly recommended that "possibility" in its occurrences in VCF theses does not denote broad metaphysical possibility, which is, very roughly, "compatibility with the laws of logic, the analytic or conceptual truths, and the propositions entailed by basic metaphysical truths (including truths about the essences of things)."[7] Rather, the sort of possibility in question is narrow possibility, the kind that corresponds to "freedom typically associated . . . with moral responsibility. . . . This sort of possibility implies that the relevant agent have a general ability to do the thing in question and also the opportunity to exercise the ability."[8] To support his recommendation, among other things, Fischer advances this example:

> Consider . . . an individual who has been reduced to a persistent vegetative state as a result of a stroke. Physicians reliably diagnose this person as terminally comatose. Presumably, in the sense of possibility relevant to the issue of whether this individual can be harmed, by (say) a betrayal [or whether a betrayal is extrinsically bad for the individual], it is *impossible* for the individual to have unpleasant experiences. But if this is correct, then the relevant notion of possibility cannot be the broad notion, for it is possible in the broad sense for the individual to have unpleasant experiences (as a result, say, of a miraculous recovery of the capacity for consciousness).[9]

Given these presuppositions, Epicureans can typically be taken to be advancing the following sort of argument against the extrinsic evil of death for the deceased.

1. One ceases to exist as an experiential person at the time of one's death. (A cleansed version of the termination thesis.)

2. A state of affairs is extrinsically bad for one only if it leads to, or can lead to, later unpleasant experiences for one. (VCF2)

3. If (1) and (2), then one's death cannot lead to later unpleasant experiences for one. (1, 2)

4. If one's death cannot lead to later unpleasant experiences for one, then one's death cannot be extrinsically bad for one. (1, 2, 3)

5. Therefore, one's death cannot be extrinsically bad for one.

3. MORAL DEATH AS A PROBLEM FOR VCF2

In what follows, I focus primarily on VCF2. Although this thesis has been called into question by others,[10] the example that I use to cast doubt on it facilitates uncovering some notable asymmetries in "agency presuppositions" of different sorts of moral appraisal. Let's start with the example.

Imagine that neurology and neurosurgery have so progressed that not only can particular pro-attitudes like desires, volitions, intentions, or goals be induced in an individual with or without the individual's consent or knowledge, but an individual can be molded psychologically to be just the kind of person the surgeon desires. Jenny is a shy, unassuming woman with no family and friends. She lacks outstanding skills or distinguished capacities, and if she were to disappear from her workplace or domicile in Brooklyn, preliminary questions would be asked only to be quickly forgotten. Jamie, an accomplished computer hacker, has successfully masterminded several lucrative "hacking" offenses. Suppose Max, the evil neurologist turned criminal, eager to test a new form of psychosurgery that, if successful, will be used to "recruit" personnel, kidnaps and anesthetizes Jenny. During her sleep, Max works on Jenny in his operating room aboard his jet and turns her into a psychological twin of Jamie. Flown to Zurich, Jenny is to begin work at Maxwell Incorporated, Max's computing firm. Max is the sole person aware of Jenny's transformation. Having settled Jenny into her new abode, he is killed in an air crash on his return to New York. Knowledge of Jenny's transformation dies with him.

Recovering from the surgery, Jenny has no suspicions that she has fallen victim to Max. She awakens with profound changes that, from her own inner perspective, she cannot but accept. The psychosurgery has endowed her with a new set of values, goals, preferences and the like while "erasing" ones she formerly had. Assume that these implanted elements are practically unsheddable. As Alfred Mele explains, an "actional" element like a desire or belief is practically unsheddable for a person at a time if, given her psychological constitution at that time, ridding herself of that attitude is not a "psychologically genuine option" under any but extraordinary circumstances.[11] Catching the morning news, Jenny learns about the new computing system installed in Barclays Bank, and after some diligent work, manages to transfer from an account in that bank a sizable sum of money into Maxwell's holdings. Although he will never know it, Max's transformation surgery has been a stellar success.[12]

The case ("Psychohacker") assumes that pre- and postsurgery Jenny are identical. Understandably, some might be troubled about this assumption. A few refinements should pacify the skeptics. Suppose presurgery Jenny and Jamie do share certain types of goals, values, and preferences. Assume that these shared elements are left intact (in presurgery Jenny) by the psychosurgery. Suppose, in addition, that some of presurgery Jenny's goals, preferences, values, and so forth that "compete" with Jamie's are also left intact, together with some of presurgery Jenny's memories. Label the set of presurgery Jenny's competing psychological elements left intact the "minimum competing set." Assume, in addition, that the members of the minimum competing set, in conjunction with the shared elements, constitute the minimal conglomeration of psychological elements required to preserve personal identity so that we can be assured that postsurgery Jenny *is* identical to presurgery Jenny. Finally, assume that the memories of presurgery Jenny's that are left intact and all her competing psychological elements that are members of her minimum competing set are "repressed"; although postsurgery Jenny does have them, it is not possible (in the narrow sense of 'possible'), unlike presurgery Jenny, for her to "access" them. It would seem that under these conditions pre- and postsurgery Jenny are identical.[13]

Presurgery Jenny suffers "moral death" as a result of the transformation surgery. I believe that her moral death—Jenny's being transformed (in the absence of free consent) from one moral or normative agent into another—is extrinsically bad for her.[14] If there are initial doubts about this assessment, simply stipulate that the life Jenny would have led had she not fallen victim to Max would have been overall better than the one she leads as a "globally" manipulated agent. What, though, does VCF2 imply about the axiological status of her moral death for Jenny? VCF2 says that something is extrinsically bad for an agent only if either (a) it causes her to have an unpleasant experience, or (b) it is possible that it may cause her to have an unpleasant experience. Now her moral death does not *cause* Jenny to have an unpleasant experience. Of course, transformed Jenny might go on to do things, like eat poisoned candy, that would lead to later unpleasant experiences for her. But then it would be these things, and not her moral death itself, that would be extrinsically bad for her. It is, roughly, the notion of proximal cause that is operative in both clauses of VCF2. Further, it also seems that it is not narrowly possibly for Jenny's moral death to cause Jenny to have later unpleasant experiences, in the manner in which, for example, initially undetected betrayal may lead the betrayed person to have unpleasant experiences. For Jenny, just like all others, with the exception of Max, has no reason at all to suspect that she has fallen victim to Max and has no means whatsoever of discovering her victimization. Discovery is not (narrowly) possible, as no one save Max knows of his dark secret, but this secret lies buried with him and will never, let's assume, be uncovered. It seems, then, that Psychohacker strongly suggests that VCF2 is false.

4. AN EPICUREAN REPLY

Epicureans, however, have a possible reply to this strategy of attack against VCF2. To develop this reply, the Epicurean might first direct our attention to ascriptions of moral responsibility. When we make judgments of moral responsibility, the Epicurean might suggest, the judgments (under normal conditions) presuppose no destruction of psychological agency, or no destruction of one psychological (or "normative") person and "replacement" by another. So, for instance, if we were unaware of her transformation, it would be sensible to judge that postsurgery Jenny *is* morally responsible—perhaps morally blameworthy—for her hacking offense. Ascriptions of moral responsibility are made, again under normal conditions, against the backdrop or presupposition that psychological agency is not disrupted. Further, when psychological agency *is* disrupted, as it is in global manipulation cases such as Jenny's, the disruption affects or bears on our (appropriate) verdicts of responsibility. Having been apprised of her manipulation, it would not be out of the ordinary to judge that postsurgery Jenny is *not* morally responsible for her offense. Or at least in transformation cases like Jenny's, it would not be out of the ordinary if we were ambivalent or unclear about our ascriptions of moral responsibility.

Similarly, the Epicurean might propose, judgments regarding whether states of affairs are extrinsically bad for agents are normally made under the assumption that psychological agency is *not* disrupted. But when this assumption or background condition does not hold, its failing to hold may well affect our judgments about the extrinsic badness of various things for persons. Or at least, we may be unsure about whether the relevant states of affairs are indeed extrinsically bad for the pertinent agents. So examples of moral death, the Epicurean might conclude, are *not* appropriate counterexamples against VCF2, as, minimally, an acceptable counterexample against a thesis should be a clear, noncontroversial example that challenges the thesis.

4.1 Responsibility and Global Manipulation

To assess this reply, consider, first, the salient claim regarding responsibility:

> JMR. Judgments or ascriptions of moral responsibility are, under normal conditions, made against the background assumption that psychological agency is intact, and that when this assumption is violated, our judgments may well be affected.

Various theorists about responsibility (or autonomy) would concede and indeed defend this claim. So, for instance, commenting on his own case of global manipulation in which Beth, a philosophy professor, is implanted with the psychological personality of Charles Manson, Alfred Mele writes:

> [E]ven though Beth is a psychological twin of Manson . . . , it does not follow that she autonomously possesses her Mansonian values. One indication of this is that, given the details of the case, we would not hold her *responsible* for her Mansonian character. Our reason for withholding attribution of responsibility (while supposing that Manson, her psychological twin, is responsible for his character) can only be that Beth was compelled to possess . . . her corrupt Mansonian values. . . . Manson, on our suppositions, is not relevantly different internally, but he autonomously possesses his values.[15]

Further, Mele makes it clear that, on his view, manipulated Beth would not be responsible for the actions that flow from a character that was engineered in her against her will.[16] Analogous judgments about responsibility for actions that issue from an implanted character are made and defended by, for example, John Martin Fischer, Mark Ravizza, and Don Locke.[17]

There are, of course, prominent accounts of responsibility that yield a contrary verdict. Harry Frankfurt's hierarchical theory very roughly holds that, assuming epistemic conditions of responsibility satisfied, a person is morally responsible for an action that issues from a first-order desire (FOD) with which she identifies. A person identifies with an FOD if (on one version of the theory) there is an appropriate "fit" between an unopposed second-order volition of hers—an unopposed second-order desire as to which first-order desire should move her to action—and the FOD that does in fact move her to action.[18] Relevant to our concerns is that this sort of hierarchical mesh condition *can* be satisfied by sundry acts of Jenny's, including her hacking offense, when she awakens from psychosurgery. The hierarchical theory, in opposition to Mele's views, would then yield the result that Jenny is indeed morally responsible for her offense. There are, though, various problems with the hierarchical theory.[19] This is certainly not the appropriate place to document and assess them. Suffice it to say that even incompatibilists about determinism and responsibility, like Robert Kane, regard cases of global manipulation as posing a serious challenge to hierarchical approaches to responsibility.[20]

I have elsewhere argued for a rationale to sustain the verdict that globally manipulated agents like postsurgery Jenny are not morally responsible for their pertinent deeds. It will be useful to summarize aspects of this rationale. My view, in outline, is that postsurgery Jenny is not responsible for her offense, as this act is generated by an evaluative scheme that is not "authentic." Beginning with the concept of an evaluative scheme, intentional deliberative action requires some psychological basis for evaluative reasoning. An agent's deliberations that issue in a practical judgment about what to do, which in turn gives rise to a decision or intention, involve the assessment of reasons for or against action by appeal to the agent's evaluative scheme. Such a scheme is composed of these constituents: (a) Normative standards the agent believes (though not necessarily consciously believes) ought to be invoked in an assessment of reasons for action, or beliefs about how the agent should go about making choices. The standards offer guidance within and across specific "domains." So, for instance, Jenny might believe that financial decisions should be made on the counsel of her stockbroker, culinary choices in accordance with Julia Child's recommendations, and moral choices on the basis of religious precepts. Norms need not be shared by agents. Unlike Jenny, Jamie might believe that decisions across all domains should be predicated on some utilitarian moral principle. To be an apt candidate for *moral* responsibility, the normative principles must include a set of moral principles or norms; the agent must be minimally morally competent. She must understand the concepts of rightness, obligatoriness, or wrongness, and she must be able to appraise, morally, various choices or actions in light of the moral norms that are elements of her evaluative scheme. (There is no requirement that appraisals be fully considered, free of error, or even conscious.) (b) The agent's long-term ends or goals he deems worthwhile or valuable. Jamie, for example, may underscore his commitment to attempting to maximize overall happiness whenever he acts. (c) Deliberative principles the agent utilizes to arrive at practical judgments about what to do or how to act. For instance, Jamie may believe that the best way to maximize utility is to rely on rules of thumb like "keep your promises," "don't cheat," "don't steal," etc. (d) Lastly, motivation to act on the basis of the normative standards in (a) and goals in (b) relying on the deliberative principles in (c).

A full account of authenticity would include, among other things, a discussion of principles governing evaluative scheme authenticity in global manipulation cases and in cases involving agents like us who do not come into existence with evaluative schemes fully "in place" but who acquire schemes gradually over time.[21] Here, attention is confined to the former sorts of case.

To help with the formulation of principles that guide ascriptions of responsibility in cases like Psychohacker, start with the idea that to be an appropriate candidate for moral praise, blame, or responsibility in general, one must be a *normative moral agent*. I propose that it is a *sufficient* condition of an individual's being such an agent at time t that the individual have at t (1) an evaluative scheme with the requisite moral elements—the agent is minimally morally competent; (2) deliberative skills and capacities—for example, the agent has the capacity to apply the normative standards that are elements of its evaluative scheme to evaluating reasons; and (3) executive capacities—the agent is able to act on (at least *some* of) its intentions, decisions, or choices. An individual (like a toddler) who fails to have deliberative or executive capacities will be able to exert much less control ("responsibility-grounding control"), if any, over its actions than an individual who does have such capacities. Construe condition (2) as entailing that the agent is (at *t*) able to engage in genuine deliberation; his deliberative activities must meet the threshold of rationality below which such activities fail to count as bona fide deliberation. Normative agents have their evaluative schemes essentially: If *E* is the evaluative scheme of normative agent *N* then having *E* is an essential property of *N*.[22]

One more concept requires elucidation prior to advancing principles bearing on responsibility ascriptions in cases like Psychohacker. Let's say that an agent *S* *broadly consents* to pro-attitude (like a desire or value) *PA*'s being induced in *S* if and only if either *S* gives ordinary consent to *PA*'s being induced in *S*, or *S* would not object to *PA*'s being induced in *S* if, given *S*'s normal deliberative capacities, *S* were to reflect on *PA*'s being induced in *S*, under conditions *S* takes to be favorable or unobjectionable to making decisions relevant to restructuring or reshaping *S*'s life. For example, suppose *S* freely consents to Max's request to implant in *S* a cluster of pro-attitudes; then *S* has given broad consent. In another example, knowing that she is trying to reduce her intake of caffeine, suppose that by various persistent suggestions, Jake tactfully induces in Jasmine a desire to cut down on the number of cokes she drinks in a day. Jasmine never gives overt free consent to the desire's being thus induced in her. But assume that if she were thinking about modifying her long-standing habit of consuming large quantities of caffeine, under conditions she deemed unobjectionable to making decisions about such things, she would not object to the desire's being induced in her in the manner in which Jake induces it in her. Again, Jasmine has given broad consent.

Now we can introduce a principle about evaluative scheme unauthenticity germane to global manipulation cases:

P1. If *S* is a normative moral agent *N* with evaluative scheme *OriginalE* at time *t*, and *S* acquires at *t* or after an evaluative scheme, *NewE*, via a process to which she did not give broad consent that either destroys *N* by destroying *OriginalE* or totally "represses" *N*, then *NewE* is not *normative-wise* authentic.

Further, we add:

P2. If an agent performs an action, *A*, that arises from an evaluative scheme of hers that is not normative-wise authentic, then the agent is not morally responsible for performing *A*.

The psychosurgery to which she did not give broad consent converts Jenny into a psychological twin of Jamie, obliterating the property of being, say, normative moral agent Jenny*, and "replacing" that property with the one of being, say, normative moral agent Jamie*. Hence, P1 and P2, together with relevant facts, imply that transformed Jenny is not morally to blame for her offense. Principles P1 and P2 are meant to capture the suggestion that agency and authenticity of actional springs both affect ascriptions of responsibility.

These considerations give us reason to believe that the Epicurean's view that ascriptions of responsibility presuppose nondisruption of psychological agency is on firm ground.

4.2 Global Manipulation and Deontic Morality

Let's now turn to the Epicurean's much more provocative suggestion about ascriptions or judgments of an axiological nature:

> JEB. Judgments of extrinsic badness made under normal conditions, just like those of moral responsibility, also assume nondisruption of psychological (or normative) agency and that violation of this assumption may significantly alter or affect such judgments.

I will assess this suggestion in a somewhat roundabout fashion by first asking about the agency presuppositions of yet another variety of moral appraisal. Let the label 'primary deontic properties' refer to the moral properties of rightness, wrongness, and obligatoriness, and call any act that instantiates one or more of these properties a "deontic act." The set of deontic acts constitutes "deontic morality." Examples of judgments of deontic morality are the judgments that Max's manipulation of Jenny is wrong, and Ella's comforting Jenny is right. The new thesis to be evaluated is this:

> JDM. Judgments of deontic morality assume nondisruption of psychological (or normative) agency and that violation of this assumption may significantly alter or affect such judgments.

Is JDM true? On one of the two broad possibilities of whether an agent like postsurgery Jenny can, for example, do moral wrong by stealing, the verdict is negative. Perhaps the strongest line of reasoning that sustains this verdict is that postsurgery Jenny's actions issue from actional springs—from elements of an evaluative scheme—that are not truly her own, and that it is only actions that issue from authentic springs that can instantiate one or more of the primary deontic properties. This verdict would then lead to a sort of symmetry: Postsurgery Jenny is not morally responsible for stealing, as one is responsible for something only if it issues from an authentic evaluative scheme, *and* she does no wrong by stealing, as one's action can be wrong (right, or obligatory) only if, again, it too issues from an authentic evaluative scheme.

However, this line of reasoning is open to challenge. To begin with, an objector might first call attention to the fact that postsurgery Jenny intentionally stole in light of the belief that she was doing wrong. Next, it might be indicated that, presumably, any plausible normative ethical theory, like versions of consequentialism or deontological theories, would rule that postsurgery Jenny *did* do wrong by stealing. The objector might then say that one shouldn't conflate different sorts of moral appraisal: whereas postsurgery Jenny did *wrong* by stealing, she is not (perhaps) to *blame* for stealing. Postsurgery Jenny's action, it might be urged, is relevantly analogous to that of a person who robs the strongbox in the throes of posthypnotic suggestion. Surely such a person, if she is totally in the dark about the hypnosis, is not morally responsible for the stealing, though she does wrong by stealing. The charge, then, would be that it is simply conflation of two different varieties of moral appraisal that leads to the verdict that a manipulated agent like postsurgery Jenny cannot do wrong.

What, then, the advocate of the first possibility might ask, should be said about the crude android that successfully executes its program of robbing the strongbox? Here, there is no question about its not being responsible for robbing, but does it do *wrong* by robbing? And if we deny that it does wrong, what is the relevant difference between its action and that of postsurgery Jenny or the person who steals under posthypnotic suggestion? The germane difference *couldn't* be that the android does not rob intentionally or that its "action" is not caused by beliefs or desires. For it might be proposed that we would not want to say of the tiger that kills the young child that its action lacks moral value or that it does wrong by killing, even though, arguably, its killing is an intentional action caused nondeviantly by appropriate beliefs and desires.

There is, though, no compelling reason to deny that what the tiger or postsurgery Jenny does has *moral disvalue*. But there is, it seems, *this* salient difference between the tiger and Jenny: the latter is a normative moral agent, whereas the former is not. Presumably the tiger is not, for example, minimally morally competent. Not having moral standards, it cannot apply these to evaluating reasons for action even if we assume that it does undertake crude evaluations of its reasons. One might plausibly propose that an entity or agent can perform actions that are right, wrong, or obligatory only if it is a normative moral agent, and one is a normative moral agent only if one is minimally morally competent. One must, on this proposal, if one is to be a normative moral agent, have a basic grasp of the concepts of rightness, wrongness, and obligatoriness, and one must be able to use these concepts in appraisals of various things.

Although I am attracted to this "moral competence model" of deontic moral agency, I suspect that its requirements are too stringent: things that fail to be minimally morally competent may, it seems, perform actions that can be right, wrong, or obligatory. Think, for instance, of hypothetical agents who are devoid of moral concepts, do perform a whole spectrum of intentional actions, and undertake aesthetic or prudential evaluations of various things like policies, courses of action, paintings, architecture, and the like. Such beings would be normative agents of a particular variety: Though normatively competent, their normative competence would not include moral competence. These beings would have (1) an evaluative scheme with appropriate aesthetic and prudential elements but not moral elements; (2) deliberative skills and capacities; and (3) executive capacities. Intuitively, such beings may well perform actions that are morally wrong, although they wouldn't know that these were morally wrong, or they wouldn't perform them in light of the belief that they were doing moral wrong. With this sort of example in mind, one might propose, in contrast to the moral competence model, a normative competence model according to which an entity can perform actions that are right, wrong, or obligatory only if it is a bona fide normative agent of some sort; it must have an evaluative scheme that includes normative standards for evaluation, deliberative skills and capacities, and executive capacities. Such an entity would be able to undertake some sort of *normative* appraisal—one that needn't be moral—of things like policies, actions, and so forth.

Some might object that whereas this relatively weak model gets the case of the hypothetical beings right, one of its drawbacks is that it rules that the tiger's act of killing the child is wrong. But this is controversial. It is debatable, for instance, whether tigers have anything like an evaluative scheme, even one that need not include moral standards of appraisal.

I shall not decide between the two models though, of the two, I'm drawn toward the weaker second. Either implies (together with relevant facts) that postsurgery Jenny does moral wrong by stealing. Introducing a bit of terminology will help. Let's say that one is morally appraisable for an action if and only if one is either morally praiseworthy or morally blameworthy for its performance. I'm inclined to believe that relatively stronger models than either of the two that I have introduced will be implausible. So, for instance, a pretty obvious flaw of the condition that an entity can do something that is morally right, wrong, or obligatory only if it can perform actions for which it is morally appraisable is that beings devoid of moral concepts but otherwise normatively sophisticated cannot be appraisable for what they do, though they may well do things that are right, wrong, or obligatory. My overall verdict is that there are fairly substantial grounds to resist the first possibility, the one that implies that postsurgery Jenny cannot do wrong by stealing.

On the second possibility, a manipulated agent like postsurgery Jenny does wrong and so can do wrong by stealing. This option derives support from either the moral competence model or the weaker normative competence model discussed above. If this second option is correct—and I think it is—we are committed to a curious asymmetry: The kind of subversion of agency that we find in Psychohacker affects ascriptions of responsibility but leaves unblemished those of deontic morality. Responsibility for an action, it seems, *does* require that the action be caused by authentic actional elements—that is, by an evaluative scheme that is normative-wise authentic—whereas deontic morality (whether an action that one performs is right, wrong, or obligatory) does not. So whereas JMR is true, JDM is false.

5. WHY THE ASYMMETRY?

Well, what accounts for the asymmetry? The answer, I believe, is affiliated with the fact that responsibility, especially appraisability, tells us something about the moral worth of a person, whereas deontic morality—a person's performing an action that is right, wrong, or obligatory—need not. Reflect, for a bit, on these aspects of the concepts of moral blameworthiness and praiseworthiness: Moral blameworthiness for a deed is composed of someone's being deserving of being judged in a certain way, the judgment recording the moral worth of the person with respect to its performance. A person of high moral standing or overall good character can be blameworthy for an action, and when she is, her moral worth is diminished as a result of its performance. Blameworthiness for an action, in Michael Zimmerman's terminology, results in a "negative mark" being entered in the person's "ledger of life."[23] Analogously, when a person is morally praiseworthy for performing an action, her moral worth vis à vis that action is augmented; praiseworthiness results in a "positive mark" being entered in her ledger. Much in keeping with this conception of responsibility is a conception, or at least an aspect of one, advanced by Gary Watson. Of the two aspects of responsibility that Watson distinguishes, the self-disclosure view holds that an agent is morally responsible insofar as he has the capacity to choose ends freely and act in accordance with them. Watson says:

> Moral accountability is only part, and not necessarily the most important part, of our idea of responsibility. The self-disclosure view describes a core notion of responsibility that is central to ethical life and ethical appraisal. In virtue of the capacities identified by the self-disclosure view, conduct can be attributable or imputable to an individual as its agent and is open to appraisal that is therefore appraisal of the individual as an adopter of ends. Attributability in this sense *is* a kind of responsibility. In virtue of the capacities in question, the individual is an agent in a strong sense, an author of her conduct, and is in an important sense answerable for what she does.[24]

Watson's self-disclosure conception of responsibility resonates with the view I proposed above that for an agent to be morally responsible for an action, that action must be "truly her own"; it must issue from an authentic evaluative scheme. If judgments of appraisability *do* reveal something about the moral worth of persons in relation to specific things they do or ends they freely adopt, then it is no wonder—it is, indeed, sensible to expect—that it is only normative moral agents that can be morally appraisable, and more broadly, morally responsible for their conduct. In contrast, it appears that deontic evaluations are or at least can be much more *act-focused* than agent-focused. If by sheer accident and nonculpable ignorance, I trip the wire that sets off the explosive that brings down the house that Jack built, my moral worth with respect to tripping the wire has not been diminished, though I have, arguably, done wrong by tripping it. If alien amoral beings who are devoid of deontic concepts and who evaluate things either aesthetically or prudentially destroy Jack's house because they judge it to be an aesthetic atrocity, their moral worth with respect to the deed of destruction has not been tarnished, though again, arguably, this deed of theirs is morally wrong.

6. WHY JEB IS FALSE

We are now in a position to see why JEB, the Epicurean's view that judgments of extrinsic badness, just like those of moral responsibility, presuppose that psychological or normative agency is not disrupted, is false. In a nutshell, ascriptions of extrinsic badness like those of deontic morality are act- and not *agent-focused*. Generally, such ascriptions do not reveal the moral worth of agents in relation to things they do or disclose ends that they have freely adopted. Rather, they reveal some moral quality—an axiological one—about various states of affairs that stand in a relation to agents. For example, it seems that Jenny's moral death is extrinsically bad for Jenny. This axiological ascription does not disclose anything about the moral worth of Jenny, or ends she has freely adopted, or whether she has acted in conformity with or violated such ends. Rather the ascription reveals a moral feature of some state of affairs that has Jenny as a constituent. Analogous things are true with other such ascriptions or judgments like, for instance, the judgments that eating poisoned candy is extrinsically bad for Cindy, or smoking is extrinsically bad for Al, or having a tummy ache is extrinsically bad for Shaheen.

Perhaps an Epicurean will object that I have misgeneralized from a limited sample of cases. Suppose Manson molests children and derives pleasure from doing so. Then, given certain assumptions, the state of affairs, *Manson's molesting children is extrinsically good for Manson* (SM), is true. But isn't SM agent-focused, the Epicurean might charge? I don't think so. Again, SM reveals nothing essential about the moral worth of Manson in relation to his molesting children, or about whether acts about molesting children are "truly Manson's own," or about the ends Manson has freely chosen and whether he has been true to those ends. SM, it appears, is no more agent-focused than is the state of affairs *smoking is extrinsically bad for Al*.

To tie some ends together, as we have reason to reject JEB, and as the Epicurean's case against Psychohacker's being an effective counterexample to VCF2 presupposes the truth of JEB, the Epicurean's case is undermined.

7. FINAL REMARKS

I want, finally, to motivate the claim that ascriptions of extrinsic badness (of the sort that state of affairs *x* is extrinsically bad for agent *A*) do not presuppose either the existence of normative moral agency or experiential agency (they do not presuppose that *A* is either a normative moral agent or an experiential agent), and then draw out the implications of this claim for whether death can be bad for the deceased. I suggested above that beings devoid of moral concepts and hence incapable of moral assessments but capable of other varieties of normative appraisals, like aesthetic or prudential ones, could perform acts that are morally right, wrong, or obligatory. Such beings would not be normative *moral* agents. Suppose Max transforms Jenny into a psychological twin of such a being. Other relevant conditions remaining unchanged, her hacking offense is, presumably, still morally wrong even though she has ceased to be a normative moral agent. Suppose, in addition, Jack's house offends Jenny's aesthetic sensibilities and she feels disgust, even pain, at the sight of it. There would, I believe, be nothing untoward about the axiological judgment that *viewing Jack's house is extrinsically bad for transformed Jenny*. Surely this judgment could be appropriate even if Jenny is not a normative moral agent. Both the deontic ascription that her stealing is wrong and the axiological one that her viewing the house is extrinsically bad for her could be true, in part, because such ascriptions are act-focused.

Finally, suppose Max, now really ambitious, succeeds in transforming Jenny into a psychological twin of a normative agent bereft of moral concepts and devoid of sensations or affections. Imagine that the agent is a highly complex android-like being capable of sophisticated reasoning and purposeful action but lacking moral concepts (the moral chip has not yet been installed) and sentience. Suppose transformed Jenny (call her Data*) is betrayed by some of her colleagues, and each person who knows about the betrayal is killed soon after Data* is betrayed. It is, in consequence, not narrowly possible for Data* ever to discover the betrayal. If Sata, a nonmoral normative but sentient agent, were betrayed under similar conditions, her betrayal could, presumably, be extrinsically bad for her. But then I see no compelling reason to deny that Data*'s betrayal could also be extrinsically bad for her. Or if we add to Sata's case that, moments after being betrayed, she is reduced to a permanent vegetative state as a result of a stroke and is thereafter no longer any sort of normative agent, her betrayal could still be extrinsically bad for her. Again, I suggest that part of the reason why the pertinent states of affairs could be extrinsically bad for these agents is that ascriptions of extrinsic badness are act-focused.

Of what significance are these observations to whether death can be bad for the one who dies? The Epicurean argument (summarized in section 2) is predicated on VCF2 *and* the termination thesis. Even if VCF2 is abandoned, the Epicurean might insist that both of the following are true: (D1) Nothing can be extrinsically bad for a person at a time unless that person exists at that time; and (D2) A person ceases to exist at the time of his death. If (D1) and (D2) are both true, then there is an alternative pathway—one that does not appeal to VCF2—to the conclusion that death is not extrinsically bad for the deceased. D2, however, is multiply ambiguous. On one reading that we have already considered, D2 says that (necessarily) a person ceases to exist as a human being at the time of his death. But this interpretation of D2 is implausible. On a second, more pertinent reading, D2 says that a person ceases to exist as a normative or a psychological agent at the time of his death. This interpretation is true, but then there would be a problem with the relevant construal of D1. D1 would now say that nothing can be extrinsically bad for a person at a time unless that person exists as a normative or psychological agent at that time. I think Sata's case, the one in which she is reduced to a vegetative state at about the time when she is betrayed, calls this interpretation of D1 into question. Finally, on a third reading, D2 says that a person ceases to exist as an experiential agent at the time of his death. This interpretation is also true, but then again the appropriate version of D1 would fail, as D1 would now say that nothing can be extrinsically bad for a person at a time unless that person exists as an experiential agent at that time. Data*'s case impugns this version of D1.

In conclusion, ascriptions of extrinsic badness, just like those of deontic morality, are *act*-focused. This fact sheds light on why versions of VCF theses presupposed by the Epicurean argument are false, and why various versions of the Epicurean argument that do not engage VCF theses are not sound.

NOTES

1. See, for example, Fred Feldman, *Confrontations with the Reaper* (New York: Oxford University Press, 1992); John Martin Fischer, "Death, Badness, and the Impossibility of Experience," *Journal of Ethics* 1 (1997): 341–53; and Thomas Nagel, *Mortal Questions* (Cambridge: Cambridge University Press, 1979), pp. 1–10, reprinted in J. M. Fischer (ed.), *The Metaphysics of Death* (Stanford, Calif.: Stanford University Press, 1993), pp. 61–9.

2. See, for instance, S. E. Rosenbaum, "How to Be Dead and Not Care: A Defense of Epicurus," *American Philosophy Quarterly* 23 (1986): 217–25, reprinted in Fischer, *Metaphysics of Death*, 119–34. Walter Glannon argues for the Epicurean view that it is not rational to be concerned about, fear, or regret death in "Temporal Asymmetry, Life, and Death," *American Philosophical Quarterly* 31 (1994): 235–44.

3. See Harry Silverstein, "The Evil of Death," *Journal of Philosophy* 77 (1980): 401–24, p. 414.

4. A relevant passage from Epicurus' "Letter to Menoeceus" is this:

> Become accustomed to the belief that death is nothing to us. For all good and evil consists in sensation, but death is deprivation of sensation. . . . So death, the most terrifying of ills, is nothing to us, since so long as we exist death is not with us; but when death comes, then we do not exist. It does not then concern either the living or the dead, since for the former it is not, and the latter are no more.

The translation is by C. Bailey and it occurs in W. H. Oates (ed.), *The Stoic and Epicurean Philosophers* (New York: The Modern Library, 1940), 30–34, p. 31.

5. "Evil of Death," pp. 414–5.

6. See "Evil of Death," p. 415, and "How to Be Dead and Not Care: A Defense of Epicurus," p. 221.

7. "Death, Badness, and the Impossibility of Experience," p. 347.

8. "Death, Badness, and the Impossibility of Experience," p. 347.

9. "Death, Badness, and the Impossibility of Experience," p. 348.

10. See Feldman's *Confrontations with the Reaper*, esp. pp. 137–8, and Fischer's "Death, Badness, and the Impossibility of Experience," pp. 344–46.

11. Alfred Mele, *Autonomous Agents: From Self-Control to Autonomy* (New York: Oxford University Press, 1995), p. 172.

12. Such cases of global manipulation have been discussed by various authors. See, for example, Daniel Dennett, *Elbow Room: The Varieties of Free Will Worth Wanting* (Cambridge: MIT Press, 1984); Richard Double, "Puppeteers, Hypnotists, and Neurosurgeons," *Philosophical Studies* 56 (1989): pp. 163–73; Mele's *Autonomous Agents*, esp., chap. 9; and Ishtiyaque Haji, *Appraisability: Puzzles, Proposals, and Perplexities* (New York: Oxford University Press, 1998).

13. Walter Glannon has argued that our practices of holding people morally and criminally responsible require only a low threshold of psychological connectedness and bodily continuity. See his "Moral Responsibility and Personal Identity," *American Philosophical Quarterly* 35 (1998), 231–49, esp. section IV. In *Autonomous Agents*, p. 175, note 22, Mele suggests that in such transformation cases, the pre- and postsurgery agents may be strongly psychologically connected, in Parfit's sense [*Reasons and Persons* (Oxford: Clarendon Press, 1984, p. 206)]. They may be such that the number of direct psychological connections between them "is *at least half* the number that hold, over every day, in the lives of nearly every actual person."

14. The notion of normative agency is explained in section 4.1.

15. *Autonomous Agents*, p. 159.

16. *Autonomous Agents*, p. 164.

17. J. M. Fischer, "Responsiveness and Moral Responsibility," in F. Schoeman (ed.), *Responsibility, Character and the Emotions* (Cambridge: Cambridge University Press, 1987), pp. 81–106; J. M. Fischer and Mark Ravizza, "Responsibility and History," *Midwest Studies in Philosophy* 19: 430–51; and *Responsibility and Control: A Theory of Moral Responsibility* (New York: Cambridge University Press, 1998); and Don Locke, "Three Concepts of Free Action I," *Proceedings of the Aristotelian Society* 86 (1975, sup. vol. 44): 95–112.

18. See Harry G. Frankfurt's "Freedom of the Will and the Concept of a Person," *Journal of Philosophy* 68 (1971): 5–20, reprinted in Frankfurt's *The Importance of What We Care About* (New York: Cambridge University Press, 1988). Other relevant papers of Frankfurt's include "Three Concepts of Free Action II," *Proceedings of the Aristotelian Society* 86 (1975, sup. vol. 44): 113–25; "Identification and Externality," in A. Rorty (ed.), *The Identities of Persons* (Berkeley and Los Angeles: University of California Press, 1976), 237–51; "The Problem of Action," *American Philosophical Quarterly* 15 (1978): 157–62; and "Identification and Wholeheartedness," in Schoeman, *Responsibility, Character and the Emotions*, 27–45. These papers are reprinted in *The Importance of What We Care About*.

19. See, for example, the works listed in note 17. See also Gary Watson, "Free Agency," *Journal of Philosophy* 72 (1975): 205–20; M. Friedman, "Autonomy and the Split-Level Self," *Southern Journal of Philosophy* 24 (1976): 19–35; and Michael Slote, "Understanding Free Will,"

Journal of Philosophy 77 (1980): 136–51. Eleonore Stump defends some of Frankfurt's hierarchical views in "Sanctification, Hardening of the Heart and Frankfurt's Concept of Free Will," in J. M. Fischer and M. Ravizza (eds.), *Perspectives on Moral Responsibility* (Ithaca, N.Y.: Cornell University Press, 1987), 211–34.

20. See Robert Kane, *The Significance of Free Will* (New York: Oxford University Press, 1996), pp. 61–7.

21. See *Appraisability*, chap. 7.

22. It should be cautioned that 'normative agent' is a *technical term*. One should not confuse, say, Ish with a normative agent and then scoff at the untenable suggestion that Ish has his evaluative scheme essentially. Presumably, Ish could have had a very different evaluative scheme than the one he in fact has. For more discussion on the notion of normative agency, see *Appraisability*, pp. 118–9.

23. Michael Zimmerman, *An Essay on Moral Responsibility* (Totowa, N.J.: Rowman & Littlefield, 1988), p. 38. Others who embrace a "ledger view" of responsibility include Joel Feinberg [*Doing and Deserving* (Princeton: Princeton University Press, 1970), pp. 30–1, 124–5]; Jonathan Glover [*Responsibility* (London: Routledge & Kegan Paul, 1970)]; B. Gert and T. J. Duggan ["Free Will as the Ability to Will," *Noûs* 13 (1979): 197–217, pp. 199–217]; and Ishtiyaque Haji [*Appraisability*, pp. 9–10]. There are alternative views. So, for example, Peter Strawson suggests that we can understand moral responsibility in terms of certain social practices. Strawson argues that, when members of a society regard a person as a responsible agent, they react or see it fitting to react to that person with a characteristic set of feelings and attitudes—the so-called reactive attitudes—like resentment, love, gratitude, forgiveness, respect, and indignation ["Freedom and Resentment," *Proceedings of the British Academy* 48 (1962): 1–25]. Jay Wallace defends an original and sophisticated variation of the Strawsonian account in *Responsibility and the Moral Sentiments* (Cambridge: Harvard University Press, 1994). Rejecting the Strawsonian account, Marina Oshana proposes that "when we say a person is morally responsible for something, we are essentially saying that the person did or caused some act (or exhibited some trait of character) for which it is fitting that she give an account" ["Ascriptions of Responsibility," *American Philosophical Quarterly* (1997) 34: 71–83, p. 77].

24. Gary Watson, "Two Faces of Responsibility," *Philosophical Topics* 24 (1996): 227–48, p. 229.

Midwest Studies in Philosophy, XXIV (2000)

Appraising Death in Human Life:
Two Modes of Valuation

STEPHEN E. ROSENBAUM

O ver the course of the last twenty-five years or so, contemporary philosophers have disagreed over whether, if death is the end of personal existence, death is bad for people who die. Most, following Aristotle, have argued that death is bad for people, perhaps even the very worst thing in human life.[1] Others, however, following Epicurus, have argued that death is not bad for those who die, apparently contradicting Aristotle's idea that death is bad for people.[2] This disagreement has resulted in a number of powerful philosophical papers, an apparent philosophical dialogue, designed to contribute to the resolution of the issue. In the various papers directed to this debate, the opposing arguments manifest a peculiar impotence. Few arguments for one of the sides seem to faze the other side. It is as if the basic premises of the different views loom so large in their proponents' fields of view that, from behind them, the basis of the opposing view is invisible. Indeed, the hypothesis that guides this paper is that the real roots of the disagreement about death have not yet been clearly identified.

Lying underneath the dispute about death and its value for individuals who die is at bottom a disagreement about value. In particular, it is an implicit disagreement about what categories of thing can have value, can be good or bad, for people. Once one understands this and identifies the notions of value involved, one discovers very surprisingly that there is a strict logical compatibility between the different views over which people have argued for years. If I am correct about the nature of this debate, the insight might have one of two effects on the debate. It might end the debate, on the ground that if the views are strictly compatible, then there is no point for those who have supported either one of the views to argue against the other. Alternatively, it might alter the nature of the debate. I am going to urge that it should change the character of the debate, and I shall try to contribute to a new, more lucid basis for the disagreement.

A large part of the purpose of this paper, then, is to show that, at least as views have been so far discussed, the view expressed by "death is bad for people" is compatible with the view expressed by "death is not bad for people," despite appearances to the contrary. This will involve showing that the views depend on different (and apparently logically compatible) views about value, on two different modes of valuation. I shall argue, however, that important questions remain to be resolved in relation to the two views, and offer ideas intended to help in the further consideration and assessment of the two views. Although the views about valuation are compatible, the apparent disagreement between them suggests that real issues remain to be addressed. My discussion will clarify the nature of the debate between the two views considerably, and it should also advance our critical understanding of the value of death in human life.

In beginning to discuss the relationship between the Aristotelian view (and its descendents) and the Epicurean view (and its descendents), one can hardly do better than to recur to the ancient Greek disagreement about death apparent between Aristotle and Epicurus. Aristotle's paradoxical discussion of courage and fear in *Nicomachean Ethics* (1115a) declared that "death is the most terrible of all things, for it is the end, and *nothing is thought to be any longer good or bad for the dead*" (emphasis added). This statement is open to different interpretations, but in a straightforward way, it is deeply puzzling. To understand why it is puzzling and how it can be reasonably understood will help reveal the shadow of one of the axiological views involved in the recent dialogue about death.

Aristotle appears here to be arguing that death is the worst thing for people, but on the ground that nothing is good or bad for those who are dead. This seems puzzling, since the claim that death is the most terrible of all things for people would seem to entail at least that death is bad for people, and, assuming that 'death' means the condition of being dead, rather than dying or the fact of becoming dead, the claim is based implicitly on the statement that there is nothing good or bad for the dead.[3] If death (in this sense) is bad for people, then it cannot be true that *nothing* has value for the dead (since being dead would be bad for them), but if *nothing* is either good or bad for the dead, then death (in the same sense) has no value for them.[4] In fact, Epicurus argued that because nothing is either good or bad for the dead, because "all good and evil lie in sentience, whereas death is the absence of sentience," death is not at all bad for the dead. Paradoxically, Aristotle's reasoning appears to be closely similar to that which supports Epicurus's seemingly contrary conclusion about death. On this initial interpretation of Aristotle's thinking, his argument appears to undermine itself. The premise seems to contradict the conclusion.

One can see, of course, several ways to reinterpret Aristotle's reasoning in order to save it from what it seems to be. To see Aristotle's reasoning to be consistent, one would have to see him as having argued not that the condition of being dead is bad for people, but that something else is bad for them. My purpose, however, is not to explore Aristotle's view deeply, but rather to show how ambiguity in axiological terminology has dogged and disabled ancient as well as contemporary discussions about the evaluation of death. To this end, I want to discuss briefly the reasoning embodied in Aristotle's comment. Specifically, I want to identify some feasible candidate for the conclusion of Aristotle's argument.

If Aristotle's passing remark about death is not inconsistent, then his conclusion should not be understood as the affirmation that the condition of being dead is bad for those who are dead, for reasons I have already given. It is hence apparently not incompatible with Epicurus's claim that being dead is not bad for the dead. If Aristotle's conclusion is not that being dead is bad for the dead, then he must be saying of something other than being dead that *it* is bad (for the dead).[5]

Again, I assume that Aristotle's words "death is the most terrible of all things" entail that something is at least bad. What might this other thing Aristotle calls 'death' be? It would not the process of dying, for that process could not be shown to be bad for people on the ground that "nothing is (thought to be) either good or bad for the dead." Dying does not take place among the dead, and its badness is because it affects the living so powerfully. Could he have meant the moment of death? There seems no feasible reason to think that the moment of death itself, in and of itself, would be bad for someone, simply on the ground that "nothing is either good or bad for the dead." Why would the moment of death be bad for someone on the ground that nothing occurring after that moment could be good or bad for the person who dies? It seems to me that the most plausible candidate for what Aristotle meant, for what he evaluated negatively, is *the fact that a person dies*. I am thus inclined to think that if Aristotle's reasoning is plausible and consistent, then his conclusion should be understood to be the proposition that the fact that a person dies is bad (for that person), based on the premise that when the person is dead, nothing is any longer good or bad for him or her.

Before leaping the long centuries between Epicurus and contemporary philosophical thinking and reviewing the contemporary debate, it will be useful to reflect briefly on the differences between Aristotle and Epicurus on death. Aristotle appears to have thought not that the condition of being dead is bad for the dead, but rather that the fact that a person dies is bad (for the person who is dead). He also seems to have believed that the fact that one dies, at a certain time, or will die in the future, is sufficient ground for (the living) fearing death.[6] Epicurus thought on the other hand that the condition of being dead is not bad for the dead, and he believed that this is sufficient ground for (the living) not fearing death.[7] These philosophers appear to have been thinking about the same thing, about death and about whether there are grounds for fearing death. However, close attention reveals that things are more complex. Although they probably had incompatible views about whether there are good grounds for people to fear death, it seems clear that their views about whether death is bad for the dead are compatible. They were considering different issues.

Aristotle and Epicurus certainly had *different* ideas about the value of death in human life, but those ideas could be maintained together. Someone who thinks that the condition of being dead is not bad for the dead might also consistently believe that the fact that a person dies is bad for that person. Later, it will be clearer why people might think that the fact that person dies is bad for the person, and it will then be easier to see how someone might believe both these things. For now, it will perhaps be enough to suggest why the argument concluding that being dead is not bad for the dead is not by itself a good reason to conclude that the fact that a person will die at a particular time is not bad for the person.

The condition of being dead (for an individual) does not begin to occur until the person becomes dead. Epicurus's premises, that "all good and bad lie in sentience" and "death is the absence of sentience," seem straightforwardly to support the conclusion that the condition of being dead is not bad for the dead. Being dead does not occur until a person dies, and if "all good and bad lie in sentience," and the dead are not *capable* of sentience, then, it seems clear, being dead cannot be bad for the dead. The dead cannot "sense" or be affected by being dead.

On the other hand, depending on what facts are, *the fact* that a person dies at a particular time or within a particular time span does not clearly exist only after the person dies and would not necessarily be prevented from having value for the person by the person's being dead and thus not being able to sense anything, or experience anything.[8] It might, for example, be a fact that a newborn child will die in the week before his or her forty-fourth birthday, and although that fact might not be *known* by anyone, it is possible to hold that it exists before the person dies, exists even when the person is gestating. Similarly, the fact that Alexander died in 323 may be said to exist now, over two centuries after his death. If *the fact that a person dies* exists, perhaps as a kind of abstractum, before the person dies, then the Epicurean reasoning that things that happen, exist, or occur after a person dies cannot thereby affect the person, and thus cannot be bad for the person, would not obviously apply to *the fact* that a person dies at a particular time. Abstracting from different views on the fear of death, Aristotle and Epicurus appear strictly to have had at one level logically compatible ideas about the value of death in human life.

This apparent compatibility between Aristotle and Epicurus is surprising. Contemporary theorists commonly accept their opposition. Differences between the views are mirrored in recent discussions of the question of death's badness, and this will be evident shortly. In spite of compatibility between the ideas of Aristotle and Epicurus, and between recent discussions among those who believe that death is bad for the dead and those who believe it is not, their discussions hide a deeper disagreement about the nature of value. On this deeper disagreement rests different appraisals of death. This implicit disagreement lurks also in the contemporary discussion of the issue of evaluating death.

Thomas Nagel initiated recent discussions of the value of death for those who die and recognized at the same time that the issue between those who think that death is bad and those who think it is not rests on "assumptions about good and evil."[9] Thinking that Epicurean ideas about value would undermine taking death to be an evil, he argued, inspired perhaps by Aristotle, for a different way of thinking about value. He insisted that

> [t]here certainly are goods and evils of a simple kind (including some pleasures and pains) which a person possesses at a given time simply in virtue of his condition at that time. But this is not true of all the things we regard as good or bad for a man. Often we need to know his history to tell whether something is a misfortune or not; this applies to ills like deterioration, deprivation, and damage. Sometimes, his experiential *state* is relatively unimportant—as in the

case of a man who wastes his life in the cheerful pursuit of a method of communicating with asparagus plants. Someone who holds that all goods and evils must be temporally assignable states of the person may of course try to bring difficult cases into line by pointing to the pleasure or pain that more complicated goods and evils cause. Loss, betrayal, deception, and ridicule are on this view bad because people suffer when they learn of them. But it should be asked how our ideas of human value would have to be constituted to accommodate these cases directly instead. (This would enable us to explain *why* their discovery causes suffering.) One possible account is that most good and ill fortune has as its subject a person identified by his history and his possibilities, rather than merely by his categorical state of the moment—and that while this subject can be exactly located in a sequence of places and times, the same is not necessarily true of the goods and ills that befall him.[10]

This important and influential passage is unclear in various ways, but does contain an almost explicit claim that value can attach both to propositions and to states of being. Nagel takes the Aristotelian view that death is bad for people, and bases his view, as Aristotle apparently does, on propositions, or facts, having value for people. Nagel also gives implicit compressed arguments for taking propositions to be objects of value, and I shall consider these arguments in turn, since they bear directly on the applicability to death of one kind of valuation.

Other writers endorse the idea that value attaches to states of being or conditions, such as pain or pleasure. In defending the Epicurean idea that death is not bad for people, for example, philosophers at least implicitly adopt the view that value attaches to states or conditions of people and argue that states must be able to affect people in order to be bad for them.[11] Even some philosophers who find the Epicurean idea insupportable and argue for the badness of death for people take value to attach to objects other than facts or propositions.[12]

The contemporary literature on the issue of death's badness for those who die shows the same two ideas about value as the writings of Aristotle and Epicurus. The recent discussion of whether death is bad for people rests on two concepts of value, as does the disagreement between Aristotle and Epicurus. This fact would explain why the dialogue on death in current philosophical literature seems so relatively impotent, and why the arguments on each side seem not to touch the other side. My hypothesis is that the term 'death' is ambiguous and veils the fact that those who argue that death is not bad for people mean by 'death' *being dead*, whereas those who argue that death is bad for people mean by 'death' *the fact that one dies at a particular time*. The strict consistency between the positions is obvious when one realizes that from the proposition that being dead is not bad for people, one cannot infer that the fact that one dies at a particular time is not bad for people. Nor, obviously, can one infer, from the proposition that the fact that a person dies at a particular time can be bad for people, that being dead can be bad for people. In order to justify such inferences, one would need to show that the different objects are so related logically that the inference can be made.

One might think that a logical compatibility between the two positions supposed for so long to be inconsistent should terminate the debate about whether death is bad for people. Although the positions are different, why should they not be maintained together? And so, why argue about them, as if a convincing proof of one of the views would refute the other? However, the consistency of the positions will help clarify them and enable them to be explored more deeply. The chief philosophical issue connected with the views concerns attitudes people take toward death. Indeed, one of the points of the discussion, among both Aristotelians and Epicureans, is to explore the fear of death. Aristotle tried to justify the fear of death by his view of the badness of death, and Epicurus tried to undermine it by his different view. Thus there perhaps remain important questions about people fearing death, even if the bases of their different ideas about the fear of death are consistent. Moreover, since the disagreement between Aristotle and Epicurus, and between those recent thinkers who believe that death is bad for people and those who believe that death is not, amounts ultimately to a difference in axiological views, a question arises about the nature of those views and their relationships to one another. After clarifying the differences between the two modes of valuation and discussing the justifications for using the modes, I shall recur to the relative importance of them in illuminating the reasonability of fearing of death.

Recognizing a possible distinction between personal or person-relative value, and impersonal or non-person-relative value, I should indicate that as I discuss the relationship between the two modes of valuation, I assume that the value involved is personal relative value. That is, I suppose for the sake of the discussion that if something has value, it has value for some particular person, or is good or bad for some particular person, or persons. This would be person-relative value. There may be impersonal value, such that things may be said to be good or bad, but not in relation to any particular person or persons. If there is such value, that is not my concern here. I shall assume that the issue concerns good or bad in relation to particular individuals and restrict my discussion to things that are or could be valuable for particular individuals.

The most obvious way to characterize the different modes of valuation in Aristotle, Epicurus, and their followers is to say that one mode of valuation takes propositions as the objects of value whereas the other takes states or conditions of people as the object of value. For Aristotle and Nagel, the fact that a person dies, or dies at some particular time, is bad for the person. If the proposition that someone dies at a particular time is bad for the person, or perhaps is good for a person, then propositions may be said to have value for people. This mode of valuation is properly called *propositional valuation*. On the other hand, the other view is that events that can causally affect people by causing them to be in certain states or conditions, as well as those conditions or states of people, can have value. Being injured, an event, can, for example, have value for a person, perhaps because it causes a state of pain or a condition of disability. Since events, states, and conditions of people are concrete things, this mode of valuation may be called *concrete valuation*. Epicurus and others used this mode of valuation in arguing that since being dead is not a condition or state that can affect one, it cannot be bad for one.

The distinctness of the two different modes of valuation is obscured by the fact that the types of valuation seem to be related. It would appear that the value of propositions for people parallels the value of states or conditions of them. Being in intense pain, a concrete condition of a person, for example, seems clearly matched to a proposition about the person, namely, *that the person is in intense pain*. If the condition were bad for the person, then it seems that the corresponding proposition would also be (or could be) bad for the person. Similarly, for a person in some condition that is good for the person, the proposition *that* the person is in that condition is also good for the person, and for the same reasons, whatever they are. If being healthy is good for someone, then it is good *that the person is healthy*. In fact, it appears appropriate to generalize and believe that every state or condition of someone, and every event that causes such a state or condition, in which the concrete item has value for someone corresponds to some proposition that has value for him or her. States and conditions can be described.

Not every description of someone, not every proposition, however, corresponds to some concrete state or condition the person is in. Some of Nagel's examples illustrate this nicely. Being betrayed in such a way that one never knows that one is betrayed and is never affected by the betrayal is such a description. To say that it is bad that he or she was betrayed in these circumstances is to endorse implicitly the idea that the propositions that are valuable for people do not necessarily correspond to states of them of which they might become aware or which might affect them. Indeed death is supposed to be like this. The proposition that a person dies at a particular time does not correspond in any neat or obvious way to the state of being dead. The separation here is the basis for the strict consistency between Aristotelians and Epicureans on death.

One can sense a kind of opposition, even inconsistency, possible between the view that there is propositional valuation and the idea that there is concrete valuation, provided of course that they are suitably qualified. Those who adopt the notion of propositional value assert implicitly that at least some value is not associated at all with concrete states or conditions of individuals or any causes of those states or conditions. They are perfectly free to allow the possibility of concrete value as well, just as Aristotle might have said that pain is bad in addition to facts not associated with concrete states. Those who believe that valuation is concrete might deny that any value attaches to propositions, unless those propositions are linked in some important way to concrete states or conditions of persons. Recalling that the issue here concerns personal, rather than impersonal, value, the advocates of concrete valuation might then believe that for a proposition to have any value for a person, that proposition must entail the existence of some state or condition of which the person is capable of being aware at some time, or it must entail the existence of some cause of such a state or condition. If there is any inconsistency between the Aristotelian view and the Epicurean, that inconsistency centers on different, and incompatible, modes of valuation, rather than on their different, ambiguous claims about death.

Suppose that opposition between the different views about death is based on a disagreement about the nature of valuation and that the propositional and concrete modes of valuation are inconsistent. They would be inconsistent, if propositional valuation held that any propositions can have value for people, even without being linked closely to states of condition of people, of which people might be aware, when, at the same time, concrete valuation holds such propositions cannot have value for people. In fact, the thesis that propositions or facts can be good or bad for people without being linked to concrete conditions of them is used implicitly by many who argue for the Aristotelian view and again the Epicurean. The crucial issue for this way of understanding the opposition between the two views would be whether propositions that do not entail the existence of concrete effects on people can have any value for them.

Most evaluations we make are, it seems, concrete, in the sense that the resulting valuations apply to concrete conditions of people, and to propositions that entail the existence of those conditions. We appraise conditions of people toward which those people have some attitude or toward which they are capable of taking some attitude, and we commonly assess the causes of such conditions. The state of depression is taken to be bad for people, and also the condition of joyfulness is taken to be good for people. We also take things that causally contribute to depression or joy to be bad or good for people. In general, we suppose that pain, pleasure, injury, health, and so on have value, and we suppose that the causes of these things have value. We commonly associate value essentially with conditions of people, or causes of those conditions, items toward which people are capable of taking some attitude.

I believe we also commonly think that if something has no effect on a person, not producing either some physical or some psychological state of which a person could at some time be aware, then it does not really have any value for the person. Some extraordinarily tragic event, say in Indonesia, tragic enough to devastate many lives, but not tragic enough to generate news in this part of the world, might, for example, never affect those living in rural Wyoming. People so remote from the event might never be caused to be in any psychological or physical condition because of the event, and they might never learn of the event. It is no more difficult to believe that such a remote event would have no value for rural Wyomingites than to believe that some temporally remote galactic event (say, 200 light years away) that, because of its temporal distance, could never affect them would have no value for them, could not be good or bad for them. One does not need to consider such remote events to understand the point that not being able to be affected by something prevents it from having any value for people not affected by it. Occurrences even in one's own neighborhood might have great value for some people, but because one is never affected by the events, they have no value for one.[13]

Such cases, reflecting what seems the customary way of evaluating events in people's lives, may be multiplied extensively, and I believe they create some presumption in favor of the thesis that human value is all concrete, that the concrete mode of valuation exhausts the kind of things that can be valuable for people. However suggestive, these examples are not conclusive. Talk about value in human life is complex and cannot readily be assimilated to concrete valuation. We frequently express serious beliefs about value that, in the context of the notion of concrete valuation, are puzzling and are perhaps inconsistent with only concrete valuation. Furthermore, several contemporary philosophers have argued that propositional valuation unconnected with concrete states of people must be used to account for manifold features of our moral thinking. In light of these beliefs and arguments, such propositional valuation may be necessary to account fully for human valuations. The arguments for this view should be considered carefully.

Nagel began the contemporary defense of the idea that death is bad for the dead, using arguments that are supposed to persuade us that abstract value is essential to how people sometimes rightly think about value. His reasoning, although influential, has not been fully appreciated, and it would be well to begin with a consideration of that reasoning. The earlier quote from Nagel incorporates a couple of arguments for the necessity of abstract valuation. One argument is the example of a "man who wastes his life in the cheerful pursuit of a method of communicating with asparagus plants." The other consists in the claim that only with a theory of abstract valuation, according to which value is not necessarily linked to conditions of a person while alive, can one explain why the discovery, for example, of hitherto unknown betrayal "causes suffering."

The example of the underinformed plant communicator is supposed to be that of a person whose life is bad (because of the supposed inutility of its overall project) but who has no bad "experiential states." Nagel invites us to conclude from this example that there must be abstract value, abstract bad, or that things may be bad for individuals without having any causal relationship to conditions of them, conditions they might mind. The plausibility of this argument depends on how one understands "experiential states." If by "experiential state" Nagel means some attitude such as liking or disliking, approving or disapproving, being satisfied or dissatisfied, where such attitudes are directed toward one's conditions, then it is easy to see why he thinks that experiential states are not required for value. It is clearly possible, as shown by the example of undiscovered betrayal, that, at the time something bad is happening to one, one need not be aware of it and need not have any attitude toward it. However, it does not follow from experience in this sense not being required for value that experience in some other sense is not required. Something could be bad (say) for one at a certain time, when he or she is not aware of it and has no attitude toward it at the time. An event could be bad for one at some time, because it might be affecting one in ways of which one could become aware later. Toxic chemicals in the environment can be bad for people in case they affect them in ways they could experience later, even when they do not experience them at the time they are affected. From this truth, it does not follow that things can be bad for people without affecting them at all or without causing them to be in some condition or other. Human ignorance does not show that abstract evaluation is necessary.

It is useful to reflect on why people might react as they commonly do to the person trying to communicate with asparagus plants. Our judgments evaluating what people do are determined in part by estimates about what is possible and by values about what is worthwhile. These in turn are determined by the advance of science and by cultural conditions. The ground of our judging the life of the plant communicator negatively, even though we know he is enjoying his activities, is therefore complex. We might think his life bad based on what we commonly think a good life would be like. We might judge his efforts futile (because it is not possible to achieve his goal, based on current scientific information) or unworthy (because we would not see his project or any of its likely results as valuable). In either case, we might think his life bad in ways that he would not, given his different assessment of it.

When we are tempted to judge that the plant communicator's life is bad, now, for him, it may be because we think that his efforts will have some sort of negative effect on his life or because we think it plausible that he will later come to regret spending all that time on his project. In this case, the evaluation of his life as bad depends on effects on him, effects of which he can become aware and to which he can react. As such, we are really using the notion of concrete valuation to appraise his life, not the notion of abstract valuation, on which Nagel's argument relies. Consequently, unless an account of the case more favorable to Nagel's conclusion is plausible, this case should not convince us that we must use abstract valuation in assessing the value of events for given individuals.[14]

Nagel supplements his example by urging that a theory of value that "directly" accommodates the cases of unknown bads "would enable us to explain *why* their discovery [when previously unknown] causes suffering." His idea is that such undiscovered bads as deterioration provoke suffering or bad feelings when the person who undergoes them learns of them. They produce suffering, so the implicit hypothesis would go, on account of their being bad. And, of course, if they produce suffering on account of their being bad, then the suffering they cause then cannot be the source of their badness. Nagel's theory, or account, of the badness is that "most good and ill fortune has as its subject a person identified by his history and his possibilities, rather than merely by his categorical state of the moment—and that while this subject can be exactly located in a sequence of places and times, the same is not necessarily true of the goods and ills that befall him."[15] The explanation introduces abstract propositional value.[16]

This account of badness goes far beyond what is necessary to explain why people suffer when they learn of previously unknown bads. Nagel appears to suppose that the only way to explain why people feel bad when they discover such bads is to make the badness of the event or situation that is bad independent of experience, independent of all states of people at all times. All the theory would need to do would be to make badness independent of feelings of the sort that might be consequent, for example, upon the discovery of hitherto unknown deterioration. This might be done by some theory that attributed badness to effects on a person of a sort of which the person might not initially be aware, but might come to be aware under appropriate conditions. Since this could be true, the theory that good and bad for persons must be independent of all effects on a person is not justified by the need to explain badness independent of feelings. Nagel's argument is based on conflating effects on a person and feelings of a person.[17] A person might be affected at some particular time without having at that time feelings about being affected, either because the person is unaware of the effect or effects, or for some other reason.

Nagel's argument is weakened by its failure to accommodate an important fact about human psychology. When people learn of events and react emotionally to them, their reactions depend more on what they consciously or unconsciously believe or think about the happenings than about the nature of the events themselves, or about the effects of those events on others. This is something Stoics tried to teach us centuries ago. When, for example, someone does not succeed in getting a job which he or she wanted and for which he or she competed intensely, not getting the job might be bad for the person or it might not be, in some sense, depending on circumstances. On the other hand, how the person feels about not getting the job is determined by what he or she believes about not getting the job. If the applicant believes that not getting the job is evidence that his or her work is not well thought of, that other jobs may not be available, or that an impecunious future looms, then the person will react badly because of those beliefs and their implications. This does not show that the event of not getting the job is bad for the person in any other sense, as if somehow the badness attaches to the event itself. Not getting the job might even be good for her in some way that is independent of how she reacts to it, say, because of its further effects on her. Suggesting that we must (or should) account for why people suffer when they learn about previously unknown events on the basis of the badness of those events is to overlook this significant fact about human psychology. Nagel makes this mistake when he supposes that we can explain why deterioration causes suffering when it becomes known by saying that it is bad independent of the suffering. Because suffering is often due to beliefs and thoughts, he overlooks an indispensible factor in the occurrence of much human suffering. The suffering is due to the beliefs forming the framework in which it occurs, rather than to the badness of the event for the person, independent of effects on the person.

Nagel's paper on death has influenced many philosophers. His reasoning that death is bad because it deprives people of good has been the benchmark by which thinking about the value of death has been measured. Few philosophers have examined closely his attractive reasoning that things can be bad for people even though they can never be caused to be in negative conditions by those things. Reflection suggests, however, that the arguments he gives that there must be abstract value for people are not convincing. For all Nagel has given, we can do without abstract value.

Other philosophers, however, have used other reasons to insist that abstract valuation is essential to human value judgments, and considering those arguments is important. Arguing that things can be bad for people without causing "intrinsic bad" such as pain or dissatisfaction, Fred Feldman gives a couple of examples that are supposed to persuade one that there must be abstract bad for people, bad unassociated with conditions of people of which they can be aware. The examples are cases in which because of various circumstances, a person's life is less good than it would have been without those circumstances.[18] However much pleasure or satisfaction is associated with such circumstances, because of conditions of life structured around those circumstances, Feldman urges, those circumstances are bad for the people involved, even though they do not result in any pain or dissatisfaction, even though they have no effects. They are bad for the individuals because if they had not occurred, the individuals would have had better lives, perhaps by having more pleasure than they otherwise had. This is exemplified in the life of a person who is very happy and has developed an abidingly satisfyingly life, but who, because of normal circumstances, misses an opportunity that would make his or her life better. Suppose that the opportunity consists in a chance to meet some person who would enrich his or her life, or in a chance to take advantage of some educational program that would enhance the person's happiness. Missing the opportunity makes the individual's life less good than it would have otherwise been, even though the individual never believes that the opportunity passed and never believes that his or her life is deficient in any way. Missing the opportunity is bad for the person, Feldman thinks.

Feldman has interestingly captured how we sometimes think and feel about people's lives. We often appraise lives in light of how they might have developed if certain things had not happened, or if certain things had happened. We sometimes even feel sorry for people whose lives circumstances prevent from being what we think would be better. Such appraisals and sentiments would be arrested sharply, however, by the realization that those about whom we have such feelings will never be affected by the circumstances in question. Although we feel bad for a person some of whose important potentials are forever undeveloped because of circumstances, we react differently in those cases in which we know that a person can never be affected by the circumstances, in those cases in which we know that a person can be affected but can never realize what happened, and in those in which we know that a person can be affected and can realize what happened. The distinctions in these cases should affect how we regard Feldman's argument and the view of those who think virtually unqualifiedly that losses are bad for people. Suppose a person misses the opportunity to get a flu vaccination during the last day on which such vaccinations are available. In the situation in which a terrible flu epidemic will sicken many people and in which the person would have been immunized by the vaccination, it would have been better for the person to have been vaccinated. Her life would have been better, as some would think. Nevertheless, consider her failure to get a vaccination in three different circumstances.

In one case, she gets the flu, suffers, and realizes that if she had only organized her life better, she would have gotten a shot and been immune. This is the worst situation for her, assuming that no further misfortunes come from not having gotten the shot, and it would be appropriate to judge that not getting the flu shot was bad for her. However, the judgment in the case lends no support to the thesis that things can be bad for people without causing any bad effects on them. Not getting the flu immunization did have a bad effect on the person, in the sense that it constituted part of the causal conditions in which the person got the flu and suffered.

In another case, she gets the flu, suffers, and never realizes that she would have been able to be immune if she had just conducted her life differently. Maybe she is ignorant of the availability of flu immunizations. Again, her life would have been better if she had gotten the flu shot. Whether this is less bad for the person than the situation in which she both is affected and knows her role in being affected is not clear. Nevertheless, it does seem clear in this case also that not getting the shot contributes to causal conditions in which she later contracts the flu and is thus bad. It is bad in the literal sense in which something bad causes or constitutes bad effects on people. Consequently, this case provides no support for the view that things can be bad for people without having any effects at all on them. It does not support the notion of abstract propositional bad.

Finally, suppose someone fails to get the flu shot under similar circumstances. Assume, too, that those circumstances constitute causal conditions in which she would get the flu three months later, and that she in fact would get the flu. Clearly, her life would be better if she had had the vaccination. Imagine, however, that events occur that prevent from happening the conditions in which she would ordinarily get the disease. That is, imagine that other events intervene that prevent her from getting the flu. If, for example, she dies in an automobile accident one week after the date on which she could have gotten the shot and at a time before she would have gotten the flu, we would have a difficult time justifying the view that not getting the flu shot was bad for her, at least in any important sense. We would also have a difficult time feeling sorry for her that she did not get a flu shot. It would have been bad for her, if she had lived, but not otherwise. In any case, whoever would judge this to be bad for the person would not think it as bad as the first two situations.

Consideration of these cases undermines the argument that things can be bad for people without having any causal effects on them. The descriptions of those cases supposed to show that there must be abstract bad as well as concrete bad are usually flawed by a failure to make the distinctions suggested by these cases. Once the distinctions are made, however, such arguments as Feldman's may be seen as insufficient for showing that there must be abstract bad.[19] In fact, the multiple case of the unfortunate person who missed her flu immunization not only does not support the notion of abstract bad, but it reinforces the idea that real bad is concrete, at least in the most basic sense. Other examples would similarly cast doubt on the need for using abstract valuation to account for human value judgments.

One of the most original efforts to support abstract valuation and to divorce bad from causal effects is due to Harry Silverstein.[20] Focusing on the idea that death is bad for people, and committed to the rejection of the idea that death is not bad for people, he sees that the problem Epicurean reasoning presents for the common idea that death is indeed bad for people is that it assumes that anything that has value for a person must antedate his or her death, because only what occurs before a person's death can causally affect the person, and only what can causally affect a person can be good or bad for the person. Focusing on what he calls this "temporality assumption," that things valuable for people must have a specific temporal location, and yet at the same time believing that values must "connect with feelings," Silverstein holds that "*temporally* distant—and hence posthumous—events (states, objects, etc.) can coherently be accorded the same status . . . as spatially distant events," and be nevertheless linked in the right way with feelings.[21] Since he realizes that temporally distant—future—events cannot causally bring about feelings (or other causal effects) in the way Epicurus's denial of death's badness requires, he argues that Epicurus would not be able to cite the futurity of posthumous events as the ground on which they could not be bad for people. Thus he seems satisfied that placing time on the same footing as space will enable one to reject the Epicurean reason why death cannot be bad for people.[22]

The difficulty with Silverstein's proposal is that it does not constitute a good reason for rejecting the principle underlying concrete valuation. Concrete valuation requires that events not be good or bad for people unless those events have some (causal) effect on them. Arguing that future events can be the objects of people's thoughts, as Silverstein argues, does not by itself negate this requirement of concrete valuation. An event's being the object of a person's thoughts is independent of whether an event's affecting the person is required for it to have value for the person. People can think about events without being affected by them. So, to reason that because temporally distant (future) events exist on a kind of par with spatially distant (past and present) events and can thus be the objects of present thoughts is not to reason that they can cause present physiological or psychological conditions—that they can affect people—nor is it to show that things can be valuable for people without affecting them. Realizing this point, Silverstein implicitly endorses the idea of abstract valuation when he says that "what seems important in any case is not the event's being the *cause*, but its being the *object*, of this feeling."[23] He adopts the view that an event need not causally affect a person in order to have value for the person. However, in the context of taking seriously the question whether things can be bad for people without causally affecting them, the reasoning here is not convincing that there must be abstract valuation. It simply assumes the necessity of abstract valuation and thus implicitly avoids engaging the question dialectically. The assumption may be based on a strong desire to reject the Epicurean idea that death is not bad for people, but this desire does not make the assumption reasonable. One must look further for a justification for abstract valuation.

Unfortunately for the idea of abstract valuation, so widely assumed among philosophers, no other efforts to show that abstract valuation is necessary seem to be available. It is important, however, to take stock of the dialectical situation and assess what it would be appropriate to conclude. Concrete valuation is common, occurring predominately in human valuations. It seems impossible to do without the idea that events that causally affect people can be good and bad for people. Accordingly, propositions that are about such events can themselves have value for people, the value of such propositions deriving from the value of the correlative events. The prevalence of concrete valuation creates some presumption that value for people is restricted to what can affect them, including the conditions in which people can be affected. Realizing the currency of concrete valuation and perhaps the questionability of the occurrence of abstract valuation in human life, some philosophers have tried to argue that abstract propositional valuation is essentially involved in some value judgments. I have reviewed those arguments and have concluded that they do not show that abstract valuation, unconnected with events people can experience, is needed to account for what we say is good and bad for people.

Debating the necessity of a concept of value, of abstract valuation (propositional valuation not linked to concrete effects on people), may seem rather odd. After all, even if the concept were not necessary for many features of human evaluation, it might nevertheless be able to be used by people to capture what they want to express in some of their evaluations. It might strike one that concepts can after all be constructed, even if uncommon or inconsistent with more customary modes of valuation, and, having been constructed, might be employed as seems useful. Nothing is necessarily objectionable in such a practice. If the concept is clear, why should anyone object to use of the concept? There are at least two grounds on which one might suitably object to the use of a concept. One might object on the ground that the concept is unwittingly employed to avoid addressing some important questions, or to beg some significant philosophical question. One might worry additionally that the concept obscures some valuable philosophical insight.

That some people use an abstract notion of propositional valuation should perhaps not really be in question. What may be reasonably considered, however, is the use of the concept in relation to the notion of concrete valuation and in relation to human concerns and various issues concerning death and the fear of death. If there is abstract valuation, does it reveal something important about the evaluation of death, especially in relation to the idea of concrete valuation? Furthermore, does it shed light on various questions surrounding the human fear of death, as Aristotle implicitly thought it did?

If abstract propositional valuation were constructed merely as a way of supporting the idea that death is bad for people, then introducing the idea would unfortunately be question-begging, in the context in which one questions whether death is bad for people, for obvious reasons. The most common idea of concrete valuation does not support the thesis that death is bad for people, as Epicurus argued, and to introduce a new idea just for the sake of supporting that thesis, without further argument, would be to reason illegitimately and unconvincingly. This is perhaps why some philosophers who use the idea of abstract valuation feel compelled to argue that it is essential to various value judgments and is not just restricted to the subject of the badness of death. Although the arguments to this effect are unconvincing, one might judge that death is not bad in one sense, namely in regard to concrete valuation, but that it is bad in another sense, in regard to abstract propositional valuation. Two important questions remain, however, and should at least be addressed before the question of the value of death is merely left to rest on a casual choice between these two modes of valuation. How are these concepts related to the traditional question whether the fear of death is reasonable? What is the relative importance of these different concepts of value in human life and among human preferences? These are difficult questions, and they are not simple matters, capable of being resolved crisply. In the remaining part of this paper, I address these questions.

First, how do these ideas of value relate to what people value, what they find good and bad? More specifically, if there are these two types of value, is one more important to people than the other, or are they equally significant in human life? I do not think this question is capable of being given a definitive, final answer, because I think the answer depends on human interests, and those interests differ from one person to another. In this issue, it seems that proofs of general theses, to which so many philosophers seem attracted, may not be possible. Perhaps this is one of those issues on which Aristotle cautioned that we should not seek precision when it is not proper to expect precision. It may be enough to raise considerations on which people may reflect, so that they can assess their assumptions about value, for the purpose of weighing the two modes of valuation and deciding whether death is importantly bad for people.

A consideration of the relative importance of these two modes of valuation may be placed in the context of comparisons of possible choices of alternative circumstances in which the two kinds of value are present. For example, if, all else equal, people preferred avoiding an abstract propositional bad to avoiding a comparable degree of concrete bad, then one might reasonably say that people regarded the propositional bad as worse than the comparable concrete bad. Moreover, if they preferred acquiring a concrete good to acquiring a comparable abstract, propositional good, then one might say that they regarded the concrete good as more important. One difficulty with this approach, however, is that it would be very hard, if not impossible, to determine whether two different types of goods or bads were comparable in degree. Perhaps the very idea that one might be able to assign degrees of intensity, for example, to any types of good or bad is insupportable and perhaps as much a fiction as the idea that pleasures can be assigned precise degrees and compared on that basis. Nevertheless, some examples may shed some light on the issue, by enabling people to consider some comparisons.

Imagine that one would need to choose between two courses of life, equal except for the occurrence of different bad things. Each course of life would have one additional bad thing, with no compensating good. The only difference is the presence of different kinds of bad, and the bad things, suppose, are comparably intense, if that be plausible. Suppose that in one future course of life, the additional bad will be concrete; one will suffer a painful injury, with, of course, no compensating advantage. Imagine, too that in the other course of life, the additional bad will be an abstract propositional bad. Suppose the bad will be that it is true of one that one is betrayed by a close friend. But, remember, for the comparison to be fair, the betrayal, in order to be truly abstract, cannot affect the course of one's life in any way. One can never come to know about it, and one can never be affected in any way by it. Otherwise it would not be an abstract propositional bad; it would be concrete. My judgment is that most people would prefer the course of life with the abstract bad, which would suggest that people would not mind the abstract bad as much as they would mind the concrete bad. If this is true, concrete value may be more important than abstract value.

If people would judge differently, it might be because they cannot imagine truly abstract bad of the sort suggested. They may not be able to think of a betrayal without its ill effects. At least, when they imagine it, they may have a difficult time thinking of it without any ill effects. Wouldn't the person betrayed somehow find out, sooner or later? Wouldn't the betrayal have some sort of negative effect, sooner or later, an effect worse than the painful injury? If people would think thus about the betrayal, they would not be regarding it as an abstract bad, for a completely abstract propositional bad would not entail any negative states or conditions or causes of such negative states or conditions. Of course, one cannot be confident that all people would judge the case similarly. Some people may feel so strongly about loyalty (abstracted from its practical effects) that they would much prefer the course of life with the concrete bad to that in which the unknowable, unaffecting, and abstract bad would occur. I suspect that if people really understand this choice, they will not prefer the abstract bad to the concrete, but I do not know how to demonstrate this. In any case, I invite readers to reflect on this case and its significance.

One could easily imagine analogous choices involving good things, choices between a concrete good and an abstract propositional (unaffecting) good with no effects, thinking of all else being equal. Between two courses of life, differing only in the respect that one has a concrete good and the other an abstract good of comparable value, which course of life would be preferable? One would need to assume that the interest of the person living the life in at least one of the goods is greater than indifference. Otherwise, the goods might be comparable, but only in their indifference. Imagine that the concrete good is a pleasant and satisfying holiday with one's family, and suppose that the abstract good is it being a fact about one that one is admired (secretly) by some of the most prominent members of one's profession. The good is abstract in that one can never be affected by it in any way. Of course, these goods might not really be equally valuable to the person, but we should suppose that they are in order to make the proper comparison. I suppose that different people might decide the issue differently, but it seems to me that most people would choose the good that can affect them and that is associated with actual experiences they have, rather than the abstract good that can have no effects on them. Why would one even care about the admiration of members of one's profession, if it could not affect one, if one could never know about it, and if one could never have experiences caused by it? If people were attracted to the prospect of professional admiration, I suspect that it would be because of the positive effects they would conceive it to have on their lives. Maybe they would think of the resulting honors, promotions, and increased pay, but, if they were attracted on this basis, the good to which they would be attracted would not be abstract. It would be concrete.

There are many different types of comparison possible, and it would not be useful to introduce more comparisons or to attempt to catalogue the various comparisons. In light of the manifold possibilities, it seems futile to think of trying to supply a demonstration of some general thesis about the relative importance of these two modes of valuation in human life. These cases suggest, however, although they of course do not "prove," that things having value according to the concrete mode of valuation are more important than things having abstract, propositional value. At least the comparisons suggest further reflections by which people may appraise the relative significance of concrete value and abstract value.

Thinking about these two modes of value in the context of death may even more clearly suggest the greater importance of concrete value. In choosing physician-assisted suicide, as we have come to call it, or in choosing active euthanasia, people display a preference for avoiding concrete bad in preference to avoiding abstract bad. Such people choose to avoid pain and suffering at the cost of accepting the fact of dying at a particular time, with whatever abstract bads they conceive the acceptance of that fact to have. People who make that choice clearly feel that they would rather accept the evil of abstract bad than to endure the evil of concrete bad, assuming of course that they think of the choice in this way. Actually, however, people probably do not make the choice in these terms. When people face the choice of euthanasia, they probably weigh the concrete bad against the concrete good they expect in the remainder of their lives, assuming that they consider the question. The point, however, is that people are not usually deterred by the prospect of abstract bad in the quest for alleviating the pain and suffering of terminal disease. Furthermore, it seems to me doubtful that people would endure very much intense pain and suffering just for the sake of trying to avoid posthumous losses and related abstract bads.

We should remember that Freud, however, chose to suffer greatly in order to continue whatever satisfactions he believed would attach to the project of finishing some of his most important unfinished writing projects. He chose to forego analgesics for the sake of continuing as long as possible having a clear and intellectually productive head. I would challenge the idea that we should interpret this as showing that Freud thus was willing to accept abstract goods, such as the good of a great posthumous reputation, in preference to alleviating the bad of intense pain. A plausible alternative interpretation is that he chose the (concrete values and) satisfactions of clearheaded work, with the accompanying pain, instead of relief of the pain at the cost of foregoing work. This does not favor the idea that he preferred abstract, propositional value to concrete value, because he might well have gotten many concrete values from the work and might have believed that they outweighed the concrete disvalue of the pain.

The most important question about death in relation to the two modes of valuation is how they relate to the fear of death, since the badness of death has been supposed to be the basis for explaining the fear of death and deciding whether it is "rational." Aristotle believed that the fear of death was reasonable, because death is "the most terrible of all things," whereas Epicurus thought that the fear of death was groundless, given that "death is nothing to us" and not at all bad. One grand difficulty for addressing this question clearly, however, is that the fear of death has many faces, and is not distinct. Some people may fear nonexistence. Some may fear the pain of dying. Others might fear an unpleasant afterlife. There is no single concept of what the fear of death is. Moreover, there is no way this might be resolved in a brief few pages. One can here only consider what attitudes people might have in relation to death toward goods and bads in the different modes of valuation. Even then, it will not be clear what one should conclude generally. Nevertheless, some considerations may shed light on the issue.

It may be that abstract value, abstract bad in particular, is not generally the object of fear in the way that concrete bad is, and can be, the object of fear. Consider a paradigm abstract bad associated with death, and compare it to a paradigm concrete bad associated with death. Think of a situation in which after one dies, he or she is betrayed by loyal friends so that his or her good reputation is completely and irretrievably destroyed. Of course in this circumstance, the person plainly cannot experience or be affected by the fact that his or her reputation is destroyed, assuming that being dead entails being nonexistent. The person could think of it in advance but could not be affected by it. Thus, the evil, supposing it is an evil, would be an abstract, unaffecting evil. Is this evil the kind of object that would commonly generate fear? Under certain circumstances, it would generate some kinds of negative feelings. For example, if the event were to happen during one's lifetime, so that one could experience it and be affected by it, it would cause great distress. It might even cause fear, depending on how one thought one was going to be affected by it. However, these comments are premised on the idea that the evil is not an abstract evil, but rather a concrete, affecting one. Would the anticipation of the event, occurring after one's death, cause one to feel negative feelings appropriately called 'fear'? The answer to this would depend of what feelings of fear were, exactly. If fear were, by definition, as it were, a negative feeling caused by the thought or anticipation of some future pain or injury,[24] it does not seem as if this future, abstract, unaffecting bad would be the object of fear. It could not be associated with future pain or injury. Perhaps it could be an object of regret or some other such negative feeling, but it is difficult to see how it could be an object of fear, unless someone could believe of it that it would have a negative effect on him or her. This abstract bad seems not to be the kind of thing that could be the object of fear. Perhaps it might be the object of other kinds of negative feelings, but not an object that would justify or explain death anxiety. Of course, this idea should be qualified by the recognition that the notion of death anxiety is not clear and univocal. However, these considerations should at least cast doubt on the claim that the fear of death is linked to the kind of valuation implicitly used by Aristotelians in their discussions of why death is bad for people and why it is rational to fear death.

On the other hand, people are concerned about concrete bad, especially in the context of death. They are concerned about physical pain and psychological anguish associated with the process of dying. They may be concerned, as Epicurus believed people were, about an unpleasant afterlife. They seem clearly concerned about concrete bads and would thus be likely to be to some extent relieved if they knew that no concrete bad would attach to their dying or to their being dead. Of course, such knowledge may be beyond the reach of mortals, but the point is that human concerns about death may largely be about value in the concrete mode.

If abstract bad were not a proper object of death anxiety and people were more concerned to avoid concrete bad than to avoid abstract bad, then it appears that the Epicurean denial of the badness of death, using as it does a concrete mode of valuation, is more relevant to human concerns about death and value than the Aristotelian view. It more directly addresses human concerns about death, since people seem more concerned about concrete bads associated with death. To argue that death, being dead, is a state in which one cannot be affected and cannot have any experiences is to address the appraisal of death in a way that could undermine the fear of bad experiences connected with death and address value of the kind that most concerns people. Although the idea of abstract valuation may capture the way some regard value for some objects supposed to have value, it is worth considering the extent to which abstract propositional valuation can explain the badness of death in such a way as to justify or support the rationality of death anxiety. The fact that one dies at a certain time may well be bad for people according to the abstract propositional mode of valuation, but a fuller consideration of the axiological assumptions used in such a view provides reason to question whether that mode of valuation shows the badness of death in any sense relevant to human concerns.

Much more might be said about all of the issues I have considered in this paper, but it would be appropriate to end the discussion with a summary of the points I have made. Surprisingly, as I said at the outset, the Epicurean and Aristotelian views of death, supported by various different philosophers in the last twenty-five years, are strictly consistent, in the sense that neither is the negation of the other. They are consistent because they implicitly employ different, and consistent, notions of value, different modes of valuation. The Aristotelian view uses an abstract notion of valuation, whereas the Epicurean view uses a concrete mode of valuation, according to which things have value for people if those things affect the people in some ways. Any dispute between the two views must amount ultimately to a disagreement about whether there is only concrete value or both concrete value and abstract value. Alternatively, it might reflect a disagreement about which of the two modes of valuation is more important in human life, in assessments of the value of death, and in relation to death anxiety. Therefore, the real philosophical issue between the views is not which is better justified, but rather which is more closely related to human concerns about death. I have argued that there is some reason to believe that the Epicurean view is more relevant to human concerns about death. The reasons may not be conclusive, but they are sufficient to show that the ongoing debate about the badness of death for those who die is deeply connected to basic questions about value and about what kinds of things have value for people. Further conversation about the badness of death for people and about the fear of death should take place in the context of the realization that the discussion so far has not focused enough on these two modes of valuation.

NOTES

1. Aristotle, *Nicomachean Ethics* III, 1115a; Thomas Nagel, "Death," *Noûs 4* (1970), 73–80, reprinted in J. M. Fischer, *The Metaphysics of Death* (Stanford, Calif.: Stanford University Press, 1993), 61–69; Martha C. Nussbaum, "Mortal Immortals: Lucretius against the Fear of Dying," *Philosophy and Phenomenological Research* 50 (1989), 303–351; Harry Silverstein, "The Evil of Death," in Fischer, 95–116; Jeff McMahan, "Death and the Value of Life," in Fischer, 231–266; Anthony Brueckner and J. M. Fischer, "Why Is Death Bad?" in Fischer, 219–229; Fred Feldman, *Confrontations with the Reaper* (Oxford: Oxford University Press, 1992), esp. pp. 127–156; *et alia*.

2. O. H. Green, "Fear of Death," *Philosophy and Phenomenological Research* 43, 99–105; Stephen E. Rosenbaum, "How to Be Dead and Not Care: A Defense of Epicurus," reprinted in Fischer, 119–134; and Rosenbaum, "Epicurus and Annihilation," reprinted in Fischer, 293–304.

3. If 'death' means something else, then of course Aristotle's reasoning might not seem so puzzling. I will argue that Aristotle must have meant something else.

4. If Aristotle meant by 'death' the dying process, his argument would make no sense, the conclusion then being logically unrelated to the premise. If he meant by 'death' the moment of death, then, although the argument would make sense, it would need further explanation. Even so, it would not clearly relate to the Epicurean point.

5. Aristotle might have thought just that death is bad, but not for the one who dies. Whatever this might mean, it also is not inconsistent with the idea that death is not bad *for the dead*.

6. Aristotle, *Nicomachean Ethics* III, 1115a.

7. Epicurus, *Letter to Menoiceus*, Diogenes Laertius, X, 125.

8. Facts, whatever they are, are commonly taken to be timeless or eternal. See, for example, George Pitcher, "The Misfortunes of the Dead," in Fischer, 157–168.

9. Nagel, "Death," 64, in Fischer.

10. Nagel, "Death," 64–65, in Fischer. Nagel also says that the "fact" that a person's life is over and that there will never be any more of it, "rather than his past or present condition, constitutes his misfortune, if it is one" (67 in Fischer).

11. See, for example, Rosenbaum's "How to Be Dead and Not Care," in Fischer.

12. See Harry Silverstein's "The Evil of Death," in Fischer.

13. Of course, such remote events might have indirect and long-term effects, and thus have value for people affected.

14. See Silverstein's discussion of Nagel and what Silverstein calls the principle that "values connect with feelings," in "The Evil of Death," in Fischer.

15. Nagel, "Death," 65, in Fischer.

16. Although there might be different specific versions of abstract propositional value, there is no need to distinguish different versions, since the issue concerns the acceptability of abstract propositional value of any sort.

17. The conflation is also sponsored by Nagel's critics. See, for example, Silverstein, in his discussion in "The Evil of Death," in Fischer.

18. Fred Feldman, *Confrontations with the Reaper*, 137–142.

19. For further discussion of Feldman's arguments, see Stephen Rosenbaum's review of *Confrontations with the Reaper*, in *Philosophy and Phenomenological Research* 60, no. 1 (1995), 233–237.

20. Silverstein's "The Evil of Death," 95–116, in Fischer.

21. Silverstein "The Evil of Death," 109, in Fischer.

22. Silverstein's idea has been discussed critically by Palle Yourgrau, in "The Dead," 141–142, in Fischer.

23. Silverstein, "The Evil of Death," 110, in Fischer.
24. As Aristotle thought it was, in *Rhetoric*, II, 5 (1382a).

Midwest Studies in Philosophy, XXIV (2000)

"For Now Have I My Death"[1]: The "Duty to Die" versus the Duty to Help the Ill Stay Alive

FELICIA ACKERMAN

For the last three days he screamed incessantly. It was unendurable. I cannot understand how I bore it; you could hear him three rooms off. Oh, what I have suffered![2]

I

Suppose you are a sixty-year-old who has worked hard and made sacrifices for your family. Now you are ill and the care necessary to keep you alive is taking up a lot of time and money, including almost all your spouse's free time and much of the money you previously set aside for your child's college education. You and your family still love one another, but you all have strong self-interested desires as well. You want to stay alive as long as possible. Your spouse, a dedicated amateur athlete who used to spend much time playing tennis, is tired of being your caregiver. Your child wants to go to college. Who has a duty to do what? Here are four possible answers.

1. You have a duty to die (possibly including a duty to commit suicide) in order to avoid burdening your family.

2. Your spouse has a duty to accept the loss of leisure time and take care of you (that is why "in sickness and in health" is in the marriage vows) and your child has a duty to accept the loss of your financial contribution to his education, in order to avoid burdening you with the premature loss of your life.

3. Either course of action can be justified; it is not a matter of duty.

4. It depends.

John Hardwig has recently argued in favor of (1), at least in some circumstances. This paper will criticize his views and argue for alternatives.

One way Hardwig seeks to support his view is by pointing out that

> [m]any older people report that their one remaining goal in life is not to be a burden to their loved ones. Young people feel this, too: when I ask my undergraduate students to think about whether their death could come too late, one of their very first responses always is, "Yes, when I become a burden to my family or loved ones."[3]

Hardwig thinks this reflects "moral wisdom."[4] He does not consider the possibility that it reflects our society's bias against systematic devaluation of the old and ill, a devaluation some old people accept uncritically, just as many women used to accept the idea that women should be subordinate to men. After all, it would hardly be surprising to discover that fifty years ago, most married women reported that they did not want careers that would burden their families. But people (or at least liberals) nowadays would have second thoughts about calling this moral wisdom, let alone using it to support an argument that married women had a duty to avoid careers that would burden their families. We now recognize two factors. First, fifty years ago there was so much social pressure on married women, if they worked outside the home at all, not to let their work inconvenience their families that any woman who dissented from this outlook risked being instantly condemned as selfish (which is not to deny that some women genuinely felt this way). Second, there was bias involved in seeing women's careers, but not men's, as a burden to their families. Many people recognize these things nowadays. But how many recognize that the same factors apply to Hardwig's uncritical report of present-day expressions of attitudes toward old age and illness? To illustrate the first factor, imagine the social reaction to a sick old person who said, "I'm sorry if it burdens my family, but my life comes first." The fact that sick old people do make "burdensome" choices often enough to give the question of a duty to die practical as well as theoretical interest suggests that many of the old and ill are less self-sacrificing than the sentiments they pay lip service to may suggest. To illustrate the second factor, consider the (deliberate) oddness of my formulation of (2), above. Sick old people are routinely called burdens to their families, but college-bound teenagers are not. It is surprising that someone who believes "life without connection is meaningless"[5] would think it shows moral wisdom for people to talk as though they did not realize that accepting the burdens of taking care of one another is part of what a family is all about. If Hardwig really holds, as much of his writing claims, the more moderate position that there are *limits* to the burdens families can be expected to assume (although I will argue that his limits are unacceptably stringent), then why does he think it shows moral wisdom to speak as though any burden, no matter how small, would be unacceptable?

Similar concerns apply to Hardwig's use of such loaded words as 'individualistic' and 'selfish.' I doubt that anyone actually believes what he condemns as "the individualistic fantasy . . . that the patient is the only one affected by decisions about her medical treatment."[6] And few would find fault, except on grounds of triteness, with his claim that "[t]hose of us with families and loved ones always have a duty not to make selfish . . . decisions about our lives."[7] We normally use the pejorative term 'selfish' only for things we want to condemn. But in order to see what sorts of decisions Hardwig condemns as selfish or unduly individualistic, we must look at the family burdens he thinks can give rise to a duty to die. He says:

> The lives of our loved ones can be seriously compromised by caring for us. The burdens of providing care or even just supervision twenty-four hours a day, seven days a week are often overwhelming. When this kind of caregiving goes on for years, it leaves the caregiver exhausted, with no time for herself of life of her own. Ultimately, even her health is often destroyed. But it can also be emotionally devastating simply to live with a spouse who is increasingly distant, uncommunicative, unresponsive, foreign, and unreachable. Other family members' needs often go unmet as the caring capacity of the family is exceeded. Social life and friendships evaporate, as there is no opportunity to go out to see friends and the home is no longer a place suitable for having friends in.

> We must also acknowledge that the lives of our loved ones can be devastated just by having to pay for health care for us. One part of [a] recent . . . study documented the financial aspects of caring for a dying member of a family. Only those who had illnesses severe enough to give them less than a 50 percent chance to live six more months were included in this study. When these patients survived their initial hospitalization and were discharged about one-third required considerable caregiving from their families; in 20 percent of cases a family member had to quit work or make some other major lifestyle change; almost one-third of these families lost all of their savings; and just under 30 percent lost a major source of income.

> If talking about money sounds venal or trivial, remember that much more than money is normally at stake here. When someone has to quit work, she may well lose her career. Savings decimated late in life cannot be recouped in the few remaining years of employability, so the loss compromises the quality of the rest of the caregiver's life. For a young person, the chance to go to college may be lost to the attempt to pay debts due to an illness in the family, and this decisively shapes an entire life.[8]

These remarks cry out for critical examination. For one thing, Hardwig's conception of what can constitute an unacceptable family burden seems astonishingly weak. Several questions immediately arise. Should being "distant, uncommunicative, unresponsive, foreign, and unreachable" really be a capital offense anywhere, let alone in a "loving" family? Does a loving family really welcome a beloved member's suicide in order to keep a young person from having to work and/or borrow his way through college? Does the view that you have a duty to spend your hard-earned money to put your able-bodied child through college rather than to prolong your own life reflect a devaluation of the old and the ill that will someday be as offensive to liberals as 1950s attitudes toward women are today?

Hardwig's bias is also reflected in his failure to extend his criticism of selfishness and individualism to a teenager's decision to accept the college tuition money that could be used to extend his father's life or to a husband's self-interested encouragement of the suicide of his ailing wife. Such failure illustrates how terms like 'selfish' and 'individualistic' can serve in a worldview promoting not altruism, but the favoring of the interests of some *individuals* over those of others. Hardwig says, "We fear death too much."[9] But to the extent that his views are widespread, I think that what we fear too much is having our lives and plans disrupted by the medical needs of our loved ones. This fear may cause us to magnify such disruptions out of proportion, to the point where having to work and borrow one's way through college or live with a distant and uncommunicative spouse seems so terrible that the sick person's death seems preferable and perhaps even obligatory.

There are other elements of bias in the quoted passage. The burden of providing "care or even just supervision twenty-four hours a day, seven days a week," far from being unbearable or unique to caretakers of the ill, is routine for many stay-at-home single mothers of babies and toddlers (and for stay-at-home married mothers with unhelpful husbands).[10] It is likewise common for "a family member [to have] to quit work or make some other major lifestyle change" or for a family to lose "a major source of income" when a baby is born. (Of course, people are aware of such needs when they choose to have children, but people who choose to marry are likewise aware of the strong possibility that their spouse will someday be ill and need care. I will discuss this matter more in the next section.) And Hardwig's claim that "[s]ocial life and friendships evaporate, as there is no opportunity to go out to see friends and the home is no longer a place suitable for having friends in" raises three questions. First, hasn't Hardwig ever heard of the telephone or e-mail? Why is he so ready to see the hardships of taking care of a sick person as reasons why that sick person has a duty to die, rather than as practical problems open to practical remedies? Second, precisely why is a home with a seriously ill person "no longer a place suitable for having friends in"? Suppose that person is unpredictable and incontinent. Is a home with a rambunctious toddler who is not yet toilet trained no longer a suitable place for having friends in? Third, does a loving spouse really welcome the suicide of a beloved partner in order to preserve the spouse's social life? What sort of values and what sort of love would this priority indicate?

The foregoing may make Hardwig look like a bigot with respect to age and health. So it is important to consider other aspects of his arguments, including the following case:

> An 87-year-old woman was dying of congestive heart failure. [The prognosis was] that she had less than a 50 percent chance to live for another six months. She was lucid, assertive, and terrified of death. She very much wanted to live and kept opting for rehospitalization and the most aggressive life-prolonging treatment possible. That treatment successfully prolonged her life (though with increasing debility) for nearly two years. Her 55-year-old daughter was her only remaining family, her caregiver, and the main source of her financial support. The daughter duly cared for her mother. But before her mother died, her illness had cost the daughter all of her savings, her home, her job, and her career.[11]

I will return to this case after looking at some general features of Hardwig's views.

II

Hardwig's approach has one great strength: he acknowledges the existence of genuine conflicts of interest between patients and their families. This contrasts favorably with the sentimentality of the hospice approach, on which "[p]atients, their families and loved ones are the unit of care."[12] In contrast, Hardwig points out that "[t]he conflicts of interests, beliefs, and values among family members are often too real and too deep to treat all members as 'the patient.'"[13] He also refuses to hide behind the claim that many of the conditions he thinks can generate a duty to die can also impair patients' lives to the point where they have self-interested reasons for wanting to die. He recognizes that the most problematic cases are those where the burdensome patient wants to live.[14] I follow him in focusing on such cases. In fact, unless otherwise specified, I assume as a background condition that the patient *greatly* wants to stay alive, and that the family's competing wants are equally strong.

Elsewhere, however, Hardwig is not so clearheaded. He uses the phrase 'duty to die' indiscriminately to apply to a duty to eschew aggressive life-prolonging medical care and a duty to commit suicide.[15] He holds that "[t]here can be a duty to die before one's illness would cause death, even if treated only with palliative measures,"[16] and that "there may be a fairly common responsibility to end one's life in the absence of any terminal illness at all,"[17] and he offers a detailed discussion of whether a person with a duty to die should carry out his own suicide or solicit suicide assistance from his loving family or from doctors.[18]

Hardwig's use of the phrase 'duty to die' to cover both a duty to commit suicide and a duty to eschew aggressive life-prolonging medical treatment leads him to exaggerate the originality and daringness of his position. The view that sick people can have a duty to commit suicide may indeed strike people as "just too preposterous to entertain. Or too threatening."[19] But this is hardly true of the view that the old and/or terminally ill have a duty not to burden their families and society by insisting on the most aggressive life-prolonging treatment possible, regardless of financial and other costs. This latter view is popular nowadays to the point of cliché. It occurs with varying degrees of explicitness in numerous newspaper and magazine pieces, as well as in highly praised, widely read, and widely influential books by Daniel Callahan[20] and Sherwin B. Nuland,[21] the latter a National Book Award winner. The *denial* of this latter view is what strikes people as "just too preposterous to entertain. Or too threatening." (When did you last hear anyone, bioethicist or otherwise, say that terminally ill old people are entitled to extend their lives as long as possible and by the most aggressive care possible, regardless of the cost to their families and society?)[22] Hardwig is conventional, not original, when he says that "we must now face the fact: deaths that come too late are only the other side of our miraculous, life-prolonging modern medicine."[23] What is amazing is his claim (in 1996!) that "[w]e have so far avoided looking at this dark side of our medical triumphs."[24]

Unsurprisingly, Daniel Callahan, who is hostile to aggressive life-extending care for the old and ill but to whom suicide is anathema, has criticized Hardwig's moral equation of suicide and the refusal of aggressive life-prolonging medical care. Since I accept neither Callahan's views about suicide nor his views about aggressive life-prolonging medical care, I will not defend this sort of criticism. Instead, I find Callahan and Hardwig similar in the low value they place on the lives of the old and the ill. Callahan's objection to Hardwig that

> it trivializes the relationship of family members to each other to act as if their mutual obligations to each other are to be judged by some benefit-burden calculus. Hardwig seems to be saying in effect: "for better or worse, in sickness and in health—well, sort of, it all depends"[25]

should be read in light of things he says elsewhere. For example:

> It is not improper for people to worry about being a burden on their families. . . . A family member should reject [a technologically extended death] for the sake of the family's welfare after he or she is gone.[26]

Callahan even says that "the *primary* aspiration of the old [should be] to serve the young."[27] He also says, "We do not need a . . . set of moral values that will impose upon families the drain of extended illness and death."[28] (Note the bias in Callahan's use of "we" here. Who are the "we" who do not need such a set of moral values? Families eager to free themselves of burdensome sick "loved ones" do not need such a set of moral values, but the sick people themselves may, if they want to stay alive. What "we" (i.e., such actual and potential sick people) do not need is a set of moral values that impose on us the drain of being pressured to forgo high-tech life-extending care and die sooner than necessary, in order to avoid burdening our families—a description of the situation that is no more biased than Callahan's own. "We" old people also do not need a set of moral values that tell us our primary aspiration should be to serve the young.) Callahan's real objection thus seems to be to suicide, rather than to a benefit-burden calculation.[29] In contrast, I have only a practical reason for finding Hardwig's views about the duty to commit suicide more objectionable than Callahan's views about the duty to refuse aggressive life-prolonging medical care: the former duty casts a much wider net. This paper will not distinguish further between these two possible duties, but will follow Hardwig's practice of using 'duty to die' to apply indiscriminately to both.

Hardwig's second conflation is also interesting. He makes no distinction between the duty to die in order to avoid burdening your children and the duty to die in order to avoid burdening your spouse. (Interestingly, none of his examples mentions young adults with a duty to die in order to avoid burdening their caregiving parents.) But there are obvious differences between parental and "adult child" cases, on the one hand, and spousal cases on the other. Parents have often made great sacrifices for their children, including an approximation of the hyperbolically described "twenty-four hours a day, seven days a week" care that Hardwig considers so onerous in the case of the old and the ill. There is a large literature on what, if anything, grown children owe their parents, but, to my mind, nothing that refutes Joel Feinberg's "My benefactor once freely offered me his services when I needed them.

... But now circumstances have arisen in which he needs help, and I am in a position to help him. Surely I *owe* him my services now, and he would be entitled to resent my failure to come through."[30] He would also be entitled to resent my hypocrisy if I claimed to love him. (What if I have significant obligations elsewhere? This issue will be touched upon later.)

Marriages differ from parent-child relationships in two ways that are relevant here. First, they do not normally begin with a long period of one-sided caregiving, let alone one-sided caregiving by the party most likely to need care later on. Second, marriages are freely entered into by both parties. This gives couples the opportunity for prenuptial discussions and agreements that will generate their own agreed-upon caregiving duties. Of course, such an approach has its own problems. The first, which also applies to living wills, is that it may be virtually impossible for many healthy young people to enter imaginatively into hypothetical situations in which they would be seriously ill and debilitated. As Ellen Goodman puts it, "No one . . . wants to live to be senile. But once senile, he may well want to live."[31] The second problem, which also applies to prenuptial financial agreements, is that such an arrangement may seem cold-blooded and destructive to the loving spirit of the marriage. Hardwig also advocates discussions in families. He even advocates having them once a person is ill, which avoids the first problem and enables people to consider the "particular and contextual"[32] details of their actual situation. But it enormously intensifies the second problem. Hardwig's sentimental claim that "[h]onest talk about difficult matters almost always strengthens relationships"[33] raises the question of just how it would strengthen a relationship to say to your father, even in response to his query, "Well, Dad, you're not pleasant to have around anymore, and if you don't die soon, your care will use up all the money you saved for my college education, so I'd really appreciate it if you killed yourself now or at least stopped getting treatment." This may be a crude formulation, but what could be a better one of such a crude thought? The plain fact is that letting your father know you value his life less than your college tuition is unlikely to strengthen your relationship. It is surprising that someone hard-headed enough to see that the slogan "the patient is the family" glosses over genuine conflicts of interest (see the material leading up to note 13) would slip into the senti-mentality of supposing that honest discussion of such conflicts will almost always strengthen relationships. Prenuptial agreements may seem cold-blooded, but at least they do not involve the cruelty of telling a sick and vulnerable person that you would welcome his death. Prenuptial discussions also give a couple the option of calling off the wedding if they find that their values are too far apart.

III

Hardwig realizes that a duty to die may seem harsh. "And yet," he says, "a duty to die will not always be as harsh as we might assume. If I love my family, I will want to protect them and their lives. I will not want to make choices that compromise their futures."[34] But if he loves his ill wife, will he want to protect her and her life? Will he want to avoid compromising her future by encouraging her to commit suicide so he will be free of the burden of caregiving? Hardwig says that "there is something deeply insulting in . . . an ethic that . . . [treats] me as if I had no moral responsibilities when I am ill or debilitated."[35] Will he also be insulted if his ill wife commits suicide because she thinks he is the sort of person who would rather have her dead than take care of her? I would be enormously insulted if a loved one had such a view of me. Hardwig tells us that his "own grandfather committed suicide after his heart attack as a final gift to his wife—he had plenty of life insurance but not nearly enough health insurance, and he feared that she would be left homeless and destitute if he lingered on in an incapacitated state."[36] Hardwig does not tell us whether his grandmother appreciated this "gift." What sort of person would she be if she did? If she welcomed this sacrifice, how could she be worth it? What sort of love could she have felt for her husband? What sort of love could he have thought she felt for him? And was there no one else in this loving family who could help his grandmother so she would not have to be left "homeless and destitute" if her husband lingered on?

This brings me to a discussion of what I have elsewhere called "the paradox of the selfless invalid."[37] In its most extreme form, the paradox goes as follows. Either the patient's loved ones want him to die quickly in order to save money or otherwise make their lives easier, or they do not. If they do not, the patient does not respect them by dying for their sake. If they do, then why is the patient sacrificing what would otherwise be left of his life for people who love him so little that they value his life less than money and/or freedom from encumbrance? Wouldn't a truly loving family find such a sacrifice appalling? Of course, families can have mixed feelings, which include both the desire to have the patient stay alive and the self-interested desire to get it all over with and to keep expenses down.[38] But the basic point remains. Decent and loving families, as part of their decency and lovingness, will recognize the latter desire as ignoble and, on balance, will not want patients to pander to it.

This extreme view is itself open to objections. Just as it is inhumane to suppose a sick person has a duty to forgo an extra year of life in order to conserve money for a child's college tuition, it is unreasonable to suppose there are no limits to what a loving family can be expected to do for a sick member, even to the point of selling literally everything they own in order to give him a minute of extra life. The devil is in the details, or, as Hardwig puts it, "the really serious moral questions are . . . how far family and friends can be asked to support and sustain the patient."[39] I have argued that some of Hardwig's answers are ludicrous. Where should we draw the line? I hardly have an exact answer, nor does Hardwig. But here are his general guidelines.

1) A duty to die is more likely when continuing to live will impose significant burdens—emotional burdens, extensive caregiving, destruction of life plans, and yes, financial hardship—on your family and loved ones. This is the fundamental insight underlying a duty to die.

2) A duty to die becomes greater as you grow older. As we age, we will be giving up less by giving up our lives, if only because we will sacrifice fewer remaining years of life and a smaller portion of our life plans. After all, it's not as if we would be immortal and live forever if we could just manage to avoid a duty to die. To have reached the age of, say, seventy-five or eighty years

without being ready to die is itself a moral failing, the sign of a life out of touch with life's basic realities.

3) A duty to die is more likely when you have already lived a full and rich life. You have already had a full share of the good things life offers.

4) There is a greater duty to die if your loved ones' lives have already been difficult or impoverished, if they have had only a small share of the good things that life has to offer (especially if through no fault of their own).

5) A duty to die is more likely when your loved ones have already made great contributions—perhaps even sacrifices—to make your life a good one. Especially if you have not made similar sacrifices for their well-being or for the well-being of other members of your family.

6) To the extent that you can make a good adjustment to your illness or handicapping condition, there is less likely to be a duty to die. A good adjustment means that smaller sacrifices will be required of loved ones and there is more compensating interaction for them. Still, we must also recognize that some diseases—Alzheimer [*sic*] or Huntington [*sic*] chorea—will eventually take their toll on your loved ones no matter how courageously, resolutely, even cheerfully you manage to face that illness.

7) There is less likely to be a duty to die if you can still make significant contributions to the lives of others, especially your family. The burdens to family members are not only or even primarily financial, neither are the contributions to them. However, the old and those who have terminal illnesses must also bear in mind that the loss their family members will feel when they die cannot be avoided, only postponed.

8) A duty to die is more likely when the part of you that is loved will soon be gone or seriously compromised. Or when you soon will no longer be capable of giving love. Part of the horror of dementing disease is that it destroys the capacity to nurture and sustain relationships, taking away a person's agency and the emotions that bind her to others.

9) There is a greater duty to die to the extent that you have lived a relatively lavish lifestyle instead of saving for illness or old age. . . . It is a greater wrong to come to your family for assistance if your need is the result of having chosen leisure or a spendthrift lifestyle.[40]

I suggest we reconceptualize the problem by asking how these and related conditions might affect the duty to make sacrifices in order to extend the life of a burdensomely ill loved one. I will call this "a duty to aid." Here are nine conditions parallel to Hardwig's.

1. A duty to aid is more likely when failing to do so will impose significant burdens, when the ill loved one wants very much to go on living and needs your help. This is the fundamental insight underlying a duty to aid.

2. Perhaps a duty to aid becomes greater as you grow older, because you will be sacrificing a smaller portion of your life plans. Alternatively, a duty to aid may be greater when you are young, because you have more stamina as well as more life ahead of you, with more opportunity to recoup your losses. At any rate, to have reached adulthood without being ready to undertake major financial burdens and changes in "lifestyle" in order to aid a seriously ill loved one is itself a moral failing, a sign of a life out of touch with life's basic realities.

3. A duty to aid is more likely when you have already lived a full and rich life. You have already had a full share of the good things life offers.

4. There is a greater duty to aid if your ill loved one's life has already been difficult or impoverished, if he has had only a small share of the good things that life has to offer (especially if through no fault of his own).

5. A duty to aid is more likely when your loved one has already made great contributions—perhaps even sacrifices—to make your life a good one. Especially if you have not made similar sacrifices for his well-being. This imbalance frequently exists between grown children and the parents who raised them.

6. To the extent that there are others able to share the burden of aiding, there is less you have a duty to do. To the extent that you cannot make a good adjustment to the duty of aiding, there is less of a duty to aid. Still, we must also recognize that unwillingness to make a good adjustment does not constitute inability to do so, nor does making a good adjustment mean you must enjoy aiding.

7. There is less of a duty to aid if you have significant obligations elsewhere. However, you must also bear in mind that your obligations to your children do not automatically outweigh your obligations to your parents. The popular slogan "The best thing you can do for your parents is to take good care of their grandchildren" is obviously false if your father needs and wants a heart transplant, which he cannot afford without your help, and your son "needs" and wants four years at Yale.

8. A duty to aid is more likely when your loved one is painfully aware that the part of him that was loved will soon be gone or seriously compromised and is terrified that his loved ones will abandon him. And if you genuinely love your "loved one," then to the extent that the part that is loved is *not* compromised, you will have a strong self-interested reason for wanting to help him stay alive; you would hate never seeing him again.

9. There is a greater duty to provide physical care to the extent that you have lived a relatively lavish "lifestyle" that has prevented you from saving enough to provide financial help.

These guidelines are not formally incompatible with Hardwig's. He grants that families "must be prepared to make significant sacrifices to respond to an illness in the family,"[41] although his examples I quoted earlier of what can constitute an intolerable family burden raise the question of just what sort of "significant sacrifices" he has in mind. His statement "I cannot imagine that it would be morally permissible for me to . . . compromise the quality of [my grandchildren's] lives simply because I wish to live a little longer"[42] illustrates the importance of this question. What deprivation could *not* be said to compromise the quality of one's grandchildren's lives? Going without private schooling? Going without summer camp? Going without tennis lessons? At any rate, my guidelines and Hardwig's reflect (although they do not entail) different orientations. Hardwig believes we can find meaning in death by recognizing our duty to die, thus engaging in an "affirmation of connections."[43] I am less inclined to find meaning in death at all. I find Malory's "Let me lie down and wail with you"[44] a much more humane response to adversity than today's relentless tendency to insist we turn adversity into an opportunity for "growth," a tendency Hardwig at any rate follows very selectively. His selectivity reflects his characteristic bias. After all, if we are going to urge people to regard death and dying as opportunities for growth and "affirmation of connections," why not urge families to seize the opportunity to grow and "affirm connections" by making loving sacrifices to prolong the life of a seriously ill loved one? Hardwig says, "Caring for the sick or aged can foster growth. . . . But it would be irresponsible to blithely assume that this always happens, that it will happen in my family, or that it will be the fault of my family if they cannot manage to turn my illness into a positive experience."[45] He does not criticize such unsuccessful families for having a "sense of community [that] is so weak."[46] He reserves this harsh judgment for old and/or ill people who are unwilling to unburden their families by dying (although he does grant that "[a] man who can leave his wife the day after she learns she has cancer, on the grounds that he has his own life to live, is to be deplored").[47]

Hardwig's guidelines, as well as his whole approach, raise another question. Why does he fail to consider cases where the sacrificial suicide of someone who is healthy and far from old could benefit his (not overly) loving family? Suppose you are a forty-year-old mid-level executive who has been downsized. The only job you can get pays the minimum wage, not enough to support your family, even with the added income of your wife, who now has to work fifty hours a week as a home health aide, doing the caregiving Hardwig finds so onerous when done for a family member. Your family is about to lose their home; you will all have to move to a rat-infested apartment in an unsafe inner-city neighborhood. "For [your children], the chance to go to college [will] be lost"[48] (if we assume, as Hardwig inexplicably does in cases involving illness, that young people's working and/or borrowing their way through college is not an option). There is, however, a solution. Like Hardwig's grandfather, you have excellent life insurance. (If your life insurance has the common two-year "suicide clause" denying payment if the insured person commits suicide within two years of purchasing the policy, that clause has long since expired.) In accord with Hardwig's guidelines, we can build in that your life so far has been rich and full, your wife has had a difficult, impoverished childhood, and your family has made sacrifices for your career (your wife sacrificed her own career and also spent much time in the tedious pseudosocializing necessary to further your ambitions, and your children endured the dislocation of frequent moves). We can even say that you lost your job not through downsizing but through your own fault and that you have little in the way of savings because you lived a "relatively lavish lifestyle instead of saving." Would Hardwig then say you could have a duty to commit suicide instead of burdening your family by depriving them of your life insurance money? If not, why not?

Like Hardwig, I cannot lay down a series of precise rules saying who owes whom what when a sick family member needs care. In Hardwig's case of the eighty-seven-year-old woman, for example, I think much hinges on her prior relationship with her daughter. How much did that mother sacrifice for her daughter? Did the mother pay, and make sacrifices to pay, for the education that enabled the daughter to have the career Hardwig is so distressed about her losing? What was their relationship like once the daughter grew up? Did the mother, like many parents nowadays, give her daughter some of the money that enabled the daughter to buy the home Hardwig is so distressed about her losing? What happened after the mother died? Did the daughter ever find another job? Hardwig does not tell us any of these things.[49] But I think it is clear that in my own example with which I opened this paper, alternative (2) is the right answer. A teenager should work and borrow his way through college in order to free up money to prolong the life of a beloved parent who raised him and sacrificed for him. A spouse should forgo tennis (even if it is not a trivial recreation but an important part of his life) in order to take care of the beloved partner "that he promised his faith unto."[50] "Sometimes, it's simply the only loving thing to do."[51]

NOTES

1. Sir Thomas Malory, *Le Morte D'Arthur* (London: Penguin, 1969), v.2, 515. As for the subtitle, for simplicity of exposition I will focus my discussion on the ill and their families. But note that the same issues can arise when people are severely enough disabled to need care, even when the disability arises not from illness, but from some other source, such as an injury. (Some disability rights activists set great store by the fact that they are disabled, not ill, and feel insulted when considered on a par with the ill. For examples of this attitude, see Joseph Shapiro, *No Pity* [New York: Times Books, 1993, 21, 22, and 49]. I consider this attitude to be morally on a par with that of a dark-skinned Caucasian who sets great store by the fact that he is white and feels insulted when considered on a par with blacks.)

2. Leo Tolstoy, *The Death of Ivan Ilych* (New York: New American Library of World Literature, 1960), 10. Tolstoy, of course, intended this remark (by a cancer patient's widow) to show monumental selfishness and callousness.

3. John Hardwig, "Is There a Duty to Die?" *Hastings Center Report* 27, no. 2 (1997), 36.

4. John Hardwig, "Dying at the Right Time: Reflections on (Un)assisted Suicide," in Hugh La Follette (ed.), *Ethics in Practice* (Cambridge, MA: Blackwell, 1996), 54.

5. Hardwig, "Is There a Duty to Die?" 41. Hardwig's book, *Is There a Duty to Die? and Other Essays in Bioethics* (New York: Routledge, 2000), was published too late for general discussion in this paper, but I will be reviewing it in a forthcoming issue of the *American Philosophical Association Newsletter on Philosophy and Medicine*. One point can be mentioned here, though. Hardwig praises a list of "Responsibilities of Those Facing the End of Life" (ibid., 197–99) compiled by a group of old people in a discussion he led. One item on the list is "Don't live so long that your loved ones will wish you were dead" (198). This treats life as a dinner party where the "loved ones" are hosts and the elderly are guests who should not be so rude as to overstay their welcome. Note that the complete lack of qualification entails that the elderly should honor *every* reason their loved ones may have for wishing them dead. Such a low valuation of the lives of the elderly is hard to take

seriously. What if your loved ones wish you were dead so they can inherit your money and buy a Jaguar?

6. Ibid., 35.

7. Ibid., 36.

8. Ibid.

9. Ibid., 40.

10. Or, more accurately, this burden is as closely approximated in both sorts of cases. Hardwig's description is, of course, hyperbole. No one actually provides care or supervision "twenty-four hours a day." (When would he sleep? Even someone whose caregiving tasks often interrupt his sleep does not actually provide care or supervision "twenty-four hours a day.") This is not a trivial stylistic point, but an illustration of Hardwig's tendency to exaggerate the horrors of taking care of the ill.

11. Ibid., 37.

12. See B. Manard and C. Perrone, *Hospice Care: An Introduction and Review of the Evidence* (Arlington, VA: National Hospice Organization, 1994), 4.

13. John Hardwig, "What about the Family?" *Hastings Center Report* (March/April 1990), 5.

14. See Hardwig, "Is There A Duty to Die?" 35.

15. See the letters to the editor from Larry Churchill, Elizabeth A. Linehan, and Daniel G. Floury, *Hastings Center Report* (November/December 1997), 4–6.

16. Hardwig, "Is There a Duty to Die?" 35.

17. Ibid.

18. See Hardwig, "Dying at the Right Time."

19. Hardwig, "Is There a Duty to Die?" 34.

20. See Daniel Callahan, *Setting Limits* (Washington, DC: Georgetown University Press, 1987), *What Kind of Life?* (Washington, DC: Georgetown University Press, 1990), and *The Troubled Dream of Life* (New York: Simon and Schuster, 1993).

21. Sherwin B. Nuland, *How We Die* (New York: Knopf, 1994).

22. Hardwig claims that "[m]ost bioethicists advocate a 'patient-centered ethics'—an ethics which claims only the patient's interests should be considered in making medical treatment decisions. Most health care professionals have been trained to accept this ethic and to see themselves as patient advocates" ("Is There a Duty to Die?" note 3, p. 42). These claims overlook the enormous influence of Daniel Callahan. They also fail to take account of the huge (and hugely influential) hospice movement, one of whose basic principles is the above-quoted "Patients, their families and loved ones are the unit of care" (Manard and Perrone, *Hospice Care*, 4). Elsewhere, however, as I have indicated (see note 13), Hardwig distinguishes the hospice sort of approach from his own.

23. Hardwig, "Dying at the Right Time," 63.

24. Ibid.

25. Callahan, letter to the editor, *Hastings Center Report* (November/December 1997), 4.

26. Callahan, *The Troubled Dream of Life*, 218–9.

27. Callahan, *Setting Limits*, 43 (italics in original).

28. Callahan, *The Troubled Dream of Life*, 218–9.

29. See my "Death, Dying, and Dignity," in K. Brinkmann (ed.), *Proceedings of the Twentieth World Congress of Philosophy. Vol. 1: Ethics* (Bowling Green, OH: Philosophy Documentation Center, 1999), 196, for another example of how Callahan professes disdain for quality-of-life considerations, but freely uses them when the issue is "letting die."

30. Joel Feinberg, "Duties, Rights, and Claims," *American Philosophical Quarterly* 3, no. 2 (1966), 139 (italics in original). Obviously, this general claim leaves much unanswered. Feinberg is not specifically discussing parents and children, but Callahan cites this passage in that context in *Setting Limits*, 91. The general issue of what grown children owe their parents has many complexities that I lack space to go into here. For more discussion of the issue, see Jane English, "What Do Grown Children Owe Their Parents?" in La Follette, *Ethics in Practice*, 174–8; Christina Hoff Sommers, "Filial Morality," *Journal of Philosophy* (1986), 439–56; and Norman Daniels, *Am I My Parents' Keeper? An Essay on Justice between the Young and the Old* (New York: Oxford University Press, 1988).

31. Ellen Goodman, "Who Lives? Who Dies? Who Decides?" in E. Goodman, *At Large* (New York: Simon and Schuster, 1981), 161. (The first part of Goodman's statement is false. I want to live to be senile. I would rather be mentally intact than senile, of course, but I would rather be senile than dead.)

32. Hardwig, "Is There a Duty to Die?" 38.

33. Ibid., 38. He gives a less sanguine picture in his earlier paper, "What about the Family?" 10. See also his reply to the letter from Daniel Callahan, *Hastings Center Report* (November/December 1997), 6.

34. Hardwig, "Is There a Duty to Die?" 40.

35. Ibid., 40–1.

36. Hardwig, "What about the Family?" 6.

37. For further discussion of this paradox, see my "Assisted Suicide, Severe Disability, Terminal Illness, and the Double Standard," in M. P. Battin et al. (eds.), *Physician-Assisted Suicide: Expanding the Debate* (New York: Routledge, 1998), 156, and my "Goldilocks and Mrs. Ilych: A Critical Look at the 'Philosophy of Hospice,'" *Cambridge Quarterly of Healthcare Ethics*, 6 (1997), 319.

38. I owe this point to Sara Ann Ketchum.

39. Hardwig, "What about the Family?" 6.

40. Hardwig, "Is There a Duty to Die?" 38–9. With respect to the third sentence of his second guideline, note that attempts to postpone death normally reflect people's (frequently attainable) goal of living *longer*, rather than the obviously unattainable goal of immortality. A similar point applies to Elizabeth A. Linehan's speculation about the "denial of mortality" (letter to the editor, *Hastings Center Report*, November/December 1997, 5) in Hardwig's case of the eighty-seven-year-old mother (discussed above) who insisted on the most aggressive possible treatment for her congestive heart failure. Like young diabetics who take insulin, this old woman was trying to prolong her life. The term 'denial of mortality' is no more appropriate to her case than to theirs, however much one may begrudge this sick old lady the extra time she craved.

41. Hardwig, "Is There a Duty to Die?" 37.

42. Ibid., 38.

43. Ibid., 41.

44. Malory, *Le Morte D'Arthur*, v.2, 172. Malory himself, as a devout Catholic, found a completely different sort of meaning in death as a passage to a better world, but when believers and disbelievers in an afterlife talk about death, what they take themselves to be talking about is very different.

45. Hardwig, "Is There a Duty to Die?" 36.

46. Ibid., 42.

47. Hardwig, "What about the Family?" 7.

48. Hardwig, "Is There a Duty to Die?" 36.

49. In "SUPPORT and the Invisible Family" (Special Supplement, Hastings Center Report, 25, no. 6, 1995, S23–5), Hardwig discusses a real-life case of this sort but considers none of these questions. He also expresses great sympathy and concern for the daughter, whom he identifies as a personal friend, but none for the mother.

50. Malory, *Le Morte D'Arthur*, v. 2, 426.

51. This is a claim Hardwig makes about killing yourself in order to avoid burdening your loved ones: "Dying at the Right Time," 57.

Midwest Studies in Philosophy, XXIV (2000)

Taking Life and the Argument from Potentiality

ROY W. PERRETT

I

It is uncontroversial that one of the fundamental issues in bioethics is just what sorts of moral constraints should govern our treatment of human fetuses. What is much more controversial is the status of arguments for prohibiting the killing of human fetuses that appeal to the supposed moral relevance of the potentialities of such organisms. This essay is concerned to evaluate the *argument from potentiality*, that is, the argument that it is wrong to kill a human fetus because it is a potential person.

The form of this argument that I shall be concerned with can be stated as follows:

1. It is wrong to kill a potential person.
2. The human fetus is a potential person.
3. Therefore it is wrong to kill a human fetus.[1]

A few preliminary comments and clarifications are in order. First, by "person" I mean "rational, self-conscious being." In other words, I take for granted the moral significance of the person/human being distinction now commonplace in bioethical circles and assume that the fetus's potential to become a human being (i.e., a member of the biological species *Homo sapiens*) is morally irrelevant.[2] Second, and again following a common convention in bioethical circles, for convenience I shall generally use the term "fetus" to cover all prenatal stages of the developing being in the womb (including what biologists might distinguish as the zygote, the pre-embryo, the embryo, and the fetus).[3]

Third, by "potential person" I mean, roughly, "a being that will (normally) develop into a person." There are various difficulties involved in giving a more precise definition of the term, but they need not detain us here.[4] It should be noted, however, that with "potential person" thus construed the argument above does not preclude abortion of defective fetuses that will not (normally) develop into persons. In other words, even if the argument from potentiality that I am concerned with is sound, this would not entail that every killing of a fetus is absolutely prohibited, though presumably most such killings would be.

Is the argument from potentiality sound? The argument is clearly valid, and the second premise is plausibly true (given the appropriate qualifications about defective fetuses). So it is only the first premise that is controversial, and there are two distinct ways that it might be defended. One way is to treat it as a *derivative* claim, that is, to maintain that the wrongness of killing a potential person presupposes and is derived from rights and interests that it is assumed all persons have. The other way is to treat it as a *detached* claim, that is, to maintain that the wrongness of killing a potential person does not depend on or presuppose any particular rights or interests.[5]

It is possible that a friend of the argument from potentiality might opt to treat the first premise as making a detached claim, in which case it is difficult to see quite how to go about defending it to someone who does not already find it intuitively obvious. However, the more common way to understand the argument is surely to construe the first premise as making a derived claim: that is, it is wrong to kill a potential person because it is wrong to kill a person, and a potential person will (normally) develop into a person. But then the problem is how to specify the *intrinsic* wrongness of the killing of the potential person, as distinct from the harm done to other actual persons like the parents. Prima facie the fetus' interests cannot be harmed because it does not have interests, since these are created by desires and preferences. And even if persons have a right to life, it is hard to see how this can justify the right to life of a *potential* person.

This skepticism is supported by the two standard objections to the argument from potentiality: the *relevance objection* and the *scope objection*.[6] The relevance objection complains that the fact that persons have certain rights does not by itself entail that potential persons have those rights too. On the contrary, it is often the case that a potential *X* does not have the rights of an actual *X*: Prince Charles is presently a potential king, but this does not now give him the rights of an actual king.

The scope objection complains that by treating the first premise as a derivative claim, the argument from potentiality threatens to prove too much. If it is wrong to kill a potential person because this deprives the world of a person, then all practices that do this are wrong, including contraception and celibacy. After all, if a fetus is a potential person with a right to life, then so too is a sperm-egg pair. Of course, some people will be willing to accept this implication, but far more would consider it a *reductio* of the argument from potentiality.

Friends of the argument from potentiality typically reject the suggestion that these two standard objections are conclusive. They insist instead that the objections only show that we need to invoke a more metaphysically nuanced account of potentiality in order to make the argument work. If this is so, however, then such an account presumably has to satisfy at least two crucial desiderata highlighted by the relevance and scope objections: it must plausibly explain why the appropriate sense of potentiality is indeed morally relevant, and it must plausibly restrict the scope of this morally relevant property so as to include fetuses but exclude sperm-egg pairs. Call these two desiderata respectively the *relevance desideratum* and the *scope desideratum*.

The crucial question, then, is whether friends of the argument from potentiality can actually delineate a metaphysical account of potential personhood that satisfies both desiderata.

II

It might be protested that the very search for such a purpose-built account of potentiality is objectionably ad hoc. But that is by no means clear. Consider again the scope objection, which implies that there is no relevant difference in the potentialities of a sperm-egg pair and a fetus. The usual argument for this is that since a sperm-egg pair is a potential fetus and a fetus is a potential person, a sperm-egg pair is also a potential person. However, the notion of potentiality is presumably to be analyzed (at least in part) in terms of subjunctive conditionals: that is, what would happen if certain conditions were to occur. Thus a (partial) analysis of "The sperm-egg pair is a potential fetus" might be "If the sperm-egg pair were to unite, then it would produce a fetus"; and a (partial) analysis of "The fetus is a potential person" might be "If the fetus were implanted and grew normally, then it would become a person." But then it seems that the usual argument for the assumed equivalence of the potentialities of the sperm-egg pair and the fetus involves an invalid inference.[7]

This is because transitivity fails for subjunctive conditionals: from A>B and B>C, we cannot infer A>C (where the conditional connective is symbolized by ">"). Here is Stalnaker's (now quaintly dated) 1968 counterexample to the claim that the conditional connective is transitive:

> *Premises.* "If J. Edgar Hoover were today a Communist, then he would be a traitor." "If J. Edgar Hoover had been born a Russian, then he would today be a Communist." *Conclusion.* "If J. Edgar Hoover had been born a Russian, he would be a traitor." It seems reasonable to affirm these premises and deny the conclusion.[8]

Moreover, though the transitivity inference fails for subjunctive conditionals, a related inference is indeed valid. From A>B, B>C, and A, we can infer C.[9] In other words, if the sperm and egg do unite to form a zygote, then that zygote is a potential person, even though the sperm-egg pair is not.

Of course, to be fully persuasive this argument requires some further bolstering. In particular, we need a fuller account of the admittedly partial analysis of potentiality in terms of subjunctive conditionals sketched above. But perhaps the general point about the nontransitivity of subjunctive conditionals is sufficient to create some space for exploring accounts of potentiality that might consistently allow us to affirm that the fetus is a potential person, yet deny that the sperm-egg pair is also (in the same sense) a potential person.

Potentiality is obviously a modal notion of some sort, involving some sort of possibility. Moreover the relevant possibility here is stronger than merely logical possibility, involving at least physical possibility. After that the metaphysics of potential persons is more controversial. One suggestion is that we should think of potentiality as admitting of degrees. This would enable us to meet the scope desideratum by holding that the sperm-egg pair is not a potential person to the same degree as is the fetus, and hence not deserving of the same degree of protection. The question then is how to cash out the notion of degrees of potentiality.

One answer is in terms of probability. According to this account, the fetus is more of a potential person than the zygote or the sperm-egg pair because the probability of its developing into a person is higher. True, this account does have a consequence that at least some friends of potentiality would find unwelcome: namely, it implies that the earlier the killing of a fetus takes place, the less bad it is.[10] But in other contexts involving potentiality something similar seems plausible. Although a sheaf of blank paper may be a potential manuscript score of *The Magic Flute*, intuitively it seems less bad to destroy this than the completed or near completed score.

In fact, Catholic moral theologian John Noonan accepted something like this implication. However, he also argued that proper attention to the real probabilities would still justify a prohibition on abortion as very significantly morally worse than contraception, since an embryo has an 80% probability of developing into an infant, compared to a chance of one in two million for a spermatozoon.[11] Unfortunately for Noonan's argument, more recent research has altered our best estimate of the real probabilities. Before implantation (within fourteen days of fertilization), the probability of a birth resulting is 25–30%. Postimplantation this increases to 46–60%, but it is not until six weeks after gestation that the probability of birth rises to 85–90%. Thus if an 80% probability of developing into an infant is taken to be the threshold for attaining moral significance, the fetus does not have this status until six weeks after conception.[12]

Of course, some friends of the argument from potentiality may well balk at setting such probabilistic thresholds at all. After all, if probability does matter morally, then why should not every nonzero probability matter? But there is a much more fundamental difficulty with the probabilistic account of potentiality: it fails to satisfy the relevance desideratum. Why should the 80% probability of becoming a X give something the rights of an actual X? Even if now true that Prince Charles has an 80% probability of becoming king, this does not presently give him the rights of actual king. Why should it be any different for fetuses?

This seems to show we need more than degrees of potentiality; perhaps we need to recognize too different *kinds* of potentiality.[13] For example, we need to be able to distinguish between the potentiality that an acorn has to become an oak tree and the potentiality that an oak tree has to become a pile of sawdust. The first kind of potentiality is *identity-preserving* in the sense that the oak tree is the same living organism as the acorn. The second kind of potentiality is *non-identity-preserving* in the sense that the pile of sawdust is not the same living organism as the oak tree. In the first case we have the acorn's potentiality to *become* an oak; in the second case we have the oak tree's potentiality to *produce* a pile of sawdust.

This account enables us to make metaphysical sense of the claim that a fetus is a potential person, though a sperm-egg pair is not. The relevant potentiality being claimed for the fetus here is an identity-preserving potentiality in the sense that the fetus is the same living organism as the person it develops into. The sperm-egg pair is not a potential person in this sense: the two individual living organisms that form the sperm-egg pair have to cease to exist in order to unite and form the zygote, which is a nonidentical living organism.

But this metaphysics of potentiality also fails to deliver quite what the friends of the argument from potentiality want. Firstly, the account implies not only that the sperm-egg pair is not a potential person, but also that the zygote is not a potential person either, since twinning is possible up to fourteen days after fertilization. Thus a very early abortion would not violate the prohibition on killing potential persons.

Secondly, distinguishing kinds of potentiality once again does nothing to satisfy the relevance desideratum. We can grant that there is a metaphysical difference between identity-preserving and non-identity-preserving potentialities. But just why is it that the fetus's identity-preserving potentiality is supposed to be morally relevant? Why should a potential X (in the identity-preserving sense) have the rights of an actual X? If Prince Charles becomes king he will be the same living organism as the prince who is presently only a potential king, so he is presumably now a potential king in the identity-preserving sense of that term. But this still does not now give him the rights of an actual king.

III

So far we have been unsuccessfully trying to locate a morally relevant sense of potential personhood by focusing on the metaphysics of potentiality. Perhaps what we need to do instead, however, is to try to connect the notion of potential personhood more directly to the notion of personhood by drawing on the metaphysics of personal identity.

Contemporary philosophical theories of personal identity have tended to be constructed in terms of a quest for the *unity relation* for persons.[14] To specify the unity relation for persons is to specify the relation between person-stages occurring at different times in virtue of which they are all stages of one and the same person. We may think of *person-stages* as temporal slices of persons; or, alternatively, we may think of person-stages as temporal slices of the biographies of persons. Either way, there are quite a number of theories on offer as to what the unity relation for persons consists in. These theories can all be classified, however, as being instances of two general types. The first and currently most popular type of theory of personal identity holds that the unity relation between person-stages can be specified in terms of a relation that does not itself presuppose identity. This is what Derek Parfit calls

> *Reductionism*: Personal identity just consists in the holding of certain facts that can be described without making reference to personal identity.[15]

The alternative type of theory is *Non-Reductionism*, which denies this claim. Non-Reductionists hold that the unity relation for persons just is identity, that is, what makes a set of person-stages occurring at different times all stages of the same person is simply that they all are stages of the same person. Personal identity is simple and unanalyzable: there is no nontrivial and noncircular analysis of the identity conditions for persons, nothing that personal identity "consists in." Currently this is very much the less popular type of theory of personal identity, but it nevertheless has able contemporary defenders, including Roderick Chisholm, Richard Swinburne, and Geoffrey Madell.[16]

Now suppose for the moment that Reductionism is not only the more popular theory of personal identity, but also the correct one. Personal identity would then be specifiable in terms of a unity relation R, which does not itself mention identity: that is, Y at t_2 is the same person as X at t_1 if and only if Y at t_2 is R-related to X at t_1 (though Reductionists might disagree intramurally about precisely what relation R consists in). We can then try to characterize a potential person in terms of the unity relation for persons: X at t_1 is a potential person if and only if there (normally) will be a person-stage at t_2 that is R-related to X at t_1. Combine this suggestion with the notion of identity-preserving potentiality and we get the theory that a potential person is an entity that, if it survives as the same living organism, will have various later person-stages R-related to it.[17]

Would such a theory satisfy the relevance desideratum? That is not entirely clear. But the theory at least has the advantage of directly connecting the metaphysical status of the fetus to that of the person via the R-relation, a relation that *is* morally relevant in the case of persons. So it does seem rather more successful in this respect than the other theories we have looked at. Moreover, incorporating into the theory the notion of identity-preserving potentiality presumably helps with the scope objection: sperm-egg pairs are not potential persons on this characterization.

From the point of view of a friend of the argument from potentiality, however, the real difficulty with the theory is that it threatens to deny potential personhood to fetuses too. Obviously much depends here on what the R-relation consists in. Suppose, for instance, that we take a Lockean view and identify the R-relation with actual or potential memory. Then we can characterize a potential person as an entity that, if it survives as the same living organism, will have various later person-stages memory-related to it. If the claims of some people to have veridical prenatal memories of being a fetus are correct, then that fetus is a potential person.

Although this suggestion seems metaphysically coherent, it is surely implausible for two distinct reasons: not only is it dubious that there are veridical prenatal memories, but memory is an unsatisfactorily narrow account of the R-relation for personal identity. However, once we switch to the more popular psychological continuity account of personal identity, it seems even less likely that the fetus will have later person-stages R-related to it. True, the claims of the fetus to potential personhood fare better on the rival physical continuity account of the R-relation. However, there are also persuasive independent arguments to suppose that physical continuity is an inadequate account of personal identity.[18] So in the end the appeal to the metaphysics of personal identity does not help the argument from potentiality very much either.

IV

It might be objected that our explorations in the metaphysics of potentiality so far have entirely failed to capture the special "naturalness" of the kind of potentiality that is enjoyed by the fetus, but not the sperm-egg pair:

> To say that a fœtus is a potential human being . . . is to say something about its natural development. . . . A thing is potentially *F* if it will become *F* of its own accord, if nothing external intervenes.[19]

Whereas a sperm-egg pair can fail to become a fetus of its own accord, a normal fetus cannot, provided nothing external intervenes.

This purported "naturalness," however, is rather more difficult to explicate than it might at first seem. In IVF (in vitro fertilization) cases, for instance, fertilization takes place outside the body, in a petri dish, and the resulting embryo is transferred to the uterus of a female. Without the benefit of considerable human intervention into its development, the IVF-produced embryo will never develop "naturally" into a person. But presumably friends of the argument from potentiality want to count IVF-produced embryos too as potential persons.[20]

One suggestion is that we need to revive something closer to the original Aristotelian conception of potentiality, particularly its recognition of the teleological character of potentiality.[21] In Book IX of his *Metaphysics* Aristotle distinguishes two kinds of potencies, active and passive. The latter are extrinsic, in that the principle of transformation comes from outside the body transformed. Active potencies, in contrast, are intrinsic, in that they do not depend upon external causes but rather upon the very nature of the entity transformed. The nature or essence of an entity is unaffected by the actualization or nonactualization of a passive potency: a person is still a person whether or not she actualizes her potential to be a musician. An active potency, however, is inherent to an entity in the sense that entity will cease to exist if such a potentiality is not actualized: an embryo dies if it cannot actualize its potential for personhood.

This Aristotelian conception of potentiality is by no means easy to characterize clearly. Indeed Aristotle himself regards potentiality as a basic independent notion, explicable only through its contrast with actuality, and by induction from particular examples (*Metaphysics* 1048). But whereas contrasting potentiality and actuality need not involve any teleological assumptions, Aristotle does require such notions in order to be able to characterize potentiality as involving more than mere possibility. For Aristotle, a being's (active) potentiality is a capacity that is part of that being's nature, a functioning that is part of its essence. Actuality is not merely what happens to be the case, but that which actualizes potentialities. Natural functioning for members of a species is the constant actualizing of their potentialities. A living being like a fetus needs to change (i.e., realize its potential) in order to persist.

Obviously an Aristotelian metaphysics of potentiality involves a number of commitments to various controversial essentialist and teleological theses. However, if these can be vindicated then perhaps we would at least have an account of potential personhood that satisfied the scope desideratum. But what about the relevance desideratum? Even if we concede *per argumentum* that the fetus (unlike the sperm-egg pair) has a special inherent potential to develop into a person, why is this property morally relevant? One traditional answer has been to appeal to natural law theory and argue that what we ought to do is act in accord with our essential human nature. If it is part of the essential nature of a fetus to develop into a person under normal conditions, then we ought not to interfere with this process.

This theory thus tries to provide both a metaphysical articulation of the special "naturalness" of the kind of potentiality that is enjoyed by the fetus and a justification of the moral relevance of that potentiality. But even if we can make sense of an Aristotelian metaphysics of potentiality in terms of biological functions, it still remains to be shown that we ought to conform with such biological functions. Descriptive facts about biological functions do not by themselves entail any prescriptive claims. What has to be added is something like the Thomistic distinction between *laws of nature* and *natural laws*, where the former are descriptive statements derived from scientific observation of regularities in nature and the latter are prescriptive statements derived from metaphysical knowledge of the essential properties of human nature. Knowledge of our essences is then supposed to tell us how we *ought* to behave because of our nature as human beings.

Thus if the Aristotelian theory of potential personhood is to satisfy the relevance desideratum not only do we have to be able to make sense of something like this obscure distinction between laws of nature and natural law, but we also have to justify the assumption that we ought not to interfere with anything that is "natural" (in this rather special sense of "natural"). It is nowadays widely conceded that traditional natural law theorists failed to deliver satisfactory answers to either of these questions. In the absence of such answers it seems reasonable to conclude that friends of the argument from potentiality would be unwise to suppose that appealing to an Aristotelian style theory of potential personhood will help their case.[22]

V

So far, then, we have failed to locate a clear account of potential personhood that satisfies both the relevance and scope desiderata. Of course, this does not show that such an account *cannot* be provided. I submit, though, that it at least justifies a modest fallibilistic skepticism about the first premise of the argument from potentiality. If the claim that it is wrong to kill a potential person is to be defended as a *derivative* claim, then it has to be shown how the wrongness of killing a potential person presupposes and is derived from rights and interests that it is assumed all persons have. But attempts to make the argument from potentiality work by invoking more metaphysically nuanced accounts of potentiality fail unless such accounts also satisfy the relevance and scope desiderata. The relevant theory of potential personhood must plausibly explain why the appropriate sense of potentiality is indeed morally relevant, and it must plausibly restrict the scope of this morally relevant property so as to include fetuses but exclude sperm-egg pairs. Such a theory, I suggest, has yet to be articulated.

Of course, some people will object that the fetus's potential personhood is *obviously* morally relevant and it is the philosopher's job to articulate this truth. But this response threatens to treat the first premise of the argument from potentiality as a *detached* claim, that is, to maintain that the wrongness of killing a potential person does not depend on or presuppose any particular rights or interests. It is difficult, however, to see quite how to go about defending such a claim to someone who (like myself) does not already find it intuitively obvious.

But perhaps the friends of potentiality can try another tack. They might argue that denying the wrongness of killing a potential person is tantamount to denying moral status to anything but actual beings. But any plausible moral theory has to acknowledge moral status to possible persons as well as actual persons, and potential persons are possible persons.

This argumentative strategy requires very careful marshaling. Although every potentiality is a possibility, not every possibility is a potentiality. It is tempting to suppose that if the rejection of the moral relevance of potentiality involves a restriction of moral relevance to the actual, then a demonstration of the moral significance of possible persons might be apposite to a defense of the argument from potentiality. But we need to be quite clear about what we are referring to when we talk of potential and possible persons A *potential person* is an *actual* being that will (normally) develop into a person. A *possible person* is a *nonactual* being. When we talk of a possible person all we mean is that if things had been arranged differently there would have existed a person who does not exist as things actually are.

One way to reject the argument from potentiality, however, involves claiming that potential persons have no more moral status than merely possible persons. Just as there is no obligation to bring possible persons into existence, so too there is no obligation to enable potential persons to develop into actual persons.[23] This way of putting the matter apparently lumps together potential and possible persons, and thereby opens something of a dialectical space for the friends of potentiality. Is it really true that we have no moral obligations to merely possible persons, only to actual persons? If it is not true, then we cannot reject the argument from potentiality by claiming that potential persons have no more moral status than merely possible persons—even though, of course, it might still be true that there is nothing intrinsically wrong with killing potential persons.

VI

The view that we have no moral obligations to merely possible persons, only to actual persons, is what Derek Parfit calls *the Person-Affecting Restriction*.[24] But Parfit has constructed a number of imaginary cases that have led many to think that the Person-Affecting Restriction is not morally defensible. Consider, for instance, the case of

> *The Fated Child.* A woman comes to know that if she now conceives a child that child will inevitably die of a heart attack at the age of twenty-five, whereas if she waits for a month her child will have a normal life span.[25]

Everyone agrees that the woman would do wrong to conceive the Fated Child. But why?

One possible answer is that by going ahead and conceiving the Fated Child the woman will harm that child. But arguably a child conceived a month later would have been a *different* child, produced from a different ovum and different sperm. Hence the mother of the Fated Child has not harmed that particular child, for it is not true that if she had refrained from conception for a month, the Fated Child's life would have been better. Rather the Fated Child would not have existed at all.

A second possible answer is that the mother is at fault because she failed to bring into existence a possible person: the child she would have had if she had waited. But this answer implies that the Person-Affecting Restriction has to be abandoned in favor of a moral view that requires us to take account not only of those who actually exist, but also of possible persons who might have existed if we had acted differently.

A third possible answer is that what the mother has done wrong is that she has failed to bring about the best possible outcome. In other words, her wrongdoing lies not in harming an identifiable child, nor in failing to bring a possible person into existence, but in bringing into existence a child with a lesser quality of life than one she could have brought into existence.

The issues raised by this hypothetical case are far too complex and controversial to be settled here.[26] However, it is worth noting that only the second of the three answers above implies that possible persons have moral status. Moreover, that answer also seems to have the intuitively unattractive implication that, other things being equal, it is always good to bring into existence children who will lead a minimally worthwhile life. Given the plausible moral requirement that we should attempt to maximize the good, it then follows that we should have as many children who would lead a minimally worthwhile life as we can possibly manage! This is a variant of what Parfit calls the *Total Principle*, and he objects to such a principle that it leads to

The Repugnant Conclusion: For any large population, all of whom enjoy a high quality of life, there is a larger imaginable population whose existence, other things being equal, would be better, even though everyone in that population would only enjoy a quality of life barely worth living.[27]

Assuming we agree that the Repugnant Conclusion really is repugnant, we might reaffirm a slightly modified version of the original claim that we have no moral obligations to merely possible people, only to actual people. We might hold that when deciding what to do we only need to consider *noncontingent future persons*, that is, persons who actually exist, prior to our decisions, or who will exist independently of our decision.

Obviously a full-scale defense of such a principle is well beyond the scope of this essay. However, I do want to say, very briefly, something about another pair of hypothetical cases of Parfit's that might seem to threaten this version of the Person-Affecting Restriction too. Imagine a couple know that if they were to have a child it would enjoy a happy life. Many would not feel that the couple were thereby morally obliged to have the child. Imagine instead, though, that a couple know that if they were to have a child it would lead a wretched life. Most people would feel that then the couple were morally obliged to refrain from having the child. But if the pain the Wretched Child would experience is a reason *against* bringing it into existence, then why is the pleasure the Happy Child would experience not a reason *for* bringing it into existence? There seems here an unexplained asymmetry in our attitudes toward cases of possible children who will have pleasant lives and of possible children who will have painful lives, an asymmetry that the modified version of the Person-Affecting Restriction just mentioned does not explain. The Total Principle, of course, admits no such asymmetry. On the Total Principle it is both bad to bring the Wretched Child into existence and good to bring the Happy Child into existence.

But perhaps we can explain the asymmetry in our intuitions about the Happy Child and the Wretched Child in terms of a different asymmetry embedded in commonsense morality.[28] Commonsense morality takes there to be a constraint against imposing harm on others but also sees the maximization of the good as optional for agents when this imposes burdens on them. Hence we do not require the couple to make the sacrifices required of parents so that there be the pleasure of their Happy Child, even if its pleasure were to outweigh the pain of their sacrifices. On the other hand, the presumption is that the parents would proceed to create the Wretched Child for their own pleasure, and this would violate the constraint against harm (even if their pleasure were to outweigh the child's pain). Of course, my appeal to these principles of commonsense morality is only supposed to be an *explanation* of the asymmetry in our attitudes toward the two cases; whether commonsense morality is *justified* in holding these views about harms and benefits is another matter.[29]

Be that as it may, I suggest that enough has been said to show that it is by no means obvious that possible persons (or at least, contingent future persons) do have moral status. Hence there is no need to be embarrassed about claiming that just as there is no obligation to bring possible persons into existence, so too there is no obligation to enable potential persons to develop into actual persons. Moreover, even if it is false that merely possible persons have no moral status, it might still be true that there is nothing wrong with killing potential persons. Thus in the absence of an account of potential personhood that satisfies both the relevance and scope desiderata, it is indeed reasonable to reject the first premise of the argument from potentiality. There is no reason to suppose that it is wrong to kill a fetus simply because it is a potential person, since there is no reason to suppose it is intrinsically wrong to kill a potential person.

NOTES

1. This formulation is a slightly modified version of that in Peter Singer, *Practical Ethics*, 2nd ed. (Cambridge: Cambridge University Press, 1993), 152.

2. See, for instance, Michael Tooley, *Abortion and Infanticide* (Oxford: Clarendon Press, 1983), chap. 4; John Harris, *The Value of Life* (London: Routledge & Kegan Paul, 1985), chap. 1; Singer, *Practical Ethics*, 83–101; H. Tristram Engelhardt, Jr., *The Foundations of Bioethics*, 2nd ed. (New York: Oxford University Press, 1996), chap. 4.

3. For a philosophically motivated review of the relevant biology see Norman M. Ford, *When Did I Begin?* (Cambridge: Cambridge University Press, 1988).

4. Cf. Tooley, *Abortion and Infanticide*, 165–169.

5. The distinction is borrowed from Ronald Dworkin, *Life's Dominion* (New York: Vintage, 1994), 11.

6. See, inter alia: S. I. Benn, "Abortion, Infanticide, and Respect for Persons," in *The Problem of Abortion*, ed. Joel Feinberg (Belmont: Wadsworth, 1973); Jonathan Glover, *Causing Deaths and Saving Lives* (Harmondsworth: Penguin, 1977); Tooley, *Abortion and Infanticide*; Bonnie Steinbock, *Life before Birth* (New York: Oxford University Press, 1992); Singer, *Practical Ethics*;

Joel Feinberg and Barbara Baum Levenbook, "Abortion," in *Matters of Life and Death*, 3rd ed., ed. Tom Regan (New York: McGraw-Hill, 1993).

7. See David B. Annis, "Abortion and the Potentiality Principle," *Southern Journal of Philosophy* 22 (1984): 155–163; Michael J. Wreen, "The Power of Potentiality," *Theoria* 52 (1986): 16–40; Edward Covey, "Physical Possibility and Potentiality in Ethics," *American Philosophical Quarterly* 28 (1991): 237–244.

8. Robert C. Stalnaker, "A Theory of Conditionals," in *Causation and Conditionals*, ed. Ernest Sosa (Oxford: Oxford University Press, 1975), 173. On the failure of transitivity for subjunctive conditionals, see also John L. Pollock, *Subjunctive Reasoning* (Dordrecht: D. Reidel, 1976).

9. Stalnaker, "A Theory of Conditionals," 173n.

10. See, for instance, Nicola Poplawski and Grant Gillett, "Ethics and Embryos," *Journal of Medical Ethics* 17 (1991): 62–69, which firmly rejects such a notion: "The total form of a human being exists through time. We can also say that a single individual makes up that form throughout its temporal existence. Therefore, if we can justify a moral value for that individual at one time, that moral value ought to be conferred on the total form throughout its temporal existence" (64).

11. John T. Noonan, Jr., "An Almost Absolute Value in History," in *The Morality of Abortion*, ed. John T. Noonan, Jr. (Cambridge: Harvard University Press, 1970).

12. Peter Singer and Karen Dawson, "IVF Technology and the Argument from Potential," in *Embryo Experimentation*, ed. Peter Singer et al. (Cambridge: Cambridge University Press, 1990).

13. Cf. Stephen Buckle, "Arguing from Potential," in *Embryo Experimentation*, ed. Peter Singer et al.; Jim Stone, "Why Potentiality Matters," *Canadian Journal of Philosophy* 17 (1987): 815–830.

14. John Perry, ed., *Personal Identity* (Berkeley and Los Angeles: University of California Press, 1975), part 1.

15. Derek Parfit, *Reasons and Persons* (Oxford: Oxford University Press, 1985), 210.

16. Roderick M. Chisholm, *Person and Object* (London: George Allen & Unwin, 1976); Richard Swinburne, "Personal Identity," *Proceedings of the Aristotelian Society* 74 (1973–74): 231–248; Sydney Shoemaker and Richard Swinburne, *Personal Identity* (Oxford: Blackwell, 1984); Geoffrey Madell, *The Identity of the Self* (Edinburgh: Edinburgh University Press, 1981).

17. This theory was inspired by a speculation of Peter Forrest's, though he should not be held responsible for my particular development of it.

18. See Parfit, *Reasons and Persons*, part 3.

19. Rosalind Hursthouse, *Beginning Lives* (Oxford: Blackwell, 1987), 80.

20. Steinbock, *Life before Birth*, 64.

21. Massimo Reichlin, "The Argument from Potential," *Bioethics* 11 (1997): 1–23.

22. Similar criticisms apply to the argument in Stone, "Why Potentiality Matters," to the effect that the infant's potential personhood grounds an interest in continued life because the infant has a nature, the actualization of which involves an great conscious good for the infant. Crucial to this argument is Stone's undefended and unobvious claim that "we have a prima facie duty to all creatures not to deprive them of the conscious goods which it is their nature to realize" (821).

23. See Tooley, *Abortion and Infanticide*, 193; Steinbock, *Life before Birth*, 66.

24. Parfit, *Reasons and Persons*, 394.

25. Don Locke, "The Parfit Population Problem," *Philosophy* 62 (1987): 137. Cf. Parfit, *Reasons and Persons*, 367.

26. See further Parfit, *Reasons and Persons*, part 4; Derek Parfit, "Overpopulation and the Quality of Life," in *Applied Ethics*, ed. Peter Singer (Oxford: Oxford University Press, 1986); David Heyd, *Genethics: Moral Issues in the Creation of People* (Berkeley and Los Angeles: University of California Press, 1992); Nick Fotion and Jan C. Heller, eds., *Contingent Future Persons* (Dordrecht: Kluwer, 1997).

27. Parfit, *Reasons and Persons*, 388; "Overpopulation and the Quality of Life," 150.

28. The diagnosis presented here was suggested to me by Mark Siderits.

29. For forceful criticism of this commonsense view see Shelly Kagan, *The Limits of Morality* (Oxford: Clarendon Press, 1989).

Midwest Studies in Philosophy, XXIV (2000)

Privatizing Death: Metaphysical Discouragements of Ethical Thinking

JOHN WOODS

1. THE LOGIC OF DEATH

In countries such as those of western Europe and North America, the second half of the twentieth century saw a substantial change in what might be called the *benignly domestic uses of death*. Unlike deaths occasioned by war with a country's enemies or triggered by a guilty verdict in a capital trial, the benignly domestic uses of death are deaths visited upon members of the human species who are in no sense our enemies or the violators of our criminal laws. In the space of a generation, we saw abortion transformed from a grave moral and legal wrong to something rather closer to a life-style choice, and as we enter the new century we see voluntary and involuntary euthanasia in the grip of much the same transition. These normative changes have been attended by two especially arresting features. One is their scale: they are huge changes. The other is their speed: they happened and are happening with striking alacrity.

Undergirding these developments is a corresponding change in the way that death is understood. When death had a dominantly theological meaning in Western countries, it harbored a difficult metaphysical problem. It is the problem of individuating an individual human being through and beyond the loss of his or her physical constitution. However since, for the most part, the theological conception of death is accepted by people who are religious believers, then their belief in the survival of death is secure and confident notwithstanding the metaphysical difficulties that dog the very idea of death so conceived. This is an important *dialectical* feature of the theological conception. In most cases, it is part of a more general religiosity that gives to the believer authoritative instruction about, among other things, constraints on the domestic uses of death. His religiosity disposes him to accept this counsel, never mind that he might be a confused theologian. By his own lights, therefore, he need not solve the metaphysical problem of the survival of bodily death in order to have assurances that satisfy him about when it's not all right to kill people.

The theological conception of death is in retreat in Western societies; it is being replaced by what might be called the secular conception. On the secular conception, one's death is one's complete and irreversible metaphysical annihilation; it is a passage that is not survived, a transition to permanent nonexistence. For this and other reasons, secular death is also a metaphysically vexed concept. Unlike the metaphysical difficulties that attach to theological death and that need not trouble the religious believer—need not be solved by him as a basis for action—the difficulties that inhere in the secular conception of death bite deeply into the whole question of the moral legitimacy of the benignly domestic uses of death. The point is worth repeating: A person holding to the theological conception of death need not be a metaphysical adept in order to know the moral limitations on killing, since these normative constraints are already manifest in the religiosity that undergirds his theological perspective on death. But someone who is a secularist about death must derive his appreciation of the moral constraints on killing in ways that cannot be detached from the metaphysical difficulties that this view of death so deeply embeds.

One of the conceptual problems thrown up by the secular appreciation of death is the following. Consider someone, Jones, who is deathly sick. If Jones dies, then a condition on his having died is that Jones does not exist. If Jones doesn't exist, then there is no one whatever who is Jones. It cannot be true if Jones is dead that there is anyone who is Jones and is dead. People who agitate over when it is all right to cause the death of fetuses or of the hopelessly ill do not typically reflect on this conundrum. In fact, once brought to their attention, it may strike them as a rather frivolous problem, as something best thought of as a brainteaser or some other form of intellectual play.

Even so, if quantifiers are understood classically, the problem is no mere intellectual recreation. If Jones has died, then no one is Jones. And if no one is Jones, then no one who is Jones is dead. The point generalizes. No one is dead. But if there are no dead, there are no victims of death; there is no one harmed or wronged by death. If there are no dead there are no dead victims. Provided quantification is understood classically, it is extremely difficult to say in what the primary and direct wrongfulness of murder consists. If I murder Jones, I may injure his loved ones; perhaps I even deprive the country of a great leader. Whatever harm I have done to Jones, it is not the wrong of murder unless Jones is dead. Yet if Jones is dead there is no one who primarily and directly wronged by the death I have wrought.

As long as "Some things don't exist" is a unsatisfiable sentence, as it is on the classical construal of quantification, then it cannot be true that death directly victimizes or wrongs anyone. This suggests the advisability of changing our understanding of the quantifiers. We should seek the accommodations of an existence-neutral quantification theory, a theory that provides for quantification over things that don't exist.

In dynamical universes, facts of change, of the passage of time, of process, need to be reflected by tense, by quantification over time and by other idioms of continuity through change. It is clearly no less so of dynamical universes in which one of the changes is death. But since all of the difficulties posed by our logical problem remain problems even for a static universe, discourse about which is tenseless and free of quantification over times, we might just as well pursue our departures from first-order logic within a tenseless object language in which there is quantification only over individuals; not over times, not properties, not relations, and so on.[1]

We might think that a better choice would be a tensed language, possibly one that also provides for quantification over times. But unless the semantics of such languages allows for the satisfiability of "Some things do not exist," unless, that is, such languages are granted a reference capability beyond that for existing objects, our central problem is left untouched. If, having Caesar in mind, someone says, "There is at least one person x who *was* alive but is now dead," or "There exists at least two times, $t_1 < t_2$, such that x is (tenselessly) alive at t_1 and x is (tenselessly) dead at t_2," how shall we understand the variable x? In the ordinary, first-order way? If so, one is saddled in either case with the (secular) absurdity of the existing dead. Or, if we decided to forego tensed predicates for tensed quantifiers, for example, "There was an x such that," "There is at present an x such that," and "There will be an x such that," it is immediate that the variables of quantification cannot be taken the standard first-order way.

We might also consider a quantified tense logic with identity, with a distinguished existence predicate and a domain of individuals that increases monotonically with time. In this way, no individual is ever "lost" as an item of reference: Once his life begins we can always speak of him even up to his death and beyond. But such a system would not permit reference to the yet-to-exist, and thus would promote an important distinction between reference by description and reference by name that, whatever its plausibility, does not strike at the heart of our present problem.

Whatever our particular choice turns out to be, it will be necessary to say with care what the quantifiers range over when the existence predicate is failed. There are interpretations that make reasonable sense out of *reference* to the nonexistent,[2] and there are possible worlds treatments in which the dead are *existent* members of worlds other than this one. There doesn't seem to be much else on semantical offer. This matters. If the best that can be done is to make it explicable that "Jones is dead" has a nonactual referent, this is far from providing an explanation of the ways in which the referent of such a sentence counts as having been victimized or wronged by the killing that made such reference possible. On the other hand, a possible-worlds semantics imbibes the same individuation problems that attach to the *theological* conception of death, and, on top of that, leave it wholly unexplained as to what it is about existence in alternative worlds, especially in worlds as similar to the actual world as is compatible with his nonexistence in it, that constitutes the wrongfulness of a person's murder.

It is not necessary to hold that any satisfactory semantics for death must leave it problematic as to what the wrongfulness of an unvolunteered and undeserved death consists in order to make the twofold point *first*, that the secular concept of death is logically tricky; and *second*, that this fact cannot but bear on the heft and the speed of the normative changes we have noted as regards the domestic uses of death.

Here is what I propose to do in the present paper. Having indicated in this section some of the conceptual difficulties that inhere in the secular conception of death,

I examine in section 2 a particular class of intractable disagreements that I call *stand-offs*. I show that although standoffs may resist substantival resolution, this needn't preclude the development of public policy that is acceptable to both parties. This outcome is delivered by a second-order conflict resolution device called **RR** (after "resolution rule"). **RR** does not require the contending parties to move from their first-order positions even slightly. More particularly, they needn't "agree to disagree" or to "split the difference." Section 2 ends with recognition of an apparently bizarre fact. It is that for all its attractions, the **RR** strategy is not actually used by parties locked in intractable disagreement about the domestic uses of death.

Section 3 attempts to explain this odd fact. It suggests that with the collapse of the theological conception of death, the standard theological prohibitions of the domestic uses of death lost their purchase. Correspondingly, anything that remained among secularists of the taboos against feticide and euthanasia were substantially damaged by the openness and aggressiveness of the attacks on such prohibitions since the early 1970s. I will suggest the existence of a dialectically central fact. We have lost our capacity to say in a rationally compelling way what the wrongfulness of such killings consist in. Correspondingly, we have—without quite noticing it—gone a long way toward privatizing the concept of murder.

2. STANDOFFS

On the face of it, whether it's all right to kill second-trimester fetuses or people in radically reduced conditions and prospects of well-being ought not be something that people find it so utterly difficult to agree on. That such disagreements exist and that they have proved to have been so intractable defeats any presumption of dialectical serenity. There is something about such matters that explains the great difficulties they throw up. One possibility is that like other kinds of intractable normative disagreement, say about whether Elvis was a great artist, the issues of domestic death are just matters of taste. Counting against this is a significant dialectical fact. Parties to disagreements about matters of taste find it natural and appropriate to agree to disagree. But it is precisely this feature that is missing in a great many of our disagreements about abortion and euthanasia.

Disagreements of this latter kind I call *standoffs*. In the present section I shall characterize this type of disagreement and then consider whether disagreements of this type are susceptible to the type of conflict resolution device that I have just sketched. Here is a preview of what we shall find. Standoffs are indeed eligible for application of this kind of conflict resolution device. But, as is worth repeating for emphasis, it is an empirical fact that disputants do not avail themselves of it. This suggests that a more radical displacement of the concept of death than our logical problem of the previous section would easily suggest. I shall describe this displacement in the section to follow.

An argument is in a standoff of *force 1* just in a case where the participants disagree on some point at issue and there is no agreement about procedures that would or might lead to agreement. Standoffs of *force 2* are standoffs of force 1 that satisfy the condition that there is no consensus to agree to disagree.

If a third condition is met, we have a standoff of *force 3*; there is no agreement to refer the dispute to third-party determination. The hallmark of a standoff is its vulnerability to the fallacies of irrelevance and question-begging. Standoffs of force 3 are of varying degrees of importance, with their importance depending on the interests of the disputants. Even so, there are cases in which the following things are true:

1. The standoff is a standoff *in a community* and so answers to certain demographic criteria. Whatever these might be in detail, they make it true not just that Bill and Sue are in a standoff, but that the *country*[3] is, for example.

2. The standoff involves a claim about what to do or should be done, and so is of an essentially normative character.

3. The matter in dispute is of a kind that places it within the legitimate authority of a third party to settle without the direct consent of the disputants. In many such cases, the standoff includes a disagreement about what the government, say, should do about the matter in dispute, concerning which it is empowered to act.

4. The matter is frequently such as to present a third party—the government or the courts—with what William James called a *forced option*,[4] in which not taking any action is equivalent to acting for one of the contending parties and against the other(s).

Concerning the normative character of standoffs, I shall say that a subject S holds a *deontic* belief B *proactively* just in a case where

a. B is a belief in the form "Nobody should do action A," and

b. holding B commits S to the truth of proposition P, "Everybody should take appropriate steps to prevent the performance of A by anyone." (For concreteness, think of B as the belief that nobody should sexually molest a young child.)

The proactive consequences of S's deontic belief B can be understood as follows: Anyone who satisfied (a) but who did not act in conformity with P would be pragmatically inconsistent[5] and guilty of wrongful omission by his or her own lights. Conspicuous by its imprecision is the requirement of the proactive deontic believer to take "appropriate steps." I shall not attempt to remove this imprecision beyond pointing out that preventative measures are held to conditions of proportionality and procedural normalcy.

A further imprecision affects the quantifiers embedded in clauses (a) and (b) of our definition of proactively held deontic beliefs. These are the expressions 'nobody', 'everyone' and 'anyone'. Quantifiers have *scopes* or ranges of applicability. They "range over" classes of individuals to whom their attached predicates are presumed to apply. If you think that everyone should try to discourage government corruption, whether you yourself are bound to take such steps will vary as between your own government and, say, the government of Italy. In other words, it may be expected that Ps frequently embody what is called sortal quantification.

Force 3 standoffs reject an important strategy for resolution. They reject the application of what could be called in a loosely figurative way the fundamental law on collective bargaining, in a form that subsumes negotiated acceptance in a rather general sense. The fundamental law is designed to discourage extremism. It supposes that negotiable disputes are those whose rational settlement involves a splitting of differences. This may be true of any dispute reasonably deemed to be negotiable, but it is definitive of force 3 disputes that at least one party sees the issue as nonnegotiable. For the antiabortionist, for example, who sees abortion as murder at any prenatal stage, it will be obvious that there are no differences to split, that the presumption of negotiability is grotesquely maladroit.

All the same, for many standoffs of force 3, although parties will not themselves negotiate resolutions, they will submit to settlements imposed by lawfully constituted third parties who (or which) appropriate the issues as their own. In these cases we may take it that parties honor the presumption of prior consent lodged in the mythic notion of the social contract. This is a case that motivates the following two definitions.

Definition 1.   A force 3 standoff meeting conditions (1) to (4) above is a *political* standoff in a population K to the extent that K subscribes or acquiesces to the presumption of prior consent to a resolution imposed by a lawfully constituted third party recognized as such in K.

Definition 2.   A force 3 standoff fulfilling conditions (1) to (4) is a *purely moral* standoff in a population K to the extent that K rejects this presumption of prior content.

It is important to note that these definitions use the terms "political" and "purely moral" in a technical sense. A disagreement is political or is moral not on account of the content of subject matter of the matter at issue, but rather because of procedural qualifications and limitations on its resolution.

Standoffs of *force 4* can now be specified. They are standoffs of force 3 that also satisfy definition 2. They are purely moral disputes, disputes of a kind that lawfully enforced settlements will not be consented to. Political disagreements are arguments that disputants are prepared to lose. Moral disagreements of force 4 are arguments people are not prepared to lose.

Central to the present distinction is the notion of withheld consent. If S is a party to a standoff of force 4 about, say, the practice of Aing, then S proactively holds a deontic belief with respect to Aing, namely, "Nobody should do A." By virtue of the conditions that qualify S's deontic belief as proactive, S is committed to take steps to prevent the practice of Aing. If S's government acts in such a way as to make Aing lawfully permissible, S must take *some* steps to resist or cancel the government's approval, and whatever those steps may be, they must be of such a character as to express S's conviction that the government's action is not morally authoritative. It is not sufficient that a "loser" in a government-resolved force 4 contention is displeased or ticked off over having "lost." It is rather that he is not happy about having "lost" by virtue of wrongful actions by his government, hence by virtue of actions by which S judges himself to be morally unbound.

It is here that the idea of proportionality of preventative measures can be seen to bear significant theoretical weight. If S believes that not even his government is morally entitled to decide a force 4 contention "against" him, then his own proactive commitments by his own lights may obligate him to a course of civil disobedience or rebellion. In this, he is not always wrong.

It is well to try to characterize the sheer impactedness of force 4 disagreements. They embed a dialectical structure that I propose to call Philosophy's Most Difficult Problem.[6] Consider, then, this familiar argument:

1. All human actions are (macro-) natural events.
2. All (macro-) natural events have a cause.[7]
3. If there are any free actions, they are uncaused.
4. Therefore, there are no free actions.

It is easy to see that we can react to this argument in either of two ways. We might hold that the argument is sound and that, notwithstanding its extreme counter-intuitiveness, its conclusion is true. It is, so to speak, a *surprising truth*. On the other hand, we might see the argument as valid, but as a reductio ad absurdum of the premises that imply it. On this view, the conclusion, far from being a surprising truth, is an utter and transparent falsehood. The disagreement is not about whether (4) is a logical consequence of the preceding lines, but rather about what is the consequence of (4)'s being a consequence of those premises. People who see the argument in the first way are determinists. Those who see it in the second way are antideterminists, and if they select premise (2) as that which the reductio argument discredits, they are libertarians.

Determinists and libertarians thus find themselves landed in an extremely tricky problem. It is

> *Philosophy's Most Difficult Problem.* Let $A = <\{P_1, \ldots, P_n\}, C>$ be a valid argument, a sequence in which C is a logical consequence of proceeding steps. Philosophy's Most Difficult Problem is that of adjudicating in a principled way the conflict between supposing that A is a sound demonstration of a counterintuitive truth, as opposed to seeing it as a counterexample of its premises.

The essence of determinism is the following argument:

> **Det:** Since the law of causality is universally true of natural events, since all human actions are natural events, and since causality contradicts freedom, no human action is free.

The essence of libertarianism is the following argument:

> **Lib:** Since at least some human actions are free, and since causality contradicts freedom, then either the law of causality fails for certain natural events or not all human actions are natural events.

It takes little reflection to see that determinism and libertarianism are almost, but not quite, the total opposites of each other. The significance of this opposition is that neither can succeed as a critique of the other. If we try to refute **Det** by forwarding **Lib**, we *beg the question* against **Det**. Similarly, if we try to refute **Lib** by forwarding **Det**, we *beg the question* against **Lib**. Something interesting follows from this. Although **Det** makes a case *for* determinism, it does not make a case *against* libertarianism; and although **Lib** makes a case *for* libertarianism, it does not make a case *against* determinism. When any two arguments find themselves in this position, we may say that a *stalemate* exists with respect to some disputed issue.

What, in greater detail, is the structure of stalemates? In schematic form **Det** is:

Schema Det: P and Q and R; therefore not-S.

On the other hand, the schematic form of **Lib** is

Schema Lib: S; therefore either not-P or not-Q or not-R.

It is notable that **Schema Det** and **Schema Lib** are equivalent arguments-schemata in elementary logic. They are the (argumental) *contrapositives* of each other.

We now see why **Det** cannot be a case against **Lib**, nor **Lib** against **Det**. If **Det** is valid, so is **Lib**; and if **Lib** is valid, so is **Det**. There is a sense, then, in which **Det** and **Lib** are the same argument. But if this is so, how can it possibly be the case that in forwarding **Det** as a refutation of **Lib**, or **Lib** as a refutation of **Det**, we would be begging the question each time?

The answer is that, as we have seen, **Schema Det** and **Schema Lib** constitute a stalemate. They do so because they can't be coforwarded in any contention space without begging the question. And they beg the question because each has a premise that is the negation of the other's conclusion.

It is easy to see that standoffs of force 4 embed stalemates in the sense we have been discussing. It is largely because of this structural feature that force 4 disagreements are so deeply impacted. Some of the more notorious (or celebrated) developments in the recent history of the domestic death dialectic exploit this feature of stalemate. Often it will be argued that such and such a view of abortion can't be correct because if it were, then (reductio) infanticide would be all right. But people like Tooley and Singer see it differently. Because that case for abortion is sound, they say, its implications for infanticide, while surprising, are likewise sound.

Even so, it is important to see that force 4 disputes are not wholly irresolvable. They are sometimes resolvable by a Pascalian minimax strategy. The abortion issue provides a useful illustration. Let us say that X and Y are in a standoff of force 4 about abortion on demand at any time during pregnancy. X is pro and Y contra. If X and Y are willing to admit the possibility that they might be mistaken in their respective views, then costs can be reckoned. The cost of the mistake if Y is mistaken is that in Canada alone, scores of thousands of women a year would be encumbered with pregnancies they did not want and need not have put up with. It is a nontrivial cost, to say the least. But the cost of the mistake if X is mistaken is the unjustified killing of that same number of unborn year in and year out. If X and Y are able to agree on which would be the greater cost, then a resolution rule drops out.

RR: Settle the issue in such a way as minimizes the realization of the greater possible cost.

What makes the **RR** strategy so interesting (some would say "attractive") is that it settles things in a second-order way without requiring any degree of first-order accord. A person who is wholly convinced of the propriety of, say, midterm abortion can agree that the prudent thing to do—indeed the prudent social policy—is not to perform them or have them. What makes this possible is that recognizing that one's view might be mistaken is nonprobative. It does not require the holder of the view to lessen his or her confidence in its truth one iota. The significance of the recognition is wholly practical. It guides action, and does so without the need to disturb conviction.

It might strike us as perplexing that in the recent history of the abortion debate in countries like Canada, resolution rule **RR** is wholly conspicuous by its utter absence. It can only be conjectured that the abortion on demand issue failed a condition that makes **RR** an applicable rule. **RR** is an applicable rule only if each party to the disagreement is prepared to admit the possibility of error. On something as *metaphysically complex* as the issue of when a member of the biological species *Homo sapiens* acquires the protection against termination of its life, it could only expected that those having views about the matter would readily admit the possibility of mistake. Yet precisely this seems to have been missing from the Canadian record. It is an omission not restricted to Canada, of course.

I said pages ago that the secular concept of death is a metaphysically fraught concept. As we saw, part of this vexation lies in the question of what would count as a satisfactory quantificational semantics for facts such as that Caesar is dead. Our present discussion discloses a second vein of metaphysical difficulty. People who doubt that the question of abortion is decisively answered strictly by way of religious authority seek an answer that turns on the right answer to a prior question, which asks for the conditions under which a member of the species *Homo sapiens* is a *person*. Not a legal person, but a *metaphysical* person. There is, as we have just seen, a huge irony lurking in that question. It is a question that notoriously produces nothing like a stable consensus with regard to prenatal stages of human existence. It is a notoriously *hard* question. Being so, it is a question that one would expect would dispose a reasonable person to acknowledge that his own answer to it carries some nontrivial prospect of *error*. If the expectation were fulfilled, the **RR** rule could hardly be ignored. But in fact it is massively ignored. Hence, *modus tollens tollendo*, contemporary abortion disputants are not metaphysically troubled by the utterly hard metaphysical problem on which their judgments of abortion turn.

Even so, the idea of the possibility of error is a theoretically elusive one. For our purposes here an economical characterization will have to do. I will say that a disputant recognizes the possibility that his own position is mistaken just to the extent that he deems **RR** an applicable rule in the argument at hand.[8] Our final category of standoffs can now be specified. An argument is a standoff of *force 5* when it is an argument of force 4 concerning which disputants are closed-minded. Closed-mindedness is not here pejoratively intended. A person is closed-minded about an issue precisely to the extent to which he is unprepared to submit the issue to **RR**-determination. Most of us are closed-minded about whether the gunning down of customers at fast-food outlets is all right as a form of relaxation. It is obvious that **RR** would decide the issue in their favor, but that they would even consider submitting it to such a strategy is mad.[9]

3. DIALECTICAL FATIGUE

My task in this section is to try to answer the question of why the **RR** strategy does not commend itself to people who find themselves locked in disagreement about the domestic uses of death. Equivalently, ours is the question of why it has it come to pass that differences of opinion about the domestic uses of death have ended up as disagreements of force 5. My answer to this question requires that we say something about the phenomenon of slippery slopes. For this I shall require the prior notion of an *argument from discountable dissimilarities*.

It frequently happens things of certain kinds are so constituted that certain of their attributes are preserved under various kinds of difference.[10] Facts exemplifying this metaphysical commonplace support what I shall call *arguments from discountable dissimilarities* (ADDs). One form of the ADD is the analogical argument. A second is the sorites argument. Concerning analogical arguments, I have in mind iterations of them that introduce with each move a new dissimilarity. In the case of sorites arguments, there is a multiplicity condition built in, but with this difference: Iterations are iterations of the same difference.[11]

Iterations produce *accumulations*, that is, accumulations of differences. This is a fact of pivotal significance for ADDs, since accumulating differences have a propensity to be target property *preservation busters*. This is not always true, needless to say. Deductive validity is preserved under arbitrary iterations of the v-introduction rule, to take just one example. Nor is it the case that analogical arguments go wrong only when they involve iterations. But I am not concerned with such cases here.

Notwithstanding their clear differences, iterated analogical arguments and sorites arguments are chains of subarguments. The chain is secure only if its subarguments to date are sound. But as the chain lengthens, the iteration of differences approaches the status of preservation-busting accretions. It is widely accepted that one of the main tasks of a practical logic is the principled identification of the degree of accumulation at which target property preservation breaks down. If this is taken to mean, "At what *single* iteration is preservation lost?" some theorists say that the question is incompetent. Its incompetence inheres, they say, in the indeterminancy that such metaphysical arrangements underwrite. Others will say that the indeterminacy is not a metaphysical fact, but rather the marker of an epistemic limitation.

ADDs of this sort go bad when they exhibit the structure of a reductio argument. In a common form, these are arguments that seem to (or actually do) start out well, only to go disastrously wrong in transit. Reductio arguments are difficult to identify in a principled way, as we have seen. The difficulty is that one of the functions of arguments is to defeat the antecedent or received view that a given proposition is false. When arguments of this sort work, they are demonstrations of the truth of a counterintuitive consequence. The difficulty is that there is no obvious *general* way of discerning when an argument is a reductio rather than the proof of a surprising truth.

I want to consider cases in which ADD arguments come up because they are used to advance proactively deontic beliefs. Iterated ADDs of this sort have an important property. It is that *if* they are defective, they subsume subsequences that aren't defective. What is more, *if* they are defective, then at some juncture what they argue for is morally insupportable. So it is important that we be able to identify defective iterated ADDs. The class of defective ADDs we are reflecting on are those that appear to contain untrue conclusions and yet at the same time acceptable subarguments. *Sorites* arguments are arguments that appear to go wrong at a point.

But if the indeterminacy issue is correctly understood, whether metaphysically or epistemically, then either there *is* no point at which they go wrong or it cannot be *known* where that point is in the argument chain. Either way, I say again that we aren't able to say in a principled way what it is that makes such an argument a reductio as opposite to a sound proof of a surprising result. Much the same difficulty pertains to iterated analogical arguments. The ones we here have in mind appear to be defective. They seem to have false conclusions and sound subarguments. If we are to discern why these are *ad falsum* arguments, we need to have access to a suitably general conception of the concept of differences that don't make a difference. But this we do not have.

Our problem, to repeat, is that we seem not to be able to demonstrate whether an ADD is a reductio argument or a sound proof of a surprising truth. In many real-life situations, this doesn't matter. Nothing particularly important hinges on whether we can know the point at which Jack becomes bald.

I will say that arguments have the *slippery slope factor* when and to the extent that they are arguments that appear to be defective, appear to have sound sub-arguments, and are arguments concerning which we lack the resources to demonstrate that they are reductio arguments, rather than sound demonstrations of surprising truths. When such arguments are about things that matter, or matter in the way that we have been discussing, it also matters that they display the slippery slope factor. For the presence of that factor provides that we lack the resources effectively to discourage people from accepting bad arguments that have slipped attractively into badness from impeccable or anyhow uncontested beginnings.

We now define *slippery slope arguments*. It is not everyone's conception of them, but it has the attraction of bearing some real theoretical weight in the context of disputations about public policy.

> A subject S makes a *slippery slope argument* with respect to a practice or policy P if and only if, or to the extent that,
>
> 1. S holds that P is an acceptable policy or practice.
> 2. There exists an ADD originating with the presumed acceptability of P that apparently licenses policy or practice P* by parity of argument.
> 3. S holds that P* is not acceptable.
> 4. S asserts that the ADD in question has the slippery slope factor, hence that he (and the rest of us, too) lacks the resources to pinpoint the defectiveness of the ADD.
> 5. In consequence, S proposes that it is ill-advised to conform our practice to the *sound subarguments of ADD*. In other words, S counsels against implementation of P.

Slippery slope arguments are risk-averse arguments. They are arguments against acting on sound arguments that license acceptable deviations from acceptable practices, on grounds that parity of reasoning considerations may take us to further deviations whose unacceptability *we lack the resources to show*. This conception of slippery slope argument resembles that of Douglas Walton, at least in its most basic sense. As Walton says,

[a] slippery slope argument is a kind of argument that warns you [that] if you take a first step, you will find yourself involved in a sticky sequence of consequences from which you will be unable to extricate yourself, and eventually you will wind up speeding faster and faster towards some disastrous outcome.[12]

What I want now to do is to examine this conception of slippery slope and slippery slope arguments in contexts of social change that I shall characterize as *collapsing taboos*.

I begin by taking some lexical license with the word "taboo." Its (European) anthropological usage appears to have originated in Captain James Cook's mention of the word in Tongean, Tahitian, and Hawaiian variations, in the journal of his third Pacific voyage in the late 1780s. A more complete understanding of the word we owe to the work of writers such as Sahlens and Valeri.[13] I shall not recount this interesting history here, except to note that, in the Hawaiian case, taboos began as something divine or closely connected with divinity, and that after the weighty encroachments of the European presence, they were merely what is out of bounds. Some of this spread of meaning is reflected in my stipulation, as we shall now see.

In my usage, a taboo is a deep cultural protection of a value, underwritten by broad and largely tacit societal consensus. So understood, a taboo is an ordered pair $<P, X>$ in which P is a principle protecting a value—usually a prohibition—and X is an exclusion, an embedded practice that excludes P itself from free enquiry, from the rough-and-tumble of dialectical probing. The more general implication of this exclusion is to avert discussion of P's merits, whether it is a justified prohibition and if so by virtue of what. Taboos, then, are special cases of principles or points of view attended by dialectically weak—or even nonexistent—track records. Of course, there are large classes of dialectically impotent statements whose lack of justificatory support is a reflection of the fact that they are seen as not *needing* defense or justification. They are "self-evident," or "common knowledge," or some such thing. With taboos, however, dialectical impotence is less a matter of a defense not being needed than that it should not even be *attempted*.

Many taboos were once religious proscriptions. This helps in understanding both the X-factor and the dialectical impotence that attaches to taboos even after they have lost their religious moorings. Though detached from this expressly religious backing, we seem to retain them out of cultural inertia. When they were religious laws, they required no justification by us; indeed to raise the question of whether something commanded by God might require our justification was to risk the sin of hubris. These features are retained as the X-factor and the pallid dialectical track record this gives rise to.

In certain respects, taboos resemble conventions. Conventions I take in David Lewis' way; they are solutions of coordination problems.[14] In a classic example, the conventions on driving—on the right in countries such as Canada and on the left in countries such as Japan—are regulators of traffic's ebb and flow. In such cases, there is no prior fact of the matter as to which side of the road is the correct side to drive on in Canada, or in Japan. The only facts of the matter are the facts that our respective conventions constitute. If taboos resemble conventions closely enough, there is reason to think that, in some cases at least, they will imbibe this feature of them. If so, the existence of the *X*-factor can now be seen to be a well-motivated constituent of such taboos. Taboos carry the suggestion of high moral dudgeon and of settled certainty. Under their influence, people are easily disgusted and quick to dismiss contrary views out of hand. If a taboo is a convention or sufficiently like a convention, there is no prior fact of the matter that the taboo reports or honors.[15] The *X*-factor inhibits open enquiry. It does so for a reason, as we now see. Open inquiry might well disclose that the taboo records no prior fact, hence no fact that could be seen as sustaining it. This in turn affords an explanation of the dialectical impotence of taboos; for to scrutinize a taboo is to collapse it.[16]

Taboos sometimes resemble the first principles or absolute presuppositions of normal science or Kuhnian paradigms. If a paradigm lapses, nothing less then a chunk of normal science is in the balance, and a scientific revolution may well be in store. If a taboo crashes, events of similar gravity portend: the loss of a large chunk of case law, or of public morality, with the prospect, even, of a more sweeping axiological revolution.

Taboos are the natural enemy of other principles we admire. One of these is our affection of free and open inquiry. Taboos embed principles *P* under the protection of dialectical exclusions *X*. The *P*s of our <*P*, *X*>s have not had occasion to win their dialectical spurs. This makes them especially vulnerable to attack should indeed they chance to be attacked. Taboos sometimes crash. Sometimes they just wear out. When this happens, violations of the *X*-factor are made in ways that are tolerated or even sponsored by decision makers and shapers of public opinion—Walter Lipmann's "dominant élites." So a practice heretofore constrained by a taboo might become the subject of a Government White Paper, a series of editorials in the *Times*, or even the "full hour" with Larry King. More significantly still, it might be given a less than hostile "treatment" in a network sitcom or drama.[17] When the *X*-factor is violated by dominant élites, this alone may constitute its retirement, and with it the *P* in question. It is now fair game for aggressive dialectical probing that its *prior* status as a taboo has given it slight capacity now to resist.

A classic part of the abortion question has been whether fetuses have a metaphysical property that secures for them what has been called "moral standing,"[18] and if so, under what conditions is it acquired? Call this metaphysical property "personhood." The mere asking of this question leaves dialectical space for the possibility that

HP: There are human organisms who (which) aren't persons.

HP in turn gives the linked corollaries:

PA: In the species *Homo sapiens*, personhood is a something that a human organism acquires in a manner consistent with the fact that personhood is not an essential property of being human.

And

> *PL*: In the species *Homo sapiens*, personhood is something that a human being might lose in ways consistent with the fact that personhood is not an essential property of being human.

PA and *PL* should give us pause. They might dispose us to think that a human being's personhood is entirely a contingent matter. If we are being careful, this is strictly true. It is not the case that a human organism x who loses personhood ceases on that account to be that same x. What may be true is that personhood is essential to beings who are human and who have the additional characteristics $K_1, \ldots, K_n$, and precisely they. The classical metaphysical problem of abortion is the problem of specifying these K_i.

Asking the *HP* question in a serious way, in a way that exposes the issue to free and open inquiry, lands us with the substantial metaphysical task of specifying the K_i. The record to date registers our failure in this regard, an utter lack of consensus. It is hardly surprising, given that metaphysical problems have sometimes been defined as problems without solutions, or anyhow problems without recognizable solutions. But here there is a particular difficulty. We seem to be faced with the same indeterminacy problem that is triggered by any sorites problem. If so, there is no fact of the matter about when personhood is achieved; or there is indeed a point at which it is achieved but it cannot be known.

Anyone who has lived in the second half of the twentieth century will be aware of a striking dialectical fact. No one has been able to make an argument against, say, midterm abortion that has attracted a stable and enduring consensus. This suggests that in societies such as ours, we find ourselves in a classic *ad ignorantiam* situation, a situation in which there is some disposition, however tacit, to favor an argument crudely in this form:

1. We don't know of a convincing case against midterm abortion.
2. Therefore, there is no such case.

It goes without saying that *ad ignorantiam* arguments are sometimes fallacious. But they commit no fallacy when they can be interpreted *either* as an autoepistemic argument such as

a. if there were a convincing case against midterm abortion we would know what it is (by now),
b. but we don't,
c. so there isn't,

or as an abductive argument such as

i. the best explanation of our not having a convincing case against midterm abortion is that there is no such case,
ii. we haven't, in fact, a convincing case against midterm abortion,
iii. so it is plausible to conjecture that no such case exists.

The autoepistemic argument is valid by *modus tollens*; and although the abductive argument is invalid if construed deductively, this is not the intended construal, as the tentativeness of its conclusion makes clear. In each case, the main weight of the argument is borne by the first premise. It is one thing to know whether these premises are actually true; it is another and easier thing to suppose that in our failure to find a convincing case against midterm abortion, we might come to believe that they are true. The key factor in this dynamic is *dialectical fatigue*. With the retirement of theological conception of death, and the violation of the X-factor in what remained of the taboo against abortion even for secularists, we find that we have nothing effective to say against abortion. This produces a dialectical lassitude that, in turn, delivers the key premise in the autoepistemic and abductive arguments here sketched.

The attack on the no-abortion-at-any-time-condition was intended to promote only a modest-seeming reform. Those pressing for this reform hadn't—for the most part anyhow—the slightest idea or intent that abortion on demand would be in the ambit of its escape. They pressed their arguments innocently. They were innocent of two things, one already noted, and another that I shall mention now. The first was that when a taboo loses the protection of its X-factor, the principle it previously protected lacks the dialectical means to defend itself. The second point is that once its X-protection is lost, the newly qualified principle stands little chance of preserving the status of a taboo, hence the protection of the X-factor. This is borne out empirically by what is known of axiological collapse on the hoof, that is, in real-life. The likely explanation is that taboos are the result of cultural evolution, and that once the taboo against abortion as such collapsed, the culture lacked the time to reset the taboo a notch below, so to speak.

We see in this, well enough, the elements of slippery slope. Slope we can see as the reduction of the number, and sometimes the weight, of the original conditions of a prohibition. Slipperiness is the lack of dialectical resources to minimize the elimination of them, indeed to cut off at any point. (And here the general pattern of iterated ADDs recurs.)[19]

Our failure in specifying the K_i is nicely reflected in a difference between a classic sorites argument and a sorites argument applied to abortion. In the classic case of baldness, the downward sorites "proves" that no one is bald (more carefully, that no one *becomes* bald), and the upwards sorites "proves" that no one becomes hirsute. As we have seen, the *classic sorites problem* can be put this way: The termini of the downward and upward baldness sorites arguments are the two propositions that no one becomes bald and that no one becomes hirsute. Whatever the epistemic status of these termini, their *dialectical* status is that there is no disposition whatever in any community of case-makers to make a case for these propositions. There exists the widest possible consensus that they are *false*. The problem is to find the cutoff point in the descent and ascent to falsehood, the point at which truth becomes falsity. Alternatively, the problem is to show why this isn't a problem.

In the case of abortion, the two termini of the downward and upward sorites arguments are the propositions that abortion is always impermissible, that is, is permissible at no stage following conception, and that abortion is never impermissible, that is, is permissible at every stage following conception. Here there can be no question of our being faced with a classic sorites problem. For the termini are rejected by so-called moderates in the abortion debate; and two other constituencies exist in which one of this pair is rejected, while the other is held dear. It is interesting to reflect on the dialectical dynamics that sort people into these radically disjoint communities. In the one constituency, in which abortion is wrong at all stages, a risk aversion argument is at work. Given that very late abortions are impermissible and that we can't be sure how to determine the K_i, we proceed with a minimax strategy. We "bet" on the decision of least "cost" should, unbeknownst, that decision be a huge mistake.

Those favoring the opposite terminus, the proposition that abortion is permissible at every fetal stage, find themselves surrendering to what we were calling a kind of dialectical fatigue. Given the permissibility of early abortion, and given that at no subsequent point is there a convincing case that *this* is the point that divides permissibility from impermissibility, there is *dialectical* room for *ad ignorantiam* arguments in either autoepistemic or abductive variations. In each case, the proposition that there *is* a cutoff point is called into question. And if there is reason to suppose that there is no divide between the permissible and the impermissible, then, given that abortion is sometimes permissible, there is reason to think that it is always permissible.

The empirical record of the past thirty years in countries such as Canada discloses a solid majority for those who hold either the moderate or the full-width positive position on the permissibility of abortion. Those who favor the risk-averse approach take the K_i to exist but to be extremely difficult to specify. Those who favor the *ad ignorantiam* approach take the difficulty of specifying the K_i to be reason for thinking that, *for fetuses*, the K_i don't exist.

The dominant Western view of abortion should also matter for issues such as euthanasia, never mind that present practice is something of a jumble. Although it matters for euthanasia, this view is far from dominating the issue. If we applied the same considerations *ad ignorantiam* to the alleged conditions that mark the *loss of personhood* but not of human life, we would grant euthanasia considerable latitude. On the other hand, if we permitted involuntary euthanasia only on grounds of presumed consent, we could never permit abortion at any stage, short of telling an as yet untellable story of the possibility of counterfactual consent by a comatose granny and the impossibility of it by her recently conceived granddaughter or granddaughter-to-be.

As we presently conceive of it, voluntary euthanasia, or assisted suicide, proceeds from the prior right of self-destruction.[20] Whatever the qualifications that may attach to this presumed right, euthanasia is interesting beyond their reach. If we are not careful, we will resort to it freely just when it is sincerely thought that this is what the patient would tell us if he could. At the crux of such imaginings is the difference between what the patient would tell us about *remaining* in his present conditions of life and what we ourselves think about *falling into* those same conditions. Either there is a difference or there is not. If there is not, then *our* view prevails, for it is also *his* view. If there is a difference, no one has yet managed to tell us what it is and how its presence or absence might be discerned. We may eventually come to see such differences as unimaginable, finding ourselves met with a recurrence of the same dialectical tension between a risk-averse approach in which we are never satisfied by our efforts to imagine the patient's condition and an *ad ignorantiam* approach in which we come to think that the unimaginability of the difference between how the patient sees his plight and how we see it on his behalf is grounds for denying the difference. If we exercise the first option, we will never agree to assisted suicide by implied consent; and if we take the second option, we will allow it whenever someone appropriately situated feels badly enough on the patient's behalf.

It is important to know whether we have the means to adjudicate the conflict between these two options. If not, that failure *itself* could reactivate the selfsame dialectical rivalry. Risk-averse people will make a risk-averse argument for the tricky option, whereas others, noting our failure to determine which is the better approach, may reason abductively that neither is. But for this to be true, it must also be true that there *is* no best approach, that there is no fact of the matter about how best to judge assisted suicide in such cases. Either way, we have deep slopes and radical slippages—upward in the one case to the point of total prohibition, and downward in the second in ways resembling license. These are things to keep an eye on.

4. CONCLUSION

In bringing this paper to a close I want to give some consideration to the abstract structure of the issues that we have been reflecting on. Let K be a class of practices $P_1, \ldots, P_n$ concerning which the following things are true:

1. Until comparatively recent times, each of the P_i was subject to a widely consented-to prohibition.
2. The structure of those prohibitions exhibited at least something of the character of what I have been calling "taboos."
3. In more recent times, events turned in ways that constituted or led to a violation of the prohibitions' X-factor.
4. Each P_i distributes the costs of mistakenly implementing it or refraining from implementing it in ways that engage the **RR**-rule.
5. The **RR**-rule "predicts" that the P_i would not be implemented even by those who are morally untroubled by them.
6. The empirical record reveals that this "prediction" was massively wrong.
7. This failure can be explained structurally. To the extent to which the P_i were the subject of taboos against them, there was the correlative lack of the means to demonstrate in what the wrongness of P_i ing consists once the X-factor was violated.
8. This occasions dialectical fatigue which, in turn, can trigger *ad ignorantiam* arguments, whether autoepistemic or abductive, to the effect that the P_i are not in fact immoral practices.

There is little in this dialectical chain of events that is probative. Dialectical fatigue may trigger an abductive or autoepistemic argument, but this is no guarantee of its soundness. The dominant significance of dialectical fatigue is dialectical. Those who hate abortion and who hate involuntary euthanasia have no case to make against those who think otherwise. This is for one of two rather different reasons. In the case of theologically based rejections of those practices, they can cut no ice with the secularist. This lands the theological apologist in the ignoratio elenchi fallacy, in which he attributes to his opponent a view he doesn't hold and then refutes it, or he derives a consequence of a view his opponent does hold but that he denies follows from that view. On the other hand, if the would-be-case-maker against the P_i favors a case that does not offend against secularist assumptions as such, then he finds simply that he has no such case to make—that is, no case that convinces the other party. The **RR**-strategy presupposes two things in the absence of which it fails. One is that the party who is the target of the strategy will admit that the moral position on P_i ing and on refraining from P_i ing alike might be mistaken. The other is that, even assuring that the possibility of error is granted, the cost of being mistaken in favoring P_i ing is greater than the cost of mistakenly refraining from P_i ing.

The total picture thrown up by these dialectical complexities is one of the collapse of moral certainties about homicide, about the conditions under which the domestic uses of death are deeply and unanswerably immoral. We see in this a widening gulf between public and private morality. In societies such as ours there has always been such a gulf. But it must be said that never has it been so wide in matters of the moral discouragement of the domestic uses of death. It is a drift, the slippery slope character of which suggests more drift still. It may soon come to be the case that feticide will be widely practiced for reasons of diagnosed genetic damage or genetically based likelihood of trouble in the fetus's later life. Abortions having this rationale are wholly "covered" by the moral presumption of the fetus's failure to have the metaphysical protection of moral standing. Should it come to pass that genetic-harm rationale loses its cover and is taken as morally sufficient for fetuses, the slippery slope character of the changes we have here been reviewing suggests that the genetic-harm rationale may come to be taken as less conditionally sufficient. In that case, we are no longer talking about *feticide*. This, too, is something to keep an eye on. But given the dialectical impotence we have been discussing, the recommended scrutiny may turn out to be more a gestural thing than an effective, consented-to constraint on practice.

NOTES

1. Thus we might elect something like the basic logic of Woods' "Essentialism, Self-Identity and Quantifying In," in *Identity and Individuation*, ed. Milton K. Munitz (New York: New York University Press, 1971), or of chapter 2 of *The Logic of Fiction: A Philosophical Sounding of Deviant Logic* (The Hague: Mouton, 1974), rather than that, say, of Cocchiarella's "Properties of Individuals in Formal Ontology," *Noûs*, 6 (1972), 165–187.

Cocchiarella's system T* or Meyer's "Identity in Cocchiarella's T*," *Noûs,* 6 (1972), 189–197, extension of it, T* =, is a second-order system and is rich with ontological promise. It is very agreeable to discover, for example, that T* = vindicates the conjecture made in "Essentialism, Self-Identity, and Quantifying In" that the principle of indiscernibility of identicals quite properly fails for properties, since properties, unlike individualism, do not themselves have properties in sufficient abundance for their individuation. Still T* = is not needed for present purposes. See also Woods, *Engineered Death: Abortion, Suicide, Euthanasia and Senecide* (Ottawa: The University of Ottawa Press, 1978), chap. 9.

2. See again Woods, *Engineered Death*, chap. 9.

3. Or the trade union, or the university, or the political party. The demographic conditions for the attribution of standoffs include group percentages involved in the disagreement, the standing of the disputants in the group, statistical distribution of the issues in contention, the momentousness of the issue, and so on. The concept of group is a particularly intractable problem for the social sciences generally, as Margaret Gilbert's *On Social Facts* (Princeton: Princeton University Press, 1993) ably attests.

4. William James, "The Will to Believe," in *Essays in Pragmatism* (New York: Hafner Publishing Company, 1957), 89.

5. At an intuitive level, a charge of pragmatic inconsistency echoes the familiar complaint against "not practicing what you preach." A deeper analysis, which I shall not pursue here, reveals how surprisingly pernicious this breed of inconsistency actually is. See John Woods, "Dialectical Blindspots," *Philosophy and Rhetoric*, 26 (1993), 251–265.

6. A problem I have discussed under the less dramatic and less accurate title of "logic's nasty problem," in "Pluralism about Logical Consequence: Resolving Conflict in Logical Theory," in John Woods and Bryson Brown (eds.), *Logical Consequence: Rival Approaches* (Oxford: Hermes Science Publications, forthcoming).

7. Here we entertain the possibility advanced by some philosophers of science that the law of causality fails in the microdomain, that is, that part of nature studied by quantum mechanics. But few doubt that the principle of causality holds in the *non*microdomain. I assume this qualification here.

8. This issue is discussed at length under the description "real possibilities" in Woods, *Theology from the Bottom Up*, in preparation.

9. Force 5 standoffs are discussed in Woods, "Deep Disagreements and Public Demoralization," in Dov M. Gabbay and Hans Jürgen Ohlbach (eds.), *Lecture Notes in Artificial Intelligence* (#1085 = *Practical Reasoning*) (Berlin and New York: Springer-Verlag, 1996), 650–662.

10. Of course, as the classical fallacies of composition and division make clear, property preservation often falls under the difference between wholes and parts.

11. The celebrated Violinist Argument of Judith Jarvis Thomson can be seen as an iterated analogical argument. If we take it that in the situation as she describes it, the violinist does not owe the intruder continuation of the circumstances of vital dependency, then the analogical argument to the same effect in cases of rape-induced pregnancies proceeds step by step. Let us say that schematically the permissibility of unplugging the violinist's "intruder" turns on the following facts of the case: $F_1, \ldots, F_n$. In the analogical argument, at each step an F_i is replaced by a different fact D_i. The analogical step is justified if there is a more general fact G_i that F_i and D_i both instantiate. In Thomson's example, the analogy is complete when every F_j is replaced with a D_j for which (she claims) there is an appropriate G_j that they both instantiate.

Sorites arguments are well-illustrated by the classical examples, for example, Bald Man. In these cases the same difference (e.g., loss of a single hair) is repeated at each step. Still, there is a huge difference between sorites arguments and iterated analogical arguments. Sorites arguments are defective at certain stages or intervals. Analogical arguments are sometimes sound at every step.

12. Douglas Walton, *Slippery Slope Arguments* (Oxford: Clarendon Press, 1992), 1. Notwithstanding the similarity of our basic conceptions, Walton and I understand the comprehensive logic of such arguments in rather different ways, which I lack the space to detail here.

13. Marshall Sahlens, *Islands of History* (Chicago: University of Chicago Press, 1985), and Valerio Valeri, *Kingship and Sacrifice* (Chicago: University of Chicago Press, 1985).

14. David K. Lewis, *Convention: A Philosophical Study* (Cambridge: Harvard University Press, 1969).

15. I am grateful to Mark Weinstein, who in conversation has explained that the Jewish taboos such as that against the eating of pork were entirely arbitrary edicts from God.

16. In a nice turn of phrase by Michael Stingl, in conversation.

17. When the main character in the ABC sitcom *Ellen* emerged, to much anticipation and hype, as a lesbian, the show would shortly be cancelled. It appears that plummeting ratings were not a reaction to Ellen's lesbianism, but rather to the program's boring didacticism about it.

18. See, for example, L. W. Sumner, *Abortion and Moral Theory* (Princeton: Princeton University Press, 1981), and Woods' critical review of it, "Utilitarian Abortion," *Dialogue: The Canadian Philosophical Review* 26 (1985), 671–682, with a reply by Sumner.

19. These matters are discussed in greater detail in Woods, "Slippery Slopes and Collapsing Taboos," forthcoming in *Argumentation*.

20. Concerning suicide, see Woods, *Engineered Death*, chap. 6.

Midwest Studies in Philosophy, XXIV (2000)

Justifications for Killing Noncombatants in War

F. M. KAMM

The doctrine of double effect (DDE) says that we may not intend evil as a means to a greater good or as an end in itself, but it is permissible to pursue a greater good as a final end by neutral or good means even if a lesser evil is a certain, foreseen side effect (if there is no other way to achieve the greater good).[1] The DDE has been used to distinguish morally between (1) terror-bombing civilians in wartime and (2) bombing military targets, foreseeing with certainty that civilians will be killed. The first is said to be impermissible; the second may be permissible. In this article, I shall be concerned with how criticism and revisions of the DDE bear on these and related cases in the morality of war. I shall try to show how consideration of this issue leads us to two new doctrines: the doctrine of triple effect and, better yet, the doctrine of initial justification. They may do better at explaining permissible and impermissible conduct than the DDE.

1

It has been suggested that, in many cases such as terror bombing, where acting is impermissible, we need not be intending harm strictly speaking. For example, although we must intend the involvement and appearance of death of noncombatants in terror bombing, we need not intend their deaths, since if they actually survive, that would not interfere with our ending the war. Of course, we know that the only thing we can do to involve them and make them appear dead will cause their deaths, but this may only be foreseen, not intended.

To deal with this problem, Warren Quinn[2] suggested that we focus on the wrongness of *intending the involvement of a person without his consent in a way that we foresee will lead to significant harm to him* (i.e., evil). This is instead of focusing on the wrongness of *intending the harm to him* (i.e., evil), as the DDE says. Let us say that Quinn's revision results in the DDE Revised (DDE(R)). Henceforth, to mark my acceptance of this revision without adding words, I shall use "evil*" to mean "evil or involvement without consent that we foresee will lead to evil,"[3] and say the DDE(R) says that we must not intend evil*.

Now consider another problem with the DDE. Suppose a doctor is called and told that organs—innocently acquired—have arrived and must be transplanted quickly into his five patients. He drives to the hospital, but on the road finds an immovable person in his path. If he takes a different route, he will be too late to do the transplants, and as he is the only one who can do them, the five will die. If he runs over the person on the road, he foresees, but does not intend, the death of the one. However, he knows (suppose) that if he gets to the hospital, he will save the five (Car Case). It seems impermissible for him to proceed.[4]

If it can be impermissible to do what causes death merely as a foreseen side effect (as in the Car Case), why is it not impermissible to engage in strategic bombing? That is, if the Car Case can raise the objection that the DDE is too liberal in allowing killing, why does this objection not undermine the defense the DDE provides for strategic bombing? I suggest that it may, and we should provide another justification for the distinction between terror bombing and strategic bombing.

Some (e.g., Philippa Foot) have concluded on the basis of cases like the Car Case that the moral distinction between intending harm and foreseeing harm must be supplemented (or replaced) by the moral distinction between harming and not aiding: acting foreseeing harm to some in order to do greater good for others is impermissible, but not aiding foreseeing harm to some in order to do greater good to others is permissible. But this conclusion banning harm is too strong: *It matters, I believe, whether harm is the result of the greater good itself or instead the result of means that cause the greater good.* For example, consider Car Case II. It is the same as Car Case I, except that the doctor need not run over anyone to get to the hospital. However, he knows that if he saves the five (by perfectly innocent means), *their being alive* (rather than dead) and behaving quite innocently will alter the causal events in the world so that germs hitherto safely closeted will kill one person who otherwise would not have been killed. It is still permissible to save the five.[5]

Can we use this point to explain the permissibility of strategic bombing? If so, we might have to distinguish whether the noncombatants were killed (a) as an effect of the means to the munitions factory blowing up or (b) as an effect of the munitions factory itself blowing up. Furthermore, we would have to be able to say that the blowing up of the factory was itself the greater good that could justify the death of bystanders. If we could say the latter, then even if the DDE(R) is incorrect, causing deaths by way of (b) would be permissible, but causing deaths by way of (a) would be impermissible.

But how can we say that the blowing up of a munitions factory is itself a greater good (comparable to saving more lives as in Car Case II)? It seems more like a *means to* the greater good, that is, if there are no munitions, more people will be alive (because not killed). There are two suggestions one might make at this point, I believe. One suggestion is to distinguish between (1) a means to a good and (2) a component of that good. The second suggestion is to distinguish between (1′) means that cause a greater good and (2′) means that have greater good as (what I call) a noncausal flip side. Consider the first suggestion. Components of a greater good are parts of it, for example, the saving of two of five people, not means to it. I believe it is sometimes true that components of a greater good may permissibly cause lesser evils that are only ultimately justified by the greater good of which the components are parts.[6] However, if a munitions factory being blown up were in this way a component of a greater good, the greater good would have to be conceived as something like "the end of arms production." But is this not itself just a means to the good of more people alive because not killed? I suspect, therefore, that the munitions factory being blown up is not a component of the greater good.

The second suggestion may be more promising. It is not only greater good itself (or its components) that is permitted to be created if we foresee they will cause lesser evil. *Means that have a noncausal relation to greater good may also cause lesser evil.* (The means that have only a causal relation to greater good are not permitted to be used if we foresee they will cause lesser evil. This is what is true in the Car Case, where driving to the hospital causes the death of a bystander and also leads by a causal chain to saving five.) Consideration of cases may help us distinguish the causal from noncausal relation I have in mind. In a version of the Trolley Case, a trolley is headed toward killing five people, but a bystander can save them (only) by redirecting the trolley. However, if redirected, it will go off in a direction where one person will definitely be hit and killed by it. Typically, nonconsequentialists think it is permissible (though not obligatory) to divert, even though this involves harming some in order to aid others.[7]

In the context where only the trolley threatens the five, the turning of the trolley threat away from them—by which I mean the moving of the trolley itself away—is the same event as their becoming free of threats, and this is the same event as their becoming saved. Hence, there is a noncausal relation between the turning away of the trolley and the five becoming saved. Furthermore, the state of affairs of their being saved is noncausally related to these events in that context.[8] Because this is true, I will say that the five being saved (the greater good) is the noncausal flip side of the turning of the trolley. Intuitively, I mean to distinguish this noncausal relation from a less "tight," ordinary causal relation that could connect the turning of the trolley and the saving of people, as in the following Van Case. A van is headed toward killing twenty people. If we turn the trolley away from hitting five, the diverted trolley will gently push into those twenty and move them away from the van. Here the saving of the twenty is simply a causal consequence of the moving trolley. It contrasts with the relation between the five being saved and the moving of the trolley away from them. This is a contrast, as slim as it seems, that I think is crucial in a correct nonconsequentialist theory of permissible harm.[9]

Intuitively, it is also permissible to do acts (e.g., pushing a button that redirects the trolley) that cause the event that has greater good as a noncausal flip side and lesser evil as an effect. We can explain this by noting that pushing the button— an event that per se does not have greater good as a noncausal flip side or aspect— also does not per se cause the death of the one. It causes the death of the one *by* causing the trolley to be diverted, and *this* diversion has the greater good as its noncausal flip side.

How does all this relate to the case of strategic bombing? Blowing up the munitions factory has as its noncausal flip side (not as a further causal consequence) the reduced ability to kill people, and in the context of war, where munitions are necessary to kill people, this is the same as a greater number of people being alive. If the factory blowing up causes the lesser evil* and also has a noncausal relation to greater good, dropping the bombs is permissible. (Suppose the bombs themselves killed the bystander and, also, as a causal consequence, blow up the factory. Then means which had a purely causal relation to the greater good [i.e., the bombs cause the factory to blow up, and the blowing up has a noncausal relation to the greater good] would cause the lesser evil. This, I believe, would not be permitted.) In terror bombing, the evil* itself is a cause of greater good—neither the greater good nor means noncausally related to it cause lesser evil. Hence, terror bombing is impermissible.

What if blowing up the munitions factory caused noncombatant deaths as a side effect but had a purely causal relation to a greater good? For example, suppose there are no munitions being produced in the plant anymore and it is fear caused in the population when they see the factory destroyed that leads to their surrender and peace. The analysis I have provided would not justify bombing the munitions factory in this case. If this conclusion seems wrong, it may show that "war is special"—that is, principles that govern action in microinteractions between people in peacetime may not apply at the macro level in wartime, where enormous goods may outweigh some acts otherwise impermissible. (Such a "war is special" justification could also justify using bombs in strategic bombing that themselves cause noncombatant deaths.)

2

So far we have considered how one objection to the DDE(R) raised by the Car Case—that it permits too much—bears on the distinction between terror bombing and strategic bombing. We have also considered how some other proposed principles of permissible harm—that is, greater good itself may cause lesser evil and means having noncausal relation to greater good may cause lesser evil—deal with terror and strategic bombing. (I have not yet said anything here about why these two principles *are* correct principles of permissible harm or what justifies them.) Now consider two more wartime cases that bear on both the correctness of the DDE(R) and the development of alternative principles of permissible harm.

Consider first the Massacre Case: A general wants to bomb through a wall so he can move 100 people who are very important to the war effort to safety. If the hundred are moved to the safe zone, however, this will lead the enemy to massacre 200 civilians. However, the collapse of the wall will stop a mudslide that was about to kill 500 other civilians. Saving these 500 is no aim of the general's, as he is obligated to attend to war-related goals only. The general allows himself to act to save the 100 only because he believes that (i.e., on condition that he believes that) the greater good (500 saved plus 100 saved) will outbalance the lesser evil (200 dead in a massacre). However, since he does not intend to stop the mudslide, he does not act with the ultimate aim of producing that greater good. (*He does not even act intending to produce the greater good as a means to his acting on his aim of saving the 100.* He need not do this, as the mudslide will stop without his intending that it do so, just if he acts. To say that he intends to stop the mudslide as a means to his acting to save the hundred suggests that if it did not occur as a side effect of his act, he would, as a rational agent, be committed to doing something in order to make the falling of the wall stop the mudslide. But as a rational agent, he need not be committed to doing this just because he wishes to take advantage of a connection that already exists between his acting to save the 100 and the greater good.)

It is permissible, I believe, for the general to act in the Massacre Case, even though he does not aim at the greater good. *But the DDE(R) says that we may produce lesser evil* as a side effect only if we are pursuing a greater good as a final end.*[10] Even intending the greater good as a means would not satisfy this condition. Acting *because* the greater good will occur is different from acting in order that it occur. In discussing the DDE, *so much attention has been paid to the issue of whether or not we may intend a lesser evil* that none has been paid to whether or how we must intend the greater good.*

But now notice that if we can distinguish conceptually between intending an effect and acting because we believe it will occur, a common test used to distinguish conceptually between intending and merely foreseeing an effect is shown to be inadequate. The Counterfactual Test says that to see if someone acts intending or alternatively merely foreseeing an effect, we should imagine (counterfactually) that the effect will not occur but everything else remains the same. If the person would not act because the effect would not occur, this shows, it is said, that he intended the effect. But in the Massacre Case, if the greater good did not occur and all else remained the same, the agent would *not* have acted. He acts only because he believes that this greater good will occur; he will not act unless he believes it will occur. His act is conditional on his belief that it will occur, but he is still not intending this greater good. So we see that the Counterfactual Test fails to distinguish effects the belief in which is a condition of action, from effects that are intended.

Now consider the Munitions Grief Case:[11] If we bomb a munitions factory and it is immediately rebuilt, it will be pointless to bomb. It is only because civilians are killed as an (unavoidable) side effect of the factory blowing up that other citizens, consumed by grief, will be unable to rebuild. Hence, if we bomb, it would be *because* we believe the civilians would die. But this does not mean that we aim at their deaths. Though we take advantage of a side effect of our act to provide us with a reason for doing it, we need not be committed (as rational agents) to doing anything especially to make our act have that side effect. I believe bombing in the Munitions Grief Case can be permissible even if terror bombing is impermissible.

If we need not intend or aim to hit the noncombatants if we act in the Munitions Grief Case, we need not violate the no-intending-evil* component of the DDE(R). But another component of the DDE(R) says that we may produce a lesser evil* *foreseen* as a side effect if we use neutral or good means with the aim of achieving a greater good. But the lesser evil* we produce in the Munitions Grief Case is not a mere foreseen side effect; we act *because* we believe it will occur. I claim that even if intending an evil* is impermissible, acting only because one believes it will occur may not be impermissible.

If we combine what I have said about the cases where action is permitted because of unintended greater good (Massacre Case) and unintended lesser evil* (Munitions Grief Case), we can revise the DDE(R) further. These cases show us that one cannot only intend an effect or merely foresee it, but also act because of it. On account of this third relation we can have to an effect, we could construct the *doctrine of triple effect* (DTE(R)): A greater good that we cause and whose expected existence is a condition of our action, but which we do not necessarily intend, may justify a lesser evil* that we must not intend but the expectation of which we may have as a condition of action.

But now, in a variation on Munitions Grief Case, suppose we had different sorts of ways of destroying the munitions plant. One of the ways would certainly involve the noncombatants leading to their death, whereas each of the other ways has diminishing probabilities of this effect to the point of zero. If we chose a way that we foresee would involve bystanders because only then would the plant not be rebuilt, we would, I claim, make this choice intending the bystanders' involvement. This is ruled out by the DDE(R) and the DTE(R). Hence, if we adhere to these doctrines, as we acquire more precise ways to do strategic bombing, it will make no sense to bomb the plant. This is because the plant will be rebuilt, given that the only permissible means of bombing will not involve harming any bystanders.

I do not endorse the DTE(R). There are problems with it. A clear problem for the DTE(R) is that like the DDE(R), it would permit the doctor to drive over the person in the Car Case, since it allows a means to a greater good to have lesser evil* as a side effect. So it does not avoid the earlier objection I discussed in section 1.

Furthermore, both it and the DDE(R) are what I call state-of-mind principles. They make what is permissible dependent on the state of mind of the agent. But this seems wrong, quite generally. If an agent bombs a munitions plant and children die as a side effect, this can be permissible even if the agent intends the deaths. If the general in the Massacre Case did not blow up the wall because the mudslide would be stopped (he would have done it even if it did not rescue the 500), his act would still be permissible in the case where the mudslide was, in fact, stopped.

At this point, I am most interested in another problem for the DTE(R), since it will lead us to another principle of permissible harm that, I believe, accounts for the permissibility of acting in the Munitions Grief Case independently of the DTE(R).

3

The DTE(R) does not properly distinguish between the permissibility of acting in the Munitions Grief Case and the impermissibility of acting in the Two Factories Case: There are *two* munitions plants. So long as one of them is operating, there is no point in eliminating the other. We are able to bomb only one of the plants, but the foreseen side effect of this is that some noncombatants will be hit by the exploding plant and die. Only if this happens will the population be too consumed by grief to operate the second plant. Our previous analysis implies that if we proceed with the bombing, this does not mean we necessarily intend the involvement or deaths of the noncombatants; we may act only because we believe the involvement will take place. Hence, we need not violate the DDE(R) or DTE(R) in bombing in the Two Factories Case. Nevertheless, I suggest that bombing one plant in the Two Factories Case cannot be justified in the way bombing in the Munitions Grief Case is.

So far, in describing principles of permissible harm that differ from the DDE(R), I have said that greater good may cause lesser evil* and means that have a noncausal relation to greater good may cause lesser evil*. Now, in arguing against the particular failure of the DTE(R) raised by the Two Factories Case, I add the claim that it is *permissible for lesser evil* that is an effect of greater good (or of means noncausally related to it) to (in a sense) sustain that greater good*. This is so even if it is not permissible for evil* *to produce* that greater good. If it *sustains* greater good, the greater good is not *produced* by it. I will try to show that in the Munitions Grief Case, the evil* sustains greater good; in the Two Factories Case, evil* produces greater good.

Consider the Munitions Grief Case: The rebuilding of the factory is a second problem that comes about as the further causal consequence of our initially blowing up the factory. The blowing up *leads to* the potential rebuilding. Independent of this further causal consequence of the blowing up, *the noncausal flip side of blowing up* exists. This is, people being rid of the problem that existed at the time we acted (i.e., the threat of death from munitions as it existed before we did anything). This noncausal flip side would completely justify bad effects on civilians of blowing up the factory *unless some new problem arose as a consequence of blowing up and this new problem were not itself eliminated*. So the noncausal flipside is a state that, when described *independent of further causal consequences of it*, would justify the lesser evil*. I shall call such a state the *structural equivalent of the justifying good* (structural equivalent, for short). This is because it has the structure of the ultimate good that justifies the death of the bystanders: more people alive.[12] This structural equivalent provides us with a possible rationale for blowing up the factory, for we see that the structural equivalent of the justifying good involves something that could outweigh *certain* of the evils* that are effects of what we do. Which evils*? Those evils* that would affect the noncombatants killed by the blowing up of the factory.

Still, the prospect of achieving the structural equivalent may not justify blowing up the factory (and killing bystanders) unless we know that the factory will not be rebuilt shortly anyway. So justification for blowing up can depend on how the further causal consequences of blowing up are likely to affect the munitions plant and the greater number of people saved as it is in the structural equivalent. It is a prerequisite of being justified in blowing up the factory that *there be a prospect that a sufficient number of the people relieved of the munitions threat in the structural equivalent will remain unthreatened*. In this way the structural equivalent becomes the greater good that all things considered justifies the lesser evil*.

Another causal consequence of blowing up the factory is that it would lead to rebuilding were it not that the dead bystanders cause grief. We could be justified in blowing up the factory if it were likely that the good that would ultimately justify the death would occur. When we are justified in acting on the structural equivalent, I shall say it provides an *initial sufficient justification* for blowing up; the blowing up and the killings are initially sufficiently justified. "Initial" refers to what exists if we blow up the factory independent of further possible causal consequences (for the munitions plant and the greater number of people). "Sufficient" refers to the fact that the number to be saved from the munitions is a large enough number of lives to outweigh the death of bystanders.

Suppose that at least the initial sufficient justification for blowing up the factory is present. Then the hitting of the bystanders *does not produce the structural equivalent of the good*. Rather, it stands outside the structural equivalent and prevents *new* threats to it that arise from blowing up the factory. *In that sense, the evil* prevents the undoing of the good, rather than bringing about or producing the good.* (We might instead say, more precisely, that evil* *produces the good by sustaining its structural equivalent* rather than producing the structural equivalent.)

Consider by contrast the Two Factories Case. In it the second problem exists independent of the further causal consequences of what we do (blowing up a factory) to get rid of one problem. Given the existence of the two problems initially, we have *no initial sufficient justification* for blowing up one factory. *For when we blow up one factory and abstract from any new problem this causes, people are still subject to as many fatal threats from the second munitions plant.* That is, the structural equivalent of the justifying good does not yet exist as a flip side of blowing up one factory. In the Two Factories Case, the structural equivalent coming into existence depends on the bystanders being hit, as this causes the second factory to stop running. I believe this is what underlies the intuitive sense that bombing in the Two Factories Case is morally different from bombing in the Munitions Grief Case.[13] When some evil* is causally necessary for the structural equivalent that helps provide (at least) an initial sufficient justification of that evil*, the structural equivalent is *produced by an evil* that is not already initially sufficiently justified.* The evil* does not stand outside the structural equivalent of good and merely prevent its being undone by new threats caused by our successfully dealing with all the problems that originally prompted our action.

We can capture the idea behind this analysis as the Doctrine of Initial Justification (DIJ) (omitting "sufficient" for brevity's sake): It should be possible for lesser evils* to be caused by what at least initially sufficiently justifies them (which involves [at least] a structural equivalent that can become what ultimately justifies them) or by means (or effects of means) having at least the structural equivalent of its noncausal flip side or aspect. I believe what motivates this doctrine is the concern for the purity of causal chains. That is, it expresses a concern that the causal chain that leads to good G, where G justifies evil* E, need not involve evils* that are not at least initially sufficiently justified by what causes them (or by what is noncausally related to what causes the cause of them). I think this is the essence of the deep structure of nonconsequentialism in the area with which we are concerned. Its motto is: The possibility of initial sufficient justification all the way down. The DIJ can be used like the DDE(R) and the DTE(R) to test acts for permissibility and is intended to supplant them for this purpose.[14]

NOTES

1. I accept that there is a delicate distinction to be drawn between intending and aiming, such that all intendings involve aimings, but not the reverse. I also accept that those who are against intending an evil should be against aiming at it even when this does not involve intending it. (I owe these points to Michael Bratman.) Hence, I shall consider aiming at an evil to violate the DDE even when it does not amount to intending. Nothing I say in this paper should depend on distinguishing intending from aiming.

2. In "Action, Intention, and Consequences: The Doctrine of Double Effect," reprinted in his *Morality and Action* (New York: Cambridge University Press, 1993).

3. The revision is not unproblematic, as it radically changes the apparent point of the DDE. Those defenders of the DDE (like Thomas Nagel) who focus on not aiming at evil per se would be reluctant to accept it, I think.

4. This case is on the model of one described by Philippa Foot in "Killing and Letting Die," in *Abortion: Moral and Legal Perspectives*, ed. J. Garfield and P. Hennessy (Amherst: University of Massachusetts Press, 1984), pp. 178–85. It is also modeled on a case she used as an objection to the DDE (in "The Problem of Abortion and the Doctrine of Double Effect," reprinted in her *Virtues and Vices* [Oxford: Blackwell, 1978]): We must operate on five to save their lives, but doing so requires that we use a gas. It is harmless to the five, but it will unavoidably seep into a neighboring room, there killing an immovable patient. We may not operate, she concluded.

5. I first argued against Foot's conclusion in "Harming Some to Save Others," *Philosophical Studies* (November 1989), and subsequently developed aspects of the larger theory I am discussing here (as well as some of its applications) in *Morality, Mortality*, Vol. 2 (New York: Oxford University Press, 1996) and in "Toward the Essence of Nonconsequentialism" (forthcoming).

6. On this, see "Toward the Essence of Nonconsequentialism."

7. The one person is typically envisioned as on a side track, but this is not necessary. He could be in another part of the country and redirection of the trolley that leads to his being hit would still be permissible, I think.

8. I thank John Gibbons for his suggestion that there are two descriptions of the same event and they are noncausally related to a state of affairs.

9. The analysis I have provided of the Trolley Case shows that diverting a trolley headed to the five is morally the same as deciding to turn a trolley at a crossroads that *must* be turned (somehow) to one rather than five.

10. This I believe is the standard way in which the DDE is presented. Different philosophers, without drawing attention to what they are doing, have described the DDE differently with respect to whether we are to intend the greater good. The traditional rendition requires aiming at a good greater than the evil side effect (not just any good). Here are three sample renditions: (1) "The agent acts with a good intention and seeks to realize a good end . . . the good end that the agent seeks to realize is not morally disproportionate to the bad consequence" (Nancy Davis in "The Doctrine of Double Effect: Problems of Interpretation," reprinted in *Ethics: Problems and Principles*, ed. J. Fischer and M. Ravissa [Fort Worth, Texas: Harcourt Brace Jovanovich, 1992]); (2) "(a) the intended final end must be good . . . and (d) the good end must be proportionate to the bad upshot" (Warren Quinn, in "Actions, Intentions, and Consequences: The Doctrine of Double Effect"); and (3) "the good effect is the intended effect" (Baruch Brody, "Religion and Bioethics," in *A Companion to Bioethics*, ed. H. Kuhse and P. Singer [Oxford: Blackwell, 1998]). In (3), Brody is pointing to the fact that the foreseen/intended distinction in the DDE's account of permissibility is meant to distinguish the two effects—one good, which is intended, the other bad, which is foreseen. If this is the correct way of understanding the "double effect" point of the DDE, then the doctrine does not so much distinguish intending a bad effect from foreseeing a bad effect as it distinguishes intending a good effect from foreseeing a bad one. If this is so, and the good must be proportionate to the bad, this implies that we must intend a good greater than the evil. One account of the DDE that does not point to an intended greater good says that conditions to be met in order to permissibly produce a bad effect include "(1) one's action also had a good effect . . . and (4) the good effect was important enough to outweigh the bad" (*Cambridge Dictionary of Philosophy*, ed. R. Audi [Cambridge: Cambridge University Press, 1995]). (This entry also requires that one "did not produce the good effect through the bad" in addition to "not seeking the bad effect as an end or means." However, the DDE does not require that the good that justifies the bad not come about through the bad, only that we not intend that it do so. For an example, see the Track Trolley Case in note 14.) This version of the DDE, which I think is unrepresentative and inaccurate, only says a greater good need occur; it is not necessary that we intend it. Of course, this account also does not state that our act is permissible only if we act *because* there was (expected to be) a greater good. For it is quite possible that we would have been willing to act even if a greater good would not have occurred. Yet this would not make our act impermissible, according to this version of the DDE, if a greater good did in fact

occur. Even if a nonstandard version of the DDE required that we *expect* a good effect great enough to outweigh the bad, this state of mind is not the same as acting because of that expectation. For we might act expecting a greater good and our act be permissible, even if we would have acted without the expectation and so did not act because of it. This nonstandard account of the DDE represents it as a non-state- of-mind principle.

11. I first discussed this case in *Morality, Mortality*, Vol. 2.

12. Strictly speaking, the structure of the flipside need not be equivalent in all respects to the structure of the final good. For example, suppose the final good involves fewer or more people saved than exists in the flipside. This is alright so long as both flipside and ultimate good share a component of good (i.e., a certain number of particular people) that is greater than the lesser evil*.

13. As it turns out, in the Two Factories Case, the *ultimate* justifying good (both factories out) is identical with the structural equivalent. This is because no further problems for the factories being out of commission are produced by what we do. But this fact, that our blowing up one factory can lead by a causal chain to the justifying good, does not mean that we have an initial sufficient justification for blowing up the factory, for we lack the structural equivalent without evil*.

14. I speak in terms of the *possibility* of the initial sufficient justification to take account of cases where evil* is not actually initially sufficiently justified, but it could have been. For example, consider the Track Trolley Case. If we press a switch, it will turn a trolley away from five and toward one on a side track, when the trolley gets to a cross point. But pressing this switch also moves that side track with one person on it into the path of the trolley before the trolley gets to the cross point. It is the person being hit that actually causes the trolley to stop. But it is not required that this happen in order that the trolley stop, as our pressing the button would result in the other route occurring later, and this other route satisfies the DIJ. I believe turning in Track Trolley is permissible. Here is a wartime case: We drop bombs on the munitions factory, whose blowing up would cause civilian deaths. We foresee, however, that dropping the bombs to destroy the factory will cause children to run in the direction of the bombs. We know that the children will be blown up by the bombs directly and their being on fire is what will actually set the factory on fire (Children Aflame Case). I believe it is permissible to drop the bombs in this case because we do not require the children's being hit as a means to destroying the factory; if they didn't run to the bombs the bombs would blow up the factory. Why do I not say that it is permissible to drop bombs because "we do not act with the intention of using the children"? Because I do not want to rely on a state-of-mind principle; I believe that even if someone did drop the bombs with the intention to use the children, the way in which their being used comes about makes it as permissible for him to act as for someone who did not intend the use of the children. For more on the DIJ, see "Towards the Essence of Nonconsequentialism."

Midwest Studies in Philosophy, XXIV (2000)

Capital Punishment and the Sanctity of Life

PHILIP E. DEVINE

A former death row lawyer, explaining his withdrawal from "death work," has observed that "capital punishment is here to stay. Important battles remain, but the war is over. We lost."[1] Since ordinary human beings, though often wrong, are not as stupid as philosophers and other intellectuals like to think, part of the reason for the failure of the abolitionist argument is likely to be internal to it.[2]

My argument here will elaborate a remark made by the leading abolitionist scholar Hugo Adam Bedau, in his discussion of hard cases for the abolitionist argument:

> Conscientious liberals . . . cannot . . . easily refuse to compromise. Do they not already compromise on other life-and-death issues—often tolerating suicide, euthanasia, abortion, the use of lethal force in social and self-defense—thereby showing that they refuse to accept a moral principle that categorically condemns all killing.[3]

I thus attempt to place the case against capital punishment on a secure footing, one in keeping with the "seamless garment" ethics advocated by the late Cardinal Joseph Bernardin. (I limit my arguments here to the death penalty for murder.) My argument will imply a challenge to at least part of the liberal compromise.[4]

I

Positions in the debate over the death penalty are not closely tied to retributive, utilitarian, or other theories of punishment. On the contrary, abolitionists and retentionists alike invoke whatever moral and political theories may seem to support positions they hold on intuitive grounds. Abolitionists direct a volley of intuitive and theoretical arguments against intuitions powerfully entrenched among people like Ernest van den Haag, who, in his own words, "value[s] the lives of murderers negatively."[5]

The abolitionists' most important rhetorical resource is the tradition, usually called Judeo-Christian,[6] that affirms the inherent worth of each human being.[7] For this tradition, even those guilty of heinous crimes are incomparable in value, and in this respect equal, to the rest of us. One representative of this tradition, Pope John Paul II, has recently condemned the death penalty—except under circumstances rare in the modern world—at the same time rejecting abortion, assisted suicide, and euthanasia.[8] By rejecting capital punishment where other ways of protecting threatened persons are available, the Pope revises, or at least develops in a radical way, a long-standing Roman Catholic view.[9] He thereby takes part in a shift in Christian moral consciousness comparable to that which took place in the nineteenth century concerning the moral acceptability of slavery.

Meanwhile, the secular case against capital punishment has run into difficulty. As Robert Holyer reported in 1994, "in recent years appeal to the sanctity of life in the death penalty debate has been largely confined to theological discussions of the issue, especially by Catholic theologians in service of 'a consistent ethic of life.'"[10] The tradition that supports the Pope's judgment on the death penalty has been undermined by defenses of other forms of killing, as well as by attempts to exclude religious voices from public discussion. As a result, it has become difficult to reject even the crassest arguments for the capital punishment, such as that the cost of feeding and housing murderers suffices to justify our killing them.

In my response, I assume only that none of the antikilling arguments on other life issues in the background of the debate over capital punishment is contemptible.[11] Although I cite theologically grounded positions as part of this background, my argument here is a strictly philosophical one, appealing to considerations of coherence. Abolitionists have been heartened by Justice Harry Blackmun's recent conversion to their cause;[12] if I am right, they ought also to be disturbed by his authorship of the charter of abortion rights, *Roe v. Wade* (1973).

II

An argument against capital punishment that I at one time found persuasive goes as follows.[13] In order to justify the killing of a person rendered harmless, two conditions need to be met. (1) He[14] has committed an act deserving of death, and his guilt has been proved by fair procedures. (2) There are strong consequentialist reasons in terms of the common good for taking his life.

Retributive considerations have their claims but are not sufficient to justify taking human life. The moral and intellectual limitations of those who impose capital punishment and the injustices—both remediable and inevitable—of contemporary social life provide powerful rejoinders to the contention that we execute criminals "out of moral necessity."[15] It does not matter whether we spell out this supposed necessity in the intellectual terms proposed by Kant or the more emotional terms suggested by Walter Berns. In either case, though God might be justified in punishing in a strictly retributive fashion, human beings should not attempt to do so. The most common beneficial consequence claimed for capital punishment is deterrence, but no one has shown that the death penalty deters more effectively than imprisonment for long periods. Hence capital punishment should be abolished.

There are, however, at least two serious difficulties with this argument. First, the extent to which the death penalty deters murder, like other issues of social causation, is largely a matter of how we place the burden of proof, and this in turn depends on our political, cultural, and religious preconceptions. Those who regard it as a matter of common sense that threats of death are powerful deterrents are unlikely to be intimidated by statistics, which among other things reflect the biases of investigators.

Second, the argument omits some of the benefits that advocates of capital punishment hope to garner. Consider the "taxpayer's argument": killing a criminal saves the state the costs of keeping him alive in prison. Bedau responds by noting that "a criminal justice system that includes the death penalty costs more than a system that chooses life imprisonment."[16] The costs of the death penalty result, however, from the endless appeals required by the search for a perfect legal process. A society comfortable with capital punishment would not experience this cost.

The unflinching application of the death penalty also promises nonmonetary benefits as well. At least some of the cruelty of the death penalty arises from the endless appeals sponsored by abolitionists. The death penalty means that the man we execute will not commit any more crimes. Effective public justice (possibly including the death penalty) is part of the implicit contract that precludes vigilante justice. There are also scarier possible benefits of the death penalty, such as the use of the condemned man as an organ bank or subject of medical experimentation.

Some of the nondeterrent benefits adduced as expected from capital punishment might be excluded from moral reasoning, like the bad pleasures adduced by critics of utilitarianism. But the satisfaction of retributive emotions cannot be so easily dismissed: a person who was not angered by the murder of a close friend or family member would be emotionally deficient in a serious way. We might try to overcome this sort of anger for spiritual reasons, but that is not the same thing as not feeling it in the first place.[17] Berns plausibly extends this argument from personal relationships to society as a whole:

> If men are not saddened when someone else suffers, or angry when someone else suffers unjustly, the implication is that they do not care for anyone other than themselves, or that they lack some other quality that befits a man.[18]

In the United States at least, there is strong public support for the death penalty, apparently arising from this sort of anger. Officials cite this fact as their justification for keeping capital punishment in place. As Mike Everett of the Arkansas Senate has put it, "If 77% of the Arkansas people want [the death penalty], they will have it."[19] The question remains, however, whether this sort of consideration warrants the taking of a human life.

III

The argument having reached deadlock, abolitionists have turned to the question of "secondary smoke."[20]

A

Capital punishment, abolitionists argue, teaches contempt for human life and a willingness to use violence to "solve" human problems. Thus the proceedings of a recent abolitionist conference were entitled *The Killing State*, something the participants took for granted was bad.[21] The state cannot, however, send the message abolitionists want it to: to continue in existence, the state must be prepared, if necessary, to fight its foreign and domestic enemies to the death. Whatever the moral merits of anarchist pacifism, it cannot be intelligibly introduced into the debate about the appropriate uses of state power; those who believe in such a philosophy are best advised to have as little to do with the state as possible.

It does not follow that a state whose power is uncontested needs to kill private criminals, however vile their deeds. But it is sentimental nonsense to take an absolutist position concerning the execution of terrorists, since they are in a continuing state of irregular war with the rest of us. Yet the trials of those suspected of terrorism are specially unlikely to reach the standards of perfection favored by jurists with abolitionist sympathies: there are always likely to be loose ends in the prosecution's theory, as well as evidence of questionable governmental conduct. Despite such difficulties, it might be clear beyond doubt that the accused did what they were accused of, even if we suspect they did not act alone.[22]

B

Abolitionists further argue that the arbitrary administration of the death penalty renders it unjust. Some proceduralist arguments focus on the remediable deficiencies of contemporary American society, others on the inevitable fallibility and moral imperfections of those who impose capital punishment in whatever social context.

For example, abolitionists argue that the death penalty is racist, on the ground that black people are executed disproportionately to their membership in the population, or that the killers of white people are executed more often than those of black people.[23] Yet I have never seen the death penalty condemned as sexist on the ground that more men than women are executed. (In America at least, the execution of a woman is a sign of severe social stress, or else an ironic triumph for feminism.)[24] A determined sexual egalitarian might protest such leniency toward women,[25] but no one has argued against the death penalty on that ground. On the contrary, some abolitionist writers blandly assure us that nonracial "claims to discrimination in the criminal justice system [represent] no more than an abstract worry."[26]

A more serious version of the racial argument conjoins the race of murderers with the race of victims. As Stephen Nathanson puts it, "blacks killing whites have the greatest chance of being executed, while whites killing blacks have the least chance of execution."[27] Discrimination according to the race of the victim is an injustice to the victim rather than the murderer, however, and the logical remedy for such discrimination is severer sentences for white people who kill black people.[28] Nor is the fact that women who kill men are treated leniently (when they are not regarded as feminist heroines) a reason not to execute a man unquestionably guilty of the brutal murder of a woman.

In my view, the attempt to play the race card in the death penalty debate, with its attendant suggestion of programs of affirmative action (or even quotas) in the imposition of capital punishment, is politically irresponsible.[29] It is one more example of the bitter fruit produced by the movement, which gained strength about 1968, away from universal human rights (or "unity in our love of man," to cite a slogan used as late as 1970) to claims on behalf of a "Rainbow Coalition" of officially recognized oppressed minorities.[30] Whatever may be the case for admission to elite universities, it is neither morally defensible nor politically prudent to make life-and-death decisions overtly a matter of the race (or other socially sensitive traits) of either the killer or the person killed.

C

Racial injustice is not the only sort in existence, however, and radicals of many sorts argue that the structural flaws in our society deprive us of the authority to take human life. Thus Jeffrey Reiman does not mention race when he writes:

> Since I believe that the vast majority of murders in America are a predictable response to the frustrations and disabilities of impoverished social circumstances, and since I believe that impoverishment is a remediable injustice from which others in America benefit, I believe that we have no right to exact the full cost of murders from our murderers until we have done everything possible to rectify the conditions that produce their crimes.[31]

If, however, social injustice deprives us of the authority to punish murder, a fortiori it deprives us of the right to punish crimes against property, which in extreme cases might be defended on grounds of need.[32] And if we are too steeped in injustice to kill human beings for their crimes, we are not entitled to imprison them for long periods, either. Reiman's expression *full cost* may suggest a way out: we are just enough as a society to make criminals pay, though only at a discount (though how to calculate this discount I do not know). But, on this reading, Reiman permits the execution of serial killers, as well as of those murderers who also rape or torture their victims.

Let us suppose that the more just a society is, the less it will require the death penalty (and, for that matter, the criminal law). It does not follow that stopping executions will make our society more just.[33] Moreover, giving the radical argument the benefit of every doubt, it applies only to poor murderers (even if, as often happens, the victim is also poor). To be sure, Clarence Darrow mimicked the radical argument when he maintained, on behalf of two rich young men who killed "for the experience," *both* that the wealth of the defendants' families had prejudiced the authorities against them, *and* that the youths themselves were victims of excessive wealth.[34] Yet even if we accepted both Darrow's argument and Reiman's, we still could execute killers from the middle class, unless of course the pressures of middle-class existence are counted as an excuse. We are entitled to worry about the presuppositions of an argument that finds excuses for everyone. (In fact, Darrow was a hard determinist, and was committed to excusing hanging judges along with everybody else.)

The deepest source of difficulty here is the attempt to link two different sorts of normative arguments: that concerning justice between individuals, and that concerning the justice of institutions. Some contemporary conservatives propose to abolish the concept of social justice: even slavery, on their view, was just a sequence of injustices by particular slavetraders and slaveholders against particular slaves (if indeed it was unjust at all).[35] Without going so far, we still have to employ some care in linking the two sorts of claims of justice, else we risk a defense of the murder of Alexis Romanov, a hemophiliac child, on the ground that his family were "oppressors."[36] Social justice does not ground moral absolutes, nor does it override the requirements of justice between individuals when these are stringent and unambiguous.[37] Moreover, we are entitled to be queasy about programs of social justice that promise us just executions. Our arguments concerning capital punishment need to be keyed to the imperfectly just society in which we live, and in which, so far as I can see, we are destined to live so long as human society endures.

D

So long as a society is not so idyllic as to abolish serious crime, David von Drehle's observation on the death penalty applies: "The problem resides in the essential enterprise—trying to define shades of evil on a consistent basis."[38]

Caprice and mistake are inevitable in the administration of any judicial system, including its decision to inflict the death penalty. Those killed are likely to be socially marginal (by whatever criteria of marginality may prevail in a given society). Hence the likelihood of miscarriage of justice in capital cases is especially high. Moreover, an error, once made, could not be corrected—a consideration that, as we shall see, has wider implications as well.[39]

We could, it is true, sharply reduce the chances of mistake by requiring that only those be executed who confess their crimes and do not recant their convictions in the face of death.[40] The effect of this narrowing would be to limit the death penalty to political criminals broadly conceived (who have special reasons not to disavow their actions and whose apparent good faith at least mitigates their guilt) and to criminals who acknowledge both moral and legal guilt (whose sensitive conscience is something of an excuse). Even in such cases, however, the possibility of error remains (as readers of Dostoevsky will be able to confirm).

These considerations support Charles L. Black's conclusion: "Though the justice of man may indeed ordain that some may die, the justice of men is altogether and always insufficient for saying who these should be."[41] But the proceduralist argument commits what I call the "taxicab fallacy." Having reached their desired argumentative destination, abolitionists of a proceduralist bent think they can pay the driver and send him away. In fact, however, mistake, caprice, and the harsher treatment of the socially marginal are vices, not just of capital punishment, but of our criminal justice system as a whole. What is done to people in existing prisons is often morally indefensible, and there are reasons to suspect that humane imprisonment is impossible. Even imprisonment for short periods raises troubling moral issues.[42] Yet abolitionists persist in assuming that imprisonment for long periods, even life imprisonment with possibility of parole, is a morally acceptable penalty.

IV

The missing premise in the abolitionist case is that all human beings have inherent worth, incomparable both to one another and to everything else, which even the least admirable of us do not forfeit. One implication of this principle is that those who act badly do not thereby lose their claim on the sympathy of the virtuous.

These premises reflect an element in our moral consciousness alien to the ancient world. Aristotle, for example, defines pity as "the feeling of pain caused by the sight of some evil, destructive or painful, which befalls one who does not deserve it, and which we might expect to befall ourselves or some friend of ours, and moreover to befall us soon."[43] Elsewhere, while admitting that the suffering resulting from a tragic flaw may engender pity, he counsels against writing tragedies in which "an extremely bad man [is] seen as passing from happiness to misery. . . . [For] pity is occasioned by misfortune, and fear by that of one like ourselves."[44] There is no place in this way of thinking for pitying generally unadmirable people who thoroughly deserve their fate.

In contrast, the core of the case against capital punishment is the notion that there is something appalling about taking the life even of a person guilty of an atrocious crime. The ancient maxim *homo homini res sacra* can be used to defend as well as to oppose the death penalty, but once we dismiss it as "nonsense on stilts," the abolitionist case is lost. A corollary principle extends sanctity even to the legally guilty: when the taking of human life is in question, it is a terrible thing to err.

Abolitionists in fact think this way. Even when the defendant is unquestionably guilty of the offense charged, they worry whether he is as culpable as alleged, and whether his trial, or the subsequent process of appeal, was fair. Mumia Abu-Jamal is a former Black Panther, convicted and sentenced to death for murdering a policemen, and thus at war with the state if anyone is. Still, Bedau asks: "Guilty or innocent, did he have a fair trial and review by the appellate courts?"[45] Yet the political and judicial context in which they make their argument artificially isolates capital punishment from other forms of killing.

David K. Blount bridges the gap by using *innocent* in a special sense, such that a patient erroneously subjected to mercy killing is "innocent" in a way other candidates for euthanasia may not be.[46] An "innocent" patient in Blount's sense would be one misdiagnosed with a terminal illness or one who has withdrawn his consent to mercy killing without the knowledge or acknowledgment of his physicians. Assisted suicide by the "innocent" means, for example, the act of a person who, though quailing before the abyss, does what is expected of him by reason of the "whorehouse effect": an inhibition on breaking off a course of action once undertaken. Abortion is the killing of the "innocent" if the fetus is older than we suppose or we are mistaken on some point of embryology affecting our preferred criterion of personhood, or if our prenatal diagnosis is in error. An aborted fetus also counts as innocent if those who take its life are guilty of some deep philosophical error affecting the abortion issue. Even Aryans killed by Nazis under the mistaken belief that they were Jews count as "innocent" on Blount's definition.

Blount's crucial premise has little to do with innocence in the moral sense, or even in most legal senses, and is best made without using the word. It is that, when taking human life is in question, it is a terrible thing to err. This premise provides a foundation for a sound argument against capital punishment. For it *is* a terrible thing to kill a human being, and if we invoke a principle that justifies or requires doing so under some circumstances, it is terrible to err either in accepting or in applying it. Hence, as Bedau puts it, "we must start from the somewhat paradoxical proposition that, for the purposes of punishment under law, society must assume that everybody's life is valuable, even though some might have little or no value"[47]—or for that matter negative value.

This argument leaves open the possibility that killing will in some instances be a social necessity. But nonlethal solutions to our problems are to be preferred wherever possible. Even terrorists might be held hostage by the state—in technical terms, placed under suspended sentence of death—if necessary to help end or prevent a civil war.

The argument also has larger consequences. It is a terrible thing to kill a person who has withdrawn his consent to euthanasia or whose consent (or active participation) results from the pressures easily exerted on the old, the sick, the disabled, and the poor (or even from the whorehouse effect). Likewise, it is a terrible thing to kill a creature when one has misapplied the relevant criterion and excluded it from the class protected by the rule against homicide. In short, the argument from error applies to the whole range of life-and-death issues. This result is unwelcome, however, to those for whom a prochoice position on the abortion question, or a defense of physician-assisted suicide, is a cornerstone of progressive politics.

V

To make my argument for a "seamless-garment" ethics of life complete I have to argue not only that people who oppose the death penalty ought also to oppose abortion and euthanasia, but also that people who oppose abortion and euthanasia should also oppose the death penalty. Opponents of mercy killing in fact use a version of the argument from error, maintaining, for example, that the opacity of death precludes genuinely rational suicide. Likewise, the argument applies to those opponents of abortion who urge that embryos and pre-embryos be given the benefit of the doubt. If, however, conservative moralists rely on a supposedly transparent and morally decisive conception of innocent human life that applies to embryos but not to convicted murderers, they will escape at least the version of the argument against the death penalty I have been developing here. I also need to refute the seamless-garment pro-*death* position, popular in Washington, which permits capital punishment, (even part-birth) abortion, and opportunistic acts of violence both at home and abroad.[48]

For the present, however, I am content to establish the coherence of a seamless-garment approach to life-and-death issues. One difficulty with the principle "do not kill in cases of doubt" is that it seems to imply both vegetarianism and pacifism, at least if we believe that their advocates have made the least case.

A

If we are not to kill human beings in cases of doubt, it might seem that the same principle requires us not to kill nonhuman animals, since their defenders present at least prima facie plausible arguments on their behalf. Even the most dedicated animal rights advocates, however, set some limits to the application of their principles and must reject the argument from doubt outside them.[49] Tom Regan, for example, limits "the word *animal* to mentally normal mammals a year old or more," and "the word *human* to all those *Homo sapiens* aged one year or more, who are not profoundly retarded or otherwise very markedly mentally impoverished."[50] But the age of one year has no significance across species: read restrictively, and contrary to his intentions, Regan's criterion is a gross bit of special pleading on behalf of abortion, infanticide, and the drowning of unwanted kittens. But when he widens the protected class on various grounds, he creates the problem of line drawing once again.[51]

One response is to stipulate that the human species provides an outer limit, beyond which no strong moral claims will be recognized. Unless good reasons are provided for drawing the line somewhere within the human species, strong moral claims will then extend all the way to this limit. Since those who suffer the death penalty are all human beings, and few people at present are prepared to defend mass euthanasia as a "solution" to the problem of homelessness, this stipulation will suffice for the purposes of the debate over the death penalty. Yet a hardcore animal rights advocate will respond, in a Calvinist vein, that such stipulations reflect nothing more than a corrupt tradition of favoring social insiders (in this case, a "speciesist" preference for members of the human race).[52] But so suspicious an approach to traditional morality undermines moral reflection at every point.

B

A second source of difficulty for seamless-garment ethics arises from the observation that "capital punishment is warfare writ small."[53] For the liberal compromises cited at the beginning of this article are not all of a piece. A defense of killing in social and self-defense follows from the attempt to develop a *political* philosophy (and it does not matter, for this purpose, whether we think of the individual citizen who kills to defend himself or his family as in a state of nature with his victim, or as a delegate of the state). Abortion and euthanasia, in contrast, are defended on grounds vaguely described as "humanistic," or "humanitarian," that could without difficulty be extended to a wide range of cases—and has, in fact, been so extended. Given reasonable judicial procedures, the slippery slope to capital punishment for minor offenses does not seem a serious concern.

Whether just wars are possible in the modern world is much disputed among moralists, though small-scale police actions are justified if any use of public force is. The justification for the use of force is to protect the lives of persons who are in danger of being killed without a scintilla of justification. We can even defend killing to prevent other crimes against the person and some crimes against property (robbery and arson, but not larceny and embezzlement, and probably not burglary) on the principle, derived from Hobbes and Locke, that there is no security for one's life when someone has one in his power who has shown himself ready to do one severe injury.[54]

Even before the age of total war, however, it was not possible to exercise as much care to avoid killing innocent people as even retentionists expect of our judicial system. Enemy soldiers are killed without a trial, and if doubt arises whether a given person is an enemy soldier, a comrade, or a civilian, military people need to make a life-and-death decision without deliberation. Moreover, as Hoyler points out, "national defense . . . involves the preservation of liberties, political and civil rights, property and financial interests, and national pride.[55] If I am right, we are entitled to kill to protect such things only if attacks on them carry with them threats to the lives of persons: about national pride and financial interests, though not about political and civil rights, we are entitled to be dubious.

Since the seamless garment is not a complete moral code but a program for moral reflection, I need not attempt a just war theory here. My argument still has one important implication for the ethics of warfare. As Tim O'Brien puts it, "You don't make war without knowing why. . . . You can't fix your mistakes. Once people are dead, you can't make them undead."[56] This principle, although it does not imply pacifism, has serious consequences for societies, like contemporary America, that lack coherent foreign policies.

VI

Bedau has raised the issue of restrictions on incursions on the human person of a sort that secular moral theories have a hard time supporting:

> Perhaps the most important philosophical question in the death penalty debate is this. Does the theory of punishment . . . recognize any principle that limits severity or cruelty in punishment? . . . The United States Constitution and international human rights law endorse such a constraining principle (prohibiting "cruel and unusual punishments," "cruel, inhumane, or degrading treatment or punishment," respectively).[57]

Put bluntly, why not rape rapists?[58] For the law now equates rape with deviant sexual assault, our prison system would have no difficulty finding willing and able "executioners," and the threat of retributive rape might, moreover, be a powerful deterrent. Secular moralists have a hard time supporting absolute constraints on what society may do to its members. It is hard, for example, to square the supposed absoluteness of Mill's harm principle with his underlying utilitarianism. Rawls begins his *Theory of Justice* with a ringing defense of the inviolability of the human person, but his subsequent retreat to overlapping consensus—that is to say, to the practical politics (or "public reason") of a pluralistic society—undermines his capacity to support for absolutes of any sort.

Kant is a partial exception to these observations. Liberal neo-Kantians repudiate or play down some aspects of his theory, most notably his ban on suicide on the ground that it treats the agent as a means merely.[59] If we reverse this secularizing tendency in the understanding of Kant, then it is easy to see how some punishments (even, despite Kant himself, the death penalty) might be barred regardless of circumstance. Even for Kant, however, the transition from respect for persons as a moral principle to specific limitations on what can be done with the human mind and body requires both an intuitive leap from abstract premises to concrete conclusions and a metaphysical leap from the noumenal to the phenomenal self. Probably any approach to moral issues generates situationist pressures, since circumstances arise when strict moral requirements appear not to apply.

Retentionists, in any case, do not usually dispute Bedau on the philosophical issue, though they draw the line at a different point. Van den Haag, for example, finds torture, but not the death penalty, "repulsive."[60] He also objects to the now popular method of execution by lethal objection by reason of its "veterinary air," preferring death by firing squad instead.[61] Those who find abortion and euthanasia acceptable on vaguely medical grounds should prefer lethal injection to other forms of execution. At the same time, those who find lethal injection horrible by reason of its aseptic air or because it requires the participation of physicians in killings ought for that reason also to reject abortion, euthanasia, and physician-assisted suicide.

<h2 style="text-align:center">VII</h2>

There are strong presumptive arguments against both the death penalty and all other forms of homicide. Taking human life is legitimate when, and only when, it is strictly necessary, and we are entitled to examine claims of necessity, moral or other, with considerable skepticism. Prudential questions remain, of course: we should yield to situationist prejudices only when they do not undermine the whole system; drawing lines is the task of the casuist when the situation in question is common and of ad hoc judgment when it is rare (which will depend in part on how precisely the situation is described).

The most worrisome attempt to overcome this presumption to warrant large-scale killing is the popular defense of abortion as necessary to the liberation of women. As Mary Anne Warren puts it, "There is only room for one person with full and equal rights within a single skin."[62] Responding to such claims requires a challenge to the social picture that underlies it, a picture that is hostile or indifferent to all social bonds, even those as crucial as that between mother and child. If liberal individualism avoids such results only by arbitrarily excluding women from free and equal personhood, this is a reason, not for supporting abortion to equalize the situation of men and women, but for modifying our social paradigm in a communitarian direction.

Seamless-garment ethics is not a complete code but a program of moral reflection. To establish its coherence is not to defend it against every possible objection, but it is to show that it is plainly superior to the "orthodox" liberalism that rejects the death penalty while condoning, or even supporting, abortion, euthanasia, and physician-assisted suicide. The attempt to make strong claims of social justice while walling off the deep sources of moral requirements is pathetically weak. Yet the affirmation of the inherent worth of (frequently obnoxious) human beings requires us to say more about exactly what makes human life so precious, a question that leads to metaphysical and religious issues neglected here.[63]

Nonetheless, at the end of most bloody of all centuries, there is a lot to say for a coherent ethics of homicide.

NOTES

1. Michael Mello, *Dead Wrong* (Madison: University of Wisconsin Press, 1997), p. 3; see generally chap. 6.

2. Throughout I use *abolitionists* and *retentionists* for the foes and friends of capital punishment, respectively, and use *capital punishment* and *the death penalty* interchangeably.

3. *Death Is Different* (Boston: Northeastern University Press, 1997), p. 243. More recently, Bedau alludes to the situationism of "modern morality" and frames his moral principles to allow for voluntary euthanasia and assisted suicide. "Abolishing the Death Penalty Even for the Worst Murderers," in Austin Sarat, ed., *The Killing State* (Oxford: Oxford University Press, 1999), pp. 40, 54n13.

4. For an example of a compromising liberal, see Robert Young, "What Is So Wrong about Killing People?" *Philosophy* 54, no. 210 (1979): 515ff.

5. "Refuting Reimann and Nathanson," in A. John Simmons et al., eds., *Punishment* (Princeton: Princeton University Press, 1995), p. 329; also in Robert M. Baird and Stuart E. Rosenbaum, eds., *Punishment and the Death Penalty* (Amherst, N.Y.: Prometheus Books, 1995), chap. 16.

6. The expression *Judeo-Christian* is somewhat unfortunate, since it conceals important differences between the two traditions that bear, upon other things, on the question of forgiveness and mercy.

7. For reasons not to use the common expression *infinite worth*, see Robert Hoyler, "Capital Punishment and the Sanctity of Life," *International Philosophical Quarterly* 34, no. 4 (December 1994): 488.

8. See his *Encyclical Letter: The Gospel of Life* (*Evangelium Vitae*) (Boston: Pauline, 1995). He reaffirmed this encyclical, with special attention to America (both North and South), in his Apostolic Exhortation *Ecclesia in America* (1999), sec. 63; trans. in *Origins* 28, no. 33 (4 February 1999): 585. The Pope's teaching was foreshadowed by Germain Grisez, for example, in *The Way of the Lord Jesus*, vol. 1 (Chicago: Franciscan Herald Press, 1983), chap. 8, sec. H, para. 10. The link between Papal teaching and Grisez's position is drawn by Gerard V. Bradley, "No Intentional Killing Whatever," in Robert P. George, ed., *Natural Law and Moral Inquiry* (Washington, D.C.: Georgetown University Press, 1998), pp. 155–173. For a view on the ground, see Sister Helen Presjean, C.S.J., *Dead Men Walking* (New York: Random House, 1993), p. 21: "Jesus Christ, whose way of life I try to follow, refused to meet hate with hate or violence with violence." For a more recent expression of Catholic abolitionism, see A. L. Stubbs, *Clemency* (New York: Clemency Books, 1999).

9. See St. Thomas Aquinas, *Summa Theologiae*, Ia IIae, Q. 64, a. 2, for the classic defense of the death penalty in the Catholic tradition. At present the traditional view is supported by John Finnis, who defends the death penalty on the grounds that "the defining and essential . . . point of punishing is to restore an order of fairness which was disrupted by the criminal's criminal act." *Fundamentals of Ethics* (Washington, D.C.: Georgetown University Press, 1980), p. 118.

10. "The Sanctity of Life," pp. 485–86 n1.

11. For an exposition of my views, see Philip E. Devine, *The Ethics of Homicide* (Ithaca, N.Y.: Cornell University Press, 1978; Notre Dame: University of Notre Dame Press, 1990), especially on abortion and euthanasia. Since I wrote this book, Richard Stith has convinced me that the language of sacredness or sanctity is appropriate to life issues. See his "On Death and Dworkin," *Maryland Law Review* 56, no. 2 (1997): 289–383.

12. *Collins v. Collins*, 510 U.S. 1141 (1994); for discussion see Sarat, ed., *The Killing State*, pp. 7–9.

13. The standard arguments about capital punishment are rehearsed in Ernest van den Haag and Joseph Conrad, *The Death Penalty* (New York: Plenum, 1983); points found in this book will be used without further citation.

14. Since those subjected to the death penalty are overwhelmingly male, the use of "inclusive" language in this context would be absurd.

15. The quotation is from Berns, "The Morality of Anger," in Stuart and Rosenbaum, ed., *Punishment and the Death Penalty*, p. 51. For a full statement of Berns's views, see his book *For Capital Punishment* (Lanham, Md.: University Press of America, 1991).

16. "The Cost of Taking Life," *U.C. Davis Law Review* 18 (1985), quoted in Bedau, *Death Is Different*, p. 239.

17. I here skate over some complex questions; see Jeffrie G. Murphy and Jean Hampton, *Forgiveness and Mercy* (Cambridge: Cambridge University Press, 1990), especially Murphy's chapter 4, "Hatred: A Qualified Defense."

18. *For Capital Punishment*, p. 155 = "The Morality of Anger," p. 153.

19. Quoted in Amnesty International, "United States of America: A Macabre Assembly Line of Death," April 1998 (http://www.amnesty.org/ailib/aipub/1998/2510298.htm), p. 25.

20. See Richard C. Dieter, "Secondary Smoke Surrounds the Death Penalty Debate," *Criminal Justice Ethics* 13, no. 1 (Winter–Spring 1994): 2ff.

21. See note 3.

22. On the trial of Timothy McVeigh for the Oklahoma City bombing, see Stephen Jones and Peter Israel, *Others Unknown* (New York: Public Affairs Press, 1998). Jones sedulously refuses to assert his client's innocence (e.g., p. 324).

23. See Samuel R. Gross and Robert Mauro, *Death and Discrimination* (Boston: Northeastern University Press, 1989).

24. Between 1977 (when a judicially imposed moratorium on executions came to an end) and 1996, 301 men and only one woman were executed in the United States. Thad Reuther, "Why Women Aren't Executed," *Human Rights* 23, no. 4 (Fall 1996): 10–11. Seventy-four people, so far as I can see all of them male, were executed in 1997; on February 3, 1998, Karla Faye Tucker was executed in Texas to protests even from retentionist quarters. Amnesty International, "Macabre Assembly Line," pp. 10–11. Of the 47 people executed between January 1 and June 1, 1999, all so far as I can see were male. Amnesty International, USA Death Penalty, Executions, 1999 (http://www.lcomm.ca/aiusa/abolish/usexec1999.html).

25. For a skeptical account of the tradition of leniency toward women who commit violent crimes, see Julia Reed, "Lady Murderesses," *Women's Quarterly* no. 19 (Spring 1999): 20–22.

26. Gross and Mauro, *Death*, p. 213.

27. "Does It Matter If the Death Penalty Is Arbitrarily Administered?" in Simmons et al., eds., *Punishment*, p. 314; also in Baird and Rosenbaum, eds., *Punishment and the Death Penalty*, chap. 14. Nathanson cites W. Bowers and G. Peirce, "Arbitrariness and Discrimination under Post-*Furman* Capital Statutes," *Crime and Delinquency* 28 (1980): 563–635. I am indebted to Tom Grzebien for urging me to take seriously this version of the argument.

28. As van den Haag points out; "Refuting Reimann," p. 322.

29. The Supreme Court rebuffed a racially based attack on capital punishment in Georgia in *McClesky v. Kemp*, 481 U.S. 279, reprinted in Hugo Adam Bedau, *The Death Penalty in America* (New York: Oxford University Press, 1997), chap. 20. The proposed Racial Justice Act, which could easily have lead to execution quotas, was defeated in conference committee in August 1994; for sympathetic commentary, see Dieter, "Secondary Smoke," esp. p. 82.

30. One version of the stock list is "lesbians, gays, blacks, hispanics [*sic*], other peoples of color and subordinated classes." Nancy Fraser, "Toward a Discourse Ethic of Solidarity," *Praxis International* 5, no. 4 (January 1986): 428–29.

31. "Justice, Civilization, and the Death Penalty," in Simmons et al., eds., *Punishment*, pp. 290–91 (also in Baird and Rosenbaum, *Punishment and the Death Penalty*).

32. *Summa Theologiae*, IIa IIae, Q. 66, a. 7.

33. This point is directed against Reiman ("Justice," pp. 306–307).

34. *On the Death Penalty* (1924; reprinted Evanston, Ill.: Chicago Historical Books, 1991). Darrow alludes to a source of prejudice of which much would be made today—the youths' homosexual relationship—but only to show that their crime resulted from "a diseased mind" (p. 93 second pagination).

35. Irving Kristol, "A Capitalist Conception of Justice," in Richard T. DeGeorge and Joseph Pichler, ed., *Ethics, Free Enterprise, and Public Policy* (Oxford: Oxford University Press, 1978). Roger Scruton, *The Meaning of Conservatism* (Totowa, N.J.: Barnes and Noble, 1980), pp. 86–90.

36. For an appeal to social justice that moves in this direction, see Sally Markowitz, "A Feminist Defense of Abortion," in Louis P. Pojman and Francis Beckwith, eds., *The Abortion Controversy*

(Boston: Jones and Bartlett, 1994). I criticize this sort of feminist argument in my book *Human Diversity and the Culture Wars* (Westport, Conn.: Praeger, 1994), pp. 122–25.

37. This claim may be too strong for the harboring of fugitive slaves and refugees from Nazi genocide; for a case study see Philip Hallie, *Lest Innocent Blood Be Shed* (New York: Harper Torchbooks, 1985). Even here, however, it is necessary to accept some limits on our responsibility.

38. "When Harry Met Scalia," *Washington Post*, 6 March 1994, as quoted by Mello, *Dead Wrong*, p. 27.

39. Douglas K. Blount, "Euthanasia, Capital Punishment, and Mistakes-Are-Fatal Arguments," *Public Affairs Quarterly* 10, no. 4 (October 1994): 279–290, compares the arguments concerning the death penalty with those concerning euthanasia; for a skeptical discussion see Michael Davis, *Justice in the Shadow of Death* (Lanham, Md.: Rowman and Littlefield, 1996), chap. 5.

40. As Blount suggests, "Euthanasia," p. 286. Blount's shift to eyewitnesses (p. 287) ignores their notorious fallibility.

41. *Capital Punishment* (New York: Norton, 1974), p. 96.

42. See Dorothy Day's account of her brief imprisonment in *Loaves and Fishes* (Maryknoll, N.Y.: Orbis, 1997), chap. 16.

43. *Rhetoric* 1385 b 12–16. Trans. W. Rhys Roberts in Richard McKeon, ed., *The Basic Works of Aristotle* (New York: Random House, 1941).

44. *Poetics* 1453a 2–6. Trans. Ingram Bywater in ibid. I am indebted to David Konstan, "Love and Compassion among the Ancient Greeks," Providence College, 25 September 1998, for pointing out the moral and political importance of these passages.

45. *The Death Penalty in America*, p. v.

46. "Euthanasia," p. 288 n2.

47. "Worst Murderers," p. 42.

48. As Mello (*Dead Wrong*, p. 17) points out, then-Governor Clinton returned to Arkansas to preside over the execution of a mentally damaged man the same weekend he and his wife appeared on television to refute the charge of his having an affair with Gennifer Flowers. The Clinton Administration's conduct of the Branch Davidian affair showed a similar indifference to human life, including that of the children supposedly being protected against abuse. See James W. Tabor and Eugene V. Gallagher, *Why Waco?* (Berkeley and Los Angeles: University of California Press, 1995); Stuart A. Wright, ed., *Armageddon in Waco: Critical Perspectives* (Chicago: University of Chicago Press, 1995); and, in a more secular vein, David Kopel, *No More Wacos* (Amherst, N.Y.: Prometheus, 1997).

49. The most principled line is that drawn by Peter Singer (*Animal Liberation* [New York: New York Review, 1979]). His utilitarianism allows for the killing of human beings (as well as other animals) on very wide grounds, which led to intense and bitter controversy when he was appointed to a bioethics chair in a program in "human values" at Princeton.

50. *The Case for Animal Rights* (Berkeley and Los Angeles: University of California Press, 1983), p. 78. For a detailed critique of Regan's view, see Mary Anne Warren, "Critique of Regan's Animal Rights Theory," in Louis P. Pojman, ed., *Environmental Ethics*, 2nd ed. (Belmont, Calif.: Wadsworth, 1998).

51. *The Case for Animal Rights*, pp. 319–320, 416–17 n30.

52. See, for example, Edward Johnson's critique of my work on the ethics of homicide in his "Life, Death, and Animals," in Tom Regan and Peter Singer, eds., *Animal Rights and Human Obligations* (Englewood Cliffs, N.J.: Prentice-Hall, 1989), pp. 142–48.

53. Robert Burt, "Disorder in the Court," *Michigan Law Review* 89 (1987): 1784, as quoted in Mello, *Dead Wrong*, p. 39.

54. I here defend an argument made in *The Ethics of Homicide*, p. 154, against the criticisms of Hoyler, "Sanctity of Life," pp. 491–92.

55. "Sanctity of Life," p. 142.

56. *The Things They Carried* (a novel about the Vietnam War) (New York: Penguin, 1991), p. 44.

57. "Capital Punishment," in Ruth Chadwick, ed., *Encyclopedia of Applied Ethics* (San Diego, Calif.: Academic Press, 1998), vol. 1, pp. 420–21.

58. Davis, *Justice*, suggests this question.

59. Rawls (along with a number of other leading liberal political theorists) has signed a "philosophers' brief" invoking the concept of public reason to veto the legal and political expression of objections to assisted suicide. It is published as "Assisted Suicide: The Philosophers' Brief," *New York Review of Books*, 27 March 1997: 41–47; for discussion see Michael J. Sandel, "The Hard Questions: Last Rights," *New Republic*, 14 April 1997: 27.

60. "Refuting," p. 330.

61. Ibid., p. 331. For a murky but suggestive discussion of the issues posed by death by injection, see John Murphy, "Technology, Humanism, and Death by Injection," *Philosophy and Social Action* 11, no. 4 (1985): 55–63; or *Dialogos* 19 (November 1984): 165–175.

62. "The Moral Significance of Birth," in Pojman and Beckwith, *The Abortion Controversy*, p. 441.

63. For a frank rejection of the traditional ethics of homicide, tightly linked to rejection of traditional religion, see Singer, *Rethinking Life and Death: The Collapse of Our Traditional Ethics* (New York: St. Martin's Press, 1955), excerpted in Michael M. Uhlmann, ed., *Last Rights: Assisted Suicide and Euthanasia Debated* (Washington, D.C.: Ethics and Public Policy Center; Grand Rapids, Mich.: Eerdmans, 1998), chap. 8.

Aesthetics: The Need for a Theory

MARY MOTHERSILL

I

Philosophers who take an interest in the arts and in criticism—in what follows I'll call them the aestheticians—raise serious and interesting questions and discuss them, often to good effect. However, except for the historians who tell us about traditional systems, aestheticians steer clear of general theory and count it a virtue to do so. Maybe they're right: if you have no adequate theory, it's better to deal with issues piecemeal than to cobble something together for the sake of appearances. But what I want to suggest in the following pages is that philosophical aesthetics *needs* a general theory, that the necessary ingredients—true and familiar generalizations—are readily available and that the aestheticians' scruples are themselves the by-products of bad theory and ought to be left behind.

Consider first four problems much discussed in the current literature. chosen more or less at random. As presented they have a vaguely Kantian flavor. They start with some phenomenon connected with appreciation or critical judgment and go on to ask: "How is this possible?" I describe the problems and then attach labels designed to remind you of their sponsors or sources.

1. Readers develop emotional attachments to characters in novels, and moviegoers are sometimes frightened by what appears on the screen. (Call this the Anna Karenina problem, alternatively the Giant Green Slime problem.)

2. Nonrepresentational arts—music, architecture, abstract paintings—invite descriptions couched in emotive terms such as sad, triumphant, joyous, and somber. (Call this the Music Is Sad problem.)

3. A work that seems marvelous in its way conveys or endorses a message that is morally repellent. (Call this the Leni Riefenstahl problem.)

4. In matters of critical judgment, people have very strong convictions but, when challenged, find it difficult to show that their opinions have any better claim to validity than competing verdicts. (Call this the Ogilby-Milton problem.)[1]

All four problems begin with phenomenogical data, collectively *P*. Such data—collectively *D*—is not contested. Why does *P* strike philosophers as problematic? When Kant asked how some conception, for example, the synthetic a priori, is "possible," he had at his disposal—after all, he invented it—a systematic theory that had various unfilled gaps. So the stage was set for a transcendental deduction. Aestheticians, however, do not have any such theory: what they find puzzling is an apparent incompatibility between *P* and some accepted generalizations, often presented as definitional. (Call them collectively *D*.) Anna Karenina and Giant Green Slime, for example, are thought to illustrate mental states misdescribed as emotions. Received opinion has it that an emotion must have an object or target, must be grounded in a set of relevant beliefs, and must be attended by physiological changes (possibly subliminal) and be manifest in appropriate behavior (or at least in a disposition to apropriate behavior). Readers who claim to feel compassion for Anna Karenina, torn as she is between her lover and her child, do not believe that there ever was such a person or that the events narrated in the novel ever occurred. Whatever such readers may say, "compassion" is not what they experience, since they lack one essential belief component, namely, the belief that the putative object of their emotion actually exists. For the same reason they do not have the appropriate behavioral disposition: to commiserate with the victim, offer to help, and so forth. So also for Charles at the movies: he recoils and shudders as the Giant Green Slime fixes its gaze on him and moves closer and closer. Afterwards Charles claims (falsely) that he was "terrified." Neither Charles nor the compassionate reader is delusional; both know that they are dealing with fiction or with cinematic illusion. Music Is Sad arises because after the concert, Verbo and his friend agree that the music was beautiful but also very sad. Verbo is unable to sleep that night because of his worry about how it can make sense to say that music is sad. Unlike his sister Cassie, who cries and carries on, music, a mere parade of notes, is inanimate, and like the instruments that produce it, can have no emotions. But then, how to account for the fact that he and his friend agreed at once that sad was what the music was? Here the *D* factor is just the assumption that nothing except what is animate and conscious can have emotions.

Leni Riefenstahl is a bit more complicated. Few people take seriously Plato's conception of virtue as unitary. It seems obvious that courageous men may be intemperate and that regard for justice in the public sphere can coexist with tyranny at home. And yet there is a tendency (worth analyzing) to drift toward the Platonic doctrine. When it comes to works of art, it seems equally obvious that great artistic merit is compatible with moral obliquity. Dante's *Inferno* would be my example but (not to get bogged down in historical or theological debate) I'll opt for Leni Riefenstahl. *Triumph of the Will* is impressive both visually and in its dramatic structure, and yet the artist's talents are exercised in a murderously evil cause. How can we enjoy and admire what we at the same time condemn? Is the *D* factor here the assumption that no good work of art can be truly vicious? Again there is drift in that direction, sufficient to put some of us in a quandary.

With Ogilby-Milton we are on familiar ground. That Ogilby (he translated Homer) was a minor poet compared to Milton is a claim that no one worth listening to would deny.[2] And yet there are those who *do* deny it, holding that Ogilby is as good as or better than Milton. Surely they are within their rights. What entitles *us* to say that their sincere conviction is not worth listening to? Here the *D* factor is the idea that aesthetic judgments either have rational grounds or are purely arbitrary. A person who insists on her own opinion without being able to offer any grounds whatever is unreasonable. For adjudicating disputes there must be some standard of taste.

The question "How is *P* possible?"can thus be understood as asking how *P*, the phenomenon in question, can be squared with *D*, which appears to exclude it. Two possibilities: either redescribe *P* in a way that makes it compatible with *D*, or, since *P* constitutes a counterexample, argue that *D* is defective and needs to be revised. The aestheticians, by and large, choose the former alternative: what we feel for Anna Karenina is not pity but imagined pity, a make-believe emotion geared to a fictional world. Similarly for Charles at the movies: if he really believed that the Giant Green Slime was out to get him, he would flee, but he remains in his seat. What he feels, according to Walton, is quasi fear. As for Music Is Sad, Bouwsma is exceptional in his willingness to revise *D*. He does not charge Verbo and his friend with making a gross category mistake. Instead he draws a distinction between an *expression* of sadness, which does require a conscious human subject (like Cassie), and what is *expressive* of sadness, which need not. The sad face of a St. Bernard—to borrow Peter Kivy's favorite example—does not betoken a sad heart, and an actor may make sadness manifest without himself being in any way affected. Nelson Goodman, in *Languages of Art*,[3] disposes of the issue briskly: with a good deal of fanfare he introduces the notion of metaphorical truth. It is literally true that the music has a certain key signature and metaphorically true that it is sad. There is no convergence of philosophical opinion about Leni Riefenstahl. My impression is that the preferred view makes aesthetic valuation dominant. The alternative carries the suggestion of censorship and suppression of free speech. It can be argued, though, that a morally obnoxious message is an aesthetic flaw and needs to be given due weight in an overall assessment of a particular work.[4] In the Ogilby-Milton case the aestheticians agree that skeptical relativism is hard to defend: nobody believes that everyone's judgment is equally defensible. But there is a choice between alternatives: you can follow Hume, who says that appeal to authority, the joint opinion as he puts it, of "the true judges" provides the standard of taste. Another line: you can brazen it out with Kant, who says in effect that, like or not, the judgment of taste does demand universal agreement and sometimes rightly so even though it appeals to no concept and hence cannot be proven or even supported by reference to principle.

Notice that although *P* records phenomena associated with appreciation of the arts and with criticism, *D* is much broader in scope. The definitional constraints that appear to rule out *P* apply to aesthetics (if they *do* apply a fortiori). *D*, in other words, has no special relevance for aesthetics. Kendall Walton's ingenious and sophisticated explanation of audience response to the representational arts takes as its model children's games of make-believe in which by stipulation, objects in the immediate environment are to be imagined as elements of an adventure that calls for participation of all the players. ("Let this stump be a bear." "Let these mud patties be pies." "We are in a spaceship headed for Mars.") The designated objects then serve as props in a game governed by conventions, and they provide a focus for an imagined world. Tolstoy's description of Anna provides a prop for readers who are thereby launched in the task of locating themselves in her fictitious world. As children are caught up in their make-believe, so readers are carried away by their imagined emotions in a make-believe world. Charles at the movies feels quasi fear as he is drawn into the possible world in which the Giant Green Slime is a genuine menace.

If Walton's view is plausible, it extends beyond the representational arts to every rhetorical exercise enhanced by graphic or by verbal imagery. Consider television commercials: the good-looking guy standing beside a BMW and smiling into the camera is a prop for me, the viewer. I am to imagine myself in a fictitous world in which I graciously accept his invitation to join him in a trial run. Consider political propaganda: the aim is to alert audiences to what is perceived as a remediable evil. Whatever it may be—drug abuse, legalized abortion, the Jews—is depicted as a cancerous growth on society, and the depiction serves as a prop in which the audience is to play the role of the benign surgeon. The hope is that the players will forget the distinction between make-believe and reality and will aquire the the desired attitudes and motives. Such an enterprise, I take it, is antithetical to the interests of those who appreciate works of art. (Walton himself notes that at least where children's games are concerned, the barriers between the game and the real world are permeable. His example is a game where daddy is a monster in pursuit of his victim: the child's initial feeling is quasi fear but as the game continues, his attempts to escape are accompanied by genuine panic.) My question for Walton is "What is so special about the *arts*?" Make-believe dramas with their props and their to-be-imagined narrative conventions are ubiquitous. If you believe that of possible worlds, all except one is fictitious, then why single out the Anna Karenina world or the Tom Sawyer world?

Nelson Goodman, as noted above, finds no difficulty in treating Music Is Sad as an example of metaphor and supposes that a general theory of metaphor will cover it. The theory Goodman has to offer is the view—by now I should think discredited—that treats metaphor as a simple variant of simile.[5] Juliet shares some properties with the sun; a piece of sad music is somewhat like a sad person—droops, moves slowly, and so forth. Although Goodman's title is *Languages of Art*, he is quite explicit in warning us that his interests are not specifically linked to the arts but concern the use of symbols in communication.[6]

The various strategies for dealing with Leni Riefenstahl have it in common that the conflict between the moral and the aesthetics is, as presented, strikingly asymmetrical. Clear and cogent accounts of the artist's responsibilities, the relevance of her intentions and motives, questions about the actual or reasonably anticipated results of her creative work give one side of the story. What is the other side? What is aesthetic value—that value that may or may not be compatible with moral disvalue? Again we find a gap; despite authorial proclamations and examples, the issue bears only incidentally on criticism and the arts. The underlying and more general question asks how a reasonable person should deal with a situation where what she likes is incompatible with the dictates of her conscience. In parallel, the proposed solutions to Ogilby-Milton are offered as consequences of some general thesis about the merits of defects of skepticism, subjectivism, or relativism.

Aestheticians confront problems (1) through (4) with varying degrees of success. What is notable is that most of their work is describable as aesthetics treated from above, or at any rate from outside. Problems are analyzed and solved by bringing to bear assumptions garnered from philosophical psychology, metaphysics, theory of meaning, ethics, and epistemology.

II

What would an aesthetic theory look like? What would it do for us? It would provide a definition of the predicate "*x* has aesthetic value" (less pretentiously, "*x* is beautiful"); it would give us a perspective on problems (1) through (4) from which they emerge as distinctive. An aesthetic theory would not guarantee a *solution* of those problems, but although it would have to acknowledge (and respect) current findings in theory of knowledge, psychology, philosophy of language, and ethics, it would not underwrite solutions that are merely spinoffs from theories in adjoining fields.

For aestheticians the first requirement, the definition of aesthetic value, is the sticking point. Why should this be so? My conjecture is that there are two explanations. First, it is assumed that there is no common ground, that those who have thought about aesthetic value through the ages will find no basis for agreement and so no point in trying to arrive at a definition. The assumption is false. There are differences of taste among philosophers: Kant found much to admire in birdsongs; Aristotle did not. An adolescent boy struck Plato as beautiful, albeit less beautiful than the ideal form of Beauty itself; Hume had no liking for music of any sort but appreciated well-appointed country houses; Hegel found Goethe's juvenilia far inferior to his mature work; Croce thought that nothing in nature is not surpassed by some work of art. Diversity of aesthetic preference does not entail disagreement about what aesthetic preference *is*. On the contrary, reflective authors, past and present, concur in the recognition that aesthetic value is a cause of pleasure, that it is a value, that is, qualifies as good, ceteris paribus because it is enjoyable. The representations that figure in Anna Karenina and Giant Green Slime are, however they may be analyzed, a source of delight. This fact provides part of an answer to the question mentioned above that Walton's theory invites. Not every game with props justifies spending time and money to play. Not every make-believe world is delightful; some possible worlds are boring, disgusting, altogether horrible. Walton's subtitle is "On the Foundations of the Representational Arts." Any account of such foundations that does not include some reference to aesthetic value must be inadequate.

The nucleus of the puzzle in Music Is Sad is that Verbo and his friend *enjoyed* listening to the sad music. Similarly in Leni Riefenstahl: a viewer who merely *discerned* aesthetic value in *Triumph of the Will* need have no conflict. To make his dilemma intelligible we must assume that it was a film that he relished, that he liked watching.

The second explanation is really an elaboration of the first. They (the aestheticians) may assume that to endorse a definition of aesthetic value is to propose a principle of critical reasoning, a rule that could be used to determine which of two opposed judgments is valid. This conception they reject (rightly) as absurd. But why the assumption? Perhaps the supposition is that a definition of aesthetic value would prescribe a criterion that would leave the critic with nothing to do except apply a rule. Does a definition of *phi* necessarily provide a criterion for *phi*? Well, in a way it does: if the *definiendum* and the *definiens* have the same truth conditions, and if the predicates of the *definiens* pick out properties that are somehow more accessible than those picked out by the predicates of the *definiendum*, then an adequate definition could be made to serve as a rule. But definitions serve many different functions; separating the wheat from the chaff is only one of them and that will work only for the relatively well-informed. I for example understand in a vague way "$E = MC^2$" and take it on trust to be adequate, but it is of no practical use to me because in such matters I am an ignoramus. Hence, if aesthetic value were definitionally linked to some esoteric property discoverable only to molecular biology or quantum mechanics (there are some who believe something of the sort), such a definition would not curtail the freedom of the critic, since she would have no idea of how to apply it.

My guess is that the real source of the aversion to definition lies elsewhere, in what looks like an insignificant stylistic preference for the term "aesthetic value" over the more traditional "beauty." The choice is convenient—it allows for the inclusion of sunsets, unimproved landscape and other items that no one wants flatly to exclude—but unfortunate in that it obscures the fact that aestheticians are really only interested in the fine arts. Aesthetics has come to be thought of as identical with philosophy of art. Labels are not copyrighted, and any observations or thoughtful reflections on one or another of the arts can be counted as a contribution to the philosophy of art, and yet there can be (or so it seems to me) no such thing as a general *theory* of art. Why then have so many reputable philosophers believed that there must be (or ought to be) such a theory? Partly because, with Hegel and Croce, they find the aesthetic value of works of art to be immeasurably greater than that of any natural phenomenon. Perhaps they are right; a case can be made out for the visual arts. From no angle and at no time of day is Mt. St. Victoire as breathtaking as a Cezanne depiction. (With literature, it's a bit harder, because one is unsure about the terms of comparison. Does it even make sense to wonder whether a field of daffodils is or is not more beautiful than Wordsworth's poem?) Or maybe this is one of those ineluctable differences of sensibility and taste that do not call for adjudication.

One important difference: natural beauties, although they need to be defended against commercial predators, are not in competition with one another. The solemn juristic lingo—references to verdicts, to witnesses, to comparisons as uninformed or unfair—do not come into play when the disputed question is whether the coast of Maine is or is not more beautiful than the coast of Oregon. But with works of art it is different: the art market, at least in our society, is highly competitive; juries decide for or against; architects fight for commissions; prices skyrocket or plummet. The idea of a verdict is *not* out of place, and people asked to reach a verdict naturally wonder whether their decision ought to be guided by principle. (Undergraduates, in unwitting sympathy with the Ogilby fans, are preoccupied with the questions of criteria for aesthetic judgment. How do you *prove* that Ogilby is not the equal of Milton?) One would expect an aesthetic theory to show why this question is misguided.

Another stumbling block is the allergic reaction to the term "beauty," which served for many generations and in many languages as a term that picks out the generic aesthetic concept. Aestheticians, invoking a tradition that is no older than the late eighteenth century, take beauty to be the mark of a particular *style*, a species of aesthetic value. In rejecting the claim that the analysis of beauty is the subject matter of aesthetics, they observe, with predictable regularity, that great works of art are not beautiful, that it would be a misuse of language so to describe *King Lear* or Grünewald's altarpiece or late Beethoven quartets. This fussiness shows an unwarranted respect for what is a mere quirk of cultural history. Kant, in his precritical days and under the influence of Burke, felt a need to find a special place for the sublime and thought of contrasting it with the beautiful. That there is such a distinction and that it is important became staple beliefs for critical theory. A good summary is offered by Elaine Scarry[7]

> the sublime is male and the beautiful female. The sublime is English, Spanish and German; the beautiful French and Italian. The sublime resides in mountains, Milton's Hell and in a sacred grove; the beautiful resides in flowers and the Elysian meadows. . . . The sublime is night, the beautiful day. . . . The sublime is great; the beautiful "can also be small"; The sublime is principled, noble, righteous; the beautiful is compassionate and good hearted.

This division with all its ethnic and sexist stereotypes came in its time to pass as the merest common sense among those who preened themselves on their sophistication. It inspired the invention of further categories such as "the pathetic," "the picturesque," and so forth. The exaltation of the sublime seems to have originated with Longinus, for whom it was a particular rhetorical technique. It got to England and Germany via France under the auspices of Boileau, whose translation of Longinus was immensely popular and influential. Although the idea of the sublime flourished well into the nineteenth century, it has more or less vanished from the critic's vocabulary, whereas beauty still carries the stigma of applying to what is mildly agreeable, nonstrenuous, and relatively insignificant. Since we have lots of terms—pretty, charming, delightful—to cover the field, it is a pity that beauty has been quarantined and devalued.

If aesthetic value is understood as a synonym for beauty, its possible range of application is unlimited. No individual—object, person, event—can be excluded in advance. A smile, a pair of gloves, a tennis shot, a cumulus cloud, a debating maneuver, a squirrel, a table setting, a leaf, a circus clown—all are eligible candidates. Some actual attributions may surprise or shock, but none is grammatically flawed or unintelligible. My suggestion has been that for aesthetic value (=beauty), so understood, the ingredients for a general aesthetic theory are at hand and should be put to use. The prospects for a general theory of art are, in contrast, exceedingly dim. It is hard even to get started: to devise a theory of art you must have at least a rough idea of what counts as art. A layman might say that a work of art is something that is useless, ornamental, and expensive, but there is more to it than that. What is taken to be a work of art gets special treatment: it is put on a pedestal, published, performed, displayed (children are taken to see it), protected from vandals, discussed by critics and teachers. There are more postulants than there are places. What are the requirements for being a postulant? Maybe there are none. What about the items that get the special treatment, are treated with reverence but don't deserve it? Should we say that they are falsely believed to be works of art or should we say that they *are* works but failures? Such questions have led aestheticians to distinguish a normative from a descriptive use of the term "work of art." Under pressure, the descriptive use turns out to be some variant of "taken (perhaps incorrectly) to be a work of art." The "institutional" theory of art gets over this difficulty by proposing that to be a work of art just *is* to be declared to be a work of art by authorities in the art world—artists, critics, and, I suppose, gallery owners. This authoritarian nominalism seems counterintuitve and raises the question that troubled (or should have troubled) Hume, namely "By what marks do you recognize the authorities, the 'true judges'"? Doesn't it seem obvious that "work of art" is an honorific term? Like "champion" or "movie star" it connotes distinctive merit—justifies special treatment, admiration, respect. And what *is* its distinctive merit? To say its aesthetic value=beauty does not get you very far.

In practice we explain by producing examples, but the examples must be tailored to the capacities of the inquirer. For a twelve-year-old, *Remembrance of Things Past* is not a good starting point. In learning her first language, a child learns what it means to see or hear something beautiful, and the item is not typically a work of art. It may be a toy or a butterfly or a kitten. It must be something that gives her pleasure, and the function of the teacher is to encourage enjoyment and admiration and to discourage the impulse to eat or tear to pieces or kill the aesthetic object. Here we find the nucleus of the concept of the aesthetic attitude. I suggested above that the search for a definition of beauty=aesthetic value might get started by recognizing that beauty is a cause of pleasure. Now we can go on to a second step, a requirement endorsed by consensus. It has to be rather vague to begin with. It is the notion that beauty grounds prescriptions negative as well as positive. They can be expressed as imperatives: if something is beautiful (=has aesthetic value), don't damage it or destroy it or interfere with it. Do what you can to protect and preserve it. Don't hide it or make it a secret. The great unsolved problem in aesthetics is how to mark off the pleasures distinctive to appreciation. To recognize that appreciation grounds practical (perhaps moral) requirements is a help. If this second step could be clarified, as it would be as an element of a general aesthetic theory, we could get a better grasp of the conflict illustrated in Leni Riefenstahl. Note again, however, that the requirement is not peculiar to works of art but is relevant to the concerns of, for example, environmental ethics.

III

The only nonnormative and uncontested generalization about works of art is that they are artifacts, which is to say that human intentions played a role in their various causal histories. This does nothing to distinguish works of art from toothbrushes, chainsaws, or polluted rivers. It is a small but genuine advance to add that works of art are artifacts that have aesthetic value=beauty. And it is a further advance to recognize that the only way of enlightening someone who doesn't grasp the concept of the beautiful in art and nature is by presenting her with examples. Now the aestheticians show themselves to be aware of both points but do not sufficiently appreciate their potentialities as elements in an aesthetic theory. Their recognition of the crucial role of examples is reflected in their oft-repeated claim that "every work of art is unique," a puzzling assertion since it appears to be either trivially true or obviously false. Sometimes the uniqueness thesis is amplified in the assertion that no generalizations about works of art are relevant to their aesthetic assessment, and this assertion is not merely false but unfair to the work of musicologists, art historians, and experts on film, novels, and architecture. Discovering features common to Elizabethan madrigals, or impressionist paintings, or post-Schoenberg atonality can enhance your appreciation of a particular example. The wrong, migraine-inducing question is "What features shared by the *Mass in B Minor*, Vermeer's *View of Delft*, and *The Tempest* account for their aesthetic value=beauty?" (Talk about the fallacy of many questions!) What makes the absurdity conspicuous is the aestheticians' habit of choosing as examples undisputed masterpieces in all the arts. But here the aestheticians, particularly authors of textbooks, do have a legitimate reason for their practice: examples are crucial, but they must be actual, not merely hypothetical examples. They must be works that are accessible to readers if only through reproductions or recordings. A masterpiece, however, although similar to lesser works in medium, genre, formal structure, and style, is by definition an extraordinary achievement. There is no reason to suppose that any two such feats can be covered by a single explanation. Why is this fact, one that lends plausibility to the uniqueness thesis, so rarely acknowledged?

The answer I believe is as follows: beauty=aesthetic value is rightly regarded as a supervenient property. When I am struck by the beauty of a particular poem, a Shakespearean sonnet, for example, then there must be features of that poem that account for my response and one thing we hope for from critics is help in discerning such features. (I am thinking here of Helen Vendler's illuminating analyses of the sonnets taken one by one.)[8] Consider, for example, Sonnet #23, and suppose that I cite two features that strike me as remarkable: the dominant auditory paradox and the poignant theatrical imagery (the actor tongue-tied by stage fright). I can pick out these two features by using ordinary predicates—I just have—but these predicates must be understood as indexical. The ordinary predicates are projectible; the indexical predicates not. The presence of an auditory paradox or the image of a tongue-tied actor need not contribute to the poetic merit of some *other* sonnet. To believe the contrary—to believe that if I correctly identify the properties of #23 that account for its beauty, it follows that any poem that has such predicates will be *pro tanto* beautiful—is to subscribe to what Kant calls a principle of taste, a normative rule from which one can infer by straightforward deduction a judgment of some hitherto unexamined poem. Kant was the first to say explicitly, loudly, and frequently that there are not and could not be any principles of taste. If there were, all the critic would need would be a handbook and she would be relieved of the chore of actually reading the next poem submitted to her for judgment.

Those caught up in the quest for aesthetic generalizations sometimes retreat from normative claims to the hope of finding aesthetic laws. Their argument parallels the argument in support of principles of taste. The advent of my pleasure in the Shakespearean case is a causal consequence of my reading of Sonnet #23. Suppose that I am successful identifying the features of that poem in virtue of which I am moved to describe it as beautiful. Then, without having to decide whether my judgment is *valid*, I have evidence that will allow me to predict my future aesthetic responses. But as argued in the preceding paragraph, this does not follow. The point is one that has been made forcefully by Donald Davidson in his account of causa-tion.[9] A singular causal statement, though true, does not entail a causal *law* linking antecedent and consequent. My headache, I surmise, is the result of my drinking a whole bottle of red wine on an empty stomach. I may well be right, but I am not thereby entitled to announce a law that correlates headaches with red-wine-drinkings.

The beauty of Sonnet #23 is supervenient, but the properties on which it super-venes are the properties of *that sonnet*. Hence the need for indexical predicates. This is a thesis for which I have argued elsewhere,[10] and I believe that its incorporation in a general aesthetic theory would throw new light on Ogilby-Milton.

CONCLUSION

None of the foregoing suggestions is novel. Indeed what I have been urging is that the elements of a general aesthetic theory have long been available and witness to a con-vergence of opinion among philosophers past and present. I explain the aestheticians' aversion to the attempt to define aesthetic value=beauty as a consequence of confu-sion about what the function of such a definition would be. My claim is that the four problems sketched above would be treated more expeditiously if framed in the light of a general theory, but this is a point that needs to be established by detailed analysis. Even plausible claims need arguments, and programmatic tub-thumping is not an argument.

I observed earlier that Kant's *Critique of Judgement* is the earliest and most impressive attempt to formulate a theory of philosophical aesthetics. It does comprise the basic elements of the definition of the beautiful. He gives full weight to the link between beauty and experienced pleasure and recognizes the need to distinguish aes-thetic pleasure from other kinds of enjoyment. His contribution to Ogilby-Milton is his resolve to take seriously the notion of the judgment of taste as *valid*, which is to say that he does not try to soften the concept of validity to make it compatible with the commonly accepted opinions about what grounds are appropriate to the support of valid judgments. Where Kant, in my view, goes astray is in insisting that a valid judgment of taste is one that is not contaminated, as he puts it, by "charm or emotion." His theory has had a bad press because it is supposed to entail a kind of radical formalism that elevates rock crystals and wallpaper designs to high aesthetic status. Although unfair and defeasible—his discussion of the sublime is a partial correction—it is understandable. It does mean that Kant has little to contribute to *Anna Karenina* or Giant Green Slime. But these are particuarly difficult issues, and since I have complained about authors who deal with problems of aesthetics from outside, that is, as nothing more than special cases of some more general theory, I should say that until philosophical psychology comes up with something less skimpy than current theory of the emotions and imagination, we are fated on some issues to remain at an impasse.

According to Aquinas, what is beautiful is that of which the mere undersanding (*apprehensio ipsa*) pleases.[11] To my mind, the most pressing problem and the most obvious challenge for aestheticians comes from the need for an adequate analysis of *apprehensio ipsa.* Metaphors, even good ones like D. W. Prall's "aesthetic surface," are not enough. How much do you need to know to appreciate the surface? Is it enough to take in formal structures—lines, planes, counterpoint? Or must you, as some believe, be familiar with a whole cultural context including artistic conventions and whatever is the accepted view of the role of beauty=aesthetic value in human life? To appreciate a novel or a film, is folk pscyhology enough? Or do you need something more *récherché*? Is ignorance of botany a prerequisite, as Kant believed, for responding to the beauty of a wildflower? Or, as seems more plausible, does scientific lore enhance enjoyment? Lots of work to be done!

NOTES

1. For Anna Karenina, see Colin Radford, "How Can We Be Moved by the Fate of Anna Karenina?" *Proceedings of the Aristotelian Society*, supp. vol. 49 (1975); for Giant Green Slime, see Kendall Walton, "Fearing Fictions," *Journal of Philosophy* 75: 5–27; for Music is Sad, see O. K. Bouwsma, "The Expression Theory of Art," repr. in W. Elton, ed., *Aesthetics and Language* (Oxford: Blackwell, 1954); for Ogilby-Milton, see "Of the Standard of Taste," repr. ed. Eugene Miller, in *David Hume: Essays Moral, Political and Literary* (Indianapolis: Liberty Classics, 1987).

2. Hume's other example, the absurdity of thinking Bunyan the equal of Addison, is less persuasive. It's hard to see them as competitors, but if they are, I would put my money on Bunyan.

3. Nelson Goodman, *Languages of Art: An Approach to a Theory of Symbols*, 2nd ed. (Indianapolis and New York: Bobbs-Merrill, 1976).

4. Cf. Mary Deveraux, *Beauty and Evil: The Case of Leni Riefenstahl's Triumph of the Will*. In *Ethics and Aesthetics*, ed. Levinson (Cambridge: Cambridge University Press, 1998), p. 227.

5. Cf. Goodman, *Languages of Art*, pp. 77–78.

6. Cf. Goodman, *Languages of Art*, p. xi.

7. *On Beauty and Being Just* (Princeton: Princeton University Press, 1999), p. 83.

8. *The Art of Shakespeare's Sonnets* (Cambridge: Harvard University Press, 1997).

9. "Psychology as Philosophy," in *Philosophy of Psychology*, ed. S. C. Brown (New York: The MacMillan Press and Barnes and Noble, 1974).

10. *Beauty Restored* (Oxford: Clarendon Press, 1984), chaps. 9–11.

11. *Summa Theologica*, Ia, IIae, 27.1, Reply to Objection 3.

Contributors

Felicia Ackerman, Department of Philosophy, Brown University
E. M. Adams, Kenan Professor of Philosophy, University of North Carolina
Christopher Belshaw, Department of Philosophy, The Open University, England
Philip E. Devine, Department of Philosophy, Providence College
Fred Feldman, Department of Philosophy, University of Massachusetts–Amherst
John Martin Fischer, Department of Philosophy, University of California, Riverside
Ishtiyaque Haji, Department of Philosophy, University of Minnesota–Morris
F. M. Kamm, Department of Philosophy, New York University
Frederik Kaufman, Department of Philosophy and Religion, Ithaca College
John Kekes, Department of Philosophy, State University of New York at Albany
Joel Kupperman, Department of Philosophy, University of Connecticut
Mary Mothersill, Senior Scholar, Columbia University
Roy W. Perrett, School of History, Philosophy and Politics, Massey University
Stephen E. Rosenbaum, Department of Philosophy, Illinois State University
Harry S. Silverstein, Department of Philosophy, Washington State University
Daniel Speak, University of California, Riverside
John Woods, Department of Philosophy, University of Lethbridge, Canada
Palle Yourgrau, Department of Philosophy, Brandeis University

Peter A. French recently served as Cole Chair in Ethics at the University of South Florida. He has taught at the University of Minnesota, Morris, served as Distinguished Research Professor in the Center for the Study of Human Values at the University of Delaware, and served as Lennox Distinguished Professor of Philosophy at Trinity University in San Antonio, Texas. His books include *The Scope of Morality* (1980), *Collective and Corporate Responsibility* (1980), and *Responsibility Matters* (1992). He has published numerous articles in the philosophical journals. **Howard K. Wettstein** is chair and professor of philosophy at the University of California, Riverside. He has taught at the University of Notre Dame and the University of Minnesota, Morris, and has served as visiting associate professor of philosophy at the University of Iowa and Stanford University. He is the author of *Has Semantics Rested on a Mistake? and Other Essays* (1992).